Memory, Conflict and New Media

This book examines the online memory wars in post-Soviet states – where political conflicts take the shape of heated debates about the recent past, and especially the Second World War and Soviet socialism.

To this day, former socialist states face the challenge of constructing national identities, producing national memories, and relating to the Soviet legacy. Their pasts are principally intertwined: changing readings of history in one country generate fierce reactions in others. In this transnational memory war, digital media form a pivotal discursive space – one that provides speakers with radically new commemorative tools.

Uniting contributions by leading scholars in the field, *Memory, Conflict and New Media* is the first book-length publication to analyse how new media serve as a site of political and national identity building in post-socialist states. The book also examines how the construction of online identity is irreversibly affected by thinking about the past in this geopolitical domain. By highlighting post-socialist memory's digital mediations *and* digital memory's transcultural scope, the volume succeeds in a twofold aim: to deepen and refine both (post-socialist) memory theory and digital memory studies.

This book will be of much interest to students of media studies, post-Soviet studies, Eastern European politics, memory studies and international relations in general.

Ellen Rutten is Professor of Slavic Literatures and Cultures at the University of Amsterdam, and is author of *Unattainable Bride Russia* (2010).

Julie Fedor is a Research Associate at the University of Cambridge, UK. She is author of *Russia and the Cult of State Security* (Routledge, 2011) and a contributing author to *Remembering Katyn* (Polity Press, 2012).

Vera Zvereva is a Research Fellow at the Princess Dashkova Russian Centre, Edinburgh University, UK, and is author of *Network Talks: Cultural Communication on the Russian Internet* (University of Bergen, 2012) and *Real Life on TV* Screen (RSUH, 2012).

Media, war and security

Series Editors: Andrew Hoskins, *University of Glasgow* and Oliver Boyd-Barrett, *Bowling Green State University*

This series interrogates and illuminates the mutually shaping relationship between war and media as transformative of contemporary society, politics and culture.

Global Terrorism and New Media: The Post Al-Qaeda Generation
Philip Seib and Dana M. Janabek

Radicalisation and the Media: Legitimising Violence in the New Media
Akil N. Awan, Andrew Hoskins and Ben O'Loughlin

Hollywood and the CIA: Cinema, Defense and Subversion
Oliver Boyd-Barrett, David Herrera and Jim Baumann

Violence and War in Culture and the Media
Athina Karatzogianni

Military Media Management: Negotiating the 'Front' Line in Mediatized War
Sarah Maltby

Icons of War and Terror: Media Images in an Age of International Risk
Edited by John Tulloch and R. Warwick Blood

Memory, Conflict and New Media: Web Wars in Post-Socialist States
Edited by Ellen Rutten, Julie Fedor and Vera Zvereva

Memory, Conflict and New Media

Web wars in post-socialist states

Edited by Ellen Rutten, Julie Fedor and Vera Zvereva

Routledge
Taylor & Francis Group
LONDON AND NEW YORK

First published 2013
by Routledge
2 Park Square, Milton Park, Abingdon, Oxfordshire OX14 4RN

Simultaneously published in the USA and Canada
by Routledge
711 Third Avenue, New York, NY 10017

First issued in paperback 2014

Routledge is an imprint of the Taylor & Francis Group, an informa business

British Library Cataloguing in Publication Data
A catalogue record for this book is available from the British Library

Library of Congress Cataloging in Publication Data
Memory, conflict and new media : Web wars in post-socialist states / edited by Ellen Rutten, Julie Fedor and Vera Zvereva.
pages cm. — (Media, war and security)
Includes bibliographical references and index.
1. Former Soviet republics—Politics and government. 2. Former Soviet republics—Social conditions. 3. World Wide Web—Political aspects—Former Soviet republics. 4. Mass media—Political aspects—Former Soviet republics. 5. Collective memory—Former Soviet republics. 6. Political culture—Former Soviet republics. 7. Post-communism—Former Soviet republics. 8. Social conflict—Former Soviet republics. I. Rutten, Ellen, 1975– II. Fedor, Julie. III. Zvereva, V. V. (Vera Vladimirovna)
JN96.A58M46 2013
303.60947—dc23

2012039647

ISBN 978-0-415-63921-7 (hbk)
ISBN 978-1-138-84761-3 (pbk)
ISBN 978-0-203-08363-5 (ebk)

Typeset in Baskerville
by Keystroke, Station Road, Codsall, Wolverhampton

Contents

Illustrations

Figures

Tables

Charts

Contributors

Editors

Ellen Rutten is Professor in Slavonic Literatures at the University of Amsterdam and Principal Investigator of the Bergen-based research project 'Web Wars: Digital Diasporas and the Language of Memory in Russia and Ukraine' (www.web-wars.org). She is founding editor of the pioneering journal in the field, *Digital Icons: Studies in Russian, Eurasian & Central European New Media.* Her publications include the monograph *Unattainable Bride Russia* (Northwestern University Press, 2010) and articles in *SEER, kultura, Neprikosnovennyi zapas* and *Osteuropa*, among other venues. Her work on digital media has been accepted for publication by the *Journal of Computer-Mediated Communication*, among other venues.

Julie Fedor (Cambridge) is a Research Associate on the international collaborative HERA-funded research project 'Memory at War: Cultural Dynamics in Poland, Russia and Ukraine' (www.memoryatwar.org). Her book *Russia and the Cult of State Security* was published by Routledge in 2011. She is co-author of *Remembering Katyn* (Polity Press, 2012) and co-editor of *Memory and Theory in Eastern Europe* (Palgrave Macmillan, forthcoming 2013). She has taught modern Russian history at the Universities of Birmingham, Cambridge, Melbourne and St Andrews. Her current research focuses on narratives of self and other in contemporary Russian and Polish 'memory wars'.

Vera Zvereva is a Research Fellow at the Russian Academy of Sciences' Institute for General History, and an Associate Professor in the Department of Art History at the Russian State University for the Humanities. An active member of the 'Future of Russian' and 'Memory at War' projects, Dr Zvereva has published extensively on media culture. She is author of two monographs, *Network Talks: Cultural Communication on the Russian Internet* (University of Bergen, 2012) and *Real Life on TV Screen* (Moscow: RSUH, 2012), and editor of the cultural studies reader *Mass Culture: Contemporary Western Studies* (Moscow: Pragmatika Kulturi, 2005).

Authors

Before joining the Ghent University Doctoral Schools Coordination Unit in 2011, **Dieter De Bruyn** taught Polish and Czech literature and culture in the Department of Slavic and East European Studies at UGent. His current research explores cultural memory in contemporary Poland, with a focus on museums, comics and the Internet. Dr De Bruyn has published extensively on Polish literary Modernism and on contemporary Polish memory cultures in *Symposium*, *Russian Literature*, *Slovo*, and *Digital Icons*, among other publications.

Hélène Dounaevsky studied at Kyiv State University (Ukraine) and the University of Corsica (France), where she obtained a Ph.D. in Communication. Dr Dounaevsky's dissertation offered an anthropological perspective on the role of media in Ukraine's Orange Revolution. She is currently affiliated to the 'Communication and Politics' Laboratory (INSHS – CNRS, France) as a Postdoctoral Fellow. Her current research interests include East European politics and new media.

Alexander Etkind (Cambridge) is Professor of Russian Literature and Cultural History at the University of Cambridge. A Fellow of King's College, he directs the international project 'Memory at War'. Professor Etkind is the author of the internationally acclaimed history of psychoanalysis in Russia, *Eros of the Impossible* (Westview Press, 1996) and many other books and essays on Russian cultural and intellectual history. Etkind's book, *Internal Colonization: Russia's Imperial Experience*, was published by Polity Press in 2011. He has also co-authored *Remembering Katyn* (Polity Press, 2012), and his *Warped Mourning: Stories of the Undead in the Land of the Unburied* is forthcoming in 2013 at Stanford University Press.

Gernot Howanitz has studied Russian Literature and Applied Computer Science in Salzburg, Moscow and Prague. Currently he is a Ph.D. student in Slavic Literatures and Cultures at the University of Passau. His research interests include contemporary Russian, Polish and Czech literature, Internet culture, computer games and digital humanities. His Ph.D. thesis focuses on (auto-)biographical strategies of Russian authors currently emerging on the Internet.

Ilya Kukulin is a literary critic and sociologist of culture. He teaches in the Department of Cultural Studies at the National Research University – Higher School of Economics in Moscow, and at the Moscow City Teacher-Training University. He is editor of the online literary journal *TextOnly*, and co-editor of several volumes of articles, including *There, Within: Internal Colonization Practices in the Cultural History of Russia* (with Alexander Etkind and Dirk Uffelmann) (Moscow: NLO, 2012); *Noncanonical Classic: Dmitrii Aleksandrovich Prigov (1940–2007)* (with Evgeny Dobrenko, Mark Lipovetsky and Maria Maiofis) (Moscow: NLO, 2010); and *Funny Little Guys: The Cultural Heroes of Soviet Childhood* (with Mark Lipovetsky and Maria Maiofis) (Moscow: NLO, 2008).

Volodymyr Kulyk is Head Research Fellow at the Institute of Political and Ethnic Studies within the National Academy of Sciences of Ukraine, in Kyiv. He has taught at the University of Kyiv-Mohyla Academy, Columbia and Stanford Universities and has been a Visiting Scholar at Harvard, the University of Alberta and University College London. Dr Kulyk is the author of three books and numerous articles on contemporary Ukrainian nationalism, politics of language and ethnicity, and media discourse. His latest book, *Dyskurs ukraïns'kykh medii: identychnosti, ideolohii, vladni stosunky* was published in 2010 in Kyiv by Krytyka. In 2010, he edited an issue on languages and language ideologies in Ukraine for the *International Journal of the Sociology of Language.* Currently he is working on an English-language book on language, identity and democracy in post-Soviet Ukraine.

Jussi Lassila studied at the Universities of Tartu, St Petersburg, Jyväskylä and Helsinki. He has been affiliated to the latter's Aleksanteri Institute (Finnish Centre for Russian and Eastern Studies) since 2006. Currently he is a Postdoctoral Fellow on the CRIM project 'Constructing Russian Identity in the Media: Between the History of World War Two and the Future of Europeanness', which is a partner of the 'Memory at War' project. His research focuses on discussions and images of Second World War-related topics in the contemporary Russian media, and state-driven commemorative projects. Dr Lassila has published articles in the journals *Demokratizatsiia, Canadian Slavonic Papers, Forum noveishei vostochnoevropeiskoi istorii i kul'tury*, and *The Finnish Review of East European Studies*, as well as contributing to numerous edited volumes. His book *The Quest for an Ideal Youth in Putin's Russia II: The Search for Distinctive Conformism in the Political Communication of Nashi, 2005-2009* was published by Ibidem-Verlag in 2012.

Aliaksei Lastouski is a Research Fellow at the Institute of Political Studies 'Political Sphere' (Minsk-Vilnius, Belarus-Lithuania), and deputy editor-in-chief of *Belarusian Political Science Review*. His chief research interests are cultural memory and national identity, especially in East-Central Europe. Since 2009, Dr Lastouski has been a core member of several international research projects on memory and identity construction in this region. He is currently a researcher on the project 'Politics of Memory and Construction of Identities in Borderlands: Belarus, Ukraine, Moldova (1991–2011)' (Carnegie Corporation Center for Advanced Study and Education), and 'Rethinking the Soviet Memory of the "Great Patriotic War" from the Local Perspective: Stalinism and the Thaw 1945–65' (Geschichtswerkstatt Europa).

Ingunn Lunde is Professor of Russian at the University of Bergen and was Project Leader of the 'Future of Russian' project 2008–12 (http://www.uib.no/rg/future_r/). She holds a part-time professorship in Russian literature and culture at the University of Tromsø. She is the author of *Verbal Celebrations: Kirill of Turov's Homiletic Rhetoric and its Byzantine Sources* (Harrassowitz, 2001). She has published widely on Russian language and literature and is editor and co-editor of ten books, among them (with Martin Paulsen) *From Poets to Padonki: Linguistic Authority and Norm Negotiation in Modern Russian Culture* (Department of Foreign Languages, University of Bergen, 2009). She has been a Visiting Scholar at Harvard University and is founder and general editor of *Slavica Bergensia*, and president of the Scandinavian Association of Slavists and the Norwegian Association of Slavists.

Galina Nikiporets-Takigawa is a Researcher on the 'Memory at War' project. She was previously Associate Professor at the Tokyo University of Foreign Studies where she taught computational sociolinguistics and mass media language, and a Researcher at the University of Edinburgh where she conducted a project on national identity construction. Currently in Cambridge, she is developing a methodology for tracking memory wars and other social and political processes. She writes on a wide range of issues related to the interplay between media and society, politics and language, and digital humanities. She was editor of the volume *Integrum: Quantitative Methods and the Humanities* (Moscow: Letnii sad, 2006).

Having studied at Moscow State University and the University of Cambridge, where she obtained an M.Phil. in Screen Media and Cultures, **Maria M. Pasholok** is currently completing her D.Phil. thesis at Magdalen College, Oxford. Her thesis examines set design and cinematic architecture in early Russian film. Ms Pasholok also covers London cultural life for a number of British publications as a freelance journalist.

Martin Paulsen is a Postdoctoral Fellow on the 'Future of Russian' project at the University of Bergen, where he studies how the increase in computer-mediated communication challenges the position of the Cyrillic alphabet as the code for writing Belarusian, Russian and Ukrainian. Alongside a series of publications on post-Soviet culture, Dr Paulsen has edited two books on contemporary Russian literature, and he is a member of the editorial board of *Petrusjka*, a publishing project for the advancement of post-Soviet literature in Norway.

Caterina Preda is a Researcher and Assistant Professor in the Department of Political Science at the University of Bucharest. Her research explores art and cultural policies in modern dictatorships, with a focus on Eastern Europe and Latin America. Dr Preda's work on post-socialist art and politics has appeared in publications by, among others, Palgrave Macmillan, Ashgate and Routledge.

Anna Reading is Professor of Communication at the University of Western Sydney, Visiting Research Professor at London's South Bank University, and Visiting Professor of Media and Communication at the University of Loughborough. From January 2013, she will be Chair of Culture and Creative Industries at King's College, University of London. She has played a leading international role in developing the field of media memory studies, particularly in relation to gender and mediated memories of genocide and terrorism.

Having co-edited the pioneering digital memories monograph *Save As ... Digital Memories* (with Andrew Hoskins and Joanna Garde-Hansen), Dr Reading is currently writing a book on how new media technologies are changing memory through 'the globital memory field', as well as co-editing a collection on media memories of non-violent struggle. Her work is making a critical contribution to the international debate on 'a right to memory', especially in relation to marginalized groups such as the European Roma.

Doreen Spörer-Wagner is a Postdoctoral Fellow on the University of Zurich's National Center of Competence in Research Democracy Project 'Institutional and Media Strategies for Post-conflict Democratization'. Dr Spörer-Wagner has previously worked on another NCCR Democracy Project, 'The Dynamics of Political Institutions in Mediated Democracies: Political Bargaining and the Transformation of the Public Sphere'. Alongside a book (*Regierungssysteme und Reforme* [Government Systems and Reforms], Wiesbaden: VS Verlag fűr Sozialwissenschaften, 2006) with a major focus on the post-communist space, she has published a number of articles and chapters on politics, power structures and media.

Acknowledgements

Work on this book was supported by a generous grant from the HERA JRP (Humanities in the European Research Area Joint Research Programme) for the research project *Memory at War: Cultural Dynamics in Poland, Russia and Ukraine*, and its pendant, *Web Wars: Digital Diasporas and the Language of Memory in Russia and Ukraine*. We also gratefully acknowledge support received from the Department of Foreign Languages at the University of Bergen; the Department of Slavonic Studies at the University of Cambridge; the Slavonic Department at the University of Amsterdam; Darwin College, Cambridge; and the anonymous reviewers of the draft manuscript.

A note on translation and transliteration

All translations are ours unless otherwise stated.

Where established English spellings of names and place names exist, these have been given preference (e.g. 'Trotsky' rather than 'Trotskii', 'Yeltsin' rather than 'E'ltsin').

Belarusian, Russian and Ukrainian have been transliterated according to the Library of Congress system.

Introduction

Old conflicts, new media: post-socialist digital memories[1]

Ellen Rutten and Vera Zvereva

Introduction

Readers of post-socialist new media find themselves embedded in a world of *web wars* – discursive online combats, where alternative histories thrive and multifarious memories compete for hegemony. Members of the blog community Ukraine_Russia (community.livejournal.com/ukraine_russia) quarrel over the roles of the two countries in the Second World War. Polish Facebook users turn to Soviet history in an attempt to commemorate and comprehend the 2010 Smolensk plane crash. Chatters on the memory site Born in the USSR (savok.name) – set up to exchange nostalgic recollections of Soviet-era material culture – turn to collective memory to debate the territorial integrity of former Soviet states. The member populations of each of these memory-related groups and chat fora are large but unknown. Discussion entries follow one another with intervals of mere minutes or seconds, and their authors post messages from all over the globe.

The examples mentioned illustrate how, with its speed, accessibility, and accommodation of anonymity, the Internet is radically transforming the way memories travel between generations and communities. In the words of one team of mediated memory experts, online we deal with 'a new hybrid form of public and private' memories – memories that are, for instance, 'not consumed . . . but produced by the audience', and that 'are not simply shared and told . . . but creatively constructed' (Garde-Hansen *et al.* 2009: 12).

This book explores how digitally mediated memory takes shape in what we call *post-socialist states*. With this (not uncontroversial) term we refer to those world countries that, in the recent past, have engaged in attempts to create a 'socialist' – that is, working-class-dominated – state.[2] Such countries as Belarus, Georgia, Poland, Romania, Russia, Ukraine – the nation states which play a lead role in one or more chapters in this book – all partook in 'the socialist experiment' and have recently undergone radical social changes as a result of its failure. Part of these 'post-socialist' changes is the challenge that former socialist states today still face of constructing national identities, producing national memories, and – in the nation states that we scrutinize here – of relating to the Soviet legacy. Without boasting any 'inherently unique' national qualities, these states do share traumatic pasts that are closely intertwined. Their inhabitants often speak one another's language (Russian, for one, has a strong presence in the linguistic repertoires of residents of the geopolitical era that our volume examines), and some of their languages are closely related.

This shared linguistic and socio-historical background on the one hand, and a set of unsolved political and economic questions (ongoing nation-building projects and socio-economic modernization processes, for instance), on the other, trigger ceaseless public negotiations about the meanings of these countries' joint social past. They involve not only a re-estimation of twentieth-century events, but also wholesale reconfigurations of national histories. Across Central and Eastern Europe and post-Soviet space, political conflicts today take the shape of heated debates about the recent past, and especially the Second World War and Soviet socialism. A team of international scholars has recently introduced the concept of the *memory war* to study this controversial and painful aspect of the transnational process of digesting the past.[3] The Memory at War team uses this term to analyse how in Poland, Russia and Ukraine – the countries that have this team's special interest – historical events are invariably utilized to legitimize ongoing political conflicts, and changing readings of history in one country generate fierce responses in others.

Within Eastern Europe's transnational memory war, digital media form a pivotal discursive territory – one that provides speakers with radically new commemorative tools. The web wars in which they engage perfectly illustrate why early claims that 'cyberspace has actually replaced traditional geography' (Spiegel 2000: 123) are today becoming obsolete. Instead of imagining the Web as a de-nationalized, de-politicized space, our analyses join with other recent studies that – while acknowledging new media's transnational fluidity – zoom in on 'the ways national boundaries can be re-imagined online, and the ways cyberspace itself can become a site onto which national feelings are projected' (Kuntsman 2009: 17).[4]

Memory, Conflict and New Media is the first book-length publication to analyse not only how, in post-socialist space, new media serve as a site of political and national identity building; but also how in this geopolitical domain, online identity construction is irreversibly affected by thinking about the past. Put somewhat differently, our volume ponders the vectors of *post-socialist digital memories*. The pages that follow serve as an introduction to this specific form of memory. They start by outlining digital memories as a novel research discipline, and then continue to position what we call post-socialist digital memories within the new field. They argue why it is necessary to embed post-socialist digital memories into the larger field, and briefly introduce the idiosyncratic forms that online memory can acquire in post-socialist space – forms which will be discussed in more detail in the chapters that follow. It is with a brief outline of these chapters' thematic and methodological focus that this opening text concludes.

Digital memories and post-socialist space

First, as stated, some words on digital memories as a scholarly field. In the course of the 2000s, digital memories scholars have posed a forceful intervention to an existing academic discipline: that of the study of *cultural* or *collective memory*. Without elaborating on this vast and constantly growing terrain of scholarly inquiry, it is necessary to stress here that rather than history proper, memory scholars explore contemporary *perceptions* or *representations* of the past. On the optimal approach to these historical representations, memory experts deliberate to this day – but canonical methodological concepts from which our analyses take inspiration are:

- the ideas on *collective memory* (the notion that apart from the existence of individual memories, a society can boast a collective or group memory) introduced by Maurice Halbwachs (Halbwachs 1950);
- the concept of *sites of memory* (the concrete spaces, people and objects that embody a national memory) as put forward by historian Pierre Nora (Nora 1992);
- the notions of *cultural memory* (collective forms of relaying and actualizing cultural meanings which refer to the past, and which are pivotal to social and cultural identity formation) and *communicative memory* (the informal, verbally shared recollections of living generations) that interest cultural historians Jan and Aleida Assmann (J. Assmann 1992, 2008; A. Assmann 2012).[5]

Halbwachs', the Assmanns', and other notions of memory all refer to social processes that are to a substantial extent affected by and shaped in public media. From the early 2000s onwards, this interrelation of (old *and* new) media and (individual, collective and cultural) memory has started to intrigue scholars as a field that requires separate investigation. When speaking of the emerging boom in memory studies, in 2003 memory expert Andreas Huyssen already observed that '[w]e cannot discuss personal, generational, or public memory separately from the enormous influence of the new media as carriers of all forms of memory' (Huyssen 2003: 18). A few years later, cultural historians Astrid Erll and Ann Rigney went as far as proclaiming cultural memory's very *existence* dependent on media. In their words, it is 'always shared with the help of symbolic artefacts that mediate between individuals and, in the process, create communality across both time and space' (Erll and Rigney 2009: 1).

Formally, Huyssen and Erll and Rigney may not have framed their claims as 'digital memory' insights, but their arguments are formative to digital memory studies as a scholarly discipline. Thus far, the nexus between specifically *new* media and memory has been probed in a range of book-length publications whose authors tackle fields ranging from literature to neurology.[6] Most importantly, perhaps, in 2009 a British team of scholars published the collected volume *Save As . . . Digital Memories*; its contributors set themselves the task to unravel 'how we embody, create and are emplaced within digital memories' (Garde-Hansen *et al.* 2009: 1).

The findings of the *Save As . . .* collective, as well as those of additional newly emerged digital memory experts, have done much to refine the field of memory studies at large. They advance a heightened sensitivity towards *memory mediation* – the insight that memory never stands on its own, but is always, digitally or otherwise, mediated.

Current digital memory studies lack, however, another sensitivity that is crucial to thinking about digital commemoration practices. This is the perceptiveness to transcultural variation. In the existing body of work on digital memories it is easy to trace explorations of, say, German or North American new media memory; but it is substantially less easy to find discussions of post-socialist (as well as, more generally, post-totalitarian) digital memory practices. Tracing post-socialist digital memory is especially hard for those researchers who, for want of knowledge of the region's own languages, are compelled to rely on today's academic lingua franca: English.

If new media studies at large have now seen various pleas for internationalization or for more 'ethnographically rooted' approaches to the field,[7] then digital memory studies still venture mostly into 'Western' – that is, Western European-cum-American and/or Anglophone – virtual space. Digital memory experts rarely take the specificities of this linguo-cultural demarcation into account. When speaking of memory on '*the* Web', they tend to refer to Facebook, for instance, without specifying that the post-Soviet and Chinese social media markets are dominated by other services (Cosenza 2012) – services whose users operate within drastically different technological ramifications than do Facebook users. Or they criticize new media's capacity to memorialize what users want to forget – as in the famous case of a promiscuous photograph that cost its owner a graduate certificate – and plea for installing expiration dates on all online data. In proposing this 'delete' solution, its inventor, media expert Viktor Mayer-Schoenberger, relies mainly on Northern American instances of *individual* memories (Mayer-Schoenberger 2009); but his proposition has implications for *collective* digital memory, too. The plea for forgetfulness quickly loses its attraction when applied to this type of collective online memory in the world region that we tackle here: post-socialist space. Boasting turbulent and often traumatic recent histories, many post-socialist states insist on collective cultural forgetting rather than commemoration[8] – and in their public spheres, it is social media that register the historical trauma discourse that is lacking elsewhere. Once situated in these amnesiac public cultures, a defence of 'forgetting' and deleting online content seems misplaced, if not downright immoral.[9]

The Facebook bias and the 'delete' credo are a mere two out of a longer series of existing digital memories theorems that sit uneasily with post-socialist practice. In fact, they are tips of an iceberg of theoretical problems that arises once one seeks to apply current digital memory discourse to the realities of life in a post-socialist state. This theoretical collision notwithstanding, to date the leading voices in digital memories scholarship devote marginal attention to developments in non-Western regions in general, and to post-socialist developments in particular. Those recent and upcoming online memory publications that do take these regions as their departure point – important as they are – are either fragmentary, or they reach limited and/or mainly region-oriented academic audiences.[10] The book series in which this volume is published – Routledge's 'Media, War and Security' series – does include explorations of non-Western new media, but it contains hardly any mention of post-socialist states. In addition, existing inquiries into post-Soviet media and memory target television rather than digital media.[11]

Introducing post-socialist digital memories

Contrary to what the status quo in online memory research suggests, digitally mediated memories are not restricted primarily to 'Western' online space. The following chapters illustrate this claim by tackling the vastly under-theorized segment of the worldwide web that is constituted by Central and Eastern Europe and the former Soviet Union. This territory features its own digital landscape – one that partly blends with and partly differs from other online cultures. We want to use this Introduction to look at some of the features of this post-socialist digital memory landscape.

For many post-socialist states, the past is as alive as the present. Glorified, mourned and condemned, memorable events and processes from the recent past have been used for contemporary identity-building projects across the world – but this process is especially poignant in 'our' post-socialist nations, which have recently witnessed such dramatic changes and drastic disintegration of existing identities.[12] In some of these states, they are privileged for building specifically a *national* identity, or to emphasize independence from Russia (Zhurzhenko 2007). In social media, which, in post-socialist nations, are as disproportionately politicized as they are popular (Lapina-Kratasiuk *et al.* 2009), Soviet memories are vividly discussed in the contents of actual politics. Collective memories, family recollections, individual historical testimonies: all may be – and have often been – read as impact factors on current political decisions.

What is more, in digital media meaningful historical events are debated unevenly. Both this irregularity of representation in online communities and the disparate importance of the mythologized events and chosen traumas of the past are linked with their topical political value (Dubin 2004, 2008; Riabchuk 2007). Put differently, in post-socialist countries, social-media discourse is influenced by old conflicts, whose memories are actualized and politically exploited in the present. Myriad groups with their own truths and ideological preferences try to establish their voices in society, and to legitimize themselves in digital space. Economic instability, political difficulties, and a non-steadily developing civil society (for some of the countries at stake here, see on these features Nikulin 2007; Wilson 2009; Dubin 2011; Gill and Young 2011; Gudkov 2011; and (sections of) Trzeciak 2012) reinforce online battles for reinterpretations of the Soviet legacy. Most contesting groups use the same technologies and representational strategies, and they apply similar discursive techniques to promote their version of memories of the past. The highly standardized online debate that emerges from their discussions is a good place to start exploring those aspects that are endemic to post-socialist digital memories.

First of all, the intensive and diffuse interactions of web users in their discussions of cultural experiences cause the semantic shift of such a basic concept as *memory*. Recollections per se rarely attract the attention of online communities' members. In their discussions of memory, new media users in the societies that we investigate are, more than users elsewhere, preoccupied with the production of group solidarity and belonging. National differences put aside, these societies share a more or less intense cultural emphasis on the past; in their social climates, the universal trend to understand historical events as a means of social and political self-identification gains particular acuity.[13] In order to construct a stable 'self' and prove their belonging to a group, users have to choose a constellation of historical interpretations and participate in rituals of online commemoration. Against this background, their production of solidarity with a virtual group becomes highly significant – more so than the traditional strategy of sharing family recollections.

In addition, post-socialist digital memories are shaped to a large extent by the official historical explanations that mark post-Soviet public discourse. Online, we meet armies of digital fighters, who struggle with media formulas and political clichés, and who try to de- and re-legitimize different versions of historical memory – in blogs, social networking sites, chat forums and wikis.

In other words, online, the concept of memory is subjected to radical changes, as is that of the *historical past*. In post-Soviet cultures, this concept is formative to the legitimization of state power. However, in social media 'the past' is appropriated by common users, who prioritize a non-professional, bottom-up knowledge of history. Web users produce interpretations and explanations which may seem paradoxical to professional historians. In their popular versions, history is not necessarily linear; significant events that happened long ago may be repeated. Singular facts are extracted from their contexts. Existing 'here' and 'now', two or three of such facts can substitute and outweigh a long range of other facts.[14]

In post-socialist online discussion groups, the past is never neutral; it is mostly painted in black-and-white tones. Attitudes towards history are passionate: debates of past events produce emotional storms. Sharing memories of a historical event only helps to channel one's affective state.[15] A built-in feature of this emotionality is *verbal aggression* – a characteristic feature of the memory battles that this volume traces. Affective approaches to history allow online followers and fighters to produce a past using both 'classic' and 'non-classic' sources: computer games on history (discussed in Chapter 12, this volume, by Gernot Howanitz) may be as valuable as a school textbook, and a victory over ideological opponents in Wikipedia (a memory war site examined here by Hélène Dounaevsky in Chapter 8) may prove more important than a scholarly search for historical accuracy.

Another specific condition of post-socialist new media is their *transparency* of production and consumption of memory. Social media, in particular, make multiple competing versions of collective memory potentially visible to vast audiences. This openness of new media tools is not unique to post-socialist space – remember how, at the start of this Introduction, we pointed out that digital memory scholars globally observe a new hybridity in public and private memory practices. It is, however, of crucial importance especially to the deconstruction of the rigidly linear and totalizing traditional historical narrative of the Soviet Union. In post-socialist societies it also allows marginalized groups – ethnic minorities, or forgotten actors of certain past events – to appear on the digital scene.[16]

However, despite the widespread expectation that media transparency inevitably promotes democratic cultural processes, in post-socialist new media this visibility often yields complicated side effects. For one, supporters of different ideological positions find themselves overloaded with contradicting historical arguments. As a result, they either express indifference when new memories contest their established versions of the past, or they employ elaborate cynical and aggressive rejection strategies for responding to uncomfortable historical interpretations.

Although digital interactions are irregular and diffuse, post-socialist web users do create *a new topography* with special places of memory discussions, commemorations and fights. Sites of mourning as well as of verbal battles are fixed, but users do subject them to seasonal renovation. Memory messages move along broad 'highways' and narrow 'paths'. As the following chapters demonstrate, new media studies allow for a problematizion of these sites, transformations and trajectories of online memory, while also permitting us to analyse the networked arrangement logic of their information flows and the developmental patterns of users' conventions.

Currently, scholars of digital memory emphasize the need for a conceptual re-equipment: in their view, Halbwachs' notion of *collective memory* – which we briefly discussed above – is more suitable to hierarchically organized mass media than to digital technologies. The alternative notion of *connective memory* highlights both the network structure of digital communities and the fluidity of digital contents (Hoskins 2011).

Studies of post-socialist online memory demonstrate with particular acuity that, in online groups, knowledge and memory are rarely stored in the form of a final text (such as a completed study in a history book). Most materials are *scattered*: information is presented in fragments. In a thematic community it is almost impossible to find comprehensive information on a historical period or event. But then 'completeness' is not what online community members are striving for. The demand for integrity that matters so much to other media is often inappropriate for online disputants. Fragmentation turns into the main mode of presentation for facts, thoughts and emotions. All materials are subjected to the procedural character of online life.

The studies of these post-socialist digital memories in *Memory, Conflict and New Media* draw attention to the phenomenon of *circulation* – circulation of any type of information, in the form of reposts, links, repetitions, quotations, etc., as well as of emotions, feelings, attention and styles of virtual behaviour.[17] Several chapters deal with the circulation of hate speech in historical online communities, and many tackle the phenomenon of *flaming* or *holy wars* – mass-scale, long-term discussions, whose dominating tone is one of insults and mutual hatred, and whose participants defend predefined socio-political positions rather than search for consensus (extensive analyses and samples of this trend are discussed in Chapter 8 by Dounaevsky, Chapter 7 by Kukulin, Chapter 10 by Lastouski, and Chapter 5 by Paulsen).[18] In these and related online memory practices, commemoration often serves as a mere trigger for getting in touch with online friends and enemies; commemoration easily turns into phatic communication.

In the web spaces that this book scrutinizes, *trivia* and *noise* also perform their functions: the limitless discussing and sharing of mundane details and irrelevant side-tracks help arrange a comfortable space for a relaxed or an intense interaction based on discussions of past events. Repetition – as in oral communication – forms the basis for these discussions. It helps stir up certain feelings about a historical event (thankfulness, sorrow, horror or pride: in Russian comment threads related to Soviet history, for instance, we find at least one person who is grateful, one who grieves or fears and one who is proud, as is perhaps best evinced by Lunde (Chapter 6), Kukulin (Chapter 7) and Preda (Chapter 13), this volume). Even the absence of any historical content proper poses no problem for participants (as in the Day without Smolensk Facebook initiative that De Bruyn discusses in Chapter 15): it is their belonging to a group that matters.

To return to the overall aims of our book, the features mentioned all contribute to a post-socialist online culture whose mediations of social and cultural memory partly overlap with but also partly divert from those prevailing in other world regions. Studies of these digital memory practices, as well as inquiries into the new media rules of the production of identity and solidarity, are of vital relevance to the social sciences. The emerging transdisciplinary field of post-socialist digital memories allows for the bringing together of diverse research endeavours in historical memory, post-totalitarian studies, sociology, cultural studies of post-Soviet space and media anthropology. It bridges gaps between three massive scholarly fields: first, inquiries into digitization that take their cues from social and cultural anthropology;[19] second, historiographic-cum-philosophical studies of the traumatic historical memory of the twentieth century that have boomed ever since the 1980s;[20] and finally, the rapidly growing body of work on Soviet and socialist memory.[21]

Memory, Conflict and New Media is our attempt at offering an analytical space where these currently divided lines of scholarly inquiry can meet and blend into one analytical discourse: that of post-socialist digital memories. Interpreting the Internet as an actual space of social interactions, they uncover processes of dealing with the traumatic past and the unsettled present in public consciousness. At the same time, the analyses in this volume have didactic and pedagogic meaning: they shed light on current reinterpretations of twentieth-century history and on the process of national and European identity formation in post-socialist cultures.

Conclusion: limitations, variations, perspectives

This volume seeks to unlock and introduce to non-region specialists the hitherto little-explored digital memory practices of post-socialist space. In doing so, it is naturally not free from its own transcultural limitations.

The following chapters, for one, do not discuss online memory in the many post-socialist nation states (some are still socialist or communist, others merely professed a socialist orientation at some point in their past) that crowd East and South Asia, Latin America, and Africa. They halt mostly at post-Soviet-aligned territory, and the book as a whole evinces a pronounced bias in favour of Russia and Ukraine. This foregrounding of two specific post-socialist nations is no random decision, but rather one that flows from institutional preconditions. In 2010, the Humanities in the European Research Area allocated a three-year grant to Memory at War, the international collaborative research project mentioned earlier in this Introduction, and which explores how in Poland, Russia and Ukraine, political conflicts take the shape of debates about the past. It was within the ramifications of this project that the research collected here was first shared and presented. More specifically, this publication evolved from an international conference – and the first attempt at synthesizing post-socialist digital memories scholarship – hosted by Memory at War's new media spin-off, Web Wars. Based at the University of Bergen, the Web Wars team has explored how the Soviet experience is debated and mediated in digital spheres.[22]

As the Web Wars team builds on expertise in Russian and Ukrainian social media in particular, it is not surprising that its geopolitical focus left a mark upon the conference – and, ultimately, on this volume. That, by implication, such life-changing 'web wars' as the 2007 cyberwar in Estonia and Russia or the 'Hackers United Against External Threats to Russia' attacks on Lithuanian sites have remained outside the scope of this volume does not make them less relevant for the study of post-socialist digital memories at large. The same is true for relevant political and memory-related events in the world region that interests us – the cluster of (mostly Central and Eastern European) post-socialist nations that was formerly somehow aligned with the Soviet Union. We have tried to do some justice to these events by providing readers of this volume with a timeline. Pages 249–60 offer a chronological schedule of (politics- , media- and memory-related) post-socialist events that impacted tangibly upon determining public perceptions of the socialist and Soviet experiment.

At the same time, despite the inevitable regional and other limitations from which this volume suffers, the chapters that follow do tackle and traverse a variety of local, national and ethnic contexts, a plethora of cultural and political experiences, and a diversity of media technologies. If sensitive to the troubled status of the 'nation state' as a coherent socio-political container (in Vincent Mosco's apt words, today, 'key economic, political, social, and cultural decisions are set by global networks of firms, many of which dwarf in wealth and power most of the world's nations' (Mosco 2004: 10)), most chapters do depart from a focus on concrete post-socialist nation states. A majority covers Russia and Ukraine, but they also unravel developments in Belarus (Lastouski), Georgia (Spörer-Wagner), Poland (De Bruyn), and Romania (Reading, Preda). The authors scrutinize top-down commemorative initiatives (Kulyk, Lassila, Spörer-Wagner) alongside grassroots projects (De Bruyn, Dounaevsky, Kulyk, Lastouski, Lunde, Pasholok, Preda, Paulsen) and practices that enhance the position of ethnic and political minorities (Reading). Many discuss social networking sites and blogs (De Bruyn, Kukulin, Kulyk, Lastouski, Lunde, Nikiporets-Takigawa, Pasholok, Preda), while the analyses also zoom in on online archives (Etkind, Nikiporets-Takigawa, Preda, Reading), multimedia art (Preda), digitized news media (Kulyk, Lassila, Spörer-Wagner), chat forums (Lastouski, Lunde), tweets (Paulsen, Nikiporets-Takigawa), wikis (Dounaevsky) and computer games (Howanitz).

Although the multiple interrelations and intersections between the individual chapters refute reductions into rigid sets of predefined categories, we did choose to divide them into three complementary parts: concepts of memory, words of memory, and images of memory. Underlying this – inescapably arbitrary – categorization is our conviction that online memory production always takes the shape of *multimodal communication*. In a helpful definition of this term, communication expert Gunther Kress explains how

> [t]he 21st century is awash with ever more mixed and remixed images, writing, layout, sound, gesture, speech, and 3D objects. Multimodality looks beyond language and examines these multiple modes of communication and meaning making.
>
> (Kress 2009: jacket text)

The multimodality that Kress discerns in online communication in general is formative, too, to online *memory* language. As the following chapters testify, the discourse of digital memories is no rigidly textual language. It is significantly more (audio)visually oriented than non-digital memory language. Admittedly, different digital services and genres may be more or less (audio)visually or textually inclined – think of the primarily visually oriented Second World War-era photo blog as opposed to some text-only Wikipedia entries – but as a rule, the line between strictly linguistic and other forms of communication is principally blurred. This means that although post-Soviet digital memory discourse includes sternly text-oriented samples, users may also express their relationship to the Soviet past through (audio)visual components: say, through retro-styled user pictures or memory-related user profile data, or by posting Soviet-related pictures of film clips.

Our book's three parts take this multimodal dimension of online memory discourse as their starting point. The chapters in Part One, entitled 'Concepts of Memory', set the stage for the other two parts. They address a variety of useful theoretical *concepts* and methodological tools for exploring the concrete instances of multimodal communication that *Memory, Conflict and New Media* examines, and that emerge on the interface of post-socialist reality, (new *and* old) media, and memory. Following Part One are two more empirically oriented parts, which each take one form of online communication as the point of departure. Part Two – 'Words of Memory' – focuses on the myriad digital memory discussions that rely mostly (although rarely exclusively) on language and textual communication. The chapters in this part investigate how web users employ *words* to rework the socialist and Soviet past online. If consisting mostly of written language, most online debates also boast audiovisual components – and those components are foregrounded in the online platforms discussed in Part Three, entitled 'Images of Memory'. The chapters in this final part all, in some way or other, deal with online representations of the Soviet and socialist past that foreground the *visual* and/or the audiovisual.

Together, the three parts vividly illustrate how – to cite another helpful definition by Gunther Kress – in our digitized age, inquiry into '[t]he question of rhetoric – how to make communication most effective in relation to [an] audience, here and now – has moved newly, urgently into the center' (Kress 2004). The book ends with a Conclusion, which not only draws out the chapters' common themes, but also sketches the future research agenda of post-socialist digital memories studies.

In short, then, this volume explores the range of multimodal rhetorical strategies for which individual web users opt when constructing memory online. In order to map out these strategies, the authors of the book's individual chapters take recourse to equally drastically varying methodological approaches. In working with new media content, some revert to statistical analysis and to quantitative or CMC-based methods, while others use discourse or conversational analysis and classic cultural studies tools to get a grasp on their material. Many contributors come at new media from disciplinary backgrounds that do not have a history of placing changes in media usage at the heart of their research practices – think (art and literary) history, political science, philology, anthropology or psychology.

In turning their gaze to digital memory, these scholars employ the same refreshing openness to constantly innovating and improving research methods that marks new media studies at large.[23] On the one hand, their receptivity to new theoretical approaches makes it difficult, at this stage, to assess the applicability and suitability of the proposed methods. As a field, digital memories studies is simply too young to have sufficiently addressed the problems that mar social media research in general – think of the public access restrictions that social media services impose upon large amounts of user details, or the filters used by search engines for presenting customized search results.[24] In the words of renowned new media expert Lev Manovich, 'if you are an anthropologist who is working for Facebook, or a sociologist working for Google, you are lucky – but the rest of us are not' (Manovich 2011).

This book reflects the undefined methodological state that still marks digital memories studies – and, to some extent, new media studies at large – as a field. On the other hand, it is precisely this relative methodological indeterminacy that allows us to present readers with a dazzlingly diverse experimental methodological laboratory – one that (however perfect or imperfect its individual instruments may ultimately prove to be) introduces a range of theoretical tools that, to the student of online memory mediation, is bound to be as inspiring as it is useful.

Together with this new set of methodological tools, *Memory, Conflict and New Media* introduces multiple alternative analytical models and theoretical paradigms – think of the *web war* that we define in this Introduction. In a more transculturally inclusive digital-memories discipline, not only the web war but an entire range of concepts indigenous to post-socialist online memory should be taken into account. The chapters that follow make a solid start in coining and elucidating such a 'post-socialist digital memories language'. By highlighting post-socialist memory's digital mediations *and* digital memory's transcultural scope, they succeed, we believe, in a twofold aim: to deepen and refine both (post-socialist) memory theory and digital memory studies.

Notes

1 We are grateful to the three anonymous Routledge reviewers as well as Volodymyr Kulyk and Julie Fedor for helpful suggestions in crafting this Introduction; needless to add, the responsibility for any remaining errors is ours alone.

2 Scholars today rightly discuss the question how long it will remain appropriate to use such a temporally limiting term as 'post-socialist', and whether it is correct to think of 'the conformity of ideology and policy under socialism . . . as relatively greater than that present in states we characterise as "capitalist"' (Stenning and Hoerschelmann 2008: 322; on the same discussion see also Rogers 2010). However, as long as a more suitable and commonly used alternative is outstanding, this term best covers the shared experience of the cluster of nation states that this volume scrutinizes ('Eastern European' – to mention some examples – is unduly context-dependent; 'post-totalitarian' and 'neoliberal capitalist' overly general; and 'post-communist' problematic, as none of the societies at stake ever evolved into a truly communist society). In this book we also use the term 'post-Soviet': in its narrow sense it refers to the experiences of the former USSR republics; however, in a broader sense we apply it to a set of social and cultural meanings which may still be found in post-socialist countries in connection with their historical links with the Soviet Union.

3 For details on Memory at War – the project whose team members build on this term – see www.memoryatwar.org.

4 On the current tensions 'between globalization and localization, centralization and decentralization, and integration and fragmentation' in our age – and their interconnection with new technologies – see also Rosenau 2000 (as well as Reading, Chapter 1, this volume, which conceptualizes so-called *globital* memory production). According to Rosenau, 'the emergent epoch is not simply one of globalization, but rather [are] its complexities . . . such that it is best thought of as an age of fragmegration [a word that combines the terms 'fragmentation' with 'integration']' (ibid.: 2).

5 According to classic memory studies like Assmann's, communicative memory is short-lived – it connects three living generations – and it does not boast any recognized or institutionalized points of fixation. Digital memories may require a modification of the term: online, memories are often fluid and non-institutionalized, but fixed at the same time. Put differently, although online memory is no 'recognized' place of fixation, it does feature 'sites' or 'points' of fixation.

6 Most importantly, we are thinking of van Dijck (2007); Garde-Hansen *et al.* (2009); Meyers *et al.* (2011); Arthur (forthcoming); and, on the interrelations between new media and cultural heritage, Cameron and Kenderdine (2007); and Kalay *et al.* (2008). German-language research on digital memories includes Claus Leggewie's research project *Visualisierung und Virtualisierung von Erinnerung. Geschichtspolitik in der medialen Erlebnisgesellschaft.*

7 Examples include Danet and Herring (2007); Goggin and McLelland (2009); Androutsopoulos (2006; 2008).

8 Influential analyses of Central and Eastern European and post-Soviet cultures of collective cultural forgetting – ranging from book-length studies to short blog posts – include Nowak (2008); Etkind (2009); and Portnov (2010, 2011a, 2011b).

9 This is not to suggest that forgetting is a cultural strategy used exclusively in post-socialist space: forgetting was a central strategy used for handling the traumas of the Second World War in Western Europe (see esp. Judt 2005: 61–62). Neither do we doubt the need to question neat binary divisions between remembering/forgetting; in Maja Zehfuss' words, 'remembering always already entails forgetting. Thus the opposition of remembering versus forgetting, that values the former over the latter, is more problematic than is acknowledged' (Zehfuss 2007: 33; see, on the same problematization, Winter 2010).

10 For examples, see Kuntsman (2010); and selected chapters in Fawns *et al.* (forthcoming).

11 For examples that tackle Russian and Ukrainian media usage and historical memory, see the two chapters included in the 'Media and Memory' section of Beumers *et al.* (2009); also Kulyk (2010, 2011).
12 Apart from the sources mentioned in note 5, see, on this process, among others, Troebst (2011); Merridale (2010).
13 The same trend has been observed in cases of constructing group identities in memory-related communities across various world regions – say, Western Europe or Israel (see Radstone and Schwarz 2010; Meyers *et al.* 2011) – but our findings indicate that it might well be unusually prominent in post-socialist societies.
14 Apart from several of this book's chapters, see, on this process (especially in Ukraine and Russia), Zvereva (2011); Trubina (2010).
15 On new media, politics/memory and emotion, see Karatzogianni and Kuntsman (2012).
16 On the latter see, among others, Edy (2011).
17 On online circulation see also Kuntsman (2010). Although, without using the term 'circulation', Richard Rogers advocates and develops digital research methods to which the 'dominant techniques employed in authoring and ordering information' online – including recommendation culture, folksonomy and reposts – are central (Rogers 2009: 29).
18 On the phenomenon of flaming, see also Oegema *et al.* (2008); Kuntsman (2009).
19 Apart from the digital memories studies mentioned, one can think here of Goggin (2011); Turner (2010); Fuery (2008); Gershon (2010).
20 Among a plethora of memory-related classics, the groundbreaking publications we have in mind are Nora (1992); Assmann (1992); Winter (1995).
21 For canonical titles on especially Russia and Ukraine see, apart from the analyses mentioned by Portnov, Dubin *et al.* (1998); Gabovich (2005); Plokhy (2008); Oushakine and Trubina (2009); Koposov (2011).
22 See www.web-wars.org for a full project description and recent project-related news.
23 For influential discussions on the question of how to tackle online data as a humanities scholar, see Rogers (2009) and Manovich (2011).
24 On these problems see, among others, Hargittai (2007); Manovich (2011); Pariser (2011).

References

Androutsopoulos, J. (2006) 'Introduction: Sociolinguistics and Computer-Mediated Communication'. *Journal of Sociolinguistics* 10(4): 419–438. Online. Available: <http://onlinelibrary.wiley.com/doi/10.1111/j.1467-9841.2006.00286.x/full> (accessed 8 March 2012).

Androutsopoulos, J. (2008) 'Potentials and Limitations of Discourse-centered Online Ethnography'. *Language@Internet* 5. Online. Available: <http://www.languageatinternet.de/articles/2008/1610/androutsopoulos.pdf/> (accessed 9 March 2011).

Arthur, P.L. (forthcoming) *History and New Media*. London and New York: Anthem Press.

Assmann, A. (2012) *Die Zukunft der Erinnerung under der Holocaust*. Konstanz: Konstanz University Press.

Assmann, J. (1992) *Das kulturelle Gedaechtnis: Schrift, Erinnerung und politische Identitaet in fruehen Hochkulturen*. Munich: C.H. Beck.

Assmann, J. (2008) 'Communicative and Cultural Memory', in A. Erll and A. Nuenning (eds), *Cultural Memory Studies*. Berlin: De Gruyter.

Beumers, B., Hutchings, S.C. and Rulyova, N. (eds) (2009) *The Post-Soviet Russian Media: Conflicting Signals*. London: Routledge.

Cameron, F. and Kenderdine, S. (eds) (2007) *Theorizing Digital Cultural Heritage*. Cambridge, MA: MIT Press.

Cosenza, V. (2012) 'World Map of Social Networks'. *Vincos Blog*, June 2012. Online. Available: < http://www.vincos.it/world-map-of-social-networks/> (accessed 30 June 2012).

Danet, B. and Herring, S. (eds) (2007) *The Multilingual Internet: Language, Culture, and Communication Online*. Oxford: Oxford University Press.

Dubin, B. (2004) '"Krovavaia" voina i "velikaia" pobeda. O konstruirovanii i peredache kollektivnykh predstavlenii v Rossii 1970–2000-kh godov ["Bloody" War and "Great" Victory. On the Construction and Transfer of Collective Representations in Russia in the Years 1970 – 2000]'. *Otechestvennie zapiski* 5. Online. Available: < http://www.strana-oz.ru/2004/5/krovavaya-voyna-i-velikaya-pobeda> (accessed 1 June 2012).

Dubin, B. (2008) 'Pamiat', voina, pamiat' o voine. Konstruirovanie proshlogo v sotsialnoi pamiati poslednikh desiatiletii [Memory, War, Memory of War. The Construction of the Past in Social Memory of the Past Decades]'. *Otechestvennie zapiski* 4. Online. Available: <http://www.strana-oz.ru/2008/4/pamyat-voyna-pamyat-o-voyne-konstruirovanie-proshlogo-v-socialnoy-praktike-poslednih-desyatiletiy> (accessed 1 June 2012).

Dubin, B. (2011) *Rossiia nulevykh. Politicheskaia kultura. Istoricheskaia pamiat'. Povsednevnaia zhizn'* [Russia in the 2000s. Political Culture. Historical Memory. Everyday Life]. Moscow: Rossiiskaia Politicheskaia Entsiklopediia.

Edy, J.A. (2011) 'The Democratic Potential of Mediated Collective Memory', in O. Meyers, M. Neiger and E. Zandberg (eds), *On Media Memory*: 37–48.

Erll, A. and Rigney, A. (eds) (2009) *Mediation, Remediation, and the Dynamics of Cultural Memory*. Berlin: De Gruyter.

Etkind, A. (2009) 'Stories of the Undead in the Land of the Unburied: Magical Historicism in Contemporary Russian Fiction'. *Slavic Review* 68(3): 631–659.

Fawns, T., Wilson, P. and McEntaggart, P. (eds) (forthcoming) *Digital Memories* (preliminary title). Freeland: Inter-Disciplinary Press.

Fuery, K. (2008) *New Media: Culture and Image*. Basingstoke: Palgrave Macmillan.

Gabovich, M. (2005) *Pamiat' o voine 60 let spustia: Rossiia, Germaniia, Evropa* [Memory of War 60 Years Later: Russia, Germany, Europe]. Moscow: NLO.

Garde-Hansen, J., Hoskins, A. and Reading, A. (eds) (2009) *Save As . . . Digital Memories*. Basingstoke: PalgraveMacmillan.

Gershon, I. (2010) *The Breakup 2.0: Disconnecting over New Media*. Ithaca, NY: Cornell University Press.

Gill, G. and Young, J. (eds) (2012) *Routledge Handbook of Russian Politics and Society*. New York: Routledge.

Goggin, G. (2011) *Global Mobile Media*. New York: Routledge.

Goggin, G. and McLelland, M.J. (eds) (2009) *Internationalizing Internet Studies*. New York: Routledge.

Gudkov, L. (2011) *Abortivnaia modernizatsiia* [Abortive Modernization]. Moscow: Rossiiskaia Politicheskaia Entsiklopediia.

Halbwachs, M. (1950) *La mémoire collective*. Paris: Presses Universitaires de France.

Hargittai, E. (2007) 'The Social, Political, Economic, and Cultural Dimensions of Search Engines'. Special issue *Journal of Computer-Mediated Communication* 12(3). Online. Available <http://onlinelibrary.wiley.com/doi/10.1111/jcmc.2007.12.issue-3/issuetoc> (accessed 4 November 2011).

Hoskins, A. (2011) 'Anachronisms of Media, Anachronisms of Memory: From Collective Memory to a New Memory Ecology', in O. Meyers, M. Neiger and E. Zandberg (eds), *On Media Memory*: 278–289.

Huyssen, A. (2003) *Present Pasts: Urban Palimpsests and the Politics of Memory*. Stanford, CA: Stanford University Press.

Judt, T. (2005) *Postwar: A History of Europe since 1945*. New York: Penguin.

Kalay, Y.E., Kvan, T. and Affleck J. (eds) (2008) *New Heritage: New Media and Cultural Heritage*. New York: Routledge.

Karatzogianni, A. and Kuntsman, A. (eds) (2012) *Digital Cultures and the Politics of Emotion: Feelings, Affect and Technological Change*. Basingstoke: PalgraveMacmillan.

Koposov, N. (2011) *Pamiat' strogogo rezhima: istoriia i politika v Rossii* [Memory of a Fierce Regime: History and Politics in Russia]. Moscow: NLO.

Kress, G. (2004) 'Reading Images: Multimodality, Representation and New Media'. *Expert Forum for Knowledge Presentation*. Online. Available: <http://www.knowledgepresentation.org/BuildingTheFuture/Kress2/Kress2.html>.

Kress, G. (2009) *Multimodality: A Semiotic Approach to Contemporary Communication*. New York: Routledge.

Kulyk, V. (2010) *Dyskurs ukraïns'kykh medii: identychnosti, ideolohiï, vladni stosunky* [Discourse of Ukrainian Media: Identities, Ideologies and Power Relations]. Kyiv: Krytyka.

Kulyk, V. (2011) 'The Media, History and Identity: Competing Narratives of the Past in the Ukrainian Popular Press'. *National Identities* 13: 287–303.

Kuntsman, A. (2009) *Figurations of Violence and Belonging: Queerness, Migranthood and Nationalism in Cyberspace and Beyond*. Oxford: Peter Lang.

Kuntsman, A. (2010a) 'Webs of Hate in Diasporic Cyberspaces: The Gaza War in the Russian-language Blogosphere'. *Media, War and Conflict* 3(3): 299–313.

Kuntsman, A. (ed.) (2010b) 'War, Conflict and Commemoration in the Age of Digital Reproduction'. Special issue of *Digital Icons* 4. Online. Available: <http://www.digitalicons.org/issue04/> (accessed 4 November 2011).

Lapina-Kratasiuk, E., Rutten, E., Saunders, R., Schmidt, H. and Strukov, V. (eds) (2009) 'Virtual Power: Russian Politics and the Internet'. Special issue of *The Russian Cyberspace Journal* 1. Online. Available: < http://www.digitalicons.org/issue01/> (accessed 9 November 2011).

Leggewie, C. (2011) 'Visualisierung und Virtualisierung von Erinnerung. Geschichtspolitik in der medialen Erlebnisgesellschaft'. Online. Available: <http://www.uni-giessen.de/erinnerungskulturen/home/teilprojekt-16.php> (accessed 10 November 2011).

Livingstone, S. (2009) 'On the Mediation of Everything'. *Journal of Communication* 59(1), Spring: 1–18.

Manovich, L. (2011) 'Trending: The Promises and the Challenges of Big Social Data'. Online. Available: <http://www.manovich.net/DOCS/Manovich_trending_paper.pdf> (accessed 7 December 2011).

Mayer-Schoenberger, V. (2009) *Delete: The Virtue of Forgetting in the Digital Age*. Princeton, NJ: Princeton University Press.

Merridale, C. (2010) 'Soviet Memories: Patriotism and Trauma', in S. Radstone and B. Schwarz (eds) *Memory. Histories, Theories, Debates*. New York: Fordham University Press.

Meyers, O., Neiger, M. and Zandberg, E. (eds) (2011) *On Media Memory: Collective Memory in a New Media Age*. Basingstoke: Palgrave Macmillan.

Mosco, V. (2004) *The Digital Sublime: Myth, Power, and Cyberspace*. Cambridge, MA: MIT Press.

Nikulin, A. (ed.) (2007) *Puti Rossii: preemstvennost' i preryvistost' obshchestvennogo razvitiia* [Ways of Russia: Continuity and Discontinuity of Social Development]. Moscow: MVShSEN.

Nora, P. (1992) *Lieux de mémoire*. Paris: Gallimard.

Nowak, A. (2008) 'History as an Apology for Totalitarianism', in A. Nowak, *History and Geopolitics: A Contest for Eastern Europe*. Warsaw: Polish Institute of International Affairs.

Oegema, D., Kleinnijenhuis, J., Anderson, K. and Van Hoof, A.M.J. (2008) 'Flaming and Blaming: The Influence of Mass Media Content on Interactions in On-line Discussions'. IE. Konijn, M. Tanis, S. Barnes and S. Utz (eds), *Mediated Interpersonal Communication*. New York: Routledge.

Oushakine, S. and Trubina, E. (2009) *Travma: Punkty* [Trauma: Points]. Moscow: NLO.

Pariser, E. (2011) *The Filter Bubble: What the Internet is Hiding From You*. London: Penguin.

Plokhy, S. (2008) *Ukraine and Russia: Representations of the Past*. Toronto: University of Toronto Press.

Portnov, A. (2010) *Uprazhneniia s istoriei po-ukrainski* [Exercises with History in Ukrainian Way]. Moscow: OGI.

Portnov, A. (2011a) 'Sites of Forgetting'. *Memory at War Blog*, 21 March. Online. Available: <http://cambridgeculturalmemory.blogspot.com/2011/03/historian-andriy-portnov-on-sites-of.html> (accessed 4 November 2011).

Portnov, A. (2011b) 'Sites of Forgetting II'. *Memory at War Blog*, 5 April. Online. Available: <http://cambridgeculturalmemory.blogspot.com/2011/04/sites-of-forgetting-ii-by-andriy.html> (accessed 4 November 2011).

Radstone, S. and Schwarz, B. (eds) (2010) *Memory. Histories, Theories, Debates*. New York: Fordham University Press.

Rogers, D. (2010) 'Postsocialisms Unbound: Connections, Critiques, Comparisons'. *Slavic Review* 69(1), Spring: 1–16.

Rogers, R. (2009) *The End of the Virtual: Digital Methods*. Amsterdam: Amsterdam University Press.

Rogers, R. (2011) 'Digital Methods'. Online. Available: <http://www.digitalmethods.net> (accessed 7 December 2011).

Rosenau, J. (2000) 'The Governance of Fragmegration: Neither a World Republic Nor a Global Interstate System'. Paper presented at the Congress of International Political Science Association, 1–5 August. Online. Available: <http://www.lanna-website-promotion.com/moonhoabinh/lunar_material/GovernanceOfFragmegration.pdf> (accessed 5 July 2012).

Riabchuk, M. (2007) 'Kul'tura pamiati i politika zabveniia [The Culture of Memory and the Politics of Forgetting]'. *Otechestvennie zapiski* 1. Online. Available: <http://www.bigyalta.com.ua/story/2626>, <http://www.bigyalta.com.ua/story/2631> (accessed 1 June 2012).

Spiegel, S. (2000) 'Traditional Space vs. Cyberspace: The Changing Role of Geography in Current International Politics'. *Geopolitics* 5(3), Autumn: 114–125.

Stenning, A. and Hoerschelmann, K. (2008) 'History, Geography and Difference in the Post-socialist World: Or, Do We Still Need Post-Socialism?' *Antipode* 40(2), Summer: 312–335.

Troebst, S. (2011) *Erinnerungskultur – Kulturgeschichte – Geschichtsregion. Ost(mittel)europa in Europa*. Stuttgart: F. Steiner.

Trubina, E. (2010) 'Past Wars in the Russian Blogosphere: On the Emergence of Cosmopolitan Memory', in *Digital Icons: Studies in Russian, Eurasian and Central European New Media* 4. Online. Available: <http://www.digitalicons.org/issue04/> (accessed 4 July 2012).

Trzeciak, S. (2012) *Poland's EU Accession*. New York: Routledge.

Turner, G. (2010) *Ordinary People and the Media: The Demotic Turn*. London: Sage.

van Dijck, J. (2007) *Mediated Memories in the Digital Age*. Stanford, CA: Stanford University Press.

Wanner, C. (1998) *Burden of Dreams: History and Identity in Post-Soviet Ukraine*. University Park, PA: Pennsylvania State University Press.

Wilson, A. (2009) *The Ukrainians: Unexpected Nation*, 3rd edn. New Haven, CT: Yale University Press.

Winter, J. (1995) *Sites of Memory, Sites of Mourning: The Great War in European History*. Cambridge: Cambridge University Press.

Winter, J. (2010) ‘Reflections on Silence’. Keynote paper presented at the Memory at War Inaugural Workshop, 4–5 June. King's College, University of Cambridge.

Zehfuss, M. (2007) *Wounds of Memory: The Politics of War in Germany*. Cambridge: Cambridge University Press.

Zhurzhenko, T. (2007) ‘The Geopolitics of Memory’. *Eurozine*, 10 May. Online. Available: <http://www.eurozine.com/pdf/2007-05-10-zhurzhenko-en.pdf> (accessed 12 July 2012).

Zvereva, V. (2011) ‘Historical Events and the Social Network ‘V Kontakte’’. *East European Memory Studies Newsletter* 7: 1–6. Online. Available: <http://www.memoryatwar.org/enewsletter-nov-2011.pdf> (accessed 30 November 2011).

Part One

Concepts of memory

If memory is today to a large extent produced, stored and consumed online, then how do we analyse the *digital memories* (Garde-Hansen *et al.* 2009) that new media generate? Which analytical tools best suit the memory practices in which web users engage – on a global scale, that is, but also specifically in post-socialist space, which is the world region that interests us here? How, in short, do we analyse *post-socialist digital memories*?

Part One of this volume provides a set of theoretical concepts and methodological tools for understanding the *multimodal memory communication* (Kress 2009, see also Introduction, this volume) of new-media users in and from post-socialist states. It consists of five chapters that offers students and scholars some methodological foothold in the labyrinth of memory wars that crowd the Web – especially in the nations that we tackle here: those formerly belonging to or aligning with the Soviet Union. Together, its contributors have woven a helpful theoretical 'safety net' for further investigation into the field.

The mazes and shapes of this 'safety net' differ from chapter to chapter, however. Some contributors are interested primarily in the new *dynamics* of online memory practices. Communication scholar Anna Reading, for instance, zooms in on Roma (and Romanian) memory to demonstrate how new technologies generate a *globital memory field* – that is, forms of memory production and consumption that are endemic to our trans-medial, globalized world of mobile connectivities. Others explain how statistical digital tools – think Google Books's Ngram Viewer, but also such less universally known tools as the Integrum database and search engine Yandex's Pulse of the Blogosphere – can help us in unravelling mediated memory conflicts. In their contributions, historian Alexander Etkind and linguist Galina Nikiporets-Takigawa focus on such milestones of socialist history as the 'Great Patriotic War' (the Soviet designation for the Second World War) to illustrate how Ngram and other statistical instruments may be put to work in tracking post-socialist digital memory practices. Their analyses indicate that, despite their obvious limitations, statistical methods can prove fruitful trackers of a *memory event*, post-socialist and global alike – that is, 'a re-discovery of the past that creates a rupture with its accepted cultural meaning' (Etkind 2010).

Both Etkind and Nikiporets-Takigawa use digital tools to explore a memory culture that unfolds either partly or wholly offline. Their chapters are followed by an analysis that provides yet more 'offline background' for the analyses that follow. Its author Volodymyr Kulyk – a political scientist with a special interest in media usage – traces how in Ukraine, on- *and* offline mediated memories have been tangibly coloured by the country's turbulent political landscape. Providing a lush historical background for the many chapters on Ukrainian new media that follow, Kulyk outlines how, in a society where politicians relentlessly interfere with and manipulate the multiple socio-political identities of its citizens, the relationship between media and memory is principally fraught.

Part One closes with a chapter that, after Kulyk's historical background, takes readers to the near-future, by monitoring events as they unfold in real time. In a chapter that inquires how memory of the Ukrainian famine of 1932–1933 is mediated via Twitter, linguist and new media expert Martin Paulsen provides a rich theoretical discussion both of Twitter as a medium and its position as a memory platform among other online media.

Together, the five chapters present a productive methodological and theoretical toolkit – to the junior and more experienced scholar alike – for explorations into the digital memories of post-socialist subjects. More importantly, perhaps, in doing so they also help in refining and grounding existing thinking on digital memories – a line of thinking that all too often sees online memory as a universal practice while reckoning only marginally with linguo-cultural varieties.

References

Etkind, A. (2010) 'Mapping Memory Events in the East European Space'. *East European Memory Studies Newsletter* 1. Online. Available: <http://www.memoryatwar.org/enewsletter%20oct%202010%20final.pdf> (accessed 10 July 2012).

Garde-Hansen, J., Hoskins, A. and Reading, A. (eds) (2009) *Save As . . . Digital Memories*. Basingstoke: PalgraveMacmillan.

Kress, G. (2009) *Multimodality: A Semiotic Approach to Contemporary Communication*, New York: Routledge.

1 Europe's other world

Romany memory within the new dynamics of the globital memory field

Anna Reading

> Slaves differed from other human beings in that they were not allowed freely to integrate the experience of their ancestors into their lives, to inform their understanding of social reality with the inherited meanings of their natural forebears, or to anchor the living present in any conscious community of memory.
>
> (Patterson 2011: 279)

Digital connective media are enabling new articulations of memory that reanimate what has been a viscous amnesia of slavery within the heartland of Europe. This chapter aims to examine how digital connective media may offer new possibilities in relation to the public memory of Roma in Europe. What may be loosely termed 'older media' have in various ways erased significant aspects of Roma – 'gypsy' – memory, including Europe's shameful history of *rrobia*, namely Roma people's enslavement for over 500 years in what is now predominantly the national territory of Romania. In escaping bondage, Roma people fled across Europe, resulting in the present-day Roma communities to be found in all countries of Europe, with substantial minorities in Poland, Hungary, the Czech Republic and Slovakia. Slavery in various forms continued until abolition, or *desrrobija*, which began as a social and legislative movement at the end of the eighteenth century. Inspired in part by other anti-slavery campaigns in Europe and North America, the anti-slavery movement continued as an ongoing social and political struggle until the end of Roma slavery in the middle of the nineteenth century.[1]

This chapter's focus is also aimed at highlighting the fact that, when considering the post-socialist context, we need to be alive to the experience not only of nations with territories, but also of transnational minorities – minorities whose memory may have been previously de-legitimated within totalitarian regimes. As Orlando Patterson's work on memory and the slavery of African people suggests, a feature of slavery is the denial of inheritance and of a community of memory (Patterson 2011). Roma people have suffered a double de-legitimation of their past which makes the study of Roma memory particularly important within any study of memory and digital media in the new Europe.

Roma are, in fact, the biggest ethnic minority in Europe.[2] They have an estimated population of 10 to 12 million people and live and work in all 27 EU

Member States (European Commission 2010), with significant minorities in Russia, Ukraine and Turkey.[3] There are historically settled communities as well as travelling communities that go back more than 600 years. In 2005 the EU launched 'The Decade of Roma Inclusion', a major programme aimed at reducing discrimination and marginalization of Roma within education, employment, healthcare and housing. Yet more than five years on, many Roma continue to experience forced evictions from their homes and are subject to violence and discrimination in education, healthcare and at work, with many forced to live on sites comprising former refuse or chemical dumps, or former industrial land, often contaminated with lead or asbestos (EU-MIDIS 2009: 5).

When Orlando Patterson wrote *Slavery and Social Death* (2011) he was particularly referring to the impact upon collective memory of making African people into property that could be bought and sold as part of the transatlantic slave trade. In his idea of natal alienation, he encapsulates how being made into property erases ancestry and with it the sense of the past. Significantly, and in keeping with Patterson's thesis, European narratives have also constructed Roma as a people without a past or a history (Trumpener 1992), often with the added 'justification' that Roma themselves are a present-centred people who supposedly have no interest in the past (Lemon 2000). The unarticulated memory of *rrobia* or Roma slavery within the public discourses of older media was then compounded with a lack of articulation in public memory of Nazi atrocities specifically against European Roma, and subsequent mistreatment after the Second World War within state socialist Eastern bloc countries that included the denial of human rights and forced sterilization of Roma women (Barany 2000; Crowe 1991; Heuss 1997).

Thus it was only in 2011, 155 years after the abolition of Roma slavery in Europe, that there was the beginning of some public recognition of *desrrobija* in the form of plans for a monument by Roma sculptor Marian Petre in Bucharest (Lakatis 2011). This came about within a context not only of political changes since 1989 in post-socialist countries, but, as importantly, also within the context of digitization. Connective technologies, such as mobile phones and social networking sites, combined with the impact of uneven processes of globalization, are developing what elsewhere I have termed a *globital memory field* that has new memory dynamics and forms of engagement.

This chapter briefly explains the six analytical dynamics of the *globital memory field*. Using the dynamics as a method of analysis enables a clearer understanding of the ways in which digital technologies are reshaping Roma mediated memory in post-socialist Europe. Analysing Roma digital memory through these dynamics suggests how Romany memories are being *dis embodied*, *dis embedded* and *dis connected*. These processes seem to be extending and enabling resilient ways of telling the past for Europe's other world. This chapter argues for a greater heterogeneity to what has largely been a Western European construction of European history and memory (Mälksoo 2009). It also signals the need for a transnational approach. This is crucial, since some memory communities such as the Roma live and travel throughout the region. A transnational approach, this chapter argues, will enable a more complex understanding of how digital media may rearticulate neglected stories within the new Europe.

I begin the chapter with a short introduction to the concept of the globital memory field. I then briefly summarize some of the ways in which Roma memory has been discursively erased within 'older media', before tracing the dynamics of the globital memory field to reveal some of the emergent articulations of Roma memory in post-socialist Europe.

The globital memory field

This chapter takes forward the work of Robert Saunders' insights on Roma identities online in his book chapter 'The Cybernetic Vanguard; The Roma's Use of the Web to Protect a Minority Under Siege' (Saunders 2010). Saunders' work examines ethno-politics and minority nationalism in relation to webs of Roma identity. Drawing theoretically on cyber-theory, his work takes this forward specifically in relation to Roma memories. Theoretically and methodically, this moves beyond his studies through an understanding of the synergetic dynamics of *globalization* and *digitization* as an immanent process in memory.

A number of scholars have argued that globalization in combination with digitization is changing memory languages, practices and forms (Assmann and Conrad 2011; Frosh and Pinchevski 2009; Garde-Hansen *et al.* 2009; Morris-Suzuki 2005; van Dijck 2007). My own work has suggested that the synergetic dynamics of globalization with digitization is developing a *globital memory field* that cuts across conventionally understood binaries of the communicative versus the cultural, the individual versus the social, or the national versus the transnational. With this come new kinds of memory practices, languages and forms that are redrawing and reshaping memory.

How, then, might the concept of the globital memory field enable new approaches and methods of analysis within the field of digital memory studies? The conceptualization seeks to understand the intersecting processes of digitization and globalization, recognizing the importance of processes of assemblage and trajectory across and between the private and the public, the individual and the collective, the digital and the analogue, the material and the energetic. The term 'globital memory field' as a term is meant to combine the word 'global' in tension with 'bit'. *Bit* is a computing term that refers to the binary values of 0 and 1. Put together as a contiguous sequence, bits make up the smallest meaningful sequence of data – a *byte*. The term 'glo*bit*al memory field' thus seeks to denote the intermeshing processes that are often interrupted through the unevenness of digitization at various levels. These include the intersecting of micro with macro memory, the collective with the individual, the cultural with the social, the mediated with the non-mediated.

Put together with the word 'field', the term 'globital memory field' borrows Pierre Bourdieu's approach to the analysis of culture: for Bourdieu, culture is a *field*. For Bourdieu, the term 'field' refers to a setting in which agents struggle over cultural production, consumption and circulation (Bourdieu 2003). The globital memory field, though, involves in particular the struggle by agents of memory (e.g. witnesses, journalists, museum curators and economic stakeholders) over what may be understood as the mobilization, assemblage and securitization of memory. With the digital media era these struggles may be engaged within largely hidden languages of the computer, based on algorithms, and are enabled through the energetic connections of electricity. Thus the modes of struggle may be economic, they may be psychological, they may be socio-political, but they are also algorithmic and electric.

The struggles take place through intersecting pluri-medial assemblages. These are articulated through different material practices and discursive formations.[4] These assemblages are subject to and combine with processes of securitization – processes that consolidate or secure the pluri-medial assemblage. At the same time, trajectories of mobilization open the assemblage to change. An example of this procedure is the way in which entries in *Wikipedia* are added to, altered and changed by Wiki developers, sometimes initially with more than one entry for the same referent. Over time, one version becomes fixed or made secure as the official *Wikipedia* entry; the entry may then be withdrawn or added to again, by different people and organizations with different interests and versions relating to the referent.

The globital memory field is characterized by six core dynamics.[5] These six dynamics may be used as an analytical framework or method to reveal new memorial emergences and engagements within the context of digital and connective communication. First, analytically there is the extent to which mediated memory is no longer secured within one medium but – through digitization and connectivity – is mobilized and transformed across different media: I call this the *dynamic of transmediality*. Second, within the globital memory field there is the speed (which may be rapid or slow) with which mediated memory assemblages can be mobilized across the electric, algorithmic, socio-political, economic and psychic dimensions of the field: analytically, this is termed the *dynamic of velocity*. Third, there is the mediated memory assemblages' limit as well as reach from the historical point of origin: this is termed the *dynamic of extensity*. Fourth, there is the degree to which a mediated memory assemblage conforms to or is secured within a general pattern, particular group or category: analytically, this is termed the *dynamic of modality*. Fifth, drawing on the idea from chemistry of how atoms are bonded onto other atoms, there is the dynamic of valency. This refers to the degree of 'sticky points' between the assemblage and other assemblages. The sixth dynamic is the *dynamic of viscosity*. In part this term is suggested by Zygmunt Bauman's idea (2000) of liquid modernity. Liquid modernity refers to the present stage of modernity characterized by liquidity, change and instantaneity. In arguing for the significance of paying attention to viscosity, however, the globital memory framework departs from the assumption that all is necessarily more liquid. Rather, the analyst is attentive to the mediated memory assemblage's particular processes of flux or change which may flow, melt, be resistant or solidify over time and space.

These six analytical dynamics may be discursively articulated across several different axes. The first axis (x) plots the material practices and discursive formations of the assemblage. These are then subject to the (y) axis – processes of mobilization and securitization.

Roma memory: forms of erasure in older media

How then might we use this model to analyse new emergences of Roma memory within the globital memory field? To track these emergences, we need first to have some picture of how Roma memory has been articulated within older media. There are, within older media, a number of fairly stable identifiable discursive frameworks that articulate particular logics of erasure in relation to the Roma past and its community of memory.[6] Earlier studies suggest that news reports nearly always frame Roma as criminals or as engaged in criminal activity, often basing this conception on the idea that Roma do not understand mainstream ideas of private property or the idea of property rights. This involves a significant discursive inversion: it erases Roma memory of slavery and the memory that it was in fact precisely the Roma in what is now the territory of Romania who were made into chattels or non-people from 1374 until the 1850s. Older media, through asserting that it is Roma who do not understand property rights or who steal from the European *gajo* (non-Roma or non-gypsy) society, invert and erase the central fact that it was *gajo* society that stole from the Roma: *Gajo* made Roma into property, held them captive and enslaved them. This discursive inversion is a clear example of 'the social death' of slaves that Patterson terms 'natal alienation'. This means that owing to their earlier history of enslavement in Europe, Roma have often been cut off from the possibility of anchoring the present in what Patterson calls a 'community of memory' (Patterson 2011: 279).

Further, studies of the representation of Roma in 'older media' such as the press show what may then be deduced as three other discursive frameworks and logics of erasure. These are summarized in Table 1.1.[7]

So, what happens to these logics of erasure within the globital memory field of post-socialist states? In tension with the older media logics there are some new dynamics that suggest the emergence of a limited recognition of Roma memory through various digitized public media.

Roma memory in the globital memory field

Let us take as a discrete example the first of these discursive frameworks and logics of erasure, the one that erases the memory of slavery through the articulation of Roma as criminals or engaged in theft or criminal activity. Within general history books on slavery, the slavery of Roma and the impact of the abolitionist movement in Eastern Europe is barely mentioned, and is kept separate from wider European history. This statement also applies, incidentally, to the work of Orlando Patterson himself, who concentrates on the transatlantic slave trade and whose work does not reference the slavery of Roma peoples. If we turn to the globital memory field, however, we see the emergence of a different picture. For example, digitization and connective media allow for the public circulation of some of the original Bills of Sale advertising Roma slaves that date from the seventeenth and eighteenth centuries. Originally, these would have been printed in local European newspapers, such as the Bucharest newspaper *Luna*, which features one such notice

Table 1.1 Discursive logics of erasure of mediated Roma memory

Discursive framework	*Logic of erasure*	*Forgotten memory*
Roma are criminals, they steal	Discursive inversion Roma do not understand property rights.	Erases fact that Roma were made into property and held captive
Roma are a nomadic people with few settled communities	Discursive inversion Roma are wanderers with no need for roots	Erases longevity of Roma in Europe Makes invisible settled Roma communities Makes invisible forced evictions, deportations
Roma are not interested in their past	Roma have no written culture They have taboos on remembering the dead	Makes invisible lack of public interest; post-war research: prohibition on memorials; continuation of anti-gypsy policies; Makes invisible impact of sterilization on genealogical memory
Roma have not contributed to European societies and therefore their past is of no national interest	Commercialism/ capitalism	Erases and 'consumes' sites and places of Roma memory

Figure 1.1 For Sale: A prime lot of serfs or slaves. Gypsy (Tzigany). Through an auction at noon at the St Elias Monastery on 8 May 1852 consisting of 18 Men, 10 boys, 7 Women and 3 girls in excellent condition.[8]

advertising 'gypsy slaves for sale' in 1852. This bill was reproduced in 2002 in another printed form, the history book, *We are the Romani People: Ame Sam RRomane džene: Volume 28* (Hancock 2002). The printed book about Roma in Europe includes an historical overview of their enslavement by the well-known Romany scholar Ian Hancock. Sections of the book have since been made available online, and the Bill advertising the slaves has subsequently been digitally copied and circulated on the Web, through multiple sources including Wikipedia. I can easily search for 'Roma, bills of sale' from any networked computer sited anywhere on the globe. I can save it, download it and reassemble it with other material.

If we apply the analytical framework of the globital memory field with its six dynamics, the resulting table brings into view the new emergences of the digitized Bill of Sale in comparison with its earlier (older media) reproduction in the printed book (Table 1.2).

I will describe in more detail what this analysis, using the six dynamics of the globital memory field, reveals:

- The original newspaper advertisement reappeared in print form when it was reprinted in Hancock's book. The digitized on-line source of the Bill of Sale is transmedial however: it becomes mobilized in multiple forms that include print media, but also screen media. It now has the *transmedial* potential to be used in other material forms, as well as to be assembled into moving images or reassembled and reworked with other images.
- The earlier *velocity* of transformation and access through older media moving from the original Bill of Sale to disseminatation in the book was 150 years;

Table 1.2 Trajectories of mediated memory within the globital memory field articulating new visibilities of Roma *rrobia* (slavery).

Analytical dynamics of globital memory field	*Mediated memory*	*Globital memory field*
Media memory example	Nineteenth-century newspaper Bill of Sale	Online source
(Trans)-mediality	Printed newspaper to printed book	Multiple digital media forms
Velocity	150 years	Seconds, minutes, hours
Extensity	Local-nation-nation	Local-nation, Europe-wide, transnational/global-local
Modality	Print to print: limited	Print media to poly-modal: Community websites; Wikipedia; Person – wearable prosthetic – network – prosthetic Multiple/contingent; bonds with wider abolitionist history
Valency	Limited bonds	Multiple and multiplying bonds
Viscosity	Fixed/solid	Liquid
Axis	X vertical	X vertical and Y horizontal

within the globital memory field, the velocity of dissemination and distribution for the Bill of Sale is transformed, with the potential for multiple access points via computer and connective and mobile technologies in seconds, minutes and hours.

- In terms of the dynamic of *extensity*, the original Bill of Sale had very limited reach from its point of origin. By contrast, the digital Bill of Sale has extensive reach. It travels and is capable of being mobilized rapidly from its local points of origin. It is being disseminated worldwide, transnationally as well as moving from the global back to the local.
- The *modalities* of the original and reproduced book image are within only two categories: the categories are situated within the conventions of an advertisement and within the conventions of the historical text. But in terms of the modalities of the Bill of Sale within the globital memory field, the digitized object of the Bill of Sale is poly-modal, articulated within a variety of different conventions that include community websites, Wikipedia, newspapers, campaigning organizations and so on. It may be downloaded to the PC but also to the mobile phone, thus moving from the public realm of the archive or public library to a personally networked wearable *memory prosthetic* – an artificial memory device that is so close to the body that it becomes an additional part of it.
- In terms of the dynamic of *valency*, the reproduced Bill of Sale in the book has very limited bonds or 'sticky points' with other historical discourses; the digital Bill of Sale has multiple and multiplying bonds with, for example, wider abolitionist history.
- Finally, in relation to the dynamic of *viscosity*, we can see that whereas the reproduced print image is fixed and travels vertically, the digital image within the globital memory field has less *viscosity*; it flows easily, being mobilized and travelling vertically as well as horizontally between different memory agents and organizations.

Conclusion

The digitized Bill of Sale is of course just one discrete and minor indicator of new emergences of Roma memory that are being mobilized. There is much research still to be done in this regard, as there is so little work generally on Roma memory and even less in terms of how it is articulated within a globalized and digitized context. For example, as well as the digitization of older print journalism within the globital memory field – newspaper to book, book to multiple assemblages – there are interesting emergences in the globital memory field, of feature-length news stories around anniversaries related to the Holocaust, for example, that are then archived on mainstream news websites. One such report by the BBC in 2009 provided new evidence of brutality during the Nazi period using original interviews with men and women from Vlasca, the Kalderash (BBC 2009). Such journalism is then digitally archived and becomes more easily accessible, at least to those with Internet access, in ways that were not possible prior to the advent of the globital memory field.

Another area to examine within the globital memory field concerns the digitization of public and state archives themselves, with analogue documents that were once obscure and difficult to access becoming digitally accessible. Where previously Roma interviews or testimonies would have required extensive travel and fieldwork, Roma people's stories are now easily mobilized across multiple sites, with more extensive reach, and access worldwide, at least from anywhere with a computer or mobile device and broadband access. These stories may then be downloaded and reassembled within a localized context of meaning; they may also be digitally stitched together with other digital fragments to enable a fuller articulation of Roma memories. Further, digital media are more able to capture performances of culture that articulate a heritage and a community of memory in ways that include artworks, videos and dance, with a community of memory developing through, for example, Roma musicians capturing their work on video and uploading it to YouTube.

These performances in turn acquire poly-medial meaning, authority and veracity. Such material can be mobilized and reassembled within other community websites, and may be quoted or hyperlinked to other news sources, with modalities becoming contingent, multiple and multilingual. Once within the globital memory field, such communities of Roma memory, instead of remaining isolated or cut off from wider or comparable communities of memory, are able to develop multiple bonds and connections with other related historical events, such as other stories of the Holocaust, or the Second World War.

It is difficult to tell at this juncture whether the mobilization of new emergences of Roma memory through digital media will actually make a difference to Roma lives in Europe or aid the elimination of discrimination and marginalization, as well as counteracting the effects of decades of denial and forgetting of Roma memory in Europe (Van Baar 2008). Yet, these new dynamics seem to make visible particular aspects of Roma memory in emergent ways. Within older media, to return to the work of Orlando Patterson, Roma were non-persons natally alienated by European discursive practices that prevented them from integrating 'the experience of their ancestors into their lives'. The globital memory field seems to allow for Roma to more freely anchor the precarious present in a conscious community of memory that may amplify centuries of Roma resilience.

Notes

1 Anti-Gypsyism has a long etiology with hostility located within a history that is much less well known than post-colonial racism. It is subsequently much less well understood in comparison. Roma were listed as property or chattels within the inventories of monasteries and landowners. Etchings and early historical ethnographies show that Roma were kept apart in slave villages. Legislation in several European countries included the right to 'hunt' 'gypsies' to death, to physically assault them with public floggings and branding, and to remove Roma children from their parents in order to give them a Christian upbringing. A disproportionate number of Roma were transported to Colonial Penal colonies such as Australia. See Hancock 2002; Hoyland 2010; Kenrick and Puxon 1995.

2 Definitions of who the Roma in Europe are vary and are much contested. Martin Kovats (2011) argues that Roma are best defined dynamically in terms of a political

and cultural identity that is highly varied and includes heterogeneous communities across the EU.

3 The Russian census (Vserossiiskaia perepis' naseleniia 2002 goda. Natsional'nyi sostav naseleniia po regionam Rossii 2002) lists the Romani population as 183,000 in Russia with 3 million Roma in Turkey <http://www.hurriyetdailynews.com/default.aspx?pageid=438&n=taiex-seminar-on-roma-people-in-turkey-2010-12-15> (accessed 4 July 2011).

4 On this process see Frosh and Pinchevski (2009: 298).

5 For earlier studies that developed these analytical dynamics see Reading 2011a, 2011b, 2011c.

6 See a number of studies of the representation of Roma in 'older media', including Balcanu 2009; Foszto and Anastasoaie 2001; Guy 2001.

7 For my more detailed analysis of the logics of erasure of Roma memory in older media based on a meta-analysis of a range of studies, see Reading 2012.

8 Source: <http://en.wikipedia.org/wiki/Image:Sclavi_Tiganesti.jpg> (accessed 4 July 2011).

References

Assmann, A. and Conrad, S. (eds) (2011) *Memory in a Global Age. Discourses, Practices, Trajectories*, Basingstoke: Palgrave Macmillan.

Balcanu, A. (2009) 'Romany Issues: The Images of Romanian Gypsies at Home and Abroad', *Transtext (e)s Transcultures*, vol. 4. Online. Available: <http://transtexts. Revues.org/index251.htm> (accessed 22 September 2010).

Barany, Z. (2000) 'Politics and the Roma in State-Socialist Eastern Europe', *Communist and Post-Communist Studies*, 33:4, Winter: 421–437.

Bauman, Z. (2000) *Liquid Modernity*. Cambridge: Polity Press.

BBC (2009) 'Roma Holocaust Victims Speak Out'. Online. Available: <http://news.bbc.co.uk/1/world/Europe/7844787.stm> (accessed 4 July 2011).

Bourdieu, P. (2003) *The Field of Cultural Production*. Oxford: Polity Press.

Crowe, D. (1991) 'The Gypsy Historical Experience in Romania', in D. Crowe and J. Kolsti (eds), *The Gypsies of Eastern Europe*. London: Armonk Sharpe, pp. 61–79.

Dautaj, Erisa (2010) 'Roma More Integrated in Turkey, EU Says' 15 December 2010. Online. Available: <http://www.hurriyetdailynews.com/default.aspx?pageid=438&n=taiex-seminar-on-roma-peoplein-turkey-2010-12-15> (accessed 4 July 2011).

EU-MIDIS (2009) '01: European Union Minorities and Discrimination Survey Data in Focus: The Roma. FRA: European Agency for Fundamental Rights'. Online. Available: <http://fra.europa.eu> (accessed 9 July 2011).

European Commission (2010) 'The European Union and Roma'. Online. Available: <http://ec.europa.eu/social/main.jsp?catId=518&langId=en> (accessed 9 July 2011).

Foszto, L. and Anastasoaie, M.-V. (2001) 'Romanian; Representations, Public Policies and Political Projects', in W. Guy (ed.), *Between Past and Future: The Roma of Central and Eastern Europe*. Hatfield: University of Hertfordshire Press, pp. 351–369.

Frosh, P. and Pinchevski, A. (2009) *Media Witnessing*. Basingstoke: Palgrave Macmillan.

Garde-Hansen, J., Hoskins, A. and Reading, A. (eds) (2009) *Save As . . . Digital Memories*. Basingstoke: Palgrave Macmillan.

Guy, W. (2001) 'Romani Identity and Post-Communist Policy', in W. Guy (ed.), *Between Past and Future: The Roma of Central and Eastern Europe*. Hatfield: University of Hertfordshire Press, pp. 3–33.

Hancock, I. (2002) *We are the Romani People: Ame Sam e Rromane džene: Volume 28*. Hertfordshire: University of Hertfordshire.

Heuss, H. (1997) 'German Policies of Gypsy Persecution 1870: 1945', in H. Asseo, K. Fings, H. Heuss and F. Sparing (eds), *The Gypsies During the Second World War: From Race Science to the Camps: Volume One*. Hatfield: University of Hertfordshire Press, pp. 15–36.

Hoyland, J. (1816, 2010) 'A Historical Survey of the Gypsies. Digital PDF 553', in *Anguline Research Archives*. Online. Available: <http://anguline.co.uk/gypsy.html> (accessed 5 May 2011).

Kenrick, D. and Puxon, G. (1995) *Gypsies Under the Swastika*. Hatfield: University of Hertfordshire Press.

Kovats, M. (2011) 'The Historical Importance of Roma Politics: Roma as a Political Identity', in M. Flasikova-Benova, H. Swaboda and J.M. Wiesma (eds), *Roma: A European Minority: The Challenge of Diversity*. Lier: European Alliance of Socialists and Democrats, pp. 161–168.

Lakatis, G. (2011) 'Bucharest Will Have a Monument Dedicated to the Abolition of Roma Slavery', *Roma Transitions*. Online. Available: <http://www.romatransitions.org/node/208> (accessed 6 July 2011).

Lemon, A. (2000) *Between Two Fires: Gypsy Performance and Romanii Memory from Pushkin to Post-Socialism*. Durham, NC: Duke University Press.

Mälksoo, M. (2009) 'The Memory Politics of Becoming European: The East European Subalterns and the Collective Memory of Europe', *European Journal of International Relations*, 15:4, Winter: 653–680.

Morris-Suzuki, T. (2005) *The Past Within Us: Media, Memory and History*. London: Verso.

Patterson, O. (2011) 'Slavery and Social Death: A Comparative Study', excerpt in J.K. Olick, V. Vinitzky-Seroussi and D. Levy (eds), *The Collective Memory Reader*. Oxford: Oxford University Press, pp. 279–282.

Puxon, G. (2008) 'Letter in Protest against Destruction of Sulukule, Istanbul, Turkey, Europe's Oldest Romani Community. Use of Turkish National Law No. 5366 – Based on "Urban Renewal Processes in the Historic City"'. Online. Available: <http://community.livejournal.com/romany_gypsy/> (accessed 20 June 2010).

Reading, A. (2011) 'Identity, Memory and Cosmopolitanism: The Otherness of the Past and a Right to Memory', *European Journal of Cultural Studies*.

Reading, A. (2011a) 'Globital Witnessing: Mobile Memories of Atrocity and Terror in London and Iran', in K. Hall and K.N. Jones (eds), *Constructions of Conflict: Transmitting Memories of the Past in European Historiography, Literature and Culture. Vol. 15. Cultural History and Literary Imagination*. Oxford: Peter Lang, pp. 73–90.

Reading, A. (2011b) 'Globalisation and Digital Memory: Globital Memory's Six Dynamics', in M. Neiger, O. Meyers and E. Zandberg (eds), *On Media Memory*. Basingstoke: Palgrave Macmillan.

Reading, A. (2011c) 'The London Bombings: Mobile Witnessing, Mortal Bodies and Globital Time', *Special Issue: Remembering the 2005 London Bombings: Media, Memory, Commemoration. Memory Studies*, 4:3, Autumn: 298–311.

Reading, A. (2012) 'The European Roma: An Unsettled Right to Memory', in P. Lee and P. N. Thomas (eds), *Public Memory, Public Media and the Politics of Justice*. Basingstoke: Palgrave Macmillan, pp. 121–140.

Saunders, R. (2010) *Ethnopolitics in Cyberspace: The Internet, Minority Nationalism, and the Web of Identity*. Lanham, MD: Lexington Books.

Trumpener, K. (1992) 'The Time of the Gypsies: A "People without History" in the Narratives of the West', *Critical Inquiry*, 18:4, Winter: 843–884.

Van Baar, H. (2008) 'The Way Out of Amnesia?', *Third Text*, 22:3, Autumn: 373–385.

van Dijck, J. (2007) *Mediated Memories in the Digital Age*. Stanford, CA: Stanford University Press.

2 Mourning and melancholia in Putin's Russia

An essay in mnemonics[1]

Alexander Etkind

Introduction

Walter Benjamin said, 'He who seeks to approach his own buried past must conduct himself like a man digging' (Benjamin 1979: 314). And we are still digging, though, after many excavations and exhumations, our spades have taken forms that are different from what Benjamin may have imagined. In this chapter on Russian cultural memory, I am experimenting with statistical methods that operate with large – very large – amounts of digital artifacts. These massive data reflect the changing representations of the past and, as I argue, also of the present. Used by various teams of scholars in the growing environment of Digital Humanities, similar methods have recently been named Culturomics and Cultural Analytics (Manovich 2009; Michel *et al.* 2010; Rogers 2009). These methods have subjected incredible amounts of cultural data to computational analyses in the hope that the sheer volume of data in combination with the new software might generate novel ways of representing – describing, explaining, or even predicting – cultural mechanisms. Operating with similar data, I am interested in bringing a cultural historian's eye to this terrain. In this chapter, I map out some preliminary contours for what I hope to develop into a new methodological approach to these data, an approach in some ways more traditional and, I believe, more realistic, than some of the existing digital humanities methodologies. In application to cultural memory, this methodology addresses the cultural – in this essay, digital – representations of the past, and therefore I call it *Quantitative Mnemonics*.

While dependent upon information technologies, scholarship is different from these technologies. What is important for scholarship is, of course, not the methods themselves but the verifiable results they help to generate, provided that these results elucidate questions of clear and understandable relevance. Since only the living community of scholars can evaluate 'relevance', relevant questions can and, in fact, should sound traditional. Relying on the supercomputers that generate the unprecedentedly large archives and help to process these archives with incredible ease and speed, I apply to these archives the traditional approach of a historian.

We historians have a long experience of working with the archives, and we have always known that even traditional, paper archives are too large to be surveyed without guiding hypotheses: a series of plausible statements to be proved, disproved or modified by the findings in the archive. As we routinely teach our students, an archival scholar should formulate her hypotheses before entering the archive. She can change these hypotheses later, and in the course of her work in the archive she can also collect bits and pieces of evidence that do not fit the initial hypotheses, in the hope that this information may in turn generate a new, testable idea. However, we know from experience that she who enters the archive without a guiding idea is doomed. This is what Benjamin wanted to say with his image of the man digging: one who seeks to approach the *buried* past never knows for sure where to start digging. Yet we cannot simply dig at random, because the ground is vast and the digging is tough.

Mapping memory's digital traces

My methodology aims at representing cultural memory as a historical process, which continuously changes over time (see e.g. Assmann 2011; Etkind 2013; Rothberg 2009). These changes leave traces in various media, and they can be dug up in the archives of these media. Given that we have the ability to identify the digital traces of particular memories, to aggregate and count them, we can represent their changing intensities against the historical timeline. This is not a new idea, but digital archives of both on-and off-line media provide us with unprecedented power in pursuing it.

While the content of cultural memory is always qualitative, we can measure its changing intensity by tracking the frequency with which this content – specific figures, events or concepts – is mentioned in the public sphere. In this way, the intensity of cultural memory may be empirically studied, statistically measured and graphically charted. I would say that the purpose is to trace and chart memory processes – temporal shifts in the balance between the multiple acts of remembering and forgetting – in the same way as one follows the charts of the stock market, which also represent a moving equilibrium between myriad choices. Ideally, this set of instruments should represent the trends and flows of memory in the intermedial space of digital communications, including electronic representations of non-digital materials such as books or public events.

From a more traditional perspective, I would describe my method as *quantitative microhistory*. Defined as the practice of searching for the answers to big questions in short stretches of time (Ginzburg *et al.* 1993), *microhistory* examines the temporal dynamics of events and meanings over weeks and years. For a cultural historian who is used to working with decades and centuries, microhistory works as a zooming instrument, a kind of microscope. The new, web-based ability to provide microhistory with a statistical dimension enriches this methodology that has, since its inception, emphasized its interpretive, qualitative aspects. With their ability to create and collect large samples of meaningful responses to political, cultural and other events covering short segments of time – and, in addition, to track the precise timing and sequence of each of these responses – web-based technologies open new and largely untested vistas for microhistory.

Using quantitative microhistory methodology to study digital representations of memory in the Russian language presents both limits and advantages. Over the past two decades, the Russian-language Internet (Runet) has developed into an alternative public sphere.[2] Given the differentiation of state control over various media, from the efficiently censored television to the loosely controlled newspapers to the free Internet and social media, the Russian public has turned to web-based sources as a major source of news and commentary.

The Russian Internet works in the Cyrillic alphabet, which helpfully limits the corpus of texts by containing all searches and computations within a large but naturally restricted universe. Mnemonic technologies work in Cyrillic as well as they work in Latin, and in some cases they are easier to access. A challenge to the cross-medial analysis of the public representations of the past, however, results from the fact that we have different computational methods for different cultural genres, which makes it difficult to compare these genres – say, books and blogs – in one pure test. For this study, I have combined three different tools:

1 Google Books Ngram Viewer for books: a graphing tool that charts *n-grams* (words or combinations of words), as found in Google Inc's digitized book collection, available until 2008.
2 Integrum for the press: the Russian rival of Nexis, Integrum is a comprehensive database of full-text digital copies of the Russian-language press; it provides sophisticated search and charting methods. Integrum full-text databases add 40,000 new documents – articles from newspapers and magazines, and transcripts of television and radio programmes – daily (see http://www.integrum.ru; the scholarly use of Integrum is surveyed in Nikiporets-Takigawa (2006)).
3 Yandex's 'Pulse of the Blogosphere' for blogs and forums: developed by Yandex, Google's Russian rival, this instrument computes and charts the Russian-language blogs and posts at LiveJournal, LiveInternet, Twitter, and several other portals. Importantly, it does not include Facebook. It adds about four million posts and notes daily (see http://blogs.yandex.ru/).

All these instruments have their problems and limitations, which my attempt to employ them together has made only more apparent.

Post-Soviet melancholia

I define amnesia as preferring the present to the past, nostalgia as preferring the past to the present, and melancholia as an inability to distinguish between the past and the present.[3] How can one possibly verify and quantify these conceptual distinctions? One idea is to go to the library, select a sample of books, read them, and then calculate to what extent these books are concerned with manifestations of the present, to what extent they are concerned with manifestations of the past, and to what extent they contaminate and blend the two. Doing essentially the same work but on a much larger scale and in the blink of an eye, I employ the

Google Books Ngram Viewer, software that reads through all the books that Google has scanned, and calculates the frequencies of selected words in these books over the years. The Ngram Viewer uses a sample of about 4 per cent of all books in existence, including Russian books. Unfortunately, Google stopped collecting these data in 2008, so the Viewer can only be used to follow books up until this year. Within this limit, however, it allows us to calculate the annual frequencies with which certain concepts, or even short sequences of words, are mentioned, and to do so separately for the Russian corpus of books, which may be compared with the English and German corpora.

An easy way to start is to trace the important dates of Soviet history, as mentioned in books and charted by Ngram Viewer (see Chart 2.1).[4] The years from 1978 to 2008 are plotted on the horizontal axis. On the vertical axis, we see how often a certain year is mentioned in Russian books relative to the total number of counted words and symbols, in fractions of percentages. The different lines trace the shifting frequencies with which these dates are mentioned: 1917, the year of the Bolshevik Revolution; 1937, the culmination of the Great Terror; 1941, the start of the Great Patriotic War with Nazi Germany; and 1945, the Soviet victory in this war.

Over the three decades, we see that two tragic dates dominate public memory. The first and most dramatic spike is associated with the start of the Great Patriotic War (1941), which was particularly relevant for books written in the late 1980s and early 1990s, 50 years after this event. The line of the Great Terror (1937) shows the most recent peak among these charts; interestingly, '1937' became a popular term of reference after 2004, surpassing even '1941'. Caused by the proliferation of popular history books that strikes any visitor to a contemporary Russian bookstore, this peak reflects the actual focus of many of those books: Stalin, his victories and his 'repressions'. Is this interest in Stalin and Stalinism patriotic and nationalist, or melancholic and mournful?

This question may sound abstract and non-measurable, but the Ngram Viewer helps to answer it with a degree of precision that no amount of reading could ever provide. Although one could expect the Russian authors' and readers' interest in the events of the Great Patriotic War, what is remarkable is their strong tendency to focus more on its tragic start than its triumphal end. The year '1941' is mentioned more often than '1945'; based on the popular idea that modern Russian nationalism is grounded in the victory in this war, we would probably expect the opposite. This focus on the most tragic dates testifies to the active and continuing, though not acknowledged, immersion into the darkest parts of the Soviet past – a feature of melancholy.

Following the proper names of Russia's political leaders provides another clue on the same question (Chart 2.2). Predictably, Lenin and Stalin dominate this chart from 1930 to 1950. Stalin then retreats and Lenin moves ahead, and stays on top until about 1990. At this point, Lenin's reputation collapses, and Stalin's rises up again. Even in the 2000s, Russian books mentioned Stalin and Lenin more often than they did more contemporary leaders, and Stalin clearly leads the chart. For the course of almost two decades, from 1991 to 2008, Stalin is

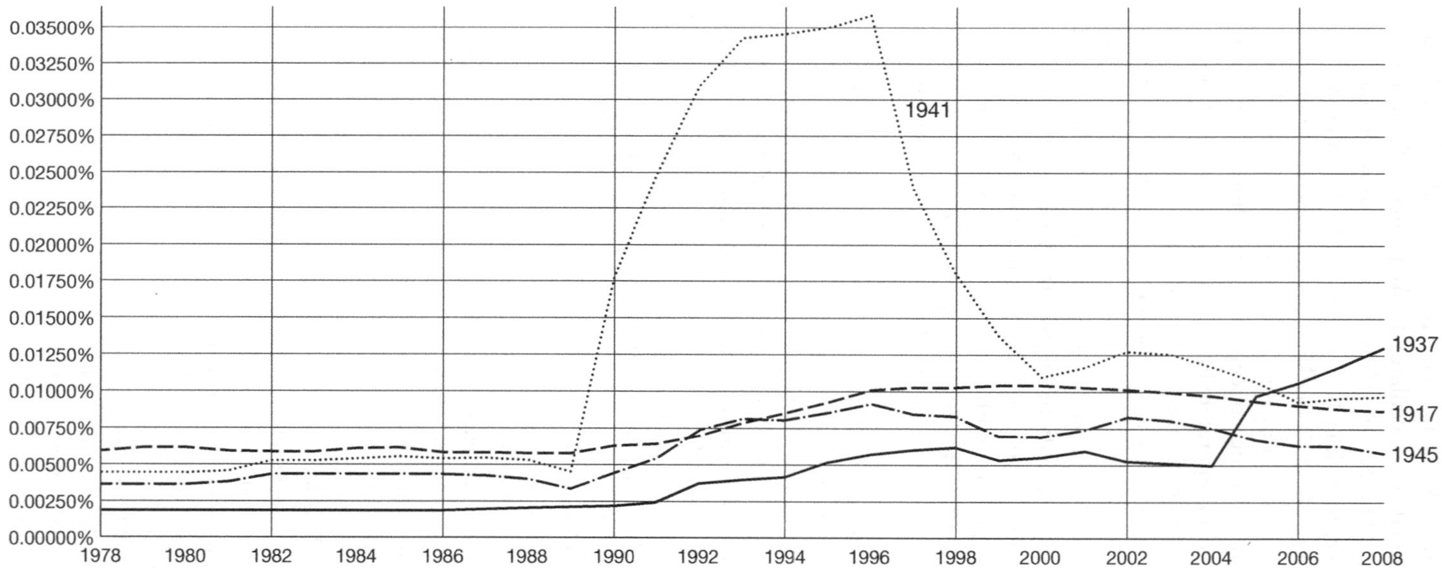

Chart 2.1 Frequencies of dates in Russian and Soviet books, 1978–2008

Source: Books Ngram Viewer, Russian Corpus

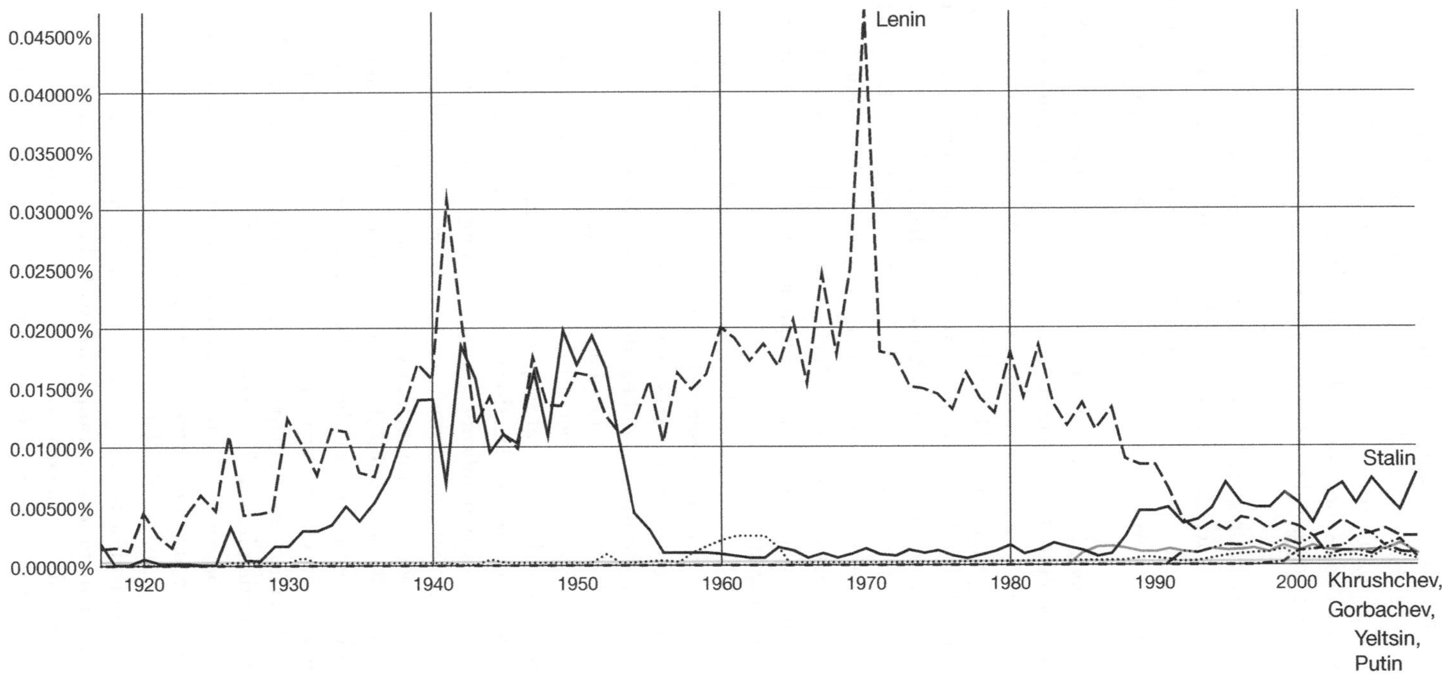

Chart 2.2 Frequencies with which leaders are mentioned in Russian and Soviet books

Source: Books Ngram Viewer, Russian Corpus

mentioned in Russian books more often than any other Russian political leader, current or recent. There is no doubt that all these books discuss Stalin in vastly different terms, from the most glowing to the most critical. However, the fact is that they discuss Stalin more often than any other of Russia's leaders. 'Moscow does not believe in tears', alleged one of the most popular Soviet films;[5] the data testify to the opposite.

To provide this finding with a comparative dimension, I asked the Ngram Viewer to chart two terms – Stalin and Hitler – separately in Russian and in German. In both cultures, their corresponding dictators were mentioned most frequently while they were in power, with the peaks following immediately after their deaths.

In subsequent decades, however, the results diverge. Starting from about 1985, the Stalin curve on the Russian chart began to rise, and this trend then continued through two decades of stable growth until 2008. We find no equivalent to this pattern on the German chart. Here, the Hitler curve descends after hitting its peak in the late 1940s, shows a minor spike in the mid-1960s, with the end of the 'inability to mourn' period (Mitscherlich and Mitscherlich 1975), and then steadily declines. While in 1980 the chances of reading about Stalin in a Russian book and about Hitler in a German book were equal (about 0.0015 per cent in both cases), in 2008, the relative frequency with which Stalin was discussed in Russian books had roughly quadrupled; the relative frequency of discussing Hitler in German books remained the same.

Does this mean that Russian authors, publishers and readers have been more preoccupied with old fears rather than with current concerns? To pursue this hypothesis, I focus on three concepts, which I have chosen to contrast local and global concerns of the Russian public: the cult of personality (*kul't lichnosti*); the vertical of power (*vertikal' vlasti*); and global warming (*global'noe poteplenie*). The cult of personality is a historical concept that Nikita Khrushchev coined in 1956 to denounce Stalinism. The vertical of power is a political concept that Vladimir Putin coined in about 2000 to describe his vision of government. Global warming is a concept of planetary significance, which connotes a danger of climate change and potential catastrophe for various parts of the world, including Russia. While the vertical of power is an important concept that the supporters of Putin use positively to describe his political system, the cult of personality is a critical concept that has been used since the 1950s to describe abuses of power.

What we see very clearly on Chart 2.3 is that in the books that have been published in Russian, the cult of personality has been a tremendously successful concept. After hitting its absolute peak in about 1964, it was suppressed during the following two decades, though it did not fall out of use. During perestroika it underwent a resurgence, and even in 2008 it was still more popular than Putin's vertical of power, though the latter was rapidly growing. By contrast, global warming – a problem of foreign origin and worldwide relevance – presents little interest for Russian authors in comparison with the two political concepts which they use to describe, explain and understand the workings of local power. Of these latter concepts, they show preference for the historical concept over the

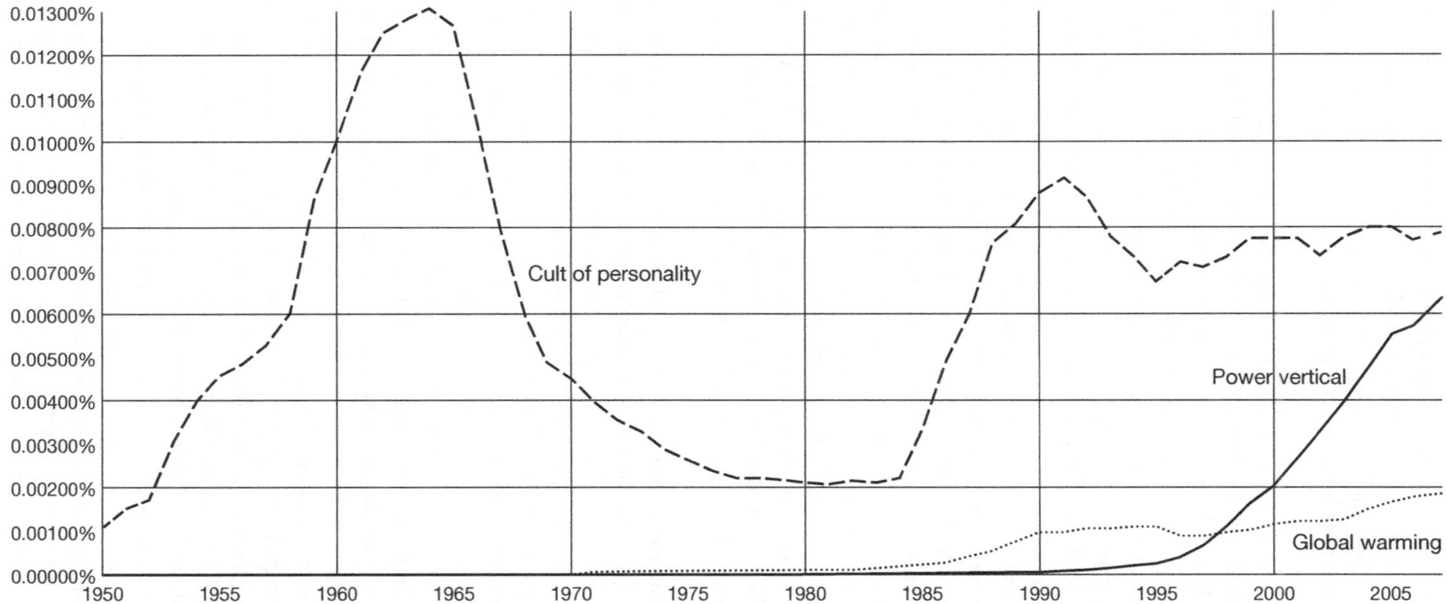

Chart 2.3 Three political concepts in Russian and Soviet books, 1950–2008

Source: Books Ngram Viewer, Russian Corpus

contemporary one.[6] Some of the books that have contributed to the creation of this curious pattern specifically discuss Stalin's cult of personality; in others, however, the cult of personality is mentioned specifically with reference to current affairs. This indistinction between the past and the present is what I call *political melancholia.*

Could the explanation for these facts be that published books respond to current concerns more slowly than other media, and that books tend, by virtue of their very genre, to be focused on the past rather than the present? Clearly, before we can answer these questions, we need both a cross-cultural and a cross-medial study of post-Soviet melancholy. Looking for a comparable case, I have charted great American presidents of the past together with not-so-great current ones, using the Ngram Viewer's 'American English' corpus. Some of these presidents share surnames, but this does not change the overall picture.

On the American chart, the current presidents are usually mentioned more often than the former ones; for example, in 2006, George W. Bush is ahead of Franklin D. Roosevelt. However, I have found one period when a current US president was upstaged by a past US president in the pages of American books. This period was the 1930s, approximately the period from the Great Depression to Pearl Harbor, and the popular point of reference here was a Civil War leader, Abraham Lincoln. It seems that the dark periods of history shape a situation in which the past becomes untypically relevant to the present. In the America of the 1930s, as in the Russia of the 1990s to the2000s, a focused immersion into the glory and the horror of the past signals both rejection of the present and fear of the future.

Obviously, it takes more time to write a book than it does an essay or a blogpost, and one can speculate that this process creates a certain chronological distance, or time lag, between books and their subject matter, while for newspapers or blogs this time lag is shorter. Comparing the Ngram Viewer for books, the Integrum databases for the press, and the Yandex 'Pulse of the Blogosphere' for blogs and forums, helps to test this inter-medial hypothesis. According to these comparisons, if (pre-2008) books mentioned Stalin more often than Putin, bloggers throughout this period and beyond have been discussing Putin more often than Stalin. On the other hand, even in these new media, the interest in the past is very robust, and the focus on Stalin is significant and stable. Charting Stalin and the twenty-first-century political leaders in Russian blogs, I have found that only Putin and Medvedev have been mentioned more frequently. Most of the time, Stalin also surpasses any foreign leader in Russian blogs, though occasionally, sensational events, such as the election of Obama or the war in Libya, dislodge Stalin's lasting grip over the Internet. Then, Obama or Qaddafi may topple Stalin for a few weeks, but later Stalin invariably regains his dominance.

Using Integrum and the Yandex Pulse of the Blogosphere, I repeated the same comparison – cult of personality vs. global warming – that I used for the Ngram Viewer. It turns out that in contrast to Russian books, the Russian press and blogs have been more interested in global warming than in the cult of personality, and the difference between these two concerns has been growing (Chart 2.4). I find

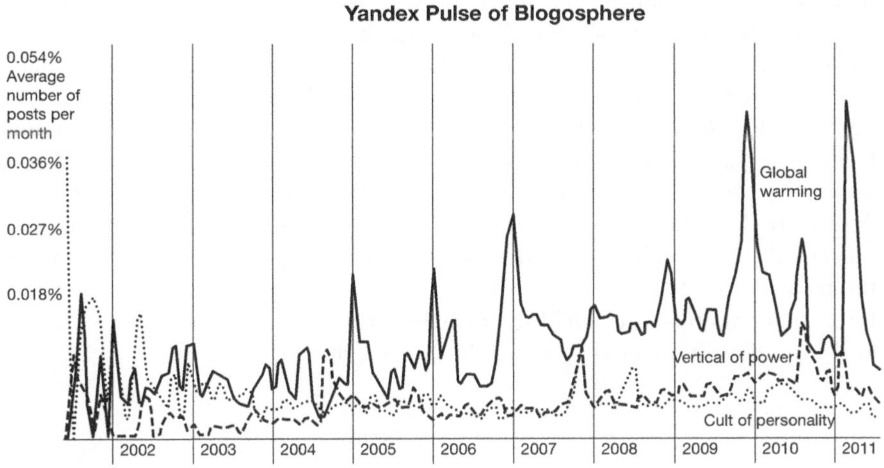

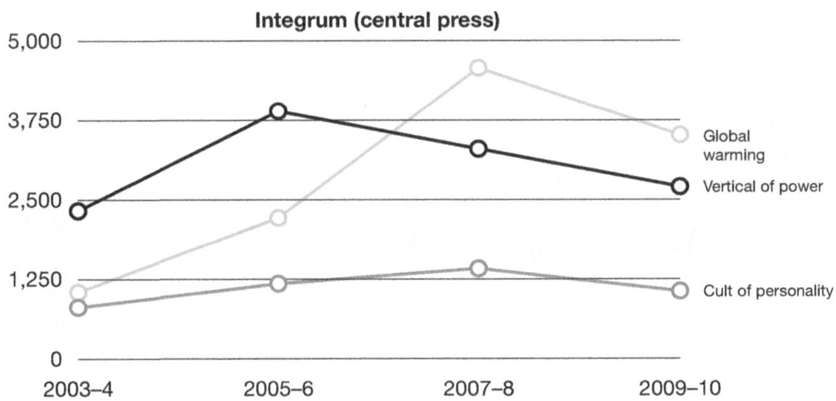

Chart 2.4 Three political concepts in Russian press and blogs, 2002–2011

this difference very instructive. Any cross-cultural comparison is rooted in the specific cultural forms and genres in question. What might be valid if we compare books may or may not be valid if we compare blogs. I see quantitative mnemonics as a multi-dimensional matrix with two axes emerging repeatedly as the most relevant:

1 The inter-cultural axis, which pursues comparisons of similar political issues and historical periods across national cultures.
2 The inter-generic axis, which pursues such comparisons across cultural genres.

Applying this two-dimensional approach, I have compared the changing public interest in two institutions of law enforcement in Russia, one that belongs to the past and another that belongs to the present and future: the gulag, on the one hand, and the jury, on the other. The gulag, the system of Soviet concentration camps, existed under this name from 1930 to 1960; this acronym has become shorthand for and symbol of the Soviet Terror. The jury (*sud prisiazhnykh*) was introduced in Russia in 1993 and functions, with many difficulties, as an optional form for criminal trials, which co-exists with the court trial without jury, a Soviet legacy. As you will see in Chart 2.5, Russian books talk about the gulag more frequently than they do about trials by jury; blogs mention these two more or less equally; and only the central press is struggling to tell the public about the relevance of the jury and its problems. Still, we can easily be disappointed by the inattention of Russian bloggers to the serious problems of the present, such as the insufficient use of the jury, or the dangers of global warming.

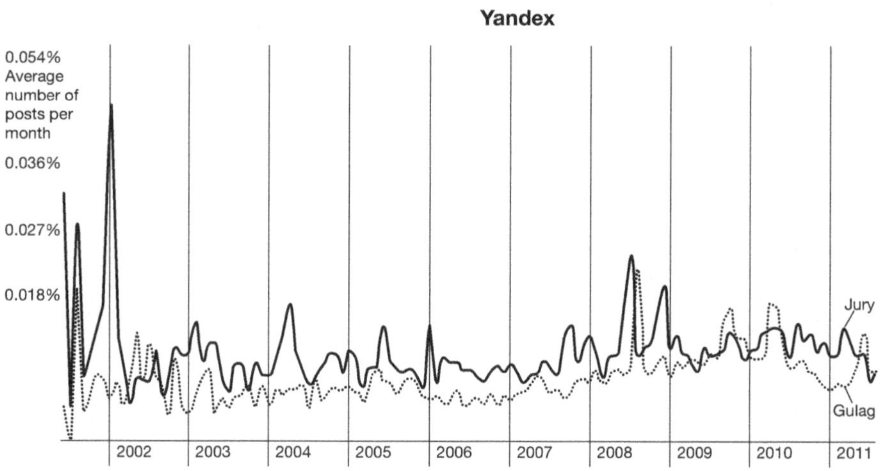

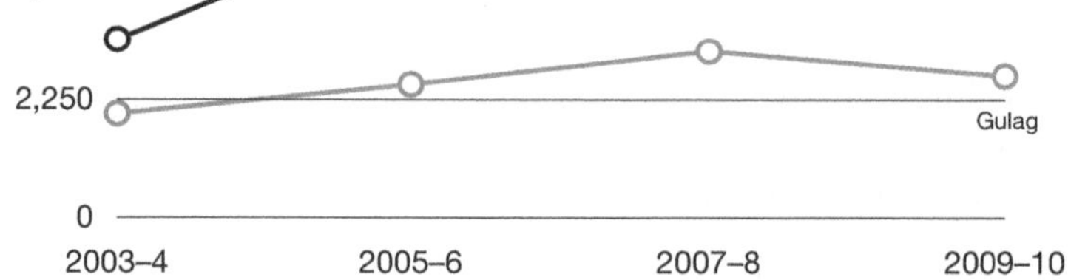

Chart 2.5 Two legal concepts in books, the press and blogs

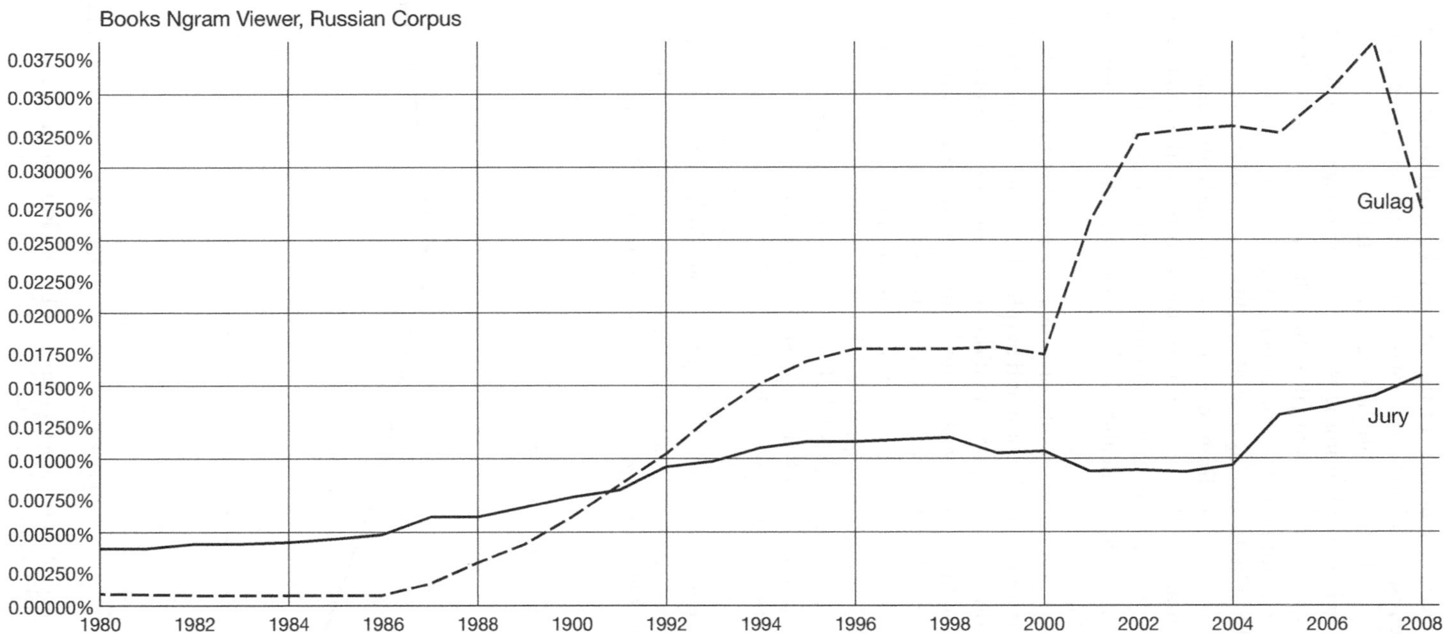

Chart 2.5 (continued)

In its coverage of the activity of the current Russian leadership, is the Russian press more interested in its leaders' involvement in present policies, say, in international affairs, or in their relations to the past? Integrum gives the opportunity to chart these relations by using a so-called *proximity search*: a search for terms occurring within a specific maximal textual distance of one another. Using this method, I have computed the frequencies with which two different concepts (say, Putin and Stalin) feature as textual neighbours, mentioned within a standard distance of three sentences from one another. Obviously, the charts do not tell us the actual meaning of this proximity, or the nature of the relationship that it reflects: in some texts, Putin and Stalin may have been compared, and in others contrasted, or we might be dealing with texts citing a recent comment by Putin about Stalin, etc.

In Chart 2.6, I present the results of proximity searches linking Putin to two of his counterparts, one from the past and another from the present. Specifically, the chart shows how often Putin is mentioned within three contiguous sentences together with Stalin, and how often he is mentioned within three sentences of Bush. We see here that the central Russian press does care more about international relations in the present than it does about the relation to the past. After President Bush left office, the press lost interest in discussing him together with Putin; but despite the fact that Stalin left his office almost 60 years ago, the press keeps telling stories in which Putin and Stalin figure together.

As the next step in using proximity searches for mapping relationships, I have centred on President Medvedev and computed how often he is mentioned in the same three sentences as some other figures, from Putin to Stalin to the ex-mayor of Moscow, Yurii Luzhkov, and several other figures. The results are dramatic (see Chart 2.7). Of course, given all the things that Putin and Medvedev have

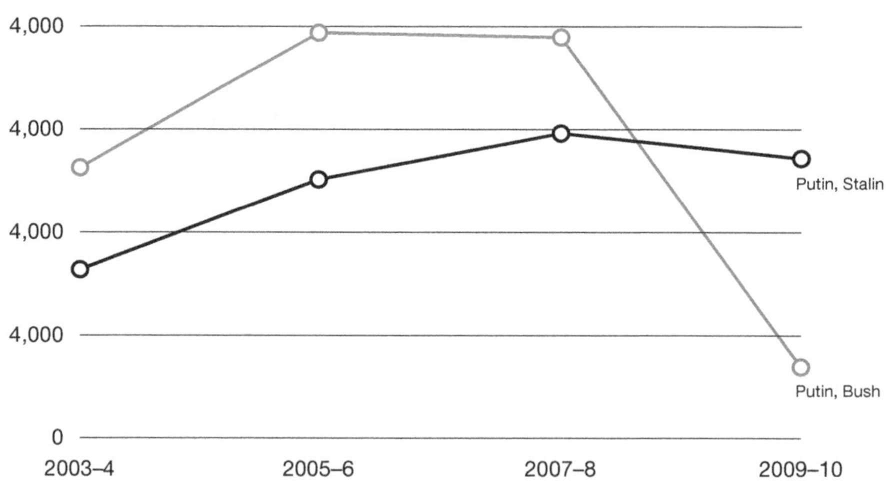

Chart 2.6 Frequency of two names mentioned by the Russian press in three adjacent sentences, 2003–2010. Source: Integrum

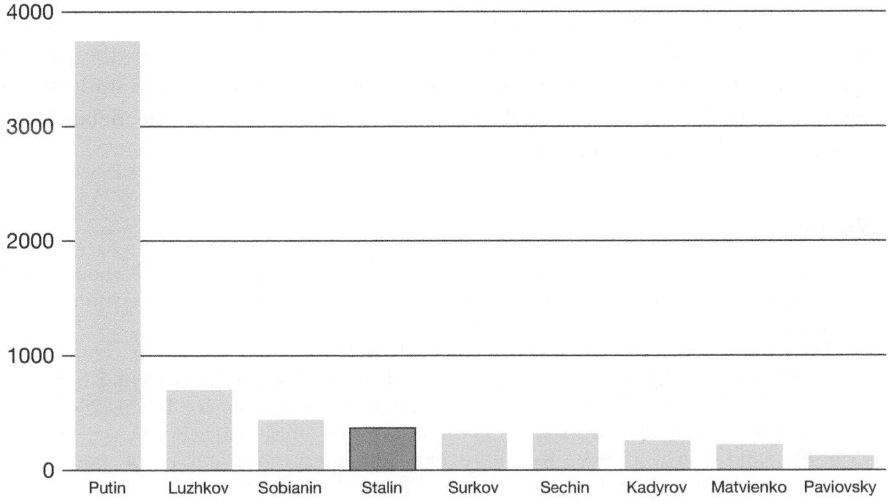

Chart 2.7 Frequency of names mentioned within three sentences of Medvedev, 2009–2011

Source: Integrum (central press)

done or failed to do together, they are mentioned together much more often than other pairs. However, Stalin is mentioned in some connection to Medvedev as often as almost any current political figure (e.g. less frequently than the Mayor of Moscow, but more frequently than the Mayor of St Petersburg, and more frequently than some of Medvedev's key advisers, allies or rivals).

Looking at the victims of the Russian state over decades, as they are mentioned in the blogs, we also see that the concentration on the past is mediated by the cultural genre. Mikhail Khodorkovsky, the oil tycoon who was arrested in 2003 and has been kept in prison since then, dominates this picture; understandably, his peaks coincide with his trials in 2005 and 2010. Between them his relevance for the bloggers is roughly equal to the relevance of Trotsky, a leader of the Russian Revolution that happened almost 100 years ago. In contrast to Russian blogs, Russian books barely mention Khodorkovsky; even in 2008, Trotsky was mentioned about ten times more frequently than Khodorkovsky. The figures of the past have their stable, grasping power over the present.

Conclusion

Methods of quantitative mnemonics have consistently demonstrated the complexity of Russian cultural space and its general bias towards the past. Russian authors, journalists and bloggers feel the past to be understandable and relevant, and this is different from their response to the confused and confusing, rapidly changing present. Their texts use the figures and stories of the past in two ways: they focus on them when they discuss the past, and they draw upon them when they discuss the present, in various comparisons and allegories. The combined result of these two processes is that the public is constantly speaking about the past, as a source of allusions, allegories and fears. The public needs the past to understand the present, and the public does not need the present to understand the past. As Walter Benjamin (1998: 185) said, 'The only pleasure the melancholic permits himself, and it is a powerful one, is allegory'.

Notes

1 I am grateful to Galina Nikiporets-Takigawa for her help with the computational aspects of this work, and to Julie Fedor for her help with the current version of this chapter.
2 See Schmidt and Teubener (2006: 71–102); Kovalenko (2005).
3 Freud's famous distinction of mourning and melancholia is instrumental here; see Freud (1984: 245–268). For a creative treatment of nostalgia, see Boym (2001). For concepts of 'geopolitical melancholia' and 'post-colonial melancholia', see Derrida (1994) and Gilroy (2004). For more detailed, interpretive studies of post-Soviet memory, mourning, and melancholia, see Etkind (2009, forthcoming).
4 All results on this and other charts were computed in August 2011.
5 *Moscow Does Not Believe in Tears,* 1980, directed by Vladimir Men'shov.
6 In 2008, the corpus of 'American English' books generated the result of 0.000375 per cent for 'global warming' and the corpus of Russian books, 0.000020 per cent. In other words, Russian books published that year mentioned global warming about 20 times less frequently than American books.

References

Assmann, A. (2011) *Cultural Memory and Western Civilization: Functions, Media, Archives.* Cambridge: Cambridge University Press.

Benjamin, W. (1979) 'Berlin Chronicle', in *One-Way Street and Other Writings.* London: Verso.

Benjamin, W. (1998) *The Origin of German Tragic Drama,* trans. J. Osborne. London: Verso.

Boym, S. (2001) *The Future of Nostalgia.* New York: Basic Books.

Derrida, J. (1994) *Specters of Marx: The State of the Debt, the Work of Mourning, and the New International,* trans. P. Kamuf. New York: Routledge.

Etkind, A. (2009) 'Post-Soviet Hauntology: Cultural Memory of the Soviet Terror', *Constellations,* 16:1: 182–200.

Etkind, A. (2013) *Warped Mourning. Stories of the Undead in the Land of the Unburied.* Stanford, CA: Stanford University Press.

Freud, S. (1984) 'Mourning and Melancholia', *The Pelican Freud Library,* trans. J. Strachey, Vol. 11. Harmondsworth: Penguin, pp. 245–268.

Gilroy, P. (2004) *After Empire. Melancholia or Convivial Culture.* London: Routledge.

Ginzburg, C., Tedeschi, J. and Tedeschi, A.C. (1993) 'Microhistory: Two or Three Things That I Know about It', *Critical Inquiry,* 20:1, Autumn: 10–35.

Google Books Ngram Viewer. Online. Available: <http://books.google.com/ngrams> (accessed 17 February 2012).

Integrum. Online. Available: <http://www.integrum.ru> (accessed 17 February 2012).

Kovalenko, P. (2005) 'Structural Dynamics of the Public Sphere in Post-Soviet Russia. Online Political Forums as an Alternative Public-Private Space', *Russian Cyberspace.* Online. Available: <http://www.ruhr-uni-bochum.de/russ-cyb/library/texts/en/kovalenko.htm> (accessed 30 June 2012).

Manovich, L. (2009) 'Cultural Analytics: Visualising Cultural Patterns in the Era of "More Media"', *Domus*, Spring. Online. Available: <http://manovich.net> (accessed 17 February 2012).

Michel, J.-B. *et al.* (2010) 'Quantitative Analysis of Culture Using Millions of Digitized Books', *Science*, 16 December. Online. Available: <http://www.sciencemag.org/content/early/2010/12/15/science.1199644.full.pdf> (accessed 17 February 2012).

Mitscherlich, A. and Mitscherlich, M. (1975) *The Inability to Mourn*. New York: Random House.

Nikiporets-Takigawa, G. (ed.) (2006) *Integrum: tochnye metody i gumanitarnye nauki*. Moscow: Letnii sad.

Rogers, R. (2009) *The End of the Virtual*. Amsterdam: University of Amsterdam Press.

Rothberg, M. (2009) *Multidirectional Memory. Remembering the Holocaust in the Age of Decolonization*. Stanford, CA: Stanford University Press.

Schmidt, H. and Teubener, K. (2006) '(Counter)Public Sphere(s) on the Russian Internet', in H. Schmidt and N. Konradova (eds), *Control + Shift. Public and Private Usages of the Russian Internet*. Norderstedt: Books on Demand. Online. Available: <http://www.ruhr-uni-bochum.de/russ-cyb/library/texts/en/control_shift/control_shift.htm> (accessed 1 July 2012).

Yandex 'Pul's blogosfery'. Online. Available: <http://blogs.yandex.ru/pulse/> (accessed 17 February 2012).

3 Memory events and memory wars*

Victory Day in L'viv, 2011 through the prism of quantitative analysis

Galina Nikiporets-Takigawa

Introduction

How does a *memory event* – 'a re-discovery of the past that creates a rupture with its accepted cultural meaning' (Etkind 2010: 4; see also Preda, Chapter 13, this volume) – arise and evolve over time? What is the correlation between the dynamics of the development and movement of memory events within and across different genres, media and discourses? This chapter explores these questions via a case study of one memory event: the World War II Victory Day holiday in the Ukrainian city of L'viv in 2011.

Controversies over Victory Day have periodically flared up across post-Soviet and post-socialist space. In the case of Western Ukraine – on which I focus here – from 1991 onwards, protests against the celebration of Victory Day have become increasingly open and active, and reached their culmination in 2011 in the West Ukrainian city of L'viv. On this occasion, Victory Day was transformed from a routinized annual event marked throughout many cities in post-Soviet space into a day of 'war' between two versions of the memory of the Second World War. Apart from violent street-fighting on the streets of L'viv on 9 May 2011, two other 'wars' were fought over this event – in the official and in media discourses – and each of these discursive wars was considered a potential cause of the physical one.

As a memory event, Victory Day offers rich material for studying the related practices characteristic of new and old media. In this chapter, I focus on how this memory event unfolded in and was shaped by social media in particular. I argue that social media may be seen as a separate event genre – one that informs the parties involved and helps them to construct and discuss a point of view, but can also serve ultimately to prevent them from mobilizing and engaging in offline actions.

Victory Day

In post-Soviet space, 9 May, commonly known as Victory Day, is the commemorative date marking the anniversary of the Soviet victory over Nazi Germany in 1945. In Russia and Ukraine, in line with the prevailing interpretation

* I am grateful to Volodymyr Kulyk for his comments on an earlier draft of this chapter.

of this victory as a grand achievement of the Soviet past, this day occupies a central place in contemporary national identity projects and on the respective official calendars. It is also a genuinely popular memorial holiday. Opinion polls indicate that Victory Day enjoys 'unique symbolic prestige in the collective consciousness' in Russia (Dubin 2005), while more than two-thirds of the citizens of Ukraine (70 per cent) believe that Victory Day is a 'great day' ('Opytuvannia' 2011).

At the same time, despite these impressive levels of popularity, the Victory Day holiday also has staunch opponents in both countries. The enormous death-tolls during the war have led many Russians and Ukrainians to believe that the victory was so overpriced that Victory Day should be a day not of celebration but of mourning. They propose that Victory Day be renamed 'Veterans' Day' (Trubina 2010), 'Day of Sorrow' or 'Memory Day'. As these and related concerns are today discussed more and more widely, Russian authorities face increasing criticism for continuing such Soviet-era practices as the military parades on Victory Day and the new post-Soviet ritual of displaying the so-called St George's Ribbon. The idea of wearing the St George's Ribbon – an important Imperial-Russian military decoration – annually on 9 May was introduced by a journalist in 2005 ('Ia pomniu?'), and was enthusiastically accepted: every May many Russians attach the Ribbon to their chests, bags, car antennas, and even more exotic places: some temporarily replace their shoelaces and belts with the Ribbon. At the same time, critics defy this implementation of the ritual as 'the apotheosis of the fact that the memory of the war is in the hands of *mankurts* in Russia' ('Kod dostupa' 2012),[1] since originally the Ribbon signified membership of the Order of St George – Russia's highest military decoration – and should hence not be worn by civilians.

In Ukraine, with its 'diversity of memory models' (Portnov 2010) and drastically varying historical experiences across different local regions, 9 May is a heavily contested date in different national identity narratives (on these narratives see also Kulyk, Chapter 4, this volume). In Western Ukraine, which was incorporated into the USSR by military conquest and which experienced large-scale nationalist resistance in the 1940s, the era when Ukraine formed part of Russia and the USSR is widely seen as one of foreign occupation. In this 'nationalist' narrative, the end of the war is interpreted as a shift from Nazi to Soviet oppression (Kulyk 2011: 300). In the same narrative – which circulates in Ukraine as well as in the Baltic States and other East European countries that were occupied by the Soviet Union – 9 May is considered a traumatic day in the national calendar. Radically contrasting this viewpoint is that of those Western Ukrainians who share the attitude towards 9 May as a Victory Day and prefer to celebrate it. The resulting controversies have led to clashes, which reached a peak in 2011 in L'viv.

Empirical cases

My research on Victory Day in L'viv in 2011 is based on a mixture of qualitative and quantitative analysis of the media coverage of this memory event. I consulted a range of official documents produced by the Ukrainian and Russian authorities, together with materials gathered from a wide selection of old and new media. *Yandex Novosti* and *Integrum* served as my source and instrument for print and online newspapers, magazines, sites, and *Yandex Blogs* (IT company Yandex uses this title for its databases of blogs, microblogs and SNS) for social media. *Integrum* and *Yandex Novosti* rank among the largest collections of Russian and Ukrainian media, but they are not exactly comparable by size and they do not always cover the same sources. For instance, *Yandex Novosti* provides more limited access to central print media than *Integrum*, but it has a larger collection of Ukrainian media. For this reason, I verified the results gathered from one database with the help of another. In the case of social media, I did not have similar cross-verification possibilities, since *Yandex Blogs* has an effective monopoly here. *Yandex Blogs* provides by far the most comprehensive access to social-media archives (as of 30 June 2011, the *Yandex Blogs* database covered and indexed 102 separate blog hosting services, 13 microblog hosting services and the popular Russian social-networking site V Kontakte).

I collected those documents in which the words 'victory', 'day', 'l'viv' were mentioned within a single sentence, using them as a signifier that the event was discussed in a particular document. My quantitative approach builds on:

- A comparison between the trends and dynamic of the discussions of this event across different media during a given period of time.
- A juxtaposition of this specific memory event with other memory events (below, I provide a comparative analysis of 'Manezhka' and 'Victory Day L'viv').

This approach allows one to work with the approximate data for a given day, to avoid many limitations of large data (such as the *Yandex* data – *Yandex* provides approximate figures, does not enable full and unrestricted access to data, and uses specific algorithms in counting the data: for one, it does not count the number of comments to blog posts, so if a post yields 1500 comments, Yandex Blogs counts these as 'one') but draws conclusions from comparison. Thus, the numbers I provide in my quantitative analysis do not give a precise answer to the question: 'How many times was the event discussed in a given medium on a given day?', but they do answer the questions: 'Was it discussed more or less in comparison with other events or across different media?' and 'Was it discussed earlier or later in one medium in comparison with another?'

In this analysis, it was important to divide the media into their Russian and Ukrainian segments, in order to test my assumption that the Ukrainian media would be likely to demonstrate greater levels of interest in the L'viv event than their Russian counterparts. The simplest solution here would be to use Ukrainian-language search queries for Ukrainian media, and Russian for Russian. However, some Ukrainian media do not duplicate content in the Ukrainian language and use only Russian, and some of them use only Ukrainian without duplication in Russian. In addition, the Ukrainian social media use both languages. Therefore,

I was forced to combine both languages into a single query for searching the Ukrainian media (my exact query was '(день перемога львів) | (день победа львов)').

Given that both *Yandex* and *Integrum* are able to divide the media by region, I added the operator 'geo=Ukraine' or 'geo=Russia' to the URL from the *Yandex Advanced Search* page (option 'From where' in *Yandex Blogs* and 'Regions' in *Yandex News*) and created two Ukrainian media corpora ('Ukrainian print media' and 'Ukrainian online media') from the Integrum databases for CIS media (option 'Personal Collection'; see how to use this option in Fruchtman 2006: 181–182 and Gershenson and Romanenko 2006: 32). Classifying newspapers and websites by geographical location is quite straightforward, but this is not the case when it comes to social media. The only way for a researcher to check how accurately search engines identify the geographical location of social media users is to check this against geographical information provided in the users' profiles and geographical *realia* in the content of posts, comments and tweets. Not only is this method time-consuming, however; it is also less than fully reliable, given the possibility of missing or fake location data in users' profiles, for example (on this phenomenon in Twitter, see e.g. Hecht *et al.* 2011). Consequently, I decided, for my quantitative analysis, to unite Russian and Ukrainian social media.

For the qualitative analysis of Ukrainian social media discourses I chose those Ukrainian forums that were most likely to express a more or less neutral viewpoint on the event. For this reason, I selected one all-Ukrainian forum (TCH.ua), and one Ukrainian local forum from Cherkasy (forum.ck.ua), a city in Central Ukraine that, according to the opinion of the participants of the forum, 'is neither east nor west', and 'holds intermediate positions' on matters of memory and identity (on regional differences in Ukrainian memory practices, see Kulyk, Chapter 4, this volume).

The official discourse war

Official discourse on the L'viv version of the 9 May celebrations opened on 6 April, in connection with debates over the use of the Soviet-era Victory Banner on Victory Day. On 5 April, the Communist faction of the Ukrainian Parliament had proposed a draft law that would allow the Soviet Victory Banner to be flown alongside the national flag of Ukraine on Victory Day. If passed, this law would bring Ukraine in line with Russia, Belarus and Transnistria, where the Soviet Victory Banner has been declared an official symbol of the Soviet Victory over Nazi Germany. It would also place Ukraine at the opposite end of the spectrum to post-Soviet countries like Lithuania and Georgia, and post-socialist countries like Hungary and Poland, where the public use of Soviet symbolism of this kind has been forbidden or restricted by law (in 2008, 2011, 1994 and 2009, respectively).

The announcement of the bill immediately sparked outrage in L'viv and official debates about the forthcoming local Victory Day celebrations. In a statement entitled 'Soviet Myths Need to Be Destroyed', the L'viv Regional Rada refused not only to display red flags, but also to celebrate Victory Day ('L'vivs'ka oblrada' 2011). Despite this negative reaction, the law was adopted by the Ukrainian

Parliament on 21 April (*Zakon Ukrainy* 2011) and duly passed to President Viktor Yanukovych for signing. Even though the law had yet to come into force on 9 May, on that day red flags were displayed in Donetsk, Sevastopol, Zhytomyr, Odesa, and several other Ukrainian cities.

Meanwhile, activists from the Odesa 'Rodina' pro-Russian organization and the Crimean 'Russian Unity' group announced their intention to come to L'viv on Victory Day with a 15-metre-long red banner, together with veterans from those regions. In an effort to prevent unrest, L'viv's regional court prohibited the organization of mass demonstrations on 9 May ('Pizno vvecherei' 2011), but the ban was ignored. The ensuing events were described by news agency Interfaks-Ukraina as follows:

> During the celebration of Victory Day in L'viv, there were numerous clashes and fights. In particular, a group of young men broke through the police cordon near the Hill of Glory, and tried to prevent the unfolding of the red victory banner. In total, 14 people were injured in the clashes. Nine people were arrested for disorderly conduct. A criminal investigation has been initiated with regard to the shooting incident – a representative of 'Svoboda' suffered a wound to the leg.
>
> ('Za sobytiiami' 2011)

In this report, the identities of the opposing sides are blurred. In fact, the group who were 'trying to prevent the unfolding of the banner' were the members and followers of a Ukrainian nationalist party, 'Svoboda', while those who were 'unfolding the red victory banner' were activists from 'Rodina' and 'Russian Unity'. As for the details of the shooting, photographs and video footage appeared first on blogs (davnym_davno 2011) and YouTube, and then in other online media ('Byvshii gaishnik' 2011). The elderly war veterans were caught up between the conflicting sides.

The event also turned into an international scandal between Russia and Ukraine, since 'Svoboda' activists had grabbed a wreath out of the hands of Russian Consul Oleg Astakhov. Subsequently, the Russian State Duma issued an address to the Ukrainian Verkhovna Rada demanding that the Rada 'punish the organizers of the sacrilegious provocations in L'viv' ('Proekt' 2011). In response, the Ukrainian Foreign Ministry recalled the case of the riots on Moscow's Manezhnaia Square in December 2010 (when thousands of football fans and/or defenders of nationalist convictions held a rally at Manezhnaia which took a violent turn) and advised Russia not to interfere in Ukrainian internal affairs ('MID Ukrainy' 2011; 'Ukraina posovetovala' 2011).

After the 9 May incidents, there were apprehensions that repeat clashes might break out in L'viv the following month, in connection with another official memorial date, 22 June. Commemorating the anniversary of the German invasion of the USSR in 1941, this day was implemented in 1996 as the Day of Memory and Sorrow in Russia and in 2000 as the Day of Sorrow and Honouring the Memory of the Victims of the War in Ukraine. Commemorative ceremonies planned for 22 June 2011 were to be especially prominent, since they marked the seventieth anniversary of the invasion. Fears of possible unrest were intensified after announcements that 'the Communist Parties of Russia (KPRF) and Ukraine (KRU) plan to hold a joint event in L'viv on 22 June with the usage of red banners' ('Kommunisty' 2011).

Despite these fears, on 20 May President Yanukovych went ahead and signed the law authorizing the use of the Victory Banner. However, on 16 June the law was cancelled by the Constitutional Court of Ukraine, which deemed the use of the Soviet Victory Banner to be unconstitutional. This decision brought the official discourse war on celebration of Victory Day in L'viv, launched by the Communist faction's proposed bill on the banner, to an end. Thus, the official discourse combat on the event lasted from 6 April to 17 June.

The media war

In order to achieve the aim of this chapter – i.e. to disentangle the connections and correlations between three overlapping wars: the official discourse war, the media war and the 'real' war – I also conducted a discourse analysis of media discussions on L'viv's 9 May celebrations. The analysis tackled the battles between Russian and Ukrainian media and between different Ukrainian media.

In retrospective news analyses, Ukrainian media accused the Russian media, mainly television, of heating up passions around the events in L'viv. One Ukrainian online newspaper stated, for example, that:

> [T]he 9 May events in L'viv were the top story on all Russian channels. Over the course of two days the Russians broadcast footage of Ukrainian police trying to cope with the onslaught of mostly young demonstrators under the flags of nationalist movements.
>
> ('Rossiiskoe televidenie' 2011)

Meanwhile, the Russian central TV channels ORT, RTR and NTV ran reports on the events in L'viv in the evening news on 9 May and in four separate news broadcasts on 10 May, but the peak activity on these channels was on 11 May, when the official reaction of the Russian Duma was issued (and broadcast along with footage from L'viv). Many other Russian media outlets covered the events, often in the form of reports criticizing the Ukrainian authorities for allowing the celebrations to take place.

The majority of Ukrainian media also blamed the violence on the Ukrainian authorities who started the discussion on the Victory Banner and failed to prevent violent responses; but they also accused Ukrainian nationalists. West Ukrainian media rejected the accusation of Ukrainian nationalists and accused 'pro-Russian organizations' of having staged a 'provocation with the red flag'. In addition, many Ukrainian media attacked various combinations of Russia–the Kremlin-Moscow–the FSB (which were said to have 'created a scenario of provocations') as well as the Russian media (which had allegedly helped to bring this scenario to life, partly by preparing the Ukrainian public for it in advance). These media also extensively replicated and discussed the next potentially violent event: the commemorations due to take place on 22 June, which Communists had pledged to come to L'viv to attend.

This media war was waged, for the most part, not over different versions of memory, but over the search for culprits, conspirators and provocateurs, as in this example:

> 'The riots that occurred on Victory Day 9 May in L'viv were a clearly orchestrated script aimed at creating high-quality pictures for the media,' the GMT Group director Anatolii Lutsenko said at a press conference in Kiev, Golos.UA reports. 'The style [*lit.* handwriting] is evident. This is clear to anyone who works with media technologies. The style is well known, it belongs to, so to speak, our "eastern neighbour",' said the political consultant. He noted that the provocateurs were working in accordance with a script, which had been announced in advance by certain mass media.
>
> (Kovalenko 2011)

Here and elsewhere, journalists often supported their statements by making reference to expert opinion. The newspaper *Segodnia*, for example, cited Vadim Karasev, a Ukrainian political analyst, leader of the Ukrainian political party 'United Centre', and Head of the Global Strategies Institute (Kiev), who stated that 'the radicalization in L'viv was artificially created by political technologists' ('Eksperty' 2011).

As a rule, the experts and journalists did not identify particular media by name. Instead, the reports included general accusations that 'the media' were fanning the flames of the information war. Commentators asserted, for example, that Victory Day had been preceded by 'many days of whipping up the information wave around the planned arrival in the town of several hundred people with guards from Crimea and Odesa, who were planning to march through the city centre with party symbols and flags' (Kazarin 2011). While the media were not blamed explicitly in this article, the description of the context provided here (for example, the use of phrases like 'information wave') suggested strongly that the media had played a significant role in the preparation and provocation of the L'viv incidents.

My findings appear to contradict this version of events: the searches turned up hardly any evidence that would point to the existence of a 'script, which some media announced in advance', which predicted clashes in L'viv on 9 May. I expected to find large amounts of discussion on the Victory Banner initiative and L'viv or of plans to cancel Victory Day celebrations and of potential violence in L'viv, but the volume of such discussion was not impressive and did not point to a specific provocative role of the media in preparing or inciting the event.

Could it be the case that the media in general, and the Russian media in particular, had provoked the violent tensions in L'viv? I set out to answer this question by measuring the intensity of discussion on the event in different media over a three-month period, from the beginning of April to the end of June, based on the assumption that the media discourse would be correlated with the official discourse. My findings are presented in Chart 3.1, where I have combined the results for the Ukrainian and Russian (central and regional) print media, online media and social media.

The findings in Chart 3.1 indicate that the above-cited claims about the media's role in provoking the war in L'viv were exaggerated. Until 9 May, in fact, media discourse about potential clashes on 9 May in L'viv was practically non-existent. It was not a media war that provoked the war in L'viv; rather, the offline war in L'viv itself provoked the media war. Hence, we can see a sharp spike in the intensity of the media coverage on 10 May. Subsequently the intensity decreased rapidly, but the theme remained a constant topic of media discourse until approximately 23 June.

As Chart 3.1 shows, different types of media covered the event to varying degrees. Ukrainian online media were most active in reporting on it (322 items on 10 May). The widespread beliefs about the special role of Russian media in allegedly preparing and provoking the event, on the other hand, are not borne out by my findings. My findings indicate that, in fact, all Russian media started to cover the event not only after it had actually taken place (something which was typical for all the media), but also later than the Ukrainian media. The Russian print media lagged behind here partly due to the timing of Russian public holidays and the preceding weekend (in 2011, 9 May fell on a Monday). The Russian regional media produced almost no coverage of the event whatsoever.

There was, however, one form of media which stood out in my findings. This was the social media. As Chart 3.1 shows, the intensification of debates over 9 May in L'viv in social media not only started, but almost reached its peak one day before the event – on 8 May.

This result suggests the hypothetical possibility that the social media may in fact be the only media capable of triggering the offline clashes on 9 May.

The war in social media

In order to investigate the social media's capacity to spark offline events in this way, I needed first to ascertain the intensity of the social media debates. Here a comparison with another similar event was required, and I chose to use the riots at Manezhnaia Square in Moscow on 11 December 2010 in this capacity. This seemed an especially relevant and useful comparison, given that parallels between the two events, between the nationalists involved in both riots, the football fans in Moscow and the 'Svoboda' supporters in L'viv, had been drawn both in the abovementioned official statement by the Ukrainian Foreign Ministry and in the social media. An illustrative online comment was made by social-media user Vitalii, who wrote on 9 May 2011: 'In Moscow, at Manezhnaia square, they were arrested and tried, there is a conveyor of "hell" working, prisons are not empty. Here [in L'viv] he will pay off or hide' (Vitalii, 9 May 2011).

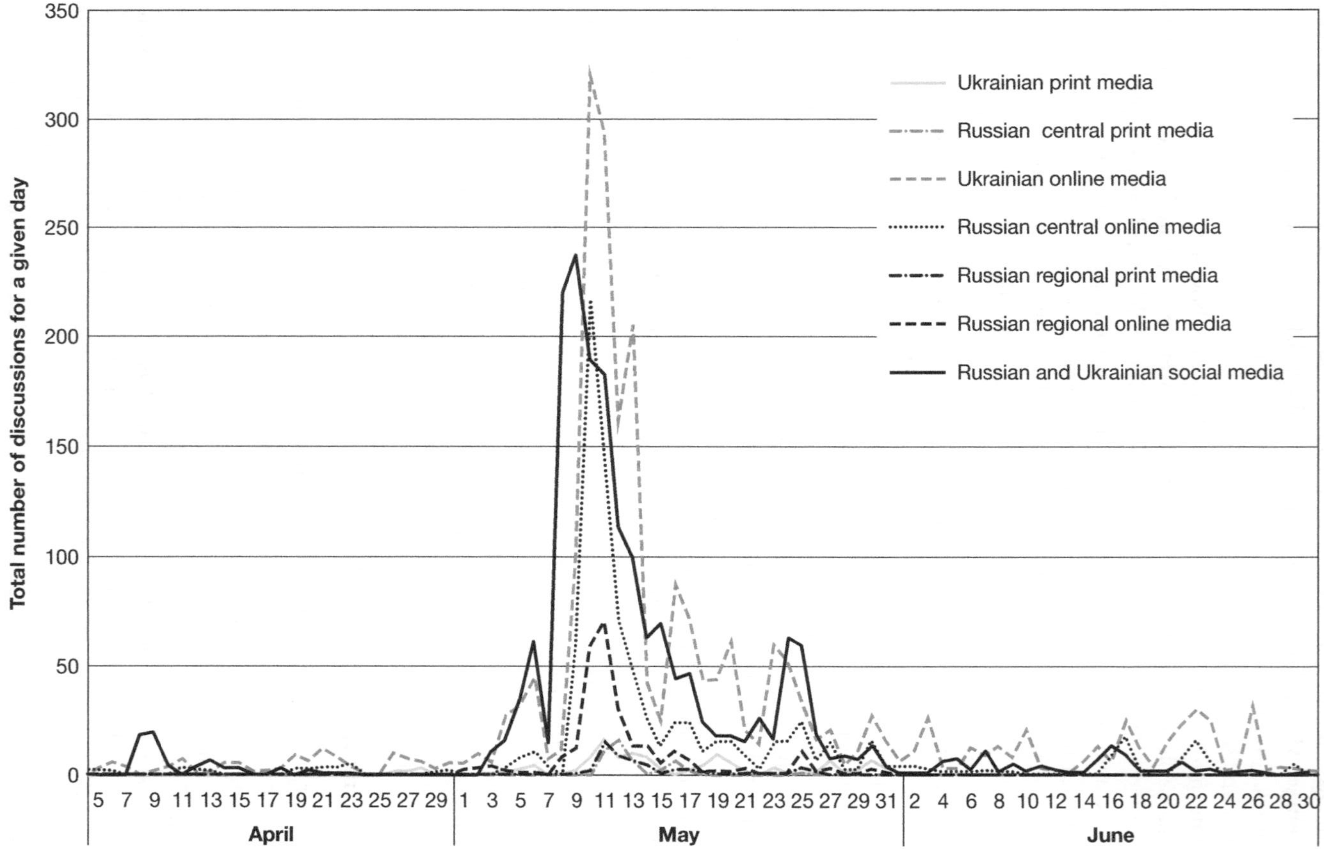

Chart 3.1 9 May 2011 in L'viv in Russian and Ukrainian print and online media, and in the social media

The dynamic of the Ukrainian and Russian social media attention paid to the Manezhnaia riots was as follows:

11 December	2,219 posts, forum comments, tweets
12 December	3,724
13 December	3,806
14 December	2,926
15 December	2,356
16 December	2,167
17 December	1,668

The combined level of attention paid by the Ukrainian and Russian social media to the riots in L'viv was:

05 May	35 posts, comments, tweets
06 May	63
07 May	14
08 May	220
09 May	239
10 May	190
11 May	183

In other words, we may conclude that the L'viv events did not resonate particularly strongly in the social media. These expressed a substantially stronger interest in the Manezhnaia Square events taking place in Moscow.

Next, I conducted an analysis of the discourses developed on the two selected Ukrainian forums before the event. My findings indicated that both forums started discussing possible clashes on Victory Day in L'viv on 6 April – immediately after the L'viv Regional Rada issued the statement that 'Soviet Myths Need to Be Destroyed', with its refusal to display red flags or to celebrate Victory Day. The dominant discourse of the debate in the Cherkasy forum (44 comments) was the condemnation of 'national fascist L'viv', Galicia, West Ukraine as a whole, and 'Svoboda' which was 'not Ukraine', where 'only banderlogi live' [*banderlog*, as well as *banderlokh* and *banderovets*, are pejorative terms for Western Ukrainians formed from the surname of Stepan Bandera – one of the World War II-era leaders of the Ukrainian national movement in Western Ukraine and head of the Organization of Ukrainian Nationalists (OUN)], and which 'should be returned to Poland', so that then 'there won't be any Bandera cities in our country'.

By the end of April, when social media users knew about the decision of the Crimean and Odesa organizations to come to L'viv bringing a red flag and veterans from those regions, the discussions touched upon a second popular topic: 'there will be a collision on 9 May, and this is a provocation' (25 comments). There were different opinions about who was behind the provocation and who would benefit from it.

The majority of users inclined to the view that it was a provocation by the Ukrainian authorities (17 comments). They claimed that the Ukrainian regime:

- '[W]ants to distract people from the rigors of everyday life. To stop people thinking about the bribes, inflation, the dead economy, the social issues. The main thing is to divert attention and win some time. It's just like the "Holodomor" wave was. After all, that worked well' (five similar comments).
- '[W]ants to split Ukraine and Ukrainian society' and has even been paying bloggers 'who stir up the topic and support divisions in society' (six similar comments).
- '[H]as started the election campaign' (three similar comments).
- '[W]ants to take benefits away from veterans' (one comment).
- '[S]upports pro-Russian organizations "Rodina" and "Russian Unity"' (one comment).
- '[W]ants to blame the nationalists for all Ukraine's modern economic and social problems' (one comment).

Some users accused the pro-Russian organizations 'Russian Unity', 'Patrol', 'Motherland' and 'United Fatherland' (four comments). Others, without identifying the authors of the provocation, blamed themselves. In the words of one blogger, 'we are the *lokhokrat* [a compound word formed from *lokh*, a Russian word describing a naïve and extremely trusting person, also used in the term *banderlokh* above, and 'electorate'], they provoke us, and we follow them' (four comments). I also found four comments in support of L'viv's Ukrainian nationalists.

At the beginning of May, the forum debates that anticipated clashes in L'viv reached a fairly high level of emotional intensity and could justifiably be described as having discussed a scenario of clashes on 9 May and, by implication, helped to provoke these clashes. Consider how the emotional mood was stepping up in the forum discussion:

1 I'll go to L'viv and look into the eyes of Bandera's nationalists as a winner, not as a slut serving the Poles (**Limonka**, 2 May 2011).
2 You will be walking between two ranks of cops [lit. *ment* – pejorative slang for police] under the dismissive eyes of L'viv's citizens, just like the Nazi prisoners walked through Moscow. Though why 'just like'? The communists-fascists are the same criminals as the Nazis, and destroyed the lives of even more innocent people. No wonder the Nazis learned from their colleagues from the NKVD how to build concentration camps, to torture and kill millions of undesirable people. Though to understand and to admit it, one needs at least an ounce of mind and conscience (**SanbI4**, 4 May 2011).
3 Simple conclusions may be drawn from the above: everything for 'ours', to the courts with the 'others'; 'Svoboda' and the nationalists have got frightened. They go all around Ukraine, but as soon as they discovered some visitors would be coming to them, they ran to the court immediately. Democracy from Ukrainian nationalists! Heil! You can shit yourself trying, but there will

be tens of millions of people coming out on 9 May with the Red Victory flags, and they will thank the veterans and commemorate the dead. And there's nothing you can do about it! All you can do is get hysterical on forums. PS. Don't strain yourself over replying, your answers are known in advance anyhow, and no-one needs them (**imperia1991**, 7 May 2011).

At the same time, the forum did not show a strong potential for mobilizing users into physical action as they did not include any concrete calls for activity:

4 **Limonka**, what about sending all of them to hell and going to the forest for a barbeque? That's exactly what I'll do. I use the whole power of the Ukrainian mentality. None of my business, I don't know (**_Clawfinger_**, 2 May 2011).

5 Presumably, 9 May will not go unnoticed either, somebody will do something weird for sure. . . . Therefore, just be human. If you don't believe 9 May is anything to celebrate, nobody is kicking you to walk around with a red flag. You can stay home or, say, go and have a barbecue in the forest. If you do [consider 9 May a festive day], then go and congratulate some elderly person, with a flag or without; it won't hurt you and it will make him feel happy. At least once a year. To all 'ours', Happy Victory day! (**ArmoR**, 8 May 2011).

Rather than discussing the question of whether or not to follow one concrete blogger (**Limonka**) to L'viv to fight the *banderovtsy* who planned to abandon the celebrations, social media users preferred to do precisely what they had previously accused the Ukrainian government of doing: they blamed everything that happened in L'viv on Ukrainian nationalists, and focused on criticizing them. The Moscow–Kremlin script was not a popular discourse on the forums under study either before or after the event (despite being broadly discussed throughout print and online Ukrainian media). On 9 May the forum started to lose interest in the event, as one blogger made very clear in his post:

6 I'm surprised! Digging in the garden all day, I thought the internet would be buzzing, after having seen the events in L'viv. But there's 'silence'. Just read a headline from Moscow: 'Ukrainian nationalists in battle with veterans'. I am struck by the indifference of society (**Brydia**, 9 May 2011).

The forum served as a platform for intense emotional moods, among them anger, hatred and aggression. It also provided information and kept the followers connected. What it did not do, however, was to engage people in offline action. The appeals to come to L'viv on 22 June likewise met with practically no support.

Conclusion

One memory event, 9 May 2011 in L'viv, fuelled by the official discourse war that began on 6 April, sparked debates in social media the following day, and then exploded in an offline war on 9 May, which in turn provoked the media war that lasted until 23 June. In this chapter, I have attempted to create as complete a map of this event as possible, with a view to illuminating the story of the evolution of the event in time, and the dynamic interweaving of the cultural genres and discourses of its representation and constitution. I have mapped this event using different tools and techniques of quantitative and qualitative analysis, based on a wide range of digital debates on the event, as well as measuring the intensity of these debates.

Relying on the outlines of this data map, I have offered a number of conclusions: about the connections between aggressive official and media debates and their potential for influencing the violent clashes on the street; on the relationship between Ukrainian and Russian media; and on the practices that characterize different types of media. The commonly accepted hypothesis about the role of the media as provocateur of this event was disproved. Instead, I have generated a new hypothesis about the existence and importance of a separate genre of event – the debates in the social media (for a similar hypothesis see Paulsen, Chapter 5, this volume). Being 'faster' than other media, the social media may in fact be the only medium capable of triggering the offline clashes. At the same time, the social media produce idiosyncratic discursive frames where no one can say a word without being immediately corrected, rejected, assessed or commented upon. This specific discursive space immediately and easily destroys any idea, disorients followers and ultimately, it would appear, fails to engage followers in offline action.

My attempts to clarify the potential of the social media for generating and shaping memory events, for foreseeing, anticipating, and even provoking or initiating events, and for mobilizing itself for real action, have raised new questions that require further research and observations of events in time. A long temporal distance will be essential to scrutinize other findings of this study. Thus, the study has highlighted the complexity of the relationship between the different discourses on the events. The official discourse war provoked a street-level war on 9 May; the media then worked hard to fix different interpretations of the offline war in popular memory; and the future will show which interpretation has won – whether 9 May has been definitively transformed into a day of struggle between different versions of the Second World War memory, or whether it has reverted to the old Victory Day format.

Note

1 The term *mankurt* has its roots in a Turkic myth that Soviet writer Chinghiz Aitmatov popularized in his novel *The Day Lasts More Than a Hundred Years* (*I dol'she veka dlitsia den'*, 1981). In the original myth, the term *mankurt* refers to a man who ranks as the perfect slave, since his life revolves strictly around the most basic human activities, and since he no longer remembers his own past.

References

'Byvshii gaishnik' (2011) 'Byvshii gaishnik: L'vovskie natsionalisty vynudili syna streliat'' [Former Traffic Cop: L'viv Nationalists Forced My Son to Shoot], *ROSBALT Ukraina*, 11 May. Online. Available: <http://www.rosbalt.ru/ukraina/2011/05/11/847467.html> (accessed 11 May 2011).

davnym_davno (2011) 'L'vov: provokatsii pod krasnym flagom' [L'viv: Provocations under Red Banner], 10 May. Online posting. Available: <http://yablor.ru/blogs/lvov-provokacii-pod-krasnim-flagom/1533342> (accessed 10 May 2011).

Dubin, B. (2005) 'Bremia pobedy' [Burden of Victory], *Kriticheskaia Massa* 2. Online. Available: <http://magazines.russ.ru/km/2005/2/du6.html> (accessed 6 September 2011).

'Eksperty' (2011) 'Eksperty: "Svoboda" nazhila sebe vo L'vove kuchu vragov' [Experts: 'Svoboda' Stirred Up a Hornet's Nest in L'viv], *Segodnia.UA*, 11 May. Online. Available: <http://www.segodnya.ua/news/14248182.html> (accessed 11 May 2011).

Etkind, A. (2010) 'Mapping Memory Events in the East European Space', *East European Memory Studies* 1. Online. Available: <http://www.memoryatwar.org/enewsletter%20oct%202010%20final.pdf> (accessed 10 July 2012).

Etling, B. *et al.* (2010) 'Public Discourse in the Russian Blogosphere: Mapping Runet politics and Mobilization', *Berkman Center Research Publication*. Online. Available: < http://cyber.law.harvard.edu/publications/2010/Public_Discourse_Russian_Blogosphere> (accessed 2 February 2011).

Fruchtman, J. (2006) 'Correlating Linguistic and Extralinguistic Developments', in Nikiporets-Takigawa, G. (ed.) (2006) *Integrum: tochnye metody i gumanitarnye nauki*. Moscow: Letnii sad.

Gershenson, L. and Romanenko, F. (2006) 'Integrum. The History of the Creation, the Operating System, the use', in Nikiporets-Takigawa, G. (ed.) (2006) *Integrum: tochnye metody i gumanitarnye nauki*. Moscow: Letnii sad.

'Ia pomniu' '"Ia pomniu? Ia gorzhus"'? Sait v zashchitu Georgievskoi lenty' ['Do I Remember? Am I Proud?' Site in Defence of St George's Ribbon]. Online. Available: <http://www.za-lentu.ru> (accessed 5 May 2011).

Hecht, B. *et al.* (2011) 'Tweets from Justin Bieber's Heart: The Dynamics of the "Location" Field in User Profiles'. Online. Available: <http://www.brenthecht.com/papers/bhecht_chi2011_location.pdf> (accessed 27 April 2012).

Kazarin, P. (2011) 'L'vovskii kozyr' Putina-Yanukovicha' [Putin-Yanukovych's L'viv Trump Card], *ROSBALT Ukraina*, 12 May. Online. Available: <http://www.rosbalt.ru/ukraina/2011/05/12/848148.html> (accessed 12 May 2011).

'Kod dostupa' (2012) 'Kod dostupa' [Access Code], radio station *Ekho Moskvy*. Online. Available: <http://echo.msk.ru/programs/code/885165-echo> (accessed 5 May 2012).

'Kommunisty' (2011) 'Kommunisty obeshchaiut L'vovu eshche bolee mashtabnye sobytiia 22 iiunia' [Communists Promise L'viv Even Bigger Events on 22 June], *Novyi Region 2*, 11 May. Online. Available: <http://www.nr2.ru/kiev/331145.html> (accessed 11 May 2011).

Kovalenko, K. (2011) 'Sobytiia 9 maia vo L'vove – stsenarii po spetsial'noi tekhnologii – politolog' [Political Scientist Says Events on 9 May in L'viv are a Scenario Using a Special Technology], *golos.ua*, 13 May. Online. Available: < http://www.golosua.com/main/article/politika/20110513_sobyitiya-9-maya-vo-lvove-stsenariy-po-spetsialnoy-tehnologii-politolog> (accessed 13 May 2011).

Kulyk, V. (2011) 'The Media, History and Identity: Competing Narratives of the Past in the Ukrainian Popular Press', *National Identities* 13:3: 287–303.

'L'viv'ska oblrada' (2011) 'L'vivska oblrada vistupila proty chervonikh praporiv' [L'viv Regional Administration is Against the Red Banners], *Galinfo*, 6 April. Online. Available: <http://galinfo.com.ua/news/85842.html> (accessed 8 May 2011).

Michel, J.B. *et al.* (2010) 'Quantitative Analysis of Culture Using Millions of Digitized Books', *Science*, 16 December. Online. Available: <http://www.sciencemag.org/content/suppl/2010/12/16/science.1199644.DC1/Michel.SOM.revision.2.pdf> (accessed 7 September 2011).

'MID Ukrainy' (2011) 'MID Ukrainy ne nravitsia, kak Rossiia reagiruet na sobytiia vo L'vove' [Ukrainian Foreign Ministry Doesn't Like Russian Reaction to L'viv Events], *Novyi Region*, 11 May. Online. Available: <http://www.nr2.ru/kiev/331099.html> (accessed 11 May 2011).

'Opytuvannia' (2011) 'Opytuvannia: Ukraintsi vvazhaiut' Den' Peremohy diisno velykym sviatom' [Poll: Ukrainians Consider Victory Day a Truly Great Day], *Tsentr Razumkova*, 29 April. Online. Available: <http://www.razumkov.org.ua/ukr/news.php?news_id=371> (accessed 2 May 2011).

'Pizno vvecheri' (2011) 'Pizno vvecheri sud zaboronyv partiiam provedennia u L'vovi aktsii u Den' peremohy' [In the Late Evening the Court Banned Actions in L'viv on Victory Day]. Online. Available: <http://portal.lviv.ua/news/2010/05/09/111827.html> (accessed 9 May 2011).

Portnov, A. (2010) 'Uprazhneniia s istoriei po-ukrainski: itogi i perspektivy. Publichnoe obsuzhdeniie s Andreem Portnovym' [Exercises in History Ukrainian-Style: Outcomes and Prospects. Public Discussion with Andrei Portnov], *polit.ru*, 26 August. Online. Available: <http://www.polit.ru/article/2010/08/26/history> (accessed 27 August 2011).

'Proekt' (2011) 'Proekt zaiavleniia Gosdumy "V sviazi s ekstremistskimi proiavleniiami v gorode L'vove vo vremia prazdnovaniia Dnia Pobedy" rassmotren na plenarnom zasedanii' [Draft Statement of the Russian State Duma 'Regarding the Extremist Manifestations in the city of L'vov during the Victory Day Celebration' discussed at the plenary session]. Online. Available: <http://pda.duma.gov.ru/news/273/75728/?sphrase_id=466017> (accessed 11 May 2011).

'Rossiiskoe televidenie' (2011) 'Rossiiskoe televidenie podogrevaet strasti vokrug sobytii vo L'vove' [Russian Television Stirs Passions around Events in L'viv], *delo.ua*, 11 May. Online. Available: <http://delo.ua/ukraine/rossijskoe-televidenie-podogre-157186> (accessed 11 May 2011).

Trubina, E. (2010) 'Past Wars in the Russian Blogosphere: On the Emergency of Cosmopolitan Memory', *Digital Icons: Studies in Russian, Eurasian and Central European New Media* 4, pp. 63–85. Online. Available: <http://www.digitalicons.org/issue04/files/2010/11/Trubina-4.4.pdf> (accessed 20 March 2011).

'Ukraina posovetovala' (2011) 'Ukraina posovetovala Rossii ne vmeshivat'sia vo l'vovskie "razborki"' [Ukraine Has Advised Russia Not to Interfere in L'viv Investigation], TCH, 11 May. Online. Available: <http://ru.tsn.ua/ukrayina/ukraina-posovetovala-rossii-ne-vmeshivatsya-vo-lvovskie-rozborki.html> (accessed 11 May 2011).

Zakon Ukrainy (2011) Zakon Ukrainy pro uvichnennia Peremohy u Velykii Vitchiznianii viini 1941-1945 rokiv [The Law of Ukraine on the Immortalization of Victory in the Great Patriotic War of 1941-1945], N 3298-VI (3298-17), 21 April. Online. Available: < http://zakon.rada.gov.ua/cgi-bin/laws/main.cgi?nreg=1684-14> (accessed 2 May 2011).

'Za sobytiiami' (2011) 'Za sobytiiami vo L'vove 9 maia ne bylo "ruki Moskvy"' ['Moscow's Hand' Not Behind 9 May Riots in L'viv], *Interfaks-Ukraina*, 24 May. Online. Available: <http://www.interfax.com.ua/rus/pol/69399/> (accessed 24 May 2011).

4 War of memories in the Ukrainian media

Diversity of identities, political confrontation, and production technologies

Volodymyr Kulyk

Introduction

As most social scientists would now acknowledge, modern collective memory is fundamentally and profoundly mediated. Technically speaking, the mediation of memories began in ancient times, with rock carvings and handwritten chronicles; but it is the advent of modernity with its state-sponsored monuments, history textbooks and daily newspapers that has made these mediated memories an inherent feature of how people deal with their perceived past.

While in the twentieth century collective memories were mainly produced and maintained by means of print and broadcast media, in the new millennium the mediation increasingly takes place via the Internet. The effects of the technological changes have been compounded by social transformations which influence the economic and political contexts of the respective media discourses and, accordingly, the identities of their participants (the latter being also constructed in those discourses themselves). In particular, while the reconfiguration of state borders has exposed millions of people to new nationalizing projects, globalization has been undermining the pre-eminence of national identity frameworks. In this new context, not only do nationwide media of various types complement and challenge each other's memory work, but they coexist with supra- and sub-national outlets whose distinctive frameworks also affect (and are affected by) the nation-centred memories. The multiplication of producers/mediators, particularly on the Internet, inevitably results in the multiplication of representations of the past and present. It thus fuels the ongoing contestation of the meaning of events, including their perception as pertaining to a particular collectivity. This is particularly true of societies undergoing radical socio-political transformations which shatter established identity structures and instigate heated controversies among proponents of various alternative visions of the country's past, present and future.

This chapter analyses mediated memories in one such society: post-Soviet Ukraine. After a theoretical discussion of the role of media discourse in the production and maintenance of identities and memories, I examine two important factors influencing memory-related discourses of the Ukrainian media, namely the diversity of citizens' identities and the ways in which this diversity has been manipulated by politicians. Turning to the discourses of various media, I focus on how they are affected by the audience structure of these media, by the state's policies on the different types of media, and by the technological conditions for particular types of media products. While analytically reducing the complexity of identities to a dichotomous structure of opposing orientations, I seek to examine the specifics of the competition between these orientations in various types of media, from newspapers to online social networks. My approach is in line with a recent

> shift from 'sites' to 'dynamics' within memory studies [which] runs parallel to a larger shift of attention within cultural studies from products to processes, from a focus on discrete cultural artefacts to an interest in the way the artefacts circulate and interact with their environment.
>
> (Erll and Rigney 2009: 3)

Memory and identity in media discourse

It seems appropriate to view a nation's collective memory as a historical dimension of national identity which, in turn, should be treated as a particular kind of collective identity. Each collective identity can vary in its *content*; that is, the prescribed meaning of membership in the collectivity, and also in the degree of *contestation* of that content within the collectivity (Abdelal *et al.* 2007). Furthermore, an individual may identify with different collectivities, in which case the multiple identities are organized into hierarchies of *salience* (Tajfel 1982). National identity may be more or less salient vis-à-vis other collective identities for individuals and subgroups within a nation, who also contest the meaning of national belonging. Identification with a nation or any other collectivity manifests itself in a wide range of beliefs or feelings, including those pertaining to the collectivity's past in general, and to certain historical events and figures in particular. Historical memory thus belongs to the content of national or other collective identity (Kulyk 2011).

The media are one of the most important among the various institutions involved in the discursive construction and maintenance of this and other dimensions of national identity. While the primary production of socially accepted historical knowledge is carried out by academics, the media play a key role in mediating communication between the academy and the general population. Moreover, in contrast to much of the academic and educational literature, the media forge relationships with the past not so much by promoting factual knowledge and 'intellectual understanding of cause and effect' as by reshaping imagination and empathy (Morris-Suzuki 2005: 22). More than facts and concepts, the very presence of bygone events in the 'imaginative landscape' and an 'empathetic relationship with the people of the past' instil in contemporary audiences a sense of belonging to certain diachronically perceived groups of people, most often national ones (ibid.). Perhaps even more importantly, the cognitive and emotive effects of the media presentations of the past tend to overshadow and thus render unnoticeable their (usually implicit) interpretation of the events and figures in question.

There are many ways in which the media, when engaging with the past, may be said to be consciously assuming the 'role of public historians' (Kitch 2005: 5). Media products such as historical dramas, documentary films and bio-pics, or news reports on the anniversaries of historical events or commemorating particular historical figures, would all fall into this category. Such products often attract very large audiences and thus play an important role both in terms of raising public awareness of particular events/figures and in defining their meanings for the audiences. At the same time, the media discourse also contributes to the production of memory through a variety of more routine and inconspicuous practices. For example, evaluative comments and background statements in news stories often refer to past events and processes and thus imply both relevant time frames and social entities to whose continuous existence current events are implicitly related. Moreover, many media representations of the past belong to the sphere of popular culture and, therefore, are largely determined by economic considerations and aesthetic conventions – conventions which are not only very different from those valid in 'high' culture, but also specific to particular media.

While historians and media critics have paid primary attention to the supposedly distorted and trivialized interpretation of historical processes in influential 'market-oriented narratives of history', no less important is the impact of the topic selection on 'our imaginative landscape of the past' (Morris-Suzuki 2005: 17). Not only does the media's selection shape the content of national history and identity by favouring some 'domestic' events and periods over others, but it can also undermine the salience of national identification vis-à-vis its competitors by favouring events from other national pasts over those of one's 'own', thereby challenging the very definition of the latter. On the one hand, the media can contribute to the democratization of national identity by 'featuring a range of class, ethnic and gendered characters' ignored or marginalized in official versions of the past (Edensor 2002: 142). On the other hand, the media can erode this identity by facilitating audiences' knowledge of and empathy with events and people in other countries. The latter effect may be particularly significant in newly founded states, where the primacy of national identification is not yet ensured by other institutions.

The advent of the Internet has contributed to both the democratization of the mediated identities and the erosion of the national framework for their reproduction. On the one hand, the unprecedented ease with which online texts can now be produced and transmitted results in the rapid multiplication of the participants in this process and, therefore, of the topics and perspectives available for everyone's consideration. In turn, this makes it harder for the elites to control the formation of the masses' views of the past and present. For instance, memorial websites, in contrast to 'physical' monuments or archives largely controlled by the political and cultural elites, 'offer a potentially significant forum for constructing, disseminating and contesting "vernacular memories"' which highlight the views of 'ordinary people'. Accordingly, these sites 'engender new opportunities for articulating dissent with the ways in which ostensibly shared events . . . are remembered' (Jarvis 2010: 76). On the other hand, the inherently transnational circulation of online discourses manifests itself, among other phenomena, in the expansion of potential online communities to include people in different countries who have a language in common. This pertains, in particular, to transnational migrants, people who are separated by borders but identify with the same ethnonation, and residents of the newly independent parts of the former empires (Lal 1999; Liu 2008). All these categories are very relevant to Ukraine and other parts of the former USSR.

This internationalization of discourses not only intensifies the contestation of the content of national identity, but it also challenges the salience of that identity and potentially even the very definition of the nation in question. At the same time, the global circulation of discourses means first and foremost the global consumption of products from a few powerful countries which thus influence the identities and memories of people in other, usually smaller and/or poorer countries. While millions of people across the world discuss controversial political and historical issues on Internet forums and in social networks, hundreds of millions watch YouTube clips or play computer games which inconspicuously present topics and perspectives from the places of their origin and thus continue the ideological work of musical cassettes and television series.

Scholars of media have traditionally focused on the ways in which events and their contexts are represented. One influential school in media studies describes these processes as *framing* (Entman 1993). When it comes to media representations of the past, each frame may be seen as an instance of a certain *(meta)narrative* – 'a global or totalizing cultural narrative schema which orders and explains knowledge and experience' (Stephen and McCallum 1998: 6) – of national history and identity. Other media scholars have been interested not so much in individual texts as in groups of texts which reach the same audience and influence audience perceptions not only individually, but also cumulatively. In particular, scholars have studied what they call media *agenda-setting*, by tracing the topical priorities of the texts produced by a certain media outlet or group of outlets over time (Protess and McCombs 1991). These topical priorities influence the audience's imaginative landscape and, therefore, identity.

The rise of the Internet has created new challenges for students of media. While newspaper or television texts only reveal the producers' propositions for the audience and need to be supplemented by analyses of audience reception, communication in online media is more interactive and thus provides insight into reception. However, we should be aware that it is only the most active members of the audience who tend to respond, and hence they should not be viewed as representative of all readers (McKenna and Bargh 1998). Finally, many Internet users 'perform' identities which are radically different from their (recognized) identities offline (Nakamura 2002). This makes it very difficult to relate particular patterns of responding to the texts to the demographic characteristics of the users and thus to assess typical responses among certain groups of the population.

Contestation of identities in post-Soviet Ukraine

Contemporary Ukraine is characterized by high levels of contestation of national identity in general and historical memory in particular. Different regions diverge sharply in their views of the country's trajectory in the past, present and future. In part, these differences reflect dissimilar historical experiences. The regions making up contemporary Ukraine belonged to different polities for many centuries. Some eastern regions were part of Russian-dominated polities for more than three centuries, while the westernmost provinces were incorporated into the Soviet Union's Ukrainian republic as late as World War II. Moreover, while the sovietization of eastern Ukraine was facilitated by relatively strong popular support for the Bolshevik Party, the west was incorporated into the USSR by military conquest and experienced a large-scale nationalist resistance movement in the 1940s. In turn, the dissimilar historical experiences partly account for differences in the ethno-linguistic profiles of the regions. The percentage of Russians is much higher in the east and south (in the Crimean autonomy they constitute a majority), where Russian has also become the first language of many ethnic Ukrainians and thus the main public language, particularly in the urban centres. In contrast, in the western provinces there are few ethnic Russians and, accordingly, the Ukrainian language prevails both in villages and cities (Magocsi 1996; Stewart 2010).

The differences in historical experiences and regional profiles translate into differing attitudes towards Russia, past and present. Many Westerners view the period when Ukraine belonged to Russia and the USSR as one of foreign occupation. This view of the past contributes to the great salience and anti-Russian content of the national identity of western Ukrainians (particularly in Galicia) – that is, their strong support for Ukraine's independence and preference for European over post-Soviet integration. For their part, the residents of the east and south tend to see tsarist Russia and the Soviet Union as instances of a common statehood of two kindred peoples – one which many would like to see restored. Their identity is not only pro-Russian in content, but also less nation-centred and more oriented towards the East Slavic commonality (Sereda 2007). Admittedly, the regions' memories and identities are also internally heterogeneous, and a large number of people hold intermediate positions, particularly in the central parts of the country, which have ambiguous historical experiences and ethno-linguistic profiles (Stewart 2010).

Current policies not only take these inherited differences into account but also perpetuate and sometimes even exacerbate them (Riabchuk 2007). As far as the historical dimension of national identity is concerned, the post-Soviet Ukrainian ruling elite – itself largely originated from the former communist *nomenklatura* – accepted some elements of the *nationalist (anti-Soviet) narrative*, which portrays Ukrainian history as an incessant independence struggle against foreign rulers. However, the regime cautiously refrained from its wholesale substitution for the *East Slavic (Soviet) narrative*, which presents the Ukrainian people as happily united with the Russian people or seeking to restore such unity. Instead, the regime combined the two versions of the national past in a number of practices such as the state calendar, commemoration ceremonies, monuments, toponymy, etc. At the same time, the central government not only allowed regional authorities to pursue policies largely reflecting the respective population's preferences, but also presented its own view of the past differently for different parts of the country. This opportunistic handling of identity was particularly noticeable during the presidency of Leonid Kuchma (1994–2004) (Jilge 2006: 64–77; Portnov 2010: 40–52).

The situation changed significantly after the Orange Revolution and the assumption of the presidency by Viktor Yushchenko in early 2005. The fierce confrontation between political elites with different regional anchoring and the unprecedented mobilization of large parts of the population from the respective regions for the defence of their perceived interests and values enhanced the role of identity matters in public discourse. Moreover, the new president, notwithstanding his calls for national unity, clearly favoured the Ukrainian language and the anti-Soviet historical narrative. Therefore, the Russian-speaking and Sovietophile citizens found their preferences rejected, particularly in the east and south where this perception was encouraged by regional elites seeking to mobilize their constituency. As far as collective memory was concerned, the policies pursued by east-southern elites mostly reflected the Soviet narrative of Ukrainian history. In contrast, western elites intensified memory politics based on the Ukrainian nationalist view of the past. At the national level, Yushchenko's initiatives were implemented to a limited extent owing to resistance by the parliamentary opposition and sabotage on the part of the government, which the president did not control. At the same time, public discourse reflected the diversity of positions, and this often escalated into fierce confrontations between the supporters of the opposing versions of identity (Portnov 2010: 79–101; Zhurzhenko 2011).

Yushchenko contributed to the contestation of historical memory in Ukraine first and foremost through his initiatives aimed at raising public awareness and boosting commemorative prominence of two key events: the Famine of 1932–1933 (the Holodomor), and the nationalist resistance of the Ukrainian Insurgent Army (Ukraïns'ka Povstans'ka Armiia, UPA) in the 1940s. His treatment of these events as, respectively, the greatest tragedy and the greatest heroic struggle in the recent history of Ukraine ran counter to the accustomed Soviet interpretation and to the view of the past propagated in Russia since Vladimir Putin came to power in 2000. By this stage, the Holodomor's political causes were no longer in doubt in mainstream discourse. Instead, the focus of the controversy now shifted to its interpretation: was this an act of genocide against the Ukrainian people, or a crime against humanity? (Riabchuk 2008; Portnov 2010: 84–90; Zhurzhenko 2011). At the same time, Yushchenko's initiative to officially recognize the UPA as 'participants in the struggle for Ukraine's independence' was fiercely opposed by south-eastern elites and some nationwide political forces which defended the Soviet-moulded view of the UPA as Nazi collaborators (Riabchuk 2007; Jilge 2008).

After Yushchenko lost the 2010 election to the anti-Orange leader Victor Yanukovych, the new president publicly renounced the view of the Holodomor as genocide and adopted its Moscow-friendly interpretation as part of a 'common tragedy of the Soviet peoples'. Moreover, he reverted to Kuchma's manner of commemorating the war against Nazi Germany, which featured Soviet veterans and excluded UPA combatants. The revision of the past was part of a bigger change in the politics of identity, which also included closer relations with Russia and a more benevolent attitude towards the public use of the Russian language (Chalupa 2010; Portnov 2011). Similarly to the negative reaction of the adherents of East Slavic commonality to Yushchenko's 'nationalist' policies, Yanukovych's 'pro-Russian' steps antagonized those favouring the anti-Russian version of Ukrainian identity. The contestation of national identity has thus continued unabated.

The role of the media in the production and contestation of identity is heavily influenced by the state policy regarding the media in general and certain types of media in particular. On the one hand, the democratization of state–society relations in the wake of the Orange Revolution enabled a pluralistic media landscape. Many media outlets, largely in response to their audiences, also began to show an increased interest in politics, culture and other 'serious' matters. This, in turn, stimulated close attention to and overt contestation of national identity. This situation was quite a contrast to that under Kuchma, when control of the media was a crucial element of the president's increasingly authoritarian power and harassment of critical media outlets led many managers to abandon political issues in favour of the safer and more profitable entertaining genres. Now, the renewed authoritarian tendencies under Yanukovych once again include tighter media control and the discontinuation or degeneration of many overtly ideological products. On the other hand, both authoritarian-minded regimes sought first and foremost to cleanse the content of the most popular (and thus electorally relevant) type of mass media, namely television. At the same time, the Internet has been exempt from official regulation and relatively free from state harassment (Dyczok 2006; Kulyk 2010: 204–214). In Ukraine, as in other parts of the world, the Internet is thus becoming a crucial arena of the politics of national identity and historical memory. The more tightly controlled traditional media tend to be predominantly entertainment-oriented and thus ideologically inconspicuous – which, of course, by no means renders them unimportant as producers of identity and memory.

Historical memory in 'old' media

Needless to say, state policy is not the only factor determining the strength and character of the media contribution to the politics of identity. No less important are socio-economic, technological and cultural factors, all of which influence the constitution of audiences and shape media products. These factors are, of course, much more medium-specific than policies are. The specificity can be clearly demonstrated by comparing two prominent types of the so-called 'old' or pre-Internet media, namely television and newspapers. In the next section, these are juxtaposed with various 'new' or online media.

Since the late Soviet decades, television has been the most popular source of both information and entertainment in Ukraine. It is a truly popular medium: very few people do not watch it at all, while almost half the population does so for at least two hours daily; an average Ukrainian spends more time watching television than reading the newspapers and listening to the radio combined (Rezul'taty 2006: 550–551). This popularity means that television audiences are inclusive both socially and geographically, and thus also linguistically and ideologically; at least this is the case for those channels transmitted on air. The most popular channels broadcast nationwide and, therefore, must provide content acceptable for people in all parts of the country, although they are particularly interested in urban residents, who are more attractive to advertisers. Linguistically, this means a combination of Ukrainian and Russian on each channel. The practice of combining the two languages has been used on television since the Soviet times, first with the heavy dominance of Russian and then with an increasing share of Ukrainian as required by post-Soviet legislation, although this requirement was strictly implemented only under Yushchenko (Kulyk 2010: 199–202). At the same time, Ukrainian speakers are more ready to consume television products in Russian, which is familiar and well known, than Russian speakers are to watch films and programmes in Ukrainian, which many of them do not know well or do not feel comfortable with. While more than half of respondents in a 2006 nationwide survey said they watched television in both languages, the distribution of those with predominantly monolingual consumption was skewed towards Russian (Kulyk forthcoming).

The greater readiness of the audience to watch in Russian encourages most channels to fill their prime-time slots with Russian-language films and serials, while scheduling the legally required Ukrainian-language products in less popular slots. The preference for Russian over Ukrainian in prime-time genres such as serials and movies is also caused by the higher economic effectiveness of production in Russian: such products may be consumed without translation in many post-Soviet countries. Moreover, as television managers point out, on the largest and most lucrative Russian market there is little demand for distinctively Ukrainian (or other post-Soviet) products, even if translated into Russian. Accordingly, both Russian and Ukrainian producers tailor their films, serials, game and reality shows first and foremost to Russian audiences, since Ukrainian viewers are not only fewer but also – so producers presume – less demanding. These products are usually shown on Ukrainian channels in Russian, while most Western products are translated into Ukrainian – a distinction both reflecting and shaping viewer preferences. Given the high cost of television production in general, most channels limit their own products to news, talk shows and occasional documentaries, while filling the lion's share of the air time with films and serials purchased from Russian, Ukrainian or Western producers (Kulyk 2010: 227–229, 465–466).

Western movies, serials, documentaries and other products influence the Ukrainian viewers' national identity by shifting their imaginative landscape from domestic to foreign places and people, and thus (to the extent that viewers identify with what they see on the screen) somewhat undermining the salience of that identity. The influence of Russian and Russian-oriented Ukrainian products can also be more direct, although not necessarily more conspicuous. They sometimes portray events in Ukraine and, much more often, Russia or elsewhere in the former USSR which are almost completely cleansed of any linguistic, ethnocultural and ideological features other than Russian and, at the same time, presented as common to the whole post-Soviet space. Thus, in effect, the producers equate that space with Russia. In announcements and advertising campaigns such movies and serials are often presented as 'our' stories about 'our' present or past which are thus implicitly contrasted with Western and other 'foreign' portrayals of 'their' societies. As far as historical memory is concerned, most movies and serials deal with the Soviet or Russian imperial past, which is explicitly or implicitly presented as a time of East Slavic commonality. If clearly identifiable Ukrainians do appear in such products, they are always an integral part of the Russian/East Slavic entity; accordingly, the only role available to the Ukrainian nationalist is that of the traitor. These products thus not only undermine the salience of Ukrainian national identity but they also present its content as prioritizing brotherly relations with the Russians.

The embodiment of the East Slavic historical narrative on Ukrainian television is supplemented by special programming on the key holidays associated with that narrative, first and foremost Victory Day on 9 May. On that day, all major channels feature movies, musical programmes and other allegedly non-ideological Soviet and post-Soviet products on the 'Great Patriotic War' – the Soviet name which is still commonly used despite attempts by opponents of the Soviet narrative to introduce the more neutral designation as the 'Second World War'. The only holiday of the nationalist narrative which television managers consider worthy of such special programming is Independence Day on 24 August, when most channels present movies and other programmes with all kinds of distinctively Ukrainian meaning, including those referring to various periods of Ukraine's history (Kulyk 2010: 306–312, 465–467).

In contrast, those domestically tailored products embodying the salient Ukrainian identity with 'balanced' or anti-Russian content usually do so much more conspicuously. The conspicuity largely results from genre conventions, as in political talk shows where memory-related issues such as the interpretation of the Holodomor or the UPA were discussed in view of the political controversies they had caused. To make a good show, such programmes should involve adherents of different positions, capable of articulating these positions clearly and engaging in energetic debate with their opponents. Even in the less obviously ideological genre of news media, stories on historical matters usually draw clear connections between past and present, which makes underlying ideological propositions more visible. The audience is thus more likely to perceive the versions of national identity embodied in such stories as partisan, compared to the versions backgrounded in movies or shows. Moreover, the cumulative share of these more visibly ideological products in daily broadcasting of most Ukrainian channels is much smaller than that of the seemingly neutral products, and the average rating is considerably lower (Kulyk 2010: 218–225), thus further limiting the nationalist narrative's chances of influencing viewer identities.

For newspapers, the relative weight of the supranational and national products is reversed. Most newspapers operate within Ukraine or even within a certain region, and the lion's share of the texts is composed by domestic authors for a domestic audience, albeit with significant reliance on foreign sources. The main reasons for this sharp difference between newspapers and television are to be found in the cost of production and the technology of delivery. As newspaper texts are relatively cheap to produce, the editors can usually afford to commission an original text aimed at giving their audience what they think it wants, rather than republishing what they hope it will find acceptable. Moreover, the relatively low delivery speed of printed copies makes it preferable to publish or at least print newspapers regionally rather than nationwide and, by the same token, to give the readers regionally adjusted texts, either in separate outlets or in regional varieties of national ones (Kulyk 2010: 190–195).

Newspapers also accommodate the linguistic preferences of their audiences. Unlike television and radio stations, whose broadcasting has combined the two languages since the Soviet period, most Ukrainian newspapers were and remain monolingual. In the 2006 survey cited above, the distribution of preferences with regard to the language of newspapers was as skewed towards Russian as it was in the case of television. However, the Russian language's lead over Ukrainian on the newspaper market is also due to the mainly urban composition of the audience: newspapers are easier to deliver in the cities, and city dwellers boast a higher purchasing capacity, which makes them both more inclined to buy newspapers and more attractive to advertisers. Accordingly, nationwide commercial newspapers tend to choose Russian as the language of publication, while many of those published in Ukrainian or in both languages are run and subsidized by the authorities. At the same time, the availability of nationwide outlets in both Ukrainian and Russian and the widespread reliance on regional newspapers allow the overwhelming majority of westerners and easterners to read in their respective languages of preference, in contrast to the predominantly bilingual consumption of television products (Kulyk forthcoming).

The enhanced ability of newspapers to accommodate audience preferences means that, while the newspaper market as a whole is characterized by much greater ideological pluralism than the television market, each individual newspaper outlet usually embodies a rather narrow range of ideological propositions. It is only elite (quality) newspapers that engage with different views on the issues under discussion, and these are presented in overtly ideological genres such as opinion articles and letters to the editor. These are the genres that are routinely used for the discussion of topics related to historical memory. Here, such discussion is not limited to aspects that have already gained public prominence; the editors also contribute to agenda-setting and awareness-raising. At the same time, elite newspapers also represent historical matters in less ideologically conspicuous genres such as historical calendars, personal memoirs and news reports on commemorative dates. It should be noted, however, that elite newspapers of considerable circulation and influence are few, not least due to the readers' increasing reliance on the Internet for political and other 'serious' topics.

It is uncontested representations and seemingly non-ideological genres of this kind that prevail in tabloids dominating the newspaper market. Unlike opinion articles in quality newspapers, tabloid texts do not set out to analyse certain events or argue with other viewpoints; rather, they tell the readers a story. The presence of history-related pages in many popular newspapers shows that the editors see history as a good source of such 'infotainment'. In order to be both informative and entertaining, the texts on these pages should deal with relatively little-known events and/or aspects of the past and present them in a reasonably concise and non-reflective manner. Disguised as ideologically neutral descriptions of events or individual life paths, the choice of topics and interpretive frames for tabloid history texts more or less consistently imbues Ukrainian history with particular content and salience vis-à-vis the histories of other nations and non-national collectivities. In other words, such texts embody one of the competing historical narratives.

Given the tabloids' orientation towards mass audiences, the more established East Slavic narrative clearly prevails in their discourse, although some nationwide newspapers and most of the western regional ones more or less clearly favour the nationalist version of the past (regional and local outlets also more or less strongly emphasize the respective subnational identity). Seeking to increase their readership, nationalist-minded editors strive to combine novel topics and/or perspectives with the typical tabloid style of entertaining storytelling. This tendency may be seen clearly, for example, in the history pages of *Hazeta po-ukraïns'ky* (Ukrainian Newspaper), one of the few nationwide tabloids published in Ukrainian. Similar to television, the newspapers usually mark East Slavic holidays by running special content or even specially structured issues. By contrast, nationalist holidays, with the exception of Independence Day, are only celebrated in those outlets favouring that narrative. Actually, 'nationalist' media do not dare to ignore important East Slavic dates such as 9 May which are observed by many of their readers, but their equal treatment of the holidays related to the two narratives nevertheless subverts the dominant interpretation of the past (Kulyk 2011).

History goes online

Estimates of the size of the Ukrainian Internet audience range from a quarter to almost half of the adult and teenage population, depending on how an Internet user is defined. There is a general consensus, however, that this audience is rapidly growing, even though it lags behind those of many other post-communist countries. Moreover, all studies agree that Ukrainian Internet users are disproportionately male, young, and tend to live in big cities, first and foremost the capital; hence they are relatively well-to-do (Geminus 2008; HiTech Expert 2010; InMind 2010). As urban residence and economic well-being are positively correlated with the use of Russian, Ukrainian Internet users are overwhelmingly Russian speaking. This, in turn, increases the odds that they will favour the East Slavic version of national identity rather than the nationalist version. Therefore, not only do most users prefer to read and post texts in Russian, but they are also likely to have no qualms about using Russian websites alongside or even instead of Ukrainian ones. Given that the Russian segment of the Internet dwarfs the Ukrainian one and that Russian sites appear more prominently in the results of Internet searches, even those made in the Ukrainian language, Ukrainians tend to use Russian Internet resources for various purposes, except for those having to do with exclusively domestic affairs. Moreover, ostensibly Ukrainian resources heavily republish texts from Russian ones, thus further blurring the line between the two segments. Last but not least, even in the Ukrainian segment most sites operate in Russian or in two languages (and sometimes three, although at times English is used *instead* of Ukrainian). Purely Ukrainian-language resources are limited to a few portals, blogs and specialized sites, primarily those originating in and/or targeted at the western region (Chornopys'ka 2005; V. B. 2011).

Notwithstanding occasional attacks on critical outlets, culminating in the infamous murder of the investigative journalist Heorhii Gongadze in late 2000, online media have been relatively free from state control and able to pursue topics of their choice. As a result, they have attracted many journalists who shun the formal and informal censorship prevalent in broadcasting and major newspapers (Krasnoboka 2002). Given the low production cost, online media can, in principle, afford not to care much about advertisements and, therefore, ratings. This, in turn, makes it possible for many outlets to focus on socio-political issues and to employ analytical formats that are marginalized in more commercial media. These factors make the Internet a particularly suitable medium for the preoccupation with memory and other aspects of identity, all the more so because the interactive nature of online communication encourages discussion of various perspectives on the topic under consideration. Not only do many online news media pay close attention to matters of history and memory, but numerous archival or discussion-oriented websites also deal exclusively or primarily with these matters. Furthermore, soon after blogs and social networks became popular in Ukraine, they came to be used, in particular, for discussions on history and the politics of memory. The proliferation of online media makes it impossible to provide an exhaustive account here; instead, I briefly review the memory-related practices employed by several different types of online media.

Online media outlets

To begin with, online media outlets with a predominantly current affairs focus also frequently raise topics related to the past and its significance for the present. Illustrative is the website of one of Ukraine's leading information agencies, UNIAN, which features a separate history section (http://culture.unian.net/ukr/rubrics/13). This section covers the 'latest news' on historical anniversaries, new archival or archaeological findings, commemorations and history-related statements by prominent figures. These are supplemented from time to time by 'publications' on certain historical events or more general issues of historical memory and identity. Some primarily offline outlets use their websites as additional means of boosting audience interest in certain key topics, including memory-related ones. The homepage of the above-mentioned *Hazeta po-ukraïns'ky*, for example, includes a section entitled 'Discussions from the Editors' (http://gazeta.ua/discuss). At the time of writing, the section featured, among others, the issue of who 'our heroes' are and what measures should be taken in order to make Ukrainian society recognize them as such – meaning, first and foremost, in order to persuade easterners to accept the prominent figures of the nationalist narrative.

In a more impressive instance of online support, the *Inter* television channel conducted a range of activities in connection to its 2007 to 2008 interactive project *Velyki ukraïntsi* (Great Ukrainians, patterned on the BBC's *Great Britons*) on a special dedicated website (http://greatukrainians.com.ua). The site continued to function even after the final broadcast programme and thus gave viewers an ongoing opportunity to discuss the results of the voting, the merits of the candidates and other topics related to history and identity. Unlike many 'old' and 'new' media, which more or less clearly favour one or the other of the competing historical narratives, the large nationwide audience of this project – combined with the interactive nature (via mobile phone texting) of the nomination and selection of candidates – made the final list of 'great Ukrainians' a somewhat 'schizophrenic' combination of opposing views of the past. Consequently, the voting became a site of contest between the supporters of these opposing views. Fearing a victory for the polarizing figure of the twentieth-century nationalist icon Stepan Bandera, the channel managers allegedly doctored the voting results in order to produce a politically correct winner, the medieval-era Prince Yaroslav, who is honoured in both narratives (Hrytsenko 2008).

Perhaps the most significant online media contributor to the production of Ukrainian historical memory is the website called *Istorychna Pravda* (Historical Truth; http://www.istpravda.com.ua), a subsidiary of one of Ukraine's leading Internet publications, *Ukraïns'ka Pravda* (Ukrainian Truth). Since its foundation in the autumn of 2010, the site has presented hundreds of original and republished texts on various aspects of Ukrainian and other countries' history. The editors of the site consciously assume the role of public historians – a role that manifests itself in their presentation of *Istorychna Pravda* as 'a site of scholarly and journalistic discussions of the politics of history and memory' as well as a 'source of news' on relevant topics and 'storage of artefacts'. The editors have declared that they are 'open to all competent views and opinions' but reserve 'the right to have [their] own view'. They have also broadly defined the topics to be covered as 'the history of Ukraine and Ukrainians, Russians, Poles, Jews, Crimean Tatars and other ethnic groups whose fate is tied to our country'. At the same time, the editors stated that the site would focus on 'the political history of the twentieth century: the struggle for statehood, human rights, scientific and technical progress, totalitarian projects and experiments, human life paths' (Kipiani and Solod'ko [2010]).

The declaration reveals both a rather inclusive approach to Ukrainian history and a preference for the nationalist narrative over the East Slavic one. While texts dealing with twentieth-century Ukraine published on the site have portrayed both the anti-Soviet struggle and the activities of the Soviet regime, in the former case the authors focus on more heroic or tragic aspects and tend to portray them in a more sympathetic light than in the latter. Most participants in the forum discussions seem to agree with the authors' interpretation of the event in question. However, a number of posts have opposed that interpretation and the underlying view of Ukrainian history in general. They provoked heated and often hostile exchanges between supporters of different views which extended well beyond the original topic – a feature typical of open and anonymous online discussions, particularly on matters of identity (cf. Liu 2008). While most Ukrainian-language posts on the site clearly support the nationalist narrative, the choice of Russian as the language of posting by no means indicates an adherence to the East Slavic narrative; rather, it reflects the above-mentioned numerical prevalence of Russian speakers among Ukrainian Internet users.

Blogs

Turning to blogs, we find a similar lack of correspondence between language choice and ideological position. Here, too, we see a tendency to devote substantial attention to issues of history and identity. Although many blogs are part of bigger websites, authored by journalists, politicians or other public figures – and used for the same purposes of influencing large audiences as their texts in other 'old' and 'new' media – numerous other blogs on various platforms are run by little-known individuals and aimed at a small group of friends and occasional random visitors. Since starting a blog has become very easy, Ukrainian blogging is rapidly growing and extending to ever-new topics. The most popular blog platform of the Russian and Ukrainian Internet, LiveJournal (http://www.livejournal.com), also functions as a social network: it allows participants to choose so-called friends, whose entries they can then easily follow, as well as starting collective blogs (communities) together with other participants.

Many blogs presented as outlets of organizations and localities limit their history pages to reference information, which is usually taken from offline encyclopaedias or other normative publications. Local history and tourist blogs, while seeking to give the audience little-known and interesting information on particular buildings, personalities or localities, likewise tend to adhere to the dominant narrative of Ukrainian history. Most such blogs reproduce the East Slavic narrative owing to the bloggers' ideological preferences and this narrative's dominance in the Soviet and post-Soviet publications on which bloggers rely for their historical entries. Even the collective blog which claims to present an 'Alternative History' (http://alternathistory.org.ua) by focusing on little-known events and unusual interpretations, while sometimes sympathetically mentioning the Ukrainian independence struggle, otherwise implicitly denies its legitimacy by portraying the Russian imperial past as common to all East Slavic peoples. The nationalist narrative is limited to a few blogs by Westerners and some individual or collective outlets by authors from other parts of Ukraine.

Some blogs, in accordance with the original purpose of this type of online media, reflect on current events, including texts by public figures and fellow bloggers. For instance, on 9 May 2008, the Russian-speaking blogger Val Petruchek (http://val.zp.ua) defended the UPA commander Roman Shukhevych from yet another online-distributed accusation of Nazi collaboration. Three days later, Petruchek sarcastically responded to attempts at penetrating the blogosphere with an official Russian symbol commemorating the Soviet victory over Nazi Germany, the so-called St George's ribbon, which was being boosted by the Russian authorities with the support of many activists in Russia and other post-Soviet countries (Chapter 3, this volume). By contrast, other blogs – particularly LiveJournal communities such as *Ukraïns'ka istoriia* (Ukrainian History, http://history-ua.livejournal.com) – aim at actively disseminating information on and 'correct' interpretations of various episodes of the past, first and foremost those that the Soviet regime supposedly silenced or falsified. Of course, some of the comments on blog entries contest the authors' views, thus undermining the narrative to which they adhere.

Social network V Kontakte

The level of contestation is particularly high in user groups within what has proven itself in recent years to be the post-Soviet answer to Facebook: the social network called V Kontakte or VK (In Contact; http://vkontakte.ru). VK is the most popular network and one of the most popular web resources in Russia, Ukraine and other post-Soviet countries, particularly among young people. According to a 2011 study, this network encompasses 67 per cent of Ukraine's Internet users, compared to 43 per cent for Facebook and 12 per cent for Twitter (Korrespondent 2011). Millions of VK users interact, among other forms, in thousands of overlapping topical groups. These groups are somewhat similar to the collective blogs in LiveJournal, but they facilitate a more equal exchange of information and opinions, as there is little status difference between original posts and comments (at the same time, the group administrators do have the power to exclude those participants seen as violating the rules of interaction). A group may be started by any user with a reproduction of an outside publication, an opinion, a question, or another means of suggesting a topic for discussion, thus provoking responses in the form of answers to the question, comments on the opinion, or republications more or less loosely related to the suggested topic. The interaction may also be continued by suggesting a new 'topic' within the same group. As a result, some groups contain dozens or even hundreds of separate exchanges with little interaction among them. Some administrators limit the membership in their groups to prevent abuse by ideologically hostile or simply irresponsible people. Most groups, however, remain open to all users of the network and, therefore, to all views of the issue under discussion. Given the predominantly Russian-speaking profile of the users, most discussions take place in Russian, although some posters use Ukrainian, which may hinder reception outside of Ukraine.

Among the millions of groups on VK, thousands focus on issues of history and historical memory in Ukraine, with group memberships ranging from dozens of thousands to the initiator alone. The number of posts in specific discussions likewise ranges widely, from thousands to only a single entry. Particularly popular are the groups focusing on controversial episodes of history such as the Holodomor or the UPA struggle, and contemporary commemorative initiatives such as the recognition of the UPA combatants as independence fighters (cf. Zvereva 2011). The exchanges differ in the degree of disagreement between the participants, which may be seen as a measure of the level of contestation of the episode under discussion among the network users. Most of the Holodomor groups are intended to commemorate the victims and, often implicitly, condemn the perpetrators; hence many users seem to see their membership as a commemorative act not warranting any textual contributions. This approach results in no more than dozens of posts in each discussion, even if some have thousands of registered members (more politicized online references to the Holodomor are discussed by Paulsen in Chapter 5, this volume). By contrast, members of the groups dealing with the UPA and/or its contemporary treatment are more polarized. They feel a stronger need to express their opinions, and this results in thousands of posts, many of which are offensive to those expressing a different opinion in this discussion or elsewhere.

At the same time, the production of Ukrainian historical memory in this network is by no means limited to discussions between adherents of the opposing narratives on controversial events of the past. Many Ukrainian participants contribute to the rather inconspicuous reproduction of familiar views of history which feature Russian contributions (military victories, scientific inventions, etc.) and implicitly present them as common to all post-Soviet or at least East Slavic peoples. However, even in these groups, some participants challenge not only statements on particular episodes, but also the underlying general assumptions about the past, including those denying the separateness of the Ukrainian people and the legitimacy of their independent statehood.

Conclusion

Although the title of this chapter refers to a war of memories, the above analysis has demonstrated that the contestation of historical memory in the Ukrainian media is by no means limited to overt discussions between adherents of the opposing narratives. No less important are inconspicuous embodiments of these narratives in supposedly non-ideological products such as television serials, newspaper stories or reference information on various websites. These embodiments can radically differ not only in the proposed content of Ukrainian history and identity, but also in the salience of its national framework vis-à-vis supra- and subnational alternatives. Moreover, the production of historical memory is medium-specific, as it depends heavily on the composition of the audience of a particular type of media; the state's policy on the media type in question; and the technology of production and distribution. Various online outlets, which play an increasingly important role in the production of historical memory, differ from offline media in various ways. On the one hand, they allow active participation by much larger numbers of people, and thus more diverse representation and more active contestation of memory and identity. On the other hand, the inherently transnational Internet communication undermines the national framework for the production of identity, all the more so because this effect is also characteristic of ideologically inconspicuous entertainment-oriented products such as music clips and computer games.

The outcome of this largely quiet war will be determined by the relative intensities of discourses embodying the competing narratives and the audiences' responses to their ideological propositions. So far we know very little about the second factor. Although interactive online communication seems to be more transparent in terms of response than the largely unidirectional discourse of print and broadcasting media, it should be kept in mind that the dialogical genres constitute only a part of memory-related practices and the responses posted by active readers are not necessarily representative of the entire audience of a given text. Scholars should examine the practices of reception in order to understand how people make sense of the diverse discourses in which they live.

References

Abdelal, R., Herrera, Y.M., Johnston, A.I. and McDermott, R. (2007) 'Identity as a Variable', *Perspectives on Politics*, 4: 695–711.

Chalupa, I. (2010) '100 Days of Change: Yanukovych's Policy Reversals', *Radio Free Europe / Radio Liberty*, 3 June. Online. Available: <http://www.rferl.org/content/100_Days_of_Change_Yanukovychs_Policy_Reversals/2061199.html> (accessed 12 October 2011).

Chornopys'ka, L. (2005) '"Zruchna" mova ukraïns'kykh internet-ZMI', *Slovo Prosvity*, 8–14 September. Online. Available: <http://slovoprosvity.com.ua/modules.php?name=News&file=article&sid=2033> (accessed 15 July 2006).

Dyczok, M. (2006) 'Was Kuchma's Censorship Effective? Mass Media in Ukraine before 2004', *Europe-Asia Studies*, 58: 215–238.

Edensor, T. (2002) *National Identity, Popular Culture and Everyday Life*, Oxford: Berg.

Entman, R.M. (1993) 'Framing: Toward Clarification of a Fractured Paradigm', *Journal of Communication*, 43(4), Winter: 51–58.

Erll, A. and Rigney, A. (2009) 'Introduction: Cultural Memory and its Dynamics', in ibid. (eds) *Mediation, Remediation, and the Dynamics of Cultural Memory*, Berlin: Walter de Gruyter.

Geminus (2008) *Auditoriia Uaneta dekabr' 2008*. Online. Available: <http://www.slideshare.net/tarastymchuk/2008-12-gemius-audience-overview-ukraineppt> (accessed 25 August 2011).

HiTech Expert (2010) *Ukrainian Internet Audience 4.6% Down in October to 19.518 Million Users*. 30 November. Online. Available: <http://en.expert.com.ua/ukrainian-internet-audience-4-6-down-in-october-to-19-518-million-users.html> (accessed 25 August 2011).

Hrytsenko, O. (2008) 'Velychannia regional'noho masshtabu', *Krytyka*, 12(12), December: 2–7.

InMind (2010) *Auditoriia internet pol'zovatelei Ukrainy*. Online. Available: <http://www.inau.org.ua/download.php?e378a9e184b2b01af8282058f060d440&target=1> (accessed 15 August 2011).

Jarvis, L. (2010) 'Remember, Remember, 11 September: Memorializing 9/11 on the Internet', *Journal of War and Culture Studies*, 3: 69–82.

Jilge, W. (2006) 'The Politics of History and the Second World War in Post-communist Ukraine (1986/1991–2004/2005)', *Jahrbücher für Geschichte Osteuropas*, 54: 50–81.

Jilge, W. (2008) 'Nationalukrainischer Befreiungskampf: Die Umwertung des Zweiten Weltkriegs in der Ukraine', *Osteuropa*, 58(6): 167–186.

Kipiani, V. and Solod'ko, P. ([2010]) 'Pro proekt'. Online. Available: <http://www.istpravda.com.ua/about> (accessed 10 December 2010).

Kitch, C. (2005) *Pages from the Past: History and Memory in American Magazines*, Chapel Hill, NC: The University of North Carolina Press.

Korrespondent (2011) 'Issledovanie: samymi populiarnymi sredi ukraintsev sotssetiami iavliaiutsia Vkontakte i Odnoklassniki', *Korrespondent*, 22 November. Online. Available: <http://korrespondent.net/business/mmedia_and_adv/1285832-issledovanie-samymi-populyarnymi-sredi-ukraincev-socsetyami-yavlyayutsya-vkontakte-i-odnoklassniki> (accessed 25 November 2011).

Krasnoboka, N. (2002) '"Real Journalism goes Underground: The Internet Underground". The Phenomenon of Online Media in the Former Soviet Union Republics', *Gazette: The International Journal for Communication Studies*, 64: 479–499.

Kulyk, V. (2010) *Dyskurs ukraïns'kykh medii: identychnosti, ideolohii, vladni stosunky*, Kyiv: Krytyka.

Kulyk, V. (2011) 'The Media, History and Identity: Competing Narratives of the Past in the Ukrainian Popular Press', *National Identities*, 13: 287–303.

Kulyk, V. (forthcoming) 'Language Policy in the Ukrainian Media: Authorities, Producers, Consumers', *Europe-Asia Studies*.

Lal, V. (1999) 'The Politics of History on the Internet: Cyber-diasporic Hinduism and the North American Hindu Diaspora', *Diaspora*, vol. 8: 137–72.

Liu, S.-D. (2008) 'Undomesticated Hostilities: The Affective Space of Internet Chat Rooms across the Taiwan Strait', *positions*, 16: 435–455.

Magocsi, P.R. (1996) *A History of Ukraine*, Seattle, WA: University of Washington Press.

McKenna, K.Y.A. and Bargh, J.A. (1998) 'Coming Out in the Age of the Internet: Identity "Demarginalization" through Virtual Group Participation', *Journal of Personality and Social Psychology*, 75: 681–694.

Morris-Suzuki, T. (2005) *The Past within Us: Media, Memory, History*, London: Verso.

Nakamura, L. (2002) *Cybertypes: Race, Ethnicity, and Identity on the Internet*, New York: Routledge.

Portnov, A. (2010) *Uprazhneniia s istoriei po-ukrainski*, Moscow: OGI, Polit.ru, Memorial.

Portnov, A. (2011) 'Ukraïns'ki obrazy Druhoï svitovoï viiny', *ZAXID.NET*, 5 September. Online. Available: <http://zaxid.net/home/showSingleNews.do?ukrayinski_obrazi_drugoyi_svitovoyi_viyni&objectId=1235328> (accessed 12 October 2011).

Protess, D.L. and McCombs, M. (eds) (1991) *Agenda Setting: Readings on Media, Public Opinion, and Policymaking*, Hillsdale, NJ: Lawrence Erlbaum.

'Rezul'taty natsional'nykh shchorichnykh monitorynhovykh opytuvan' 1992–2006 rokiv' (2006), in V. Vorona and M. Shul'ha (eds), *Ukraïns'ke suspil'stvo 1992–2006: Sotsiolohichnyi monitorynh*, Kyiv: Institute of Sociology, National Academy of Sciences of Ukraine.

Riabchuk, M. (2007) 'Kul'tura pamiati i politika zabveniia', *Otechestvennye zapiski*, 34 (1), Spring: 42–55.

Riabchuk, M. (2008) 'Holodomor: The Politics of Memory and Political Infighting in Contemporary Ukraine', *Harriman Review*, 16(2), Summer: 3–9.

Sereda, V. (2007) 'Regional Historical Identities and Memory', in Y. Hrytsak, A. Portnov and V. Susak (eds), *Lviv-Donetsk: sotsial'ni identychnosti v suchasnii Ukraïni* [special issue of *Ukraïna Moderna*], Kyiv and Lviv: Krytyka.

Stephen, J. and McCallum, R. (1998) *Retelling Stories, Framing Culture: Traditional Stories and Metanarratives in Children's Literature*, New York: Garland.

Stewart, S. (2010) 'Das unsichtbare Zentrum: Regionale Unterschiede in der Ukraine', *Osteuropa*, 60(2–4): 153–162.

Tajfel, H. (1982) 'Social Psychology of Intergroup Relations', *Annual Review of Psychology*, 33: 1–39.

V.B. (2011) 'Shcho take "ukraïnomovnyi Internet"?' 14 June. Online. Available: <http://ukr-net.info/2011/06/14/scho-take-ukrajinomovnyj-internet> (accessed 15 August 2011).

Zhurzhenko, T. (2011) '"Capital of Despair": Holodomor Memory and Political Conflicts in Kharkiv after the Orange Revolution', *East European Politics and Societies*, 25: 597–639.

Zvereva, V. (2011) 'Historical Events and the Social Network "V Kontakte"', *East European Memory Studies*, 7. Online. Available: <http://www.memoryatwar.org/enewsletter-nov-2011.pdf> (accessed 25 March 2012).

5 #Holodomor

Twitter and public discourse in Ukraine

Martin Paulsen

Introduction

In 1932–1933, a disastrous famine struck the Ukrainian Soviet Socialist Republic and left several million people dead. In recent years, this historical event has become a heavily contested topic in contemporary public debate in Ukraine, as well as internationally. The term 'Holodomor', a compound word that refers to the Ukrainian phrase *moryty holodom* – meaning to starve someone to death – indicates that the famine was the result of planned action. This understanding of events is disputed among ordinary citizens and scholars in Ukraine and Russia, and the issue has become a matter of politics at state level (Guseinov 2008).[1] In late and post-Soviet Ukraine, it has become a matter of national interest (Wemheuer 2009), and in 2003 the Ukrainian Parliament adopted a resolution which stated, among other things, that the Holodomor was deliberately organized by the Stalinist regime and should be condemned as an act of genocide (Verkhovna Rada 2003). Even though the Russian authorities have declared the Holodomor 'a national tragedy' of the Soviet Union they have contested the understanding of Holodomor as a genocide (Martin 2011).

In present-day Ukraine, as in the rest of the world, Twitter is one of the most popular Internet services. This fact makes Twitter a relevant subject for studies of public discourse on topics of vital interest to Ukrainian society. This chapter is devoted to a study of public discourse about the Holodomor on Twitter, and as such forms part of the research paradigm known as computer-mediated communication. At the centre of my attention is the memory of the Holodomor, and how it is mediated by Twitter. I am interested in establishing whether there is a 'conversation' – an exchange of opinions – about the Holodomor on Twitter. Is Twitter an arena for such conversations at all? If so, how do different statements in this conversation relate to each other? What are the *specificities* of this discourse, and how do Ukrainians negotiate the features of Twitter? This approach gives us the opportunity to observe how Twitter relates to other online media, such as news sites and blogs. Given the wide interest in the Holodomor across Ukrainian society and the strong opinions on the matter, I embark upon this investigation with two basic hypotheses:

1 The Holodomor is likely to be a recurrent topic on Twitter.

2 Given the contested nature of the topic, conversations about the Holodomor on Twitter are likely to be manifestly aggressive.

After giving a short introduction to Twitter as a medium, I shall go on to set out the methods of this study, and then turn to the main findings.

Theoretical framework: on Twitter as a medium

Twitter is a micro-blogging-cum-social networking service that allows users to publish messages – tweets – of up to 140 characters. These tweets can be read either from Twitter's website or through specially designed programs on computers or on other digital devices such as mobile phones and tablet computers. Indeed, the rapid spread of Twitter may be partly explained by the simultaneous spread of smartphones ideally suited for using the medium (Hutchins 2011).

Following its launch in 2006 and take-off in 2007 (Glaser 2007), Twitter has become highly popular worldwide, including in Ukraine. As of March 2010, the Russian Internet search company Yandex had counted almost 20,000 active users (defined here as users who tweet at least once a month) in Ukraine, compared to almost 100,000 in Russia and 10 million worldwide. The average daily volume of tweets in Ukraine exceeded 25,000 (Anon. 2010). According to Alexa.com, the internationally renowned website statistics service, in October 2011 Twitter was the twentieth most popular website in Ukraine.[2]

Twitter is designed as a social service where you can *follow*, or subscribe to, the updates of others and react to these by *replying* to them or forwarding – *retweeting* – them. While a tweet may be seen as the opening of a conversation, replies and retweets may be seen as ways of entering into this conversation. In general, a reply is the most direct way of engaging in a conversation on Twitter, while a retweet signals a desire to include more people in the conversation. A tweet usually consists of a short statement on what the user is doing or of a reaction to something experienced, quite often including a link to material on webpages or to photos (boyd *et al.* 2010).

Twitter is a markedly public medium: even though the messages can be protected as private, most users allow them to be openly accessible to everyone, including people who do not have Twitter accounts themselves. Each tweet is assigned a unique URL, a permanent address in the Internet infrastructure that can be reached without logging on to the service. This means that it is easy to integrate Twitter into other web services, such as in the form of a constantly updated Twitter feed on a particular topic on a news site. The social aspect of following others, combined with the open access to the published material, places Twitter in a position in between blogs and social network services such as Facebook and V Kontakte.

Another important feature of Twitter today is the *hashtag*. While a basic way of using Twitter is to read updates from the people you follow, hashtags allow users to follow tweets related to a specific topic, regardless of who you follow (Bruns and Burgess 2011a). In this way you can tune into discussions of a specific political event or, say, your favourite TV show. Importantly, given Twitter's sheer size, this feature of searching trends as they unfold challenges Google's monopoly on web search (boyd *et al.* 2010).

A hashtag is a signal of what the author of the tweet sees as the key issue in the tweet. It serves as a headline or keyword for the contents of the tweet. In addition, a hashtag allows others, who are not connected as followers of the person who posted the tweet, to join in the conversation. Simplifying slightly, we could say that more hashtags indicates that there are more conversations taking place. The full functionality of hashtags now includes hyperlinks from a hashtag to a continuously updated list of other tweets using the same hashtag. Hyperlinked hashtags are a quicker and more convenient way to search Twitter. This function was added to Twitter in 2009 (Rao 2009), but was made available for languages using Cyrillic script – such as Ukrainian – only in the summer of 2011 (Anon. 2011a). It had been possible to combine hashtags with Cyrillic script before, but this combination did not generate a separate *thread*, or list of related tweets for that topic, as the case had been for hashtags with Latin script.

In a study of the conversational character of Twitter, danah boyd and colleagues (2010) distinguish between the concepts *information diffusion*, the spreading of information to a larger audience, and *diffuse conversation*, participation in a multiplicity of conversational contexts at once. They relate both concepts to the use of hyperlinks in blogs and the use of retweets in Twitter. To my mind these concepts are equally valid as approaches to engagement with Twitter as a medium and are also relevant for other ways of engaging with the service. Both retweeting and the use of URLs in tweets may be seen as examples of information diffusion, while replying or the use of hashtags may be interpreted as willingness to engage in a wider conversation on a given topic – a conversation that is not limited to one's own followers.

On the method

The data material for this Twitter study was collected over four months, from 1 February to 31 May 2011. In total, 413 tweets mentioning the word 'Holodomor' in Cyrillic Ukrainian or Russian were collected manually, via the search function in Twitter and with the help of the Twitter research tool Twapper Keeper.[3] The word 'Holodomor' (in Cyrillic) was chosen because, in addition to its political and cultural significance, its orthography is identical in Ukrainian and Russian, which means that we can include both languages in the same analysis.

Since the debate about the Holodomor has been most active in post-Soviet Ukraine, the primary focus in this chapter is on Ukraine. However, there are important reasons why it makes sense to examine tweets from Russia, and other countries too. First, this is a matter of necessity, since it is, within the framework of this study, technically impossible to determine national borders online. The methods used for the collection of data do not deliver sufficiently reliable information to determine the geographical position of all the individual users, and so we cannot use geography as an analytical perspective here.[4] In addition, the current language situation in Ukraine, where the Ukrainian and Russian languages exist side by side, means that a number of the Russian-language tweets will be from Ukraine. Politically, too, the inclusion of Russian tweets is entirely appropriate. The public debate in Ukraine is not cut off from the outside world, and is known to be influenced by perspectives from Russia. Thus, the material studied here may also give an idea of how Ukrainian public debate is influenced by Russian perspectives.

In addition to this geographical issue, there are certain challenges relating to data collection. First, Twitter's creators do not like to share more information about their service than is absolutely necessary (Bruns and Burgess 2011b; Glaser 2007). In fact there are several obstacles to collecting data from Twitter. For instance, if you search for a specific word within Twitter, you will only get the results for the past five days. This does not mean that earlier tweets are deleted; they are just not available via Twitter's search function. Thus, material needs to be collected continuously, and it is impossible to trace the results back historically.[5] Second, Twitter has been developed in an Anglophone environment and is therefore best suited to English or similar languages. As mentioned above, it was only in June 2011, after I had already collected my material, that Twitter started to support hashtags in Cyrillic. In addition, my study reveals that the search function in Twitter does not include inflected variants of single words. Thus, my results include only 'Holodomor' in the nominative case. This is quite unfortunate, since this excludes important findings, such as the Ukrainian and Russian equivalents of the genitive form 'of the Holodomor' (*Holodomoru*/*Holodomora* in Ukrainian and Russian respectively) – which is used in such frequently occurring phrases as 'victims of the Holodomor'.

In addition, there are challenges related to the analysis of tweets, as described by boyd, *et al.* (2010). For instance, the 'retweet' – the forwarding of someone else's tweet – is a crucial feature of Twitter, but the syntax of these retweets varies from user to user, to the extent that one does not always know whether one is dealing with a retweet or something else. Similar issues apply to the relationship between different tweets in a conversation: it is not always obvious how they are related. These classifications need to be established by the researcher in the individual instances.

Findings

Information diffusion

A total of 413 tweets for the 120-day period from February to May amounts to a daily average of 3.4 tweets. The shortest month, February, was by far the most active, with 138 tweets, while the total numbers for the three ensuing months were very similar, ranging from 93 tweets in March to 90 in May. This means that the Holodomor is mentioned on Twitter in Ukrainian or Russian on a daily basis. The relatively high frequency in February was the result of three Ukrainian news stories which received wide attention that month. One was related to a discussion about the place of literature on the Holodomor in the Ukrainian school curriculum (a case to which I will return); one to the release of WikiLeaks documents about the Armenian authorities' refusal to allow the Ukrainian ambassador to commemorate the Holodomor; and finally, a third news story referred to statements made by the Ukrainian president Viktor Yanukovych, where he called the Holodomor a genocide for which Stalin was responsible (Anon, 2011b, 2011c). Crucially, all three of these news stories, which dominated the Twitter search for the Holodomor in February, are related to Ukrainian realities, indicating that, notwithstanding the fact that Russians outnumber Ukrainians in terms of active users on Twitter by approximately five to one, the Ukrainian and Russian discourse on the Holodomor on Twitter is mainly related to Ukrainian society or politics.

The data material contains 283 tweets in Russian, 119 tweets in Ukrainian, seven tweets in a mixed language or where it was impossible to distinguish the language, and four tweets in English where the word Holodomor is included in Cyrillic. The ratio between Russian and Ukrainian tweets is approximately two to one. This comes close to the linguistic profile ascribed to Ukrainian Twitter by Yandex: according to statistics from the summer of 2010, 27 per cent of Twitter users in Ukraine wrote in Ukrainian (Anon. 2010).[6] As explained above, it has not been possible, with the methods used in the current study, to establish where all the different Twitter users in my material come from. However, these figures for Ukrainian- and Russian-language tweets show that the Holodomor is of interest to both Ukrainophones and Russophones, which is significant in itself, as it shows that it is a topic of interest to both language communities, whether the Russian-language community in this context is limited to Ukraine or not.

Existing research on Twitter has been concerned with the frequency of technologically salient features such as hashtags, URLs and retweets. For instance, boyd *et al.* (2010) demonstrated that 5 per cent of the tweets in their English-language material collected in 2009 contained hashtags. In my material, the amount of hashtags is similar: 5.6 per cent.[7] As discussed above, the use of hashtags tells us something about the degree to which Twitter serves as an arena for communication on particular topics. At the same time, hashtags allow us to identify the topic of conversation.

One of the surprising findings of this study is the absence of hashtags for the Holodomor. Not a single tweet in my material used a hashtag with the word Holodomor. This may be explained in at least two ways. First, Twitter only started to support hashtags in non-Latin alphabets after my period of data collection. In my material, only one hashtag is in Cyrillic (#история) [i.e. #history], while there are 40 instances of hashtags in English (#ukraine), transliterated Ukrainian (#prostiistyny) or Russian (#novosty). Some of them occur several times (such as #ua [i.e. Ukraine's national domain name] or #news).

Second, the absence of hashtags with Holodomor may indicate that the topic is not regarded as a central one for conversations on Twitter by people writing in Ukrainian or Russian. It may be mentioned in ongoing debates on other topics, or in single tweets, but it is not discussed at length in itself. This preference for contemporary questions over history is in line with Vera Zvereva's research findings on the discourse on Ukrainian and Russian history on the social network V Kontakte. Zvereva writes:

> The majority of users who communicate in these groups are not profoundly interested in history itself. What is more important is contemporary politics, the shaping of one's identity, the confirmation of the markers that define one's membership in a group, and communication.
>
> (Zvereva 2011; see also Kukulin, Chapter 7, this volume)

This point is also central to this volume as a whole, and one to which I shall return below.

Another unexpected finding – next to the lack of hashtags – concerns the use of URLs in my material. Ukrainian and Russian tweets differ significantly from the English-language material studied by boyd and colleagues, who found that 22 per cent of tweets contained URLs. Research by Yandex indicates that 67 per cent of Ukrainian tweets include links. In my material the percentage was similar to the results from Yandex: 63 per cent of the tweets included links to web material, mostly news stories or blog posts.[8] Referring to boyd *et al.*'s concepts, one could say that, in general, a higher proportion of URLs indicates a stronger focus on information diffusion. A closer look at these links reveals that 48.5 per cent led to news sites.[9] This is much higher than the figures in Yandex's study, which gave only 12 per cent for the same category. Some 32.3 per cent of the URLs in the Holodomor material led to blogs, web forums or other social networking sites,[10] while 18.1 per cent of the URLs were dead links six months after they had been published.[11] The high percentage of tweets with links from news sites indicates that, in general, when it comes to discussion of the Holodomor, the agenda is set by established, editor-run media rather than by bloggers and citizen journalists. Based on my material, then, the role of Twitter is more about recirculating the perspectives on Holodomor offered by traditional media than about offering new perspectives on this historical event.

One example of how the agenda is set by established media was seen in early February 2011, in what may be dubbed the school curriculum affair. Fourteen tweets then referred to a heavily contested decision by Ukrainian Minister of Education Dmytro Tabachnyk to remove Vasyl Barka's 1963 novel on the Holodomor, *Zhovtyi kniaz* (*The Yellow Prince*) from the obligatory portion of the school curriculum, and to the reactions that followed. The first three tweets mentioned the Minister's decision and referred to news stories on the Ukrainian news sites vidgolos.com and gazeta.ua. A couple of days later, several tweets referred to a campaign to collect money to buy Barka's book for the Minister, initiated by L'viv students. These tweets also referred to news sites, mainly lvivnews.info. Finally, a week after the story about the curriculum changes broke, several tweets mentioned the fact that the L'viv students had given the novel to Tabachnyk as a present. These final tweets also referred to news sites, mainly tsn.ua.

The Barka debate shows how the agenda on the Holodomor on Twitter is set by news sites, not bloggers or other individuals. What is interesting in this case is that, given the grass-roots initiative by the L'viv students to collect money to buy a copy of the novel for Tabachnyk, one might have expected to see tweets with links to material from blogs or forums where this student campaign was presented or discussed. This did not happen, however, and it suggests – albeit only very tentatively – that the social media do not serve as an arena for grass-roots activism for Ukrainian students.

Another example is to be found in the data material from May 2011. At that time, 11 tweets shared a link to a blog post by the well-known Russian blogger and journalist Nikolai Starikov entitled 'Holodomor the American way' (Starikov 2011). At first glance, the tweets appear to illustrate how a blogger sets the agenda. A closer look at the blog post, however, reveals that Starikov had reposted a piece that was initially written by historian Boris Borisov and published on the editor-run news site novchronic.ru.

As already discussed, it is hard to tell where *all* the users who retweeted Starikov's initial tweet come from. Their profiles reveal that, aside from Starikov himself, four come from Russia, four have not indicated their location, one is from Ukraine and one is from Kazakhstan. This, then, is one counter-example to the general impression drawn from my material that the Twitter discourse on Holodomor is dominated by Ukrainian perspectives. In fact, the message in the rather conspiratorial story written by Borisov is very much about blaming the American government for creating a myth about the Holodomor in Ukraine in order to undermine Russia's international reputation, while at the same time showing that the consequences of the contemporaneous Great Depression in the USA were just as dire. This gives us an indication of how perspectives from Russia can trickle down to the public debate in Ukraine through Twitter.

Yandex found that, overall, 5 per cent of Ukrainian tweets were retweets (Anon. 2010). Again, my material produces fairly similar results, with 4.8 per cent retweets.[12] Boyd *et al.* (2010) emphasize that, by retweeting, users contribute to the conversation on Twitter by acknowledging that they have received the original tweet and by bringing new people into the conversation. In addition, a retweet implies a certain recognition of the original tweet. This recognition may be modified by editing the tweet. It is sometimes a challenge to determine whether a retweet has been edited, but in my material at least two of the 20 retweets have been edited. The following is an example:

> **wuthutter** RT @**MaartseHaas**: Мы спасены! Голодомор, о котором говорил Ющ отменили!♻@newsua:Гречка из Китая прибудет в Украину не раньше 23-24 апреля http://bit.ly/g7Eue4.[13]

> [**wuthutter** RT @**MaartseHaas**: We are saved! The Holodomor that Yush[chenko] talked about has been called off!♻@newsua: Buckwheat from China will arrive in Ukraine not earlier than 23-24 April URL.]

We can see that this is actually a retweet of a retweet. **wuthutter** retweets **MaartseHaas's** retweet of newsua's original tweet. **MaartseHaas** was also the one who related the simple news story to a possibly ironic political discourse involving the Holodomor and the former president. While **MaartseHaas** has modified the significance of the original tweet, **wuthutter** is content to forward **MaartseHaas's** message as it is. In addition, we also see two different ways of retweeting: while **MaartseHaas** uses the recycling sign '♻', **wuthutter** uses the more classic 'RT'.

Interestingly, 52.8 per cent of the tweets in my material were generated automatically.[14] This implies that the users behind these tweets, upon reading something of interest to them, clicked a 'tweet this' button on a blog or news site. This action results in a generated tweet, often made up of the headline of a news story and a URL. Some 52.8 per cent appears to be a rather high share. While URLs in tweets tell us something about the degree to which Twitter relates to the World Wide Web and to other social media, the use of generated tweets may be said to imply a reduced inclination to engage with the message, compared to tweets that people compose themselves. At the same time, it is also possible to edit a tweet that has been generated, something that signals an increased level of engagement with the message. In my material there were five generated tweets that had been edited, or 2.3 per cent of the generated tweets.[15]

Let us look at two examples of generated tweets, both taken from the school curriculum case discussed above. The first one is a regular, generated tweet in Ukrainian:

> **gazetaua_twit** Табачник викреслив зі шкільної програми роман про Голодомор: Міністерство освіти опублікувало на своєму са . . . http://tinyurl.com/4bbbwr8.[16]
>
> [**gazetaua_twit** Tabachnyk excluded a novel on Holodomor from the school curriculum: The Ministry of Education published on their we . . . URL.]

If we compare this tweet with the news story to which it is linked, we see that the tweet recycles the title and opening words of the original news story. It was posted from the account of the Ukrainian news site gazeta.ua.

The second example was posted by an individual, **skf2009**, Twitter nickname for Konstantyn Seryodkin. It is also generated from a Ukrainian news site, vidgolos.com, but we see that Seryodkin has added his own Russian comment to the generated Ukrainian tweet:

> **skf2009** Роман про Голодомор викинули зі шкільної прогр http://t.co/TJkvHGc via @AddThis *гордиться тем что рожали детей голодные матери?! так и надо!*[17]
>
> [**skf2009** Novel on Holodomor thrown out of school progr URL via @AddThis *to take pride in the fact that children were born to starving mothers?! that's the way to do it!*]

By adding the comment, Seryodkin engages with the story as presented by the news site and shows his support for the Ministry's decision.

My material includes several clusters of these generated tweets referring to the same or similar news stories. The most notable cluster relates to the WikiLeaks story mentioned above, about the Armenian authorities' refusal to allow the Ukrainian ambassador to commemorate the Holodomor. This cluster included 23 generated tweets, and only one of them had been edited by the user. Again, these clusters of similar tweets underline the information diffusion aspect and show that Twitter is widely used as a means to spread material from other media.

The amount of generated tweets is also a result of one of the main features of this material – the high volume of spam (Ingram 2010). In my material, spam takes different forms. Some of it comprises tweets posted by fake accounts that serve as commercial advertisements for different products. The tweets themselves do not include any advertisement, but the information on the profile pages does. The idea seems to be that the tweets should draw attention to the profiles and, thereafter, to the products. Some of the spam in my material has been generated by robot accounts that simply repeat things which others have posted, or post meaningless tweets.

One example of a spam account is @**perfect_worlds**. The tweet below was posted on 8 February 2011:

> **perfect_worlds** Голодомор. Кого Украина обвиняет в геноциде?: Кто победил? В прямом эфире на канале НТВ. Российский историк Нико . . . http://bit.ly/ia7OTe.[18]
>
> [**perfect_worlds** Holodomor. Whom is Ukraine accusing of genocide? Who won? Live to air on the NTV channel. Russian historian Niko . . . URL.]

Lately, though, the same account has only posted tweets with links to websites with girls in bikinis, and hence appears to be producing spam rather than politically committed tweets on the Holodomor.

In my material, 10 per cent of the tweets were spam-related. This rather high number is no coincidence. According to Spamhaus, an international organization tracking spam-related activity, by 2011, seven out of the world's ten worst spammers are located in the former Soviet Union, three of them in Ukraine (Anon. 2011d). Needless to say, by flooding the service with irrelevant information, spam significantly impedes the potential of Twitter to serve as an arena for public discourse.

Diffuse conversations

Having looked at *diffusion of information*, let us now turn to the *diffuse conversations*. This is an area where we should expect to find some of the manifestly aggressive material that I referred to in my second hypothesis in the introduction. In their study on the conversational aspect of retweets, boyd *et al.* (2010) found that 'rather than participating in an ordered exchange of interactions, people instead loosely inhabit a multiplicity of conversational contexts at once'. Similarly, Courtenay Honeycutt and Susan C. Herring (2009) have found that communication on Twitter was moderately coherent, and that it worked best in small groups. There were some direct conversations in my material: 13.3 per cent of the tweets interacted through replying or addressing the tweets to one or more other users on Twitter.[19] Most of these were conversations between two users, but some conversations involved at least three people.

The longest conversation in my material took place on 2 May, between the users **AnnLotovska** and **_lyubaHusak**, a conversation which also included a third user, **Yarumil**. The conversation started with **AnnLotovska's** indignation over the fact that the Soviet flag had been raised alongside the Ukrainian flag in some Ukrainian cities on the occasion of the commemoration of the victory in the Second World War (see Galina Nikiporets-Takigawa, Chapter 3, this volume). Altogether, it includes more than 50 tweets. The conversation is mainly about the legacy of the Soviet Union, and the Holodomor is brought into the conversation by **AnnLotovska** after **_lyubaHusak** points out that it is improper to compare the politics of the Soviet Union to the Holocaust:

> **AnnLotovska** @_lyubaHusak ти напевно забула про голодомор 32-32рр.І це також було під прапором СРСР.[20]
>
> **_lyubaHusak** **@Yarumil** **@AnnLotovska** голодомор і голокост. під час голодомору постраждали купа інших націїй,а голокост-ціленапрямлене знищення євреїв.[21]
>
> **[@_lyubaHusak** you obviously forgot about the holodomor of 1932–32 [*sic*!]. And that was also under the Soviet flag.
>
> **@Yarumil @AnnLotovska** holodomor and holocaust. during the holodomor several other nations suffered, while the holocaust was a purposeful extermination of Jews.]

The discussion is heated, but it is obvious that the three know each other well, and it never becomes uncivil. At the same time, there are examples in my material of very uncivil conversations, such as the one that took place between the Moscow-based user **Nordische** and a user with a Ukrainian name, **Andrij_Shatrov**, on 4 February. After **Nordische** had claimed that the word Ukraine derives from the Russian word for stealing (*ukrast'*), **Andrij_Shatrov** told him to 'go to hell'. **Nordische** replied that **Shatrov** '[had] the Holodomor' (да у тебя ГОЛОДОМОР).[22] There are some other examples of similar uncivil behaviour in the material, but in general the conversations are more polite.

Another conversation focusing on the relationship between Ukrainians and Russians took place between the well-known Russian blogger **navalny** and two others on 5 May:[23]

navalny Понимаю, что спровоцирую АДЪ, но: а в чем проблема, если я говорю ‘на Украине’?[24]

vladislavski @navalny Да нет никаких проблем. просто это унижает и ранит коренных жителей Украины.[25]

vladislavski @vladislavski @navalny Меньшую их часть, что не очень любят Русских. Голодомор.)[26]

[**navalny** I understand that I will be provoking HELL, but: what is the problem if I say ‘na Ukraine’?

vladislavski @navalny There is no problem. it is just that it humiliates and hurts the *original* inhabitants of Ukraine.

vladislavski @vladislavski @navalny The minority of them who do not love Russians very much. Holodomor.)]

Navalny’s initial tweet was retweeted by four others, but **vladislavski’s** reply did not lead to any further discussion. However, the same tweet from **navalny** also resulted in a parallel conversation involving the users **lenazavrik** and **semenychevroman**:

navalny Понимаю, что спровоцирую АДЪ, но: а в чем проблема, если я говорю ‘на Украине’?

lenazavrik @navalny нет проблемы) просто по русски правильно в украине, а сами украинцы говорят на украине)).[27]

semenychevroman @lenazavrik @navalny НЕТ! ГОЛОДОМОР! МОСКАЛИ ВИНОВАТЫ В ГОЛОДОМОРЕ![28]

lenazavrik @romansemenychev @navalny да ну ладно . . .[29]

semenychevroman @lenazavrik, прррововокация).[30]

[**navalny** I understand that I will be provoking HELL, but: what is the problem if I say ‘na Ukraine’?

lenazavrik @navalny no problem) it is just that in Russian ‘v ukraine’ would be correct, but the Ukrainians themselves say ‘na ukraine’)).

semenychevroman ‘@lenazavrik @navalny NO! HOLODOMOR! THE MUSCOVITES ARE TO BLAME FOR HOLODOMOR!

lenazavrik @romansemenychev @navalny yeah right . . .

semenychevroman @lenazavrik, prrrovocation).]

What is interesting is that both conversations, independently of each other, turned from a linguistic discussion of prepositions to the Holodomor within a couple of tweets. Both **vladislavski** and **semenychevroman** made the link between ideologically loaded language use and the contested issue of the Holodomor in the relationship between Ukrainians and Russians. While **vladislavski** keeps a straight face and uses Holodomor as an explanation for why Ukrainians are so aggravated by Russians, **semenychevroman** is – as he openly admits himself – merely trying to provoke, and uses the contested issue of the Holodomor to achieve this.

The explanation for this link between an ideologically loaded language discussion and the Holodomor may be found in another conversation in my material, between the user **foxtrotru** and **ottenki_serogo**:

ottenki_serogo плиз, подкиньте темы холиваров в жж, нужно для статьи. ну типа никон/кэнон, РПЦ, роды на дому, питбуль покусал ребенка . . . Что еще?[31]

foxtrotru @ottenki_serogo Playstation/xBox, win/MAC, на/в Украину, Билайн/МТС/Мегафон, голодомор, 42.[32]

[**ottenki_serogo** please, give me some topics for holy wars on LiveJournal, I need it for an article. You know, like Nikon/Canon, Russian Orthodox Church, home births, a pitbull bit a child. . . . What else?

foxtrotru @ottenki_serogo Playstation/xBox, win/MAC, na/v Ukraine, Beeline/MTS/Megafon, holodomor, 42.]

A *holy war* – the term that **ottenki_serogo** uses – is a central element in Ukrainian and Russian Internet culture, a discussion between people with diametrically opposed opinions which they have no plans to change. The Russian web encyclopedia of Internet culture *Lurkmore* explains that, as a discussion, a holy war is futile, since none of the participants has any plans to listen to or consider the arguments of the opponent. Rather, their aim is to look as good as possible in the eyes of those who are following the discussion (Lurkmore 2012).

Holy wars are pivotal to the discussions cited above. As **foxtrotru** indicates, both the issue of which preposition to use with 'Ukraine' in Russian and the Holodomor are examples of such holy wars. The risk of initiating a holy war was what **navalny** understood when he noted that he might 'provoke hell', and what **semenychevroman** was openly courting with his provocation. Again, these examples illustrate that the Holodomor is frequently invoked not due to a genuine interest in history, but rather to gain currency in contemporary disputes over identity and politics.

Conclusion

This study has focused on computer-mediated communication in Ukraine and on the memory discourse on the Holodomor. While the material collected includes twice as many tweets in Russian as in Ukrainian, the findings provide strong indications that the discourse is mainly anchored in and generated by Ukrainian realities. With one exception, the most frequently tweeted and retweeted messages related to news stories from Ukraine that had been published on Ukrainian news sites, and, in addition, the linguistic profile of the material coincides with the linguistic profile of Ukrainian Twitter as identified by Yandex in earlier research.

The figures from Yandex's research on Twitter in Ukraine are largely confirmed by the findings in my material. The one significant deviation relates to the share of links that led to news sites: the share in my material was much higher (48.5 per cent) than in Yandex's material (12 per cent). Assuming that the classification of news sites was the same, this indicates that the agenda for the Twitter discourse on the Holodomor is much more driven by news sites than is generally the case for Ukrainian Twitter.

To a large degree, the material does also reflect the findings on Twitter reported by boyd *et al.*, with the exception of the use of URLs, which was much more widespread in my Ukrainian and Russian material (63 per cent) than in the English material in their study (22 per cent). Again, my findings are supported by the Yandex study (67 per cent). This indicates that information diffusion is a more important aspect of Twitter in Ukraine than in the Anglophone world.

It is important to realize that the data material I have gathered and discussed here is not necessarily representative of what Ukrainian users encounter when they use Twitter. Depending on who they follow and how they use Twitter, they may not have come across any of the tweets discussed here. This, however, is not unique to Twitter, but is characteristic of media usage in general. We all read different newspapers, watch different TV channels, listen to different radio shows. This is the importance of the information diffusion mentioned by boyd and colleagues. The meaning of retweeting, of including URL links to news stories, or of including hashtags, is precisely to diffuse information to a larger audience – and hence, to make it more visible on Twitter as a whole.

Information diffusion stands out as the most important aspect of the way Twitter is used in Ukraine, given the high frequency of URLs and the high frequency of URLs linking to news sites, and also the popularity of generated tweets. At the same time, there is also an element of (diffuse) conversation. The most basic way of engaging in a conversation is through replying to other users' tweets, but we have also seen that retweets and the editing of retweets and generated tweets can contribute to the conversational aspect of Twitter communication. These are actions that add an extra element to the original tweet, and add new elements to the communication circuit.

Through information diffusion and diffuse conversations, Twitter contributes to the mediation of news and opinions on the Holodomor in Ukraine. The result of this study, largely supported by earlier research by Yandex, shows that, in Ukrainian, Twitter diffusion dominates over conversation. In the case of the

Holodomor, the agenda of public discourse on Twitter appears to be dominated by established news sites, rather than by individual bloggers. Thus, the introduction of Twitter has not yet implied a challenge to the role of the traditional media as news-makers.

My findings show that Holodomor is mentioned on Twitter by Ukrainian and Russian users on a daily basis. At first glance this seems to support my first hypothesis, but frequent mentions do not necessarily make the Holodomor a topic on Twitter in its own right. Indeed, the absence of a hashtag for the Holodomor indicates that it is not. Thus, I would say that the hypothesis of the Holodomor as a recurrent topic on Twitter is only partially supported by the findings in my study. This conclusion is also relevant to the second hypothesis: that conversations about the Holodomor on Twitter are likely to be quite aggressive. As we have seen, there are some examples of both heated and rude debates involving the Holodomor, but these debates are only rarely about the Holodomor proper. More often they focus on other issues, especially on the relationship between Ukraine and Russia, and the Holodomor is mentioned in passing, a point that is also made in the introduction to this volume and appears to be a common feature of memory debates in post-Soviet space at large. Again, the hypothesis is only partially supported by the findings.

We have seen how these passing mentions are related to the phenomenon of 'holy war', where the Holodomor is used as a way to identify with one of the warring sides. As Vera Zvereva has shown, this lack of interest in the Holodomor as a historical phenomenon and its use as a resource in contemporary discussions has parallels on another popular online platform in Ukraine, V Kontakte. We have seen that these are frequently contemporary discussions on the relationship between Ukraine and Russia, where the Holodomor serves as a powerful means to emphasize the political distance between the two countries. Thus – albeit somewhat indirectly, as a point of departure, rather than as the main topic of discussion – memory comes to play an important role in the contemporary public discourse on Ukraino–Russian political relations.

Notes

1 See also Volodymyr Kulyk (Chapter 4, this volume).

2 According to statistics on the website Alexa.com, at the end of October 2011 Twitter ranked ninth worldwide and twentieth in Ukraine among the most popular websites.

3 www.twapperkeeper.com. Until it was taken over by HootSuite Archives in 2012, Twapper Keeper was an easily available service for collecting data material from Twitter for the purposes of research.

4 Since 2009, Twitter has included a geotagging option that allows its users to indicate where the tweet is sent from, but by default this option is turned off. This makes geotagging an unreliable source for a study such as the current one (Sarver 2009).

5 This was the case until February 2012 when the Russian search engine Yandex struck a deal with Twitter that made such historical searches possible through Yandex's dedicated Twitter search, which specializes in languages using the Cyrillic alphabet, such as Ukrainian and Russian (Lunden 2012).

6 Note that the statistics reported by Anon. (2010) are based on a strictly Ukrainian selection, whereas my material has not been controlled for geographic location.
7 23 tweets with hashtags out of a total of 413 tweets.
8 260 tweets with links out of a total of 413 tweets.
9 126 tweets out of a total of 260 with links.
10 84 tweets out of a total of 260 with links.
11 47 tweets with links that led to some kind of 'not found' error message in October 2011.
12 20 retweets out of a total of 413 tweets.
13 Tweeted by **wuthutter** on 4 April 2011. The orthography of all tweets has been kept intact.
14 218 tweets generated out of a total of 413 tweets.
15 Five tweets out of a total of 218 generated tweets.
16 Tweeted by **gazetaua_twit** on 3 February.
17 Tweeted by **skf2009** on 3 February, italics added for clarity.
18 Tweeted by **perfect_worlds** on 8 February.
19 55 tweets out of a total of 413 tweets.
20 Tweeted by **AnnLovotska** on 2 May.
21 Tweeted by **_lyubaHusak** on 2 May.
22 Tweeted by **Nordische** and **Andrij_Shatrov** on 4 February.
23 Only the final tweets in these two conversations included the word Holodomor and turned up in the material. Thus, these conversations have been reconstructed through a manual search in the Twitter history of the individual users involved in the conversation.
24 Tweeted by **navalny** on 5 May. The use of 'na Ukraine' versus 'v Ukraine' is roughly equivalent to the distinction between 'in Ukraine' and 'in the Ukraine', and is a strongly politicized question of Russian grammar.
25 Tweeted by **vladislavski** on 2 May.
26 Tweeted by **vladislavski** on 2 May.
27 Tweeted by **lenazavrik** on 2 May.
28 Tweeted by **semenychevroman** on 2 May.
29 Tweeted by **lenazavrik** on 2 May.
30 Tweeted by **semenychevroman** on 2 May.
31 Tweeted by **ottenki_serogo** on 10 May.
32 Tweeted by **foxtrotru** on 10 May.

References

Anon. (2010) 'Za danymy Iandeks tviter v Ukraiini za ostanni pivroku zbilshyvsia vdvichi', *Twitter.in.ua*. Online. Available: <http://twitter.in.ua/page/za-danimi-jandeks-tviter-v-ukrayini-za-ostanni-pivroku-zbilshivsja-vdvichi> (accessed 18 June 2012).

Anon. (2011a) 'Twitter Introduces Cyrillic Keywords', *RIA Novosti*. Online. Available: <http://en.rian.ru/society/20110713/165172395.html> (accessed 18 June 2012).

Anon. (2011b) 'Ianukovich priznal Golodomor genotsidom', *Focus.ua*. Online. Available: <http://focus.ua/politics/172318> (accessed 18 June 2012).

Anon. (2011c) 'Ianukovich priznal Golodomor genotsidom, no ne tol'ko ukraintsev', *TCH.ua*. Online. Available: <http://ru.tsn.ua/ukrayina/yanukovich-priznal-golodomor-genocidom-no-ne-tolko-ukraincev.html> (accessed 18 June 2012).

Anon. (2011d) 'The 10 Worst Spammers', *Spamhaus*. Online. Available: <http://www.spamhaus.org/statistics/spammers/> (accessed 15 November 2011).

boyd, d., S. Golder and G. Lotan (2010) 'Tweet, Tweet, Retweet: Conversational Aspects of Retweeting on Twitter', *HICSS-43*. Online. Available: <http://www.danah.org/papers/TweetTweetRetweet.pdf> (accessed 18 June 2012).

Bruns, A. and Burgess, J. (2011a) 'The Use of Twitter Hashtags in the Formation of Ad Hoc Publics', *European Consortium for Political Research Conference*. Online. Available: <http://snurb.info/node/1533> (accessed 18 June 2012).

Bruns, A. and Burgess, J. (2011b) 'New Methodologies for Researching News Discussions on Twitter', *Future of Journalism*. Online. Available: <http://snurb.info/files/2011/New%20Methodologies%20for%20Researching%20News%20Discussion%20on%20Twitter%20%28final%29.pdf> (accessed 18 June 2012).

Glaser, M. (2007) 'Twitter Founders Thrive on Micro-Blogging Constraints', *MediaShift*. Online. Available: <http://www.pbs.org/mediashift/2007/05/twitter-founders-thrive-on-micro-blogging-constraints137.html> (accessed 18 June 2012).

Guseinov, G. (2008) 'Iazyk i travma osvobozhdenia', *Novoe Literaturnoe Obozrenie* 94: 130–147.

Honeycutt, C. and Herring, S.C. (2009) 'Beyond Microblogging: Conversation and Collaboration via Twitter', *HICSS-42*. Online. Available: <http://ella.slis.indiana.edu/~herring/honeycutt.herring.2009.pdf> (accessed 18 June 2011).

Hutchins, B. (2011) 'The Acceleration of Media Sport Culture: Twitter, Telepresence and Online Messaging', *Information, Communication & Society* 14: 237–257.

Ingram, M. (2010) 'Twitter Has Definitely Arrived – It Has Astroturf Now', *Gigaom*. Online. Available: <http://gigaom.com/2010/11/02/twitter-has-definitely-arrived-it-has-astroturf-now/> (accessed 18 June 2012).

Lunden, I. (2012) 'Yandex, Google's Russian Rival, is Twitter's New Real-Time Search Partner', *TechCrunch*. Online. Available: <http://techcrunch.com/2012/02/20/yandex-googles-russian-rival-is-twitters-newest-real-time-search-partner/> (accessed 18 June 2012).

Lurkmore (2012) 'Kholivar'. Online. Available: <http://lurkmore.ru/холивар> (accessed 18 June 2012).

Martin, B. (2011) *The Holodomor Issue in Russo–Ukrainian Relations from 1991 to 2010*, MA thesis, Geneva Graduate Institute of International and Development Studies.

Rao, L. (2009) 'Twitter Makes Hashtags more #Useful', *Techcrunch.com*. Online. Available: <http://techcrunch.com/2009/07/02/twitter-makes-hashtags-more-useful/> (accessed 18 June 2012).

Sarver, R. (2009) 'Think Globally, Tweet Locally', *Twitter Blog*. Online. Available: <http://blog.twitter.com/2009/11/think-globally-tweet-locally.html> (accessed 18 June 2012).

Starikov, N. (2011) 'Holodomor po-amerikanski', 12 May. Online posting. Available: <http://nstarikov.ru/club/9663> (accessed 18 June 2012).

Verkhovna Rada (2003) 'Postanova Verkhovnoii Rady Ukraiiny No. 789-IV'. Online. Available: <http://www.president.gov.ua/content/golodomor75_12.html> (accessed 18 June 2012).

Wemheuer, F. (2009) 'Regime Changes of Memory: Creating the Official History of the Ukrainian and Chinese Famines under State Socialism and after the Cold War', *Kritika* 10: 31–59.

Zvereva, V. (2011) 'Historical Events and the Social Network "V Kontakte"', *East European Memory Studies* 7. Online. Available: http://www.memoryatwar.org/enewsletter-nov-2011.pdf (accessed 18 June 2012).

Part Two

Words of memory

In the post-socialist nations that we examine, social media platforms thrive with constant clashes of memories and testimonies, verbal stories, and visual images of the past. They brim with online memory wars – wars that enhance web users' sensibility towards *words*: to language and discourse. Together with a heightened self-reflexivity towards diverse communicative tools – think blogs, Twitter, social networking services – this idiosyncratic feature of digital memory construction results in a working out of strategies of rational and emotional discussion; in ironic and sarcastic treatments of opposite views; and in new forms of verbal and linguistic expression.

The chapters in Part Two address this new set of discursive communication effects. They do so by tackling the myriad online memory debates that are mostly – if rarely exclusively – language- and text-oriented. This part opens with a chapter by linguist and new media specialist Ingunn Lunde to which the linguistic dimensions of digital memories are of prime interest. Interrogating chat comments on Soviet language in online chat discussions, Lunde argues that online metadiscourse about historical language cultures is a major and largely untapped source for 'studying the articulation of personal human linguistic experience'.

Personal human language experience is at the centre, too, of poet and sociologist of culture Ilya Kukulin's contribution. His chapter maps the argumentative practices that Russian-speaking bloggers employ in controversies over historical – and especially Stalinist-era – memory. Kukulin focuses on debates on the restoration of Stalinist metro architecture in the late 2000s – but points out that Russian digital memory discourse has since undergone radical transformations, related primarily to the fierce political protests of 2011 to 2012.[1]

In Chapter 8, media anthropologist Hélène Dounaevsky triggers a very different web war site from that of the weblog. Her analysis of Russian-language Wikipedia entries on Ukrainian history demonstrates that rather than a stable historical text, Wikipedia offers users a historical laboratory – one that produces a principally pluralistic, continually contested type of historical knowledge.

If memory is formative to the 'Wiki wars' that Dounaevsky outlines, it occupies a surprisingly *non*-prominent place in online news reporting on the 2008 Russo-Georgian war – a political controversy that political scientist Doreen Spörer-Wagner examines in Chapter 9. Providing a comparative study of conflict framing in Georgian print and online media discourse, Spörer-Wagner argues that – in line with the post-Soviet insistence on cultural forgetting (see Introduction) – memory-related frames are marginal to both.

Cultural forgetting is equally formative to Belarusian memory politics, which eagerly paint over the darker sides of Soviet history. In the final chapter of Part Two, sociologist Aliaksei Lastouski monitors web-based responses to this top-down approach to memory. His analysis of Second World War-memory discourse in webfora and blogs illustrates how in Belarus, digital memory oozes 'a new ethos of expression and debate, where rational argumentation gives way to provocation, visual impressiveness, cynicism, and resonance'.

Novel affective strategies, sarcastic discourse, new linguistic forms: both within and outside post-socialist space, the extent to which this set of communication effects defines social networks and blogs – and, in turn, how the shape of online conversations informs both on- and offline relationships and events – is largely understudied. In digital memory research, communication can easily be taken for secondary matter, which must be set aside in order to gain access to the truly 'important' content. The chapters in Part Two take up the challenge of rethinking its relevance. Put more broadly, they help us in reconsidering the status of the noise, the incompleteness, the constant and often emotionally charged repetition, as well as the discursive trifles and debris that accompany the everyday production of memory in online communication.[2]

Notes

1 We are referring to a widespread socio-political protest movement triggered by the 2011 Russian legislative election process, which journalists and election observers considered to be falsified. On the nexus between the 'Russian Winter', as the protests are popularly called, and new-media usage, see Schmidt (2012) and Moroz (2012).

2 On the role of the 'mediation' factor for studies of social and cultural phenomena, see Livingstone (2009).

References

Livingstone, S. (2009) 'On the Mediation of Everything'. *Journal of Communication* 59(1), Spring: 1–18.

Moroz, A. (2012) 'Krysa, khomiachki, pingviny i drugie zhivotnye. *Azbuka protesta: narodnyi plakat* [Rat, Guinea Pigs, Penguins, and Other Animals. [Review of] *Protest ABC: People's Poster*]'. *Booknik*, 16 May. Online. Available: <http://booknik.ru/reviews/non-fiction/alefbet/> (accessed 11 July 2012).

Schmidt, H. (2012) 'The Triple P of RuNet Politics: Protest, Political Technology, Public Sphere'. *Euxeinos: Governance and Culture in the Black Sea Region* 4. Online. Available: <http://www.gce.unisg.ch/~/media/Internet/Content/Dateien/InstituteUndCenters/GCE/Euxeinos%20Folder/Euxeinos%204_2012%20update.ashx?fl=de> (accessed 11 July 2012).

6 'A stroll through the keywords of my memory'

Digitally mediated commemorations of the Soviet linguistic heritage

Ingunn Lunde

Introduction

Among the many facets of post-socialist digital memories are reflections on linguistic practices of the past, on the meaning of specific words, their references, ideological content and implications. How does digitally mediated memory capture the linguistic experience, personal and collective, of the totalitarian, socialist era? This chapter seeks to shed light on this question by analysing discussions of the Soviet linguistic heritage in an online forum.

A challenge inherent in handling the Soviet linguistic heritage – for today's scholars and language users alike – is that it is not always recognized as something 'inherited'. It is, to a certain degree, still part of the Russian linguistic mentality and practice. While certain slogans and phrases are easily recognized as 'Soviet' even by younger generations of Russians, it takes a special effort of linguistic reflection – or even a philologist – to pin down the Soviet element of much Russian political and everyday talk today, or to draw a broader picture of 'the Soviet language'. In Gasan Guseinov's terms, Soviet socio-political language culture may be viewed as a 'linguistic experience', or even competence, accumulated, developed and refined during more than 70 years of Soviet rule. In his comprehensive dictionary of Soviet socio-political language, Guseinov (2003) treats the Soviet linguistic heritage from the point of view of its *implications* today, more than two decades after the collapse of the Soviet Union. This is an important and necessary perspective, and one that may partly explain the nature of much memory talk on Soviet language culture both online and offline today.

Meanwhile, it is important to keep in mind that, today, Soviet language culture is not only talked about; elements of this language are alive and thriving in various genres: in bureaucratic, official speech, political speech, in sayings, formulaic expressions, but also in linguistic humour, in satirical language, and the like. This is clearly a *competence in flux*; a linguistic practice which, one would expect, is decreasing among the average population, or at least changing in nature and depth. The various forms and degrees of this competence are in part a question of generations, and of shifting political cultures – with accompanying shifts in attitude towards the Soviet linguistic heritage.

Attitudes is a keyword when it comes to the material under scrutiny in this chapter, *digitally mediated commemorations of Soviet linguistic language.* Attitudes may be implicit or explicit; the latter articulate a meta-discourse about Soviet language culture, about this particular linguistic competence or experience. And by naming it an experience we approach this volume's central thematics of memory.

The Soviet linguistic heritage

After the fall of the Soviet Union, the role and function of typical Soviet-style language – sometimes named by the Orwellian term 'newspeak' – were transformed in several ways. A considerable part of the lexicon has been 'de-sovieticized' in one way or another: certain words have become marginal, or even historicisms, because what they denote is no longer of any relevance to post-Soviet reality; words have been de-ideologized and may have changed their connotation from positive to negative, or vice versa, or become altogether neutralized; and words may have changed their meanings. Certain elements of newspeak have been retained in a particular type of bureaucratic style, within certain political groups, and partly in the provincial press. The greater part of what is considered typical of Soviet political language has disappeared from post-Soviet political speech culture, above all the predictable and ritualistic elements. Today, political language is characterized by spontaneity, unpredictability and a polemical and rhetorical style, as well as a high degree of stylistic and lexical heterogeneity (Weiss 2000).

Meanwhile, elements of Soviet newspeak are used and reused today in a quite different context: in slang, ironic word play and linguistic humour. Linguistic clichés are inverted, played upon and re-contextualized in an ironic manner which often verges on the absurd. This particular response to the Soviet linguistic heritage is especially frequent in the mass media, but also in literature and in informal speech.

Within this context of re-functionalization and re-contextualization, Soviet language culture has also become the subject of intensive study – both documentary and critical. In the decade from 1995 to 2005 there appeared a number of important publications which dealt, in various ways, with Soviet language culture (Guseinov 2003, 2004; Kheveshi 2002; Kupina 1995, 1999; Mokienko and Nikitina 1998; Pikhurova 2006; Sarnov 2001).[1] What is covered by 'Soviet language' in these books? As it turns out, a great many different things. The notion includes, of course, the official genres – political slogans, phraseology, concepts and terms – but also a considerable amount of everyday Soviet terminology, engendered by the social and political reality, such as *dostat'* ('get hold of') or *stoiat' za* ('line up for') for *kupit'* ('buy'); *sidet'* ('sit') for *sidet' v tiur'me* ('be in prison'), etc. Furthermore, several books include personal names, toponyms, names of institutions, enterprises, products, pets, and not least many slang expressions which demonstrate the unofficial 'double or parallel life' of Soviet language culture, both during the Soviet period and afterwards.

The sources from which the studies mentioned take their cues are not only political speeches, handbooks or newspaper editorials, but also literature, anecdotes, listeners' responses to *Radio Svoboda* (*Radio Liberty*), *chastushki* (a folk genre of short, often humoristic and ironic verses), and a variety of other genres. In this respect, almost all the publications mentioned above employ a very broad notion of 'Soviet language', and 'the unofficial double life' of this language is, more often than not, a main, if not the main, focus. These various kinds of 'countercultural' reaction to official newspeak include puns, jokes (*anekdoty*) and similar phenomena – in short, the popular tradition of 'counterspeak' (*protivoiaz*, Sarnov), what Nataliia Kupina (1999) calls 'linguistic resistance' (*iazykovoe soprotivlenie*), and both Gasan Guseinov (2003) and Anna Wierzbicka (1993) call 'the language of self-defence' (*iazyk samooborony*).

I believe that the philologists' focus on the 'double life' of Soviet linguistic practices captures something essential about this language culture, and it is quite impressive that scholarly books are able to successfully document such an elusive phenomenon. However, Soviet language culture is, as argued above, also a particular *linguistic experience*, and this aspect is probably even harder to 'document' than Sovietspeak's 'double life'. The book that comes closest to doing so is Benedikt Sarnov's *Our Soviet Newspeak* (*Nash sovetskii novoiaz*, 2001), written in a genre oscillating between the dictionary and the personal memoir. Lexical items are loosely arranged here according to the following general structure: the item itself is usually listed as an element of 'official newspeak', such as *doska pocheta* ('roll of honour'), *strana sploshnoi gramotnosti* ('a country of universal literacy'), or *kommunisty, vpered!* ('Communists, forward!'). Its official meaning is illustrated by a definition from an authoritative dictionary or simply by an explanation. There frequently follows a further definition or explanation taken from, for example, Mokienko and Nikitina's dictionary of Soviet language, which brings in other, alternative meanings of the word or phrase. After this short introduction, we get Sarnov's personal, and very subjective, response to the term in question. It consists of a number of linguistic reactions in the form of anecdotes, short verses, *chastushki*, the author's own reminiscences, and so forth. In short, here Sarnov is engaged in 'humanizing' Soviet reality, and Soviet political discourse, through language. These responses are usually humoristic and illustrate the great capacities of humour and irony to confront pathetic and ritualistic linguistic practices.

Most people do not publish their linguistic experiences as a personal memoir. But new technology, and the Internet in particular, has created a new, broad venue for *digitally mediated commemorations* of the Soviet past, including its linguistic heritage.[2] From time to time, the concept of a 'Soviet language' pops up in forums and blogs, and people are invited to share their associations and memories of typical Soviet linguistic expressions. In the remainder of this chapter, I focus on a selection of such sources. In doing so, I ask two questions:

1. What distinguishes these kinds of linguistic commemorative reflections from the academic collections?
2. What do they add in terms of new information or perspective?

In addition to the obviously broader picture provided by the sheer mass of people taking part in online commemorative practices, three aspects lend themselves to particular attention:

- personal reminiscences (including reflections, assessments and associations arising in connection with concrete examples of Soviet language culture);
- reflections on the process of commemoration;
- references to the language culture of today.

By highlighting these factors, I suggest some ways in which online commemorations and thematizations of Soviet language culture may add both to historical and contemporary understandings of this phenomenon.

A short but important note on the material for this study: discussions of 'Soviet language' are scattered all over the Web. This becomes clear when one searches blogs for such material. For this chapter, the material gathered stems mainly from a research project with a broader thematic scope: discussions of the Russian language on Runet ('The Future of Russian' 2008–2012). Thus, it is not a systematic corpus of discussions on 'Soviet language', but a selection of sources from my primary material where 'Soviet language' or language culture are discussed or mentioned. My main source for this case study is an online discussion following a radio broadcast by the BBC on *sovetizmy* in 2005. It lies six years back in time, but is thus more easily compared with the philological contributions mentioned earlier. Additional sources include blog posts with comments and forum discussions from the state-run Internet portal gramota.ru. My analysis is based on a qualitative close reading of this material.

Before proceeding to the three above-mentioned aspects, we need to see whether the particular focus of the philological publications on the 'countercultural response' to Soviet language culture is also reflected in online commemorative practices. What is understood by 'Sovietism' in this material? The answer emerges from the scope of the examples people provide. *Sovetizmy* are clearly not thought to comprise only the official genres, ideological slogans and political styles, but also the 'other side of the coin', the satirical, ironical twist, word play, linguistic humour, and everyday lexicon from the Soviet period. This becomes clear in the way users bring in all kinds of Sovietisms without explicitly distinguishing between 'official' and 'unofficial' ones. Obviously, they all belong to the same, broad linguistic reserve of expressions 'made in the USSR'. The examples below are given without any introductory context or motivation: individual voices add up to a collective response to the question 'What is a *sovetizm*?'

> (1) *Ob''iavlenie v gazetnom kioske: 'Pravdy' - net. 'Rossiia' - prodana. Ostalsia 'Trud' za 3 kopeiki.* [. . .]
> *Ogromnymi bukvami na dome № 101 po prospektu Mira visel plakat: 'STAL' - RODINE!'*
> [. . .]
> ***Viktor Rossiia***

> [Announcement in the newspaper kiosk: No 'Pravda' ['truth'], 'Rossiia' ['Russia'] has been sold out. All that's left is 'Trud' [work] for 3 kopeks. . . . House no 101 on Mir Avenue had a poster on it with gigantic letters saying: 'STEEL FOR THE HOMELAND!']
>
> (2) *'Ty nachal'nik – ia durak. Ia nachal'nik – ty durak'.*
> *'Nachal'nik delaet vid, chto platit mne zarplatu – ia delaiu vid, chto rabotaiu'.*
> *'Pust' loshad' dumaet, u nee golova'.*
> *'Zakon kak dyshlo, kuda povernesh' tuda i vyshlo'.*
> *'Partiia chest' i sovest' sovetskogo naroda'.*
> *'Partiia nash rulevoi'.*
> *'Rossiia rodina slonov'.*
> *'Sovetskoe - znachit otlichnoe'.*
> *'Byl by chelovek, a delo na nego naidetsia'. (V smysle, posadit' v tiur'mu mozhno liubogo.)*
> *'Khochesh' zhni, a khochesh' kui – vseravno poluchish' . . .' (V smysle, v Soiuze voobshche rabotat' ne stoit.)*
> ***David Israel***
>
> ['If you're the boss, I'm the fool. If I'm the boss, you're the fool.'
> 'The boss pretends to pay me, I pretend to work.'
> 'Let the horse think – it's got a big head.' [I don't like to think too much. Let others think if they want to].
> 'The law is like a pillar – you can't jump over it, but you can bypass it.'
> 'One law for the rich, and another for the poor.'
> 'The Party is the honour and conscience of the Soviet people.'
> 'The Party is our helmsman.'
> 'Russia is the homeland of elephants.'
> 'Soviet – that means: excellent.'
> 'As long as you provide someone, we'll find a case on him.' (In the sense that anyone can be imprisoned.)
> 'You may reap or forge – either way, you'll get f*** all.' (In the sense that in the Soviet Union it doesn't make sense to work at all.)][3]

We see here that official slogans stand side by side with ironic distortions, humoristic or sarcastic sayings, or an anecdote – without any further commentary on the mixture of genres. This demonstrates the degree to which the official and alternative linguistic practices of Soviet language culture were intertwined and interdependent.

The personal experience

Let us start by looking at an example:

> (3) *Vspominaiu lozung u zdaniia partkoma sela Bogatoe togda Kuibyshevskoi oblasti. Byl samyi rastsvet khrushchevshiny i poetomu nam vnushali: 'Budet miaso i smetana, kolbasa*

sortov liubykh, esli vsiudu seiat' stanut kukuruzu i boby!' A v produktovom magazine sela i v pomine ne bylo ni sakhara, ni kolbasy, voobshche nikakikh produktov pitaniia, tol'ko konservy s kil'koi i vodka. A bukhanku khleba, esli uspeesh' kupit', nazyvali 'shlakoblokom', do togo ona byla cherna, spekshaiasia, syra i tiazhela. V mestnoi stolovoi dezhurnym bliudom byla tol'ko otvarnaia vermishel' - kholodnaia i sklizkaia. Cherez neskol'ko mesiatsev takogo pitaniia ia zarabotal 'zheltukhu'.
Igor' Besprosvetnyi Rossiia

[I remember a slogan in front of the *partkom* building in the village of Bogatoe in what was then the Kuibyshevskaia oblast. This was at the height of the Khrushchev era and therefore everywhere we heard: 'There will be meat and sour cream, sausages of all sorts, if maize and beans are sown everywhere!' But in the village grocery store there was no trace of sugar, no sausages, no food at all, only canned sprats and vodka. A loaf of bread, if you were lucky to get one, was called *shlakoblok* ['cinder block'] – that's how black, clotted, raw and heavy it was. The local canteen had just boiled noodles – cold and slimy. After a few months of this sort of food, I got jaundice.]

This is a typical example which neatly brings out the wide gap between ideological language and real life in Soviet times. It provides a context, a couple of concrete examples, and some reflections and thoughts, all of which add up to provide a personal experience. It does not make any attempt at generalization – but we, as readers, are free to do so, holding up our own experience or knowledge alongside the examples and comments provided.

With the possible exception of Sarnov's book (cf. above), this opposition between official language culture and real life is not particularly prominent in the philological literature on the subject, but very much present in all the online commentaries I have seen.

Not unexpectedly, many users recall *funny constellations* between official slogans and the surrounding realities:

(4) *Vspominaetsia ogromnaia fotografiia L.I. Brezhneva s vytianutoi rukoi i nadpis'iu 'Pravil'noi dorogoi idete, tovarishchi!' V obshchem nichego osobennogo, esli by v napravlenii kuda ukazyvala ruka Leonida Il'icha ne nakhodilas' izvestnaia vsem mestnaia pivnaia . . .*
Slava Chekhiia

[I remember a huge photo of Leonid Brezhnev with an outstretched arm and the inscription 'You are on the right path, comrades!' Nothing special about that, if the hand of Leonid Brezhnev wasn't pointing at a well-known local pub . . .]

(5) *V nashem gorodke bylo dva lozunga. Odin stoial metrov 300 ot drugogo. 1-Nasha tsel' – kommunizm, 2-Kazhduiu bombu - tochno v tsel'.*
Yura Panchenko Ukraine

[In our garrison town, there were two slogans. One stood about 300 metres from the other. 1. Our goal (target) is communism, 2. Every bomb – right on target.][4]

These and similar examples bring up personal reminiscences, mostly concerning one person, and one concrete memory (as opposed to attempts to generalize, inherent in the genres of dictionary and monograph). The format means that these personal memories can be supplemented by all sorts of commentaries, sometimes in a laconic manner, sometimes with more passion:

(6) *'Narod i partiia – ediny!' Eta neonovaia nadpis' na GORKOMe ne gasla dazhe kogda v okruge ne bylo elektrichestva.*
Evgenii F. Israel

['People and Party are one!' This neon sign on the *Gorkom* building did not turn off even when the area had no electricity.]

(7) *Videl vo Vladikavkaze lozung v neone – Pobeda kommunizma neizbezhna. (fatal'no kak-to eto, kak sama smert')*
Mukha-Khomukha Rossiia

[I saw a slogan in neon in Vladikavkaz – The victory of communism is inevitable. (Sounds fatalistic in a way, like death itself)

Comments like this add a lot in terms of reflection, views, characteristics, associations, assessments and emotions. They provide glimpses into a *private linguistic history*, examples of individual encounters between the official language culture and a personal linguistic, cultural and social horizon.

Reflections on the process of commemoration

Of particular interest for the present context are reflections on the process of commemoration. Such comments are often made in passing:

(8) *Ot saksofona do nozha odin shag!*[5] *Tletvornoe vliianie zapada! Partiia skazala: nado! Komsomol otvetil: est'! V to vremia, kogda vsia strana... Sud'bonosnoe vremia. Boius' gluboko uiti v vospominaniia.* ;))))
Anatolii Vadimouich Rossiia

[From the saxophone to the knife is only one step! The pernicious influence of the west! The party said: We must! The Komsomol said: We will! At a time when the whole country ... A crucial time. I'm afraid to delve deep into my memories. ;))))]

In this example, we can see how the flow of memory results in a flow of language: it proceeds from one example to the other, before adding a couple of comments and finally a spontaneous reaction to the very process of commemoration.

(9) *A teper' dlinnaia tsitata Lenina po pamiati: Kommunistom mozhno stat' lish' togda, kogda obogatish' svoiu pamiat' znaniem vsekh tekh bogatstv, kotorye vyrabotalo chelovechestvo ... (bred, no v golovu vbili na vsiu zhizn')*.
Il'ia New York, USA

[And now, a long quotation of Lenin I know by heart: you can become a Communist only when you extend your mind with the knowledge of all the riches created by mankind . . . (nonsense, but rammed into my head for ever).]

(10) *Ia – byvshii kievlianin. Kak i vse naselenie SSSR, byl pogruzhen v 'sovetizmy'*. Dazhe kollektsioniroval chuvstva, ispytyvaemye sovetskimi liud'mi, sudia po gazetam*: 1. Goriachego odobreniia. 2. Ogromnoi blagodarnosti. 3. Bezgranichnoi predannosti. 4. Zakonnoi gordosti. 5. Vsestoronnei podderzhki. 6. Bol'shogo pod"ema. 7. Bezzavetnoi samootverzhennosti. 8. Iskrennei priznatel'nosti. 9. Monolitnoi splochennosti. 10. Nebyvalogo entuziazma. 11. Bezrazdel'noi monolitnosti. 12. Polnoi soprichastnosti. 13. Nevidannogo geroizma. 14. Vsemernoi otvetstvennosti. 15. Glubokogo udovletvoreniia. 16. Tverdoi uverennosti v zavtrashnem dne. 17. Grazhdanskogo edinstva. 18. Polnovlastnogo khoziaina svoei strany. 19. Proletarskogo internatsionalizma. 20. Velichiia dela, kotoromu sluzhish'. 21. Revoliutsionnogo obnovleniia. 22. Preispolnennogo dolga. 23. Glubokoi skorbi. Dariu, t.k. kollektsiia davno ne popolniaetsia. Ed.* [my emphasis][6]
Eduard shkol'nik SShA

[I'm a former resident of Kiev. Like the rest of the USSR's population, I was immersed in 'Sovietisms'. *I even collected the feelings experienced by Soviet people as described by the newspapers*: 1. Fierce approval. 2. Immense gratitude. 3. Boundless devotion. 4. Legitimate pride. 5. Universal support. 6. Major surge. 7. Unwavering self-sacrifice. 8. Sincere gratitude. 9. Monolithic unity. 10. Unprecedented enthusiasm. 11. Unbreakable unity. 12. Complete engagement. 13. Unprecedented heroism. 14. Utmost responsibility. 15. Profound satisfaction. 16. Unflinching confidence in the future. 17. Civil unity. 18. Sole master of his country. 19. Proletarian internationalism. 20. The majesty of the cause you are serving. 21. Revolutionary renewal. 22. Filled with a sense of duty. 23. Profound sorrow. I offer it here, as the collection hasn't been supplemented for years. Ed. [my italics]]

The highlighted phrase in the above passage illustrates, in a striking way, the same opposition between ideological language and real life we saw above – now within one sentence, simply combining, without commentary, the incompatible.

My final example in this section describes the essence of much of the material gathered:

> (11) . . . *Voobshche-to interesno proguliat'sia po kliuchevym slovam pamiati.*
> ***Ivan d'Urak SU***
>
> [It's actually quite interesting to stroll through the keywords of my memory.]

Again and again we come across 'keywords', signal words, slogans, which obviously surface immediately in the minds of the respondents as soon as they are asked to think about Sovietisms. In a similar vein, a word or phrase by another commentator triggers a response: a similar slogan, a new context, a different interpretation. Such keywords activate the flux of commemorative language at work in these settings.

References to the language culture of today

Finally, I bring in just one example, by way of generalization, concerning the third aspect: the ways in which discussions on Soviet language culture often turn into discussions on the language culture of today. In the philological literature, the contemporary dimension comes to the fore in Gasan Guseinov's dictionary (see note 1), which comprises not only Sovietisms of the Soviet era, but also the afterlife of Soviet language culture in post-Soviet Russia. In the current material, the link to today's culture has a slightly different emphasis, referring, more often than not, to the chief issues of today's language debates, rather than the twists and turns of the Soviet linguistic heritage. Here is a typical example:

> (12) . . . *Pochemu vmeste s ischeznoveniem sovetskoi epokhi dali duba takie slova, kak 'tysiacheletie' (nyne millenium), 'beg trustsoi' (dzhogging), 'ocharovatel'nyi, shikarnyi' (glamurnyi), 'pokhod po magazinam' (ne risknu proiznesti)? Mne lichno bol'she vsego zhal' 'bifshteks'*!
> ***Staryi pen'***
>
> [. . . Why, with the disappearance of the Soviet era, did we see some words die out, such as '*tysiacheletie*' (now *millennium*), '*beg trustsoi*' (now *dzhogging*), '*ocharovatel'nyi, shikarnyi*' (now *glamurnyi*), '*pokhod po magazinam*' (I dare not utter this one)? Personally, I miss 'bifshteks' the most!]

Meta-discourses about language are very frequent in all segments of Runet today. As I read comments in the style of (12), they take up typical arguments from this broader discussion about today's language situation and relate them to the more specific issues of the Soviet linguistic heritage.

Conclusion

What may the digitally mediated commentaries and discussions yield in terms of new information, and what can they offer as we try to understand the phenomenon of Soviet language culture, its historical role and its contemporary incarnations?

First, it is obvious that such discussions contain contributions from all over the world and from a wide variety of participants of all ages (and this is, naturally, different from the philological corpus, where the commentating voice is usually restricted to one or two editors). This also means that I have not found 'the typical online commentator of Soviet language culture'. Instead, the online material provides a broader scope and many instances of dialogical encounters, spontaneous responses to suggestions, memories, associations, etc., which involve, on the one hand, disagreements (*Chto na samom dele? My, navernoe, v raznykh SSSRakh zhili* 'What do you mean? We seem to have lived in different USSRs' (Zotikov 2011)) and, on the other, the creation of what is in no way a full picture, but a more nuanced picture at the level of detail. The general tone of voice of the comments oscillates between nostalgia and derision, horror, sarcasm and irony. Users quarrel over the origin and exact wording of famous Sovietisms such as 'There is no sex in the Soviet Union', lament the present-day language culture, and relish reminiscences of absurd, appalling or simply comic expressions.

The parallel listings of official and satirical Sovietisms show that the emphasis on the 'double life' and countercultural aspects of Sovietspeak, which, as we saw above, are prominent in philological writings on the Soviet linguistic heritage, not only reveal some particular interest of philologists, but are a feature firmly grounded in the general Russian-speaking community of the present day.

The three aspects I have focused on here – personal reminiscences, reflections on the process of commemoration, and references to today's language culture – are, I believe, the ones that are particular to, or at least more typical of, online discussions, when compared to what the professional philological contributions provide. We are dealing with personal, often spontaneous reflections on, and assessments of, the question of the Soviet linguistic heritage, which testify, above all, to the individual's reaction to the profound disparity between abstract ideological language and everyday human life. We see the ways in which keywords and associations arise and trigger new associations, memories add to memories, and we witness the typical turns and ways of thinking about language cultures as such – as many discussions on Soviet language culture turn into a discussion or even argument about today's linguistic situation. In this way, online commemorations of Soviet language culture provide a unique and invaluable source for studying the articulation of personal human linguistic experience.

Notes

1 For a detailed examination of these and similar works, see Lunde 2008.

2 While post-socialist digital memory studies is a new, but rapidly growing field of research, I am not aware of any studies that target digitally mediated commemorations of post-socialist or post-totalitarian *language*, in particular. As the body of research on

totalitarian languages, such as National Socialist (NS) language in Germany and newspeak in Russia and other countries with a socialist past, is substantial, I do not rule out the possibility that such studies exist already. If not, I am quite certain that they will appear in the near future.

3 Unless otherwise indicated, quotations are taken from the BBC Russian Service forum on *Sovetskii iazyk* from 11 October 2005 ('Sovetskii iazyk' 2005). The punctuation and orthography of the source have been retained. All translations are my own.

4 This example turns up in a couple of variants in other forums, which may indicate that it is, perhaps, an urban legend or anecdote (which does not mean that the situation did not exist, of course).

5 The saying stems from Soviet propaganda against jazz.

6 The popular tradition of cataloguing official terms or phrases and embedding them in new genres or contexts was a widespread practice of language play in Soviet times. A famous example is Vladimir Vysotskii's song *Pis'mo rabochikh tambovskogo zavoda* (A Letter from Workers in a Tambov Factory).

References

Guseinov, G. (2003) *D.S.P. Materialy k russkomu slovariu obshchestvenno-politicheskogo iazyka XX veka*. Moscow: Tri kvadrata.

Guseinov, G. (2004) *D.S.P. Sovetskie ideologemy v russkom diskurse 1990-kh*. Moscow: Tri kvadrata.

Kheveshi, M. (2002) *Tol'kovyi slovar' ideologicheskikh i politicheskikh terminov sovetskogo perioda*. Moscow: Mezhdunarodnye otnosheniia.

Kupina, N. (1995) *Totalitarnyi iazyk: slovar' i iazykovye reaktsii*. Ekaterinburg: ZUUNC.

Kupina, N. (1999) *Iazykovoe soprotivlenie v kontekste totalitarnoi kul'tury*. Ekaterinburg: Izd-vo Ural'skogo universiteta.

Lunde, I. (2008) 'LIS (Lingua imperii sovietici): filologiens håndtering av den nære språklige fortid i Russland', in I. Lunde and S. Witt (eds) *Terminal Øst: Totalitære og posttotalitære diskurser*. Oslo: Spartacus.

Mokienko, V.M. and T.G. Nikitina (1998) *Tolkovyi slovar' iazyka Sovdepiia*. Moscow: Ast (2nd edn 2005).

Pikhurova, A. (2006) *Sud'ba sovetizmov v russkom iazyke kontsa XX–XXI vekov (na materiale slovarei i tekstov)*. Unpublished thesis, University of Saratov.

Sarnov, B. (2001) *Nash sovetskii novoiaz: malen'kaia entsiklopediia real'nogo sotsializma*. Moscow: EKSMO (2nd edn 2005).

'Sovetskii iazyk' (2005) BBC Russian Service forum, 11 October. Online. Available: <http://news.bbc.co.uk/hi/russian/talking_point/newsid_4291000/4291692.stm> (accessed 13 March 2012).

'The Future of Russian: Language Culture in the Era of New Technology' (2008–2012) Research project, University of Bergen. Online. Available: http://www.uib.no/rg/future_r/research/the-future-of-russian-language-culture-in-the-era-of-new-technology (accessed 18 June 2012).

Vezhbitska [Wierzbicka], A. (1993) 'Antitotalitarnyi iazyk v Pol'she: Mekhanizmy iazykovoi samooborony'. *Voprosy iazykoznaniia* 4:107–125.

Weiss, D. (2000) 'Der posttotalitäre politische Diskurs im heutigen Rußland', in L. Zybatow (ed.) *Sprachwandel in der Slavia: Die slavischen Sprachen an der Schwelle zum 21. Jahrhundert: Ein internationales Handbuch*. Wiesbaden: Peter Lang.

Zotikov, D. (2011) 'Novoiaz. Chto my poteriali i priobreli za 20 let', 11 May 2011. Online posting. Available: <http://gidepark.ru/user/1224334622/article/332151> (accessed 13 March 2012).

7 Memory and self-legitimization in the Russian blogosphere

Argumentative practices in historical and political discussions in Russian-language blogs of the 2000s

Ilya Kukulin

Introduction

Researchers of political discussions on the Internet have suggested that in societies that are politically (more or less) free, online debates reshape the language and inner structure of democracy (Stromer-Galley and Wichowsky 2011). In societies where civil rights and freedoms are substantially restricted, these online discussions may also construct online spaces of resistance (Kulikova and Perlmutter 2007). In the case of early twenty-first-century Russia, which may be labelled semi-free, political blogging and other online discussions served as major forms of social and cultural self-expression for a variety of Internet communities and subcultures. As a result, the mutual alienation that existed between many of these communities both increased *and* weakened. In this chapter, I explore the emergence and mutual recognition of these virtual groups, with a special eye for the argumentative practices that they employ in online political discussions. My approach views the Internet as a space of micro-social interactions, which have specific literature-like genres of communication and cultural functions. My focus is on the most striking feature of the online political discussions in blogs, primarily on LiveJournal, in the late 2000s, namely: controversies over historical memory.

Then and now, in Russia, such controversies are not really about memory (or, more precisely, *not only* about memory). Their underlying goal is the elaboration of the political and cultural self-definitions, or, we might say, identities of the participants of those discussions. Emotional posturing over more or less mythologized historical events is not only a subject or a frame for Web conversations; it is also a *tool* for self-legitimization. Such practices are most likely widespread in many different national sectors of the Internet, but they were especially important for the Russian blogosphere of the 2000s.

From the sociological point of view, blogs and similar forms of Internet activity are located on the border of the public and the private. This 'frontier' (intermediate) state is especially significant in the case of Russian society, where these two spheres often clash (Schmidt and Teubener 2006). The semi-private space of the Internet acquired special significance in Russia in the 2000s, as other spaces for public debate were increasingly closed off.

The prominent role that new media acquired in public life in the Russia of the 2000s was especially marked when it came to questions of public memory. This was a decade in which top-down-produced collective memory was 'normalized' in Russia, while other forms were 'closed down' (Koposov 2011; Miller 2012). The discussions of the 1990s – or, more precisely, their sequels – were largely concentrated in the printed media, independent radio, television (more rarely, since television is largely under state control) and educational spheres, and especially on the Internet. Those school history textbooks that called into question the official and unofficial historical myths of the Soviet period were 'not recommended' for further usage in Russian schools (Dolutskii 2004; Sveshnikov 2004; Sokolov 2008; Ermol'tsev and Koliagina 2012). In these conditions, the Russian Internet (Runet) was increasingly used by researchers as a key source of information on public opinion in contemporary Russia. Some scholars describe Runet as the primary field in which public opinion was disclosed and exposed (Lapina-Kratasiuk 2009; Aron 2011; Etling *et al.* 2010; Rogoża 2012). This approach has some hidden limitations, for example, concerning the social and geographical unevenness of the spread of the Internet in Russia; these issues are important, but beyond the scope of this chapter.

With few exceptions, the 'heroes' of my chapter are not prominent figures from the world of politics, business or literature. Instead, I examine non-specific blogs, supported by men and women in Russian-speaking space who use the Internet as a tool for communicating about all kinds of different subjects – not just politics. It is in these 'ordinary' blogs that the modes of usage and transformation of discourses of legitimation are especially visible.

Social setting: memory wars

One of the important features of the Runet of the 2000s is the 'memory wars' that raged throughout that decade within the international Russian-speaking educated society. In some cases their intensity and degree of verbal aggression warrants labelling them as manifestations of a kind of 'cold civil war'. Key examples here included a series of high-profile 'battles' over quasi-Stalinist history textbooks produced for secondary schools and universities, and heated debates on how to commemorate the victims of Stalinist terror. These discussions generally hinged on the basic issue of how to relate to the Soviet past. Some groups – conservative, neo-Stalinist, nationalist or statist – considered Russian history to be non-controversial, aesthetically sublime and centred on imperial 'greatness', often represented by Stalin personally. Others – liberals, 'non-Soviet' leftists and so on – argued that it was imperative to learn from the terrible dramas and traumas of the Soviet past in order to chart the way forward to a more humane future society. These irreconcilable polemics (which, like many other polemics, will brook no compromise) are known on Runet as *холивары* – a dark-ironic slang word, 'kholivar' (plural 'kholivary'), from the English 'holy war' (on kholivary, see also Dounaevsky (Chapter 8, this volume) and Lastouski, Chapter 10, this volume)).

The causes of these 'battles' may be briefly outlined as follows. The sociologist Lev Gudkov has described the post-Soviet Russian identity as a 'negative' identity (Gudkov 2000; Shliapentokh and Gudkov 2001). By this he means that the images of 'I' and 'we' are constructed primarily as a result of distancing from various Others, from 'them' – from foreigners, from cultural or social 'others', or from the political authorities. This is an astute observation, but the picture it paints is rather static. Examining the Russian blogosphere allows us to see a more dynamic process, namely: the endless quest for rhetorical and semantic instruments for redefining one's personal place in society and in history. Here again, the frontier state of the blogosphere becomes important. Any blog text is situated between the private and public spheres: a blogger redefines him- or herself in the course of an argument, explicitly polemicizing with particular opponents.

The socio-political situation in Russia of the 2000s provoked the endless calling into question of the historical legitimacy of both the political authorities and the oppositional social actors. All political actors were constantly challenged to justify and position themselves in terms of historical precedents. We might identify two primary causes of this seemingly permanent crisis of historical legitimacy that now plagues all public events in Russia:

1 The gradual weakening and fading of Soviet interpretations of history, but without the successful creation and dissemination of 'non-Soviet' interpretations to replace them.
2 The strikingly eclectic nature of the official historical narrative, such that it forms a kind of ideological 'patchwork' (Dubin 2010; cf. also Pavlovskii 2012).

The Russian authorities and the ideologists supporting them attempted to construct their historical legitimacy with the help of references to such varied historical precedents as Stalin's National Bolshevism (Brandenberger 2002, 2009); Solzhenitsyn's conservative and collectivist, but anti-totalitarian slogans; and the liberal rhetoric of the perestroika era, to cite just a few examples. This ideological eclecticism was necessary in order to justify the authorities' contradictory and often authoritarian political decisions, but various social movements went further in their interpretation, reading this eclecticism as heralding the whole-scale installation of a dangerous new state ideology. Indeed, the official historical narratives lent themselves to a range of sharply diverging and seemingly incompatible interpretations. An example that triggered heated online discussions is the nationalists' consideration of the regime as 'neoliberal', while liberals view it as a kind of nationalist heir to Soviet totalitarianism.[1]

In the 2000s, relations between the Russian political elites and society became more and more intense. The authorities gradually increased the rights of police and state employees to intervene in the private lives of citizens, as well as dismantling the elements of the social welfare system. Citizens responded by protesting and resorting to corruption as a means of surviving and escaping the state's reach. Ideologically, however, these relations were suspended in a state of fragile and uneasy equilibrium.

Throughout the decade, this instability intensified due to the weak differentiation of the Russian public sphere, the lack of socially rooted identities in contemporary Russian society, and the collective feeling of alienation from history. In the 2000s the underlying instability of state–society relations tended to be obscured by the disoriented and fragmented state of Russian society and public life, and the absence of integrating figures and symbols. The structures of new digital online media were arguably especially well suited to expressing, reflecting and enhancing these features and tendencies, and both of these factors (the social phenomena, and their digital mediation and reshaping) contributed to the high degree of verbal aggression characteristic of historical Runet discussions.

All of these features of Russian society and public discourse also gave rise to a less obvious consequence: the extremely limited rhetorical vocabulary of self-legitimation on the part of the participants in the online memory 'battles'. In these debates, the notion of personal responsibility is more or less entirely absent. Instead, history is used as a tool for personal self-justification.[2] The argumentative practices used to this end comprise two main categories:

1. Genealogical references to private family pasts.
2. Archaeological references redefining the traumatic past as an ethically neutral source of 'cultural values', as a kind of 'grand museum'.

The various discursive and cultural positions adopted by the participants in these discussions have one common trait. Their versions of historical memory have been constructed using a mixture of 'Soviet' and 'non-Soviet' elements. The differences are not only ideological or ethical, but also structural: the types of *cultural glue* binding together the heterogeneous elements of these 'versions of memory' are diverse.[3] In turn, the various kinds of 'glue' determine the different positions represented in the blogosphere discussions.

Case study: the Kurskaia metro station controversy

The main case study of my chapter is the Internet discussions about the restoration of inscriptions glorifying Stalin in the vestibule of Kurskaia metro station in Moscow in August 2009. Like many other Soviet underground stations, Kurskaia had been 'de-Stalinized' in 1961, when the inscriptions, together with a large statue of Stalin, were removed following Nikita Khrushchev's second condemnation of Stalin at the Twenty-Second Party Congress. The decision to restore the station's pro-Stalin inscriptions in 2009 caused a huge wave of comments in the Russian blogosphere, numbering in the thousands; one single post by **russos** (the blog nickname of Aleksandr Popov, a popular Internet photographer of Moscow life), featuring a picture-spread of the reopening of the vestibule, attracted 1,375 comments (Popov 2009). Many of these comments challenged the claim that the restoration had been carried out in the interests of cultural heritage preservation. They noted the historically inaccurate and highly selective nature of the restoration, such that, for example, the sculpture of Stalin was not replaced (the directors of the Moscow metro claimed that the statue could not be located), and the inscription on the pseudo-classical frieze over the pillars was only selectively restored, omitting the lines from the old version of the Soviet anthem dedicated to Lenin.[4]

As we have already seen, contemporary Russian society is divided by positive and negative attitudes to Stalin (on the sociological data and their interpretation, see Cherepova 2010; Levinson 2009, 2010). The restoration of the Kurskaia station entrance hall was not the first sign that 'Stalinist tastes' were prevalent in certain circles of the contemporary Russian political elite. In 2007, a major scandal had broken out over plans – apparently originating within or at least supported by the Presidential Administration – to publish a handbook for history teachers which interpreted Stalinist terror as a hard but necessary modernization measure. In this case, however, the debates tended to be concentrated mainly in online 'regular' media and on independent radio station Echo Moskvy talk shows more than in blogs. By contrast, the 2009 Kurskaia metro station case was an issue that clearly aroused strong reactions among bloggers in particular. The intensity of the blogosphere's response to the Kurskaia restoration as opposed to the history handbook in part reflects the difference between the symbolic forms at stake in these two cases. A handbook for schoolteachers is very important in a social sense, but its status as an incarnation of the common symbolic order is less obvious or immediate. A deliberately restored architectural monument, on the other hand, is a direct, 'concrete' embodiment of such an order, and hence bloggers felt bound to respond.

Selective archaeology and the 'grand museum'

Many architectural monuments in Moscow were neglected, destroyed, or incompetently restored in the 1980s to 2000s, and their plight did not attract any attention from society, with the exception of a few small groups of civil activists, such as the Arkhnadzor heritage protection group. Very few stations of the Moscow metro were restored to their 'primordial' form. This general indifference shown by the Moscow authorities to architectural monuments prompted speculation that the 2009 restoration of Kurskaia station was a 'demonstrative' act, in the words of the sociologist Boris Dubin (Dubin 2009), or a 'purely political gesture', as the coordinator of the Arkhnadzor group put it (Samover 2011). We might draw a parallel here between the Kurskaia restoration and other performative symbolic gestures carried out by the Russian authorities in other spheres. Thus, for example, if the arrest and persecution of the former business tycoon Mikhail Khodorkovskii may be seen,[5] as liberal commentators have argued, as an act of 'selective law enforcement' aimed at sending a political message, then we might see the Kurskaia restoration as an act of 'selective archaeology'. Many bloggers and experts argued that the Stalinist inscriptions had been restored to the station not out of any architectural or urban development considerations, but in order to send a political signal.

The new Kurskaia entrance hall seemed to be not only a site of public memory, but *a fragment modelling a new symbolic order* in which Stalin's rule featured as the crucial, defining era in Russia's recent past. The success of this 'breakthrough' was described by Kirill Nikolenko – a member of the Communist Party of the Russian Federation (perhaps more accurately described today as a state-socialist nationalist populist party), historian, journalist and political speechwriter, living in the city of Vladimir. On 5 August 2011 Nikolenko wrote in his blog:

> [W]e must not permit any re-locations or destructions of monuments. Let the current and future generations of Russian citizens, as they stroll the streets of our cities, see signs of various historical epochs in the country's development.
>
> If you don't like the Soviet era with its ideas and principles and their expression in the names of streets, cities and monuments, then build new streets and cities, put up other monuments on other squares, but don't touch what you can't understand.
>
> Historical justice is beginning to triumph!
>
> After the completion of the restoration of the vestibule of 'Kurskaia' metro station its composition was returned to its original form: the lyrics of the Stalinist anthem were restored: 'Stalin raised us to be faithful to the people, he inspired us to labour and feats'. Our fighters for tolerance and card-carrying s[o]-c[alled] 'democrats' were wild with anger. . . .
>
> Everything is only just beginning. . . .
>
> We, citizens of Russia, are beginning to see the light and to shake off the nonsense imposed on us for 20 years. Intellectuals are speaking out in favour of Stalin. . . .
>
> In this way, step by step, we shall be victorious!
>
> (Nikolenko 2011a)

The emblematic status which the case of Kurskaia metro station has acquired in the blogosphere is exemplified by a blog post by the right-wing and neo-Soviet popular historian Grigorii Pernavskii. In January 2010 Pernavskii used the image of Kurskaia station as part of his verbal attack on liberal human rights activist Liudmila Alekseeva, ranting that she would soon be going 'to hell, to the eternal vestibule of "Kurskaia" metro station' (Pernavskii 2010). In another example, in November 2011 the prominent liberal blogger Andrei Mal'gin used an image of the Kurskaia frieze not only as visual shorthand signifying neo-totalitarian tendencies, but even as a kind of metonym for the current regime (Mal'gin 2011).

It would be incorrect to view the creation of this 'projected symbolic order' as driven by a yearning to return to a repressive political system. Instead, we can identify different emotions at work here. Conservative pro-Soviet commentators generally view the contemporary Russian state as having been 'humiliated'. They are motivated by a desire to see the Russian state restored to its former position as something tremendous, terrible and thrilling, first and foremost, on the symbolic level, as well as by the individual desire to exact collective revenge against the liberal critics of Soviet history, the 'culprits' allegedly responsible for this sense of humiliation and loss. Speaking more analytically, pro-Stalinist tendencies of these kinds express a desire to compensate for speakers' personal alienation from a history that is interpreted – in Soviet propaganda style – as a forced progress made possible by the Soviet state and the Bolshevik Party. The resulting confusion is exemplified by the fact that alongside his pro-Stalin posts, the above-cited communist blogger Kirill Nikolenko has also published online articles calling for the development of civil society and political openness, and condemning Putin for attempting to institute a new Stalinist-style orthodoxy in school history textbooks (Nikolenko 2011c).

The blogosphere discussions on the Kurskaia station issue may be divided into *external* and *internal wars of memories*. The *external memory wars* were waged between Kurskaia's defenders, who identified with Russia, and detractors, who identified with other countries of the former USSR. It is important to note that many of the participants in these debates did not live in Moscow or even in Russia. A very emotional attitude to this issue was expressed, for instance, by authors from Ukraine, Estonia and Georgia. They read the glorification of Stalin as a project with ramifications beyond the borders of Russia, aimed at transforming the entire post-Soviet symbolic order. These memory wars were obviously entangled with other political issues. In the case of the Georgian commentary in the polemics in the **moya_moskva** community, for example, debates over Kurskaia quickly moved on to highly emotional debates about the Russian–Georgian war of August 2008.

The *internal memory wars* divided those persons who identified themselves with Russian culture, variously defined. Some defenders of the restoration openly admired Stalin and argued that he deserved a personal site of commemoration, but a considerable number of them used other reasons for their defence of Kurskaia. They argued that removing Stalin's name from architectural monuments constituted an 'act of censorship': 'It's time to put an end to the tradition when each successive generation of rulers begins by destroying everything that was built before them. The communists dismantled the tsarist monuments, the "democrats" are dismantling Soviet monuments' (comment by **rst37_2** on a blog post by **russos**: **rst37_2** 2009). One of the most active defenders of Kurskaia – the Russian nationalist and anti-Semitic blogger **mozg_cow**, a resident of the

Ukrainian city of Lugansk – wrote in one of his (numerous) comments on a post by **russos**:

> We shall demand they keep their hands off our history. We are citizens and not just taxpayers; we have a right to demand the return of our authentic history and authentic architecture. [Note that it is now rather popular to frame such appeals using elements of 'civil society' lexicon).]

In response to a comment by **dnkpm** which stated that 'Remembering does not mean praising, especially when dealing with such a monster', **mozg_cow** asked:

> What do you mean, 'monster'?
>
> The lyrics of the USSR state anthem are included in the [building's] design. Do you understand what an architectural ensemble is?
>
> (Popov 2009)[6]

Other defenders of the 'restored' vestibule labelled the calls to remove Stalin's name from the frieze as incitements to 'vandalism'. This charge was first made in the discussion in the **moya_moskva** community. Next, some pro-Stalinist civil activists (strange as this phrase may sound) sent a letter to Moscow mayor Yurii Luzhkov in which they argued that removing Stalin's name from the Kurskaia frieze would be an act of 'vandalism' and 'an encroachment against the people's right to study and evaluate its own past'. Strikingly, they labelled the approach of their opponents as 'totalitarian' (!) (Letter to Yurii Luzhkov 2009).[7]

We might describe this kind of rhetoric, which employs the language of contemporary civil society for the purposes of self-legitimization, as mimicry, but it is also more than that. This type of rhetoric paradoxically inverts two key motifs of the liberal media of the perestroika era:

1 Appeals to 'reveal the whole truth about history'; that is, to allow information about the history of Soviet state terror to be published.
2 Calls to defend the 'monuments of the past' – first and foremost, the churches, monasteries and other buildings erected before the October Revolution.[8]

These motifs of perestroika journalism were aimed at preserving the memory of the victims of state terror and reviving and rehabilitating non-Soviet cultural traditions. In the writings of bloggers like **mozg_cow**, by contrast, the rhetoric of the imperative to preserve memory and historical authenticity is pressed into the service of very different goals. The new neo-Stalinist rhetoric is aimed at representing historical memory as a kind of great museum, in which there is no place for ethical or political judgements. For example, Kirill Nikolenko argues that:

> We should not destroy the monuments of a different historical era, of a different regime.

> There should be continuity.
>
> So let there be monuments to Lenin, Stalin, Dzerzhinskii, Alexander III, Sakharov and so forth.
>
> If that's how the Kurskaia station originally looked, then this must be preserved. It must not be touched.
>
> . . . We might not be happy with it, we might refuse to accept it, we might not understand its nature, but we must preserve all this so that the connection between generations is not severed.
>
> One cannot evaluate the events of the past using modern concepts. This kind of 'modernization' of history is not to be tolerated.
>
> (Nikolenko 2011b)

This representation of memory as a museum, which exists beyond personal evaluations and personal responsibility, is the first type of *glue*, uniting 'Soviet history' and 'non-Soviet counter-history' in the writings of the conservative and nationalist bloggers (on counter-history see Ferro 1984). The image of such a museum is based on monuments, that is, on symbolic artefacts that function as *prostheses* of the 'lost' – i.e. alienated – history. Meanwhile, however, bloggers positing the existence of this museum usually also share the view that in the projected future, 'anti-Soviet' narratives and artefacts, given their perceived anti-statist potential, will nevertheless occupy a subordinate place in this grand museum.

One of the media for the above-mentioned inversion of perestroika-era rhetoric on historical memory is the so-called *normalization* discourse employed in the Russian authorities' contemporary political PR.[9] This 'normalizing' discourse represents Russian history as a pathetic drama or melodrama, such that the meaning of its traumatic events is not ethical or social, but primarily aesthetic and psychological. On this account, the contemporary individual's relationship to historical memory resembles the attitude of a spectator, who may only observe or pay for symbolically meaningful historical representations.

Family narratives: the rhetoric of tragic heredity

Self-definition based on genealogical references is the second main category of self-legitimizing practices used in online discussions about Russian historical memory. Here the participants set out to define themselves as *heirs*, whether of the victims or the victors in Russia's traumatic past. Family memory is thus the second type of *cultural glue* joining together the 'Soviet' and 'non-Soviet' components of historical memory.

The opponents to the selective restoration of Kurskaia entrance hall wrote about the anti-humanist face of Stalin's regime and about its millions of victims. But commentators from both camps in the Kurskaia debates used family narratives: they wrote about the role played by the Stalinist regime in the history of their own families. 'My great-grandfather, a priest', user **flavianos** wrote, for instance,

> was shot in nineteen thirty seven. Six children, including my grandmother, were left orphaned.
>
> So I won't tell my mother what happened at Kurskaia. I'll have some pity on her. She might not notice it when she goes to Moscow.
>
> Because her mother is that same grandmother of mine, who was left without a father.
>
> (Matveev 2009)[10]

Political journalist and blogger Denis Iaroshenko posted the following comment on the Kurskaia case in the community 'World Association of Ukrainians' on the 'Gide Park' blog service:

> Stalin was guilty of mass repressions, in the course of which hundreds of thousands of people were destroyed. This was one of the bloodiest tyrants. . . . For many his name has become a synonym for evil, for the evil that broke and disfigured the lives of several generations. But the point is not even the fact that *it is not hard to imagine the kind of emotions aroused by the lines of the old anthem, for both the surviving victims of the repressions themselves and for their children and grandchildren, when they find themselves by chance at this station of the Moscow metropolitan.* And we can say with all certainty that this concern for the restoration of the historical face of the underground station is a slap *in the face for those who perished or miraculously survived the bloody grinders of the Stalinist repressive machine.*
>
> (Iaroshenko 2011, italics added)

The defenders of the new-old entrance hall also used the family narrative to answer their opponents:

> In my family there were no 'snitches' and no 'loyal slaves'. My great-grandfather was a merchant of the first guild and did not live to see the Revolution, my grandfather was a director of the 'Metallist' plant during the siege [of Leningrad] and died there during a bombing raid. My grandma raised my mother and my uncle. During the siege my father was in an orphanage. All in all, that's the full extent to which the regime ever touched my family. They never informed on anyone and they never kowtowed. They lived their lives, just as ordinary citizens of the country are supposed to.
>
> (**billy_madbull** 2009)[11]

Moreover, the defenders of Stalin as a symbolic 'site of memory' often claim that all anti-Stalinists are themselves the descendants of those who were arrested (and perhaps, it is sometimes insinuated, of 'bandits'). Take, for example, the following exchange regarding the notorious 'Stalinobuses' project, whereby buses decorated with Stalin's portrait were introduced in a series of Russian cities.[12] Theatre researcher Liubov' Shaporina commented in this connection: 'I'm always surprised when people choose butchers as heroes and idols – this is some kind of sado-masochism!' The Stalinist and anti-Semitic blogger **pppdddnnn** (in his user profile, his interests include cats, tulips and embroidery[13]) answered her:

> By the way, in Moscow, I take it that you avoid the vestibule of Kurskaia metro station, right?. . .
>
> Generalissimus Stalin is an historic figure. He was Supreme Commander-in-Chief of the army that was victorious in the Great Patriotic war. *Why* can't we display his portraits? How is this 'sado-masochistic'? Was your grandmother repressed? Were any of your relatives repressed? I simply don't understand, *what* is the problem here?
>
> (**pppdddnnn** 2012, emphases in original)

Here we can see a conjugation of both types of self-justification discussed in this chapter: the 'grand museum' discourse ('Generalissimus Stalin is an historic figure'), on the one hand; and the negative variant of the 'family discourse' ('only the descendants of victims have any reason to hate Stalin'), on the other.

The authors of the open letter to Mayor Luzhkov, which condemned the liberals for their call to remove Stalin's name from the Kurskaia frieze, likewise appealed to 'our grandfathers and great-grandfathers':

> We must take into account the fact that those people imposing their position on us are the very same people who supported the recent decisions of the OSCE revisionists, the ones who are ready to place on the same level Hitler's SS men and Soviet liberator-soldiers, our grandfathers and great-grandfathers.
>
> (Letter to Yurii Luzhkov 2009)[14]

A direct connection may be discerned here between this type of rhetoric and the liberal historical and political discourses of the perestroika period of the late 1980s, on the one hand, and Soviet discourses of historical memory of the so-called 'stagnation' era of the 1970s, on the other. At first glance, this combination may seem incongruous, given the extent to which the semantic content of Soviet family historical narratives in the eras of stagnation and perestroika were so diametrically opposed. The stagnation era was a period characterized by the 'soft' rehabilitation of Stalinism and the 'normalization' of history – or, more precisely, of the collective memory of the twentieth century. The main form that this normalization took was the propagandist reinvention of the mythology of family ties as transcending historical traumas. One of the main genres in late Soviet mass culture comprised literary and TV pop sagas that followed a single family across several generations, tracing the way in which the family stayed loyal to Soviet power throughout various historical ordeals and traumas.[15] One of the subplots might feature a family member who had been arrested and imprisoned but 'was not embittered'.

This representation of memory served a modelling function: it was assumed that the history of every family could be understood as a melodramatic saga – one from which one could 'remove' ethical problems and transform them into aesthetic effects. In books and series that foregrounded this view of history, Stalin's rule and the Second World War were not ethical problems but only transpersonal ordeals, serving to highlight the hero/heroine's 'internal truth' and 'strength of soul'.

In 1975 the historian of Soviet culture Marietta Chudakova published a popular book, *Conversations about Archives*, which proclaimed the high value of private home collections of documents. In sharp opposition to the dominant late Soviet 'memorial melodramatism', Chudakova called for family and private histories to be made the subject of individual investigation and reflection (Chudakova 1975).

In the late Soviet period, family historical knowledge became a hidden political problem. The official support lent to the 'Soviet family sagas' made it possible to hijack some forms of anti-institutional memory. The modelling performance of the 'common' memory in late Soviet sagas was necessary to legitimate psychological loyalty to Soviet power and to morally reproach the representatives of the young generation of the 1970s. This 'last Soviet generation', to use the term coined by Alexei Yurchak (2006), did not want to feel obligated to the older Soviet generations and were interested in Western and/or Russian pre-revolutionary and émigré culture, or in Western consumer goods. Moreover, their performance of memory was socially demobilizing.

There was another kind of family historical knowledge, which was totally unofficial: this was the traumatic knowledge of, for example, relatives who had the 'wrong' ethnicity (such as Jews, or members of the 'repressed nations' [Otto Pohl 1999]), or who had served time in the camps. This knowledge could be diluted by the 'official sagas' discourse but it remained repressed, non-public and also non-mobilizing.

In the late 1980s, by contrast, family memory became a powerful mobilizing factor in public discussions. Remembrances of the traumatic events and traumatic aspects of Soviet self-consciousness invaded the public sphere. Appeals to family memory and private archives became a tool for de-normalizing Soviet history. The melodramatic performance of eternal collective survival led by the 'true communists' gave way to many local performances of the authorities' abuses against private life.

The archives served as both evidence and explanation in those performances. The main justificatory element of family memory as represented in the perestroika period was its claim to constitute 'true' – effectively synonymous here with 'traumatic' – knowledge. That period slowly drew to a close in the early 1990s.

In twenty-first-century Russia, family memory still occupies a very important place among other memorial discourses, but its social outlines have changed once again. In the 2000s the rhetoric of family memory was used by governmental 'political technologists' in unexpected ways. Historian Natal'ia Potapova has noted that appeals to family memory have today become a justification for the irrationality of 'first-hand' historical knowledge, rejecting any reflection or conceptualization, and that this 'irrational' trend was supported by the Russian political and official academic authorities (Potapova 2009 cited in Koposov 2011). A high-profile example was the May 2011 social PR campaign run in Moscow under the slogan: 'Thanks for the Victory, Grandpa', 'Victory' being shorthand in Russia for the Soviet victory in the Second World War. I would like to add: family history in the pro-government mass media has become a tool for shaping an emotional connection to the Soviet, 'non-Soviet' and pre-revolutionary history of Russia.

Here, then, we are dealing with an unusual phenomenon: whereas previously the rhetoric of family ties was used in blogs as an appeal to a family connection with the victims of Stalin's regime, now this rhetoric has been appropriated in official rhetoric as a tool of normalization – both in mass media and PR. This ambivalence shows the ambiguity of the notion of 'first-hand' memory in contemporary Russia.

In any case, an individual who invokes the family narrative constructs him- or herself emphatically as an *heir* or an *heiress* of the heroic or martyred dead ancestors. He or she may be an 'oppositional heir' of the victims or a 'pro-governmental heir' of the 'honest toilers', but in both cases the underlying assumption tends to be that it is only the status of 'being a family heir' that may force a person to adopt an ethical attitude towards history.

Conclusion

All the forms of rhetoric outlined in this chapter concern the most traumatic events of Soviet Russia's twentieth century – the Second World War and Stalin's repressions. In the collective consciousness, these events subsume, transform and stand in for the equally (or even more) painful remembrances of the Civil War of 1918 to 1922. This war has been forced out of social memory, perhaps because, in this case, pointing to an external and/or powerful perpetrator is a less straightforward business.

It may well be the case that this chapter describes a vanishing reality that will be swept out of existence by the widespread social protest movement that began in Russia in 2011 and which has seen the old rhetoric of historical continuity and legitimacy in the online discussion rapidly giving way to a new rhetoric of justice and social goal setting. Before these unpredictably large protests, any political activity not connected with the official political parties was suppressed more or less roughly, especially in the late 2000s. In those conditions the position of the victim or non-participant of the historical process was a popular and powerful form of personal historical self-definition. The Internet, and the blogosphere in particular, with its location on the border of the private and the public, was an ideal platform for these personal and virtual appeals to historical memory and the effective crafting of historical 'alibis'.

Many political jokes and anti-regime caricatures moved from the Internet sites and blogs to the cardboard or plywood slogans erected over the crowds of demonstrators in December 2011 and January 2012.[16] What were *not* transmitted to these offline protests, however, were the appeals to history as a museum or to family predecessors. The different social forces – Stalinists, anti-Stalinist communists, liberals, social democrats, nationalists – began to discuss the political agenda for the immediate future – not for the past. This offline process may well be transforming the semantics of the 'frontier space' between the public and the private in Runet.

If we are in fact dealing with a vanishing reality here, then the task of detecting its meaning becomes all the more urgent. It may be that we are currently witnessing a new stage in the process of the integration of the public and private versions of selfhood in Russia. If this is the case, then the 2000s may be viewed as a transitional period. In the initial developmental stages of online political discourse in Russia, the division of these two notions of the self was appreciable. In the 2000s, public and private selves were conjugated – a process that was marked by the genealogical argumentative practices used in the online history discussions described in this chapter. At a later stage, however, the imperative to legitimate the 'whole political self' provoked the diffusion – and, ultimately, perhaps, even the disappearance – of the old dividing and alienating boundary.

Notes

1 This crisis of social legitimacy in Russia would also seem to be connected to the broader global crisis of traditional forms of political legitimacy arising out of the specificities of online public opinion formation (Castells 2009: 286–298).

2 For an exchange reflecting on this issue, see Nosik 2011 (including comments section).

3 I have borrowed the glue metaphor from Elena Trubina's important article on Russian blogs (Trubina 2010).

4 The 'Lenin line' was later added, in October 2009. It is difficult to ascertain whether this was done as a result of the public response in the blogosphere and mass media.

5 Khodorkovskii, a tycoon whose arrest and trial in 2003 were apparently linked to his political activities, is considered a prisoner of conscience by Amnesty International.

6 These comments were accessed on 25 August 2011 but are no longer available online (as at 30 June 2012). A similar example of a comment by **mozg_cow** in defence of the Kurskaia restoration may be found in the comments to another related post (Kuraev 2009; **mozg_cow** 2009).

7 The above-mentioned letter to Luzhkov was published on the site za-stalina.ru (containing only this letter) and gathered 1,832 signatures.

8 We might note here that the late Soviet civil 'movement for the protection of monuments' was, from the 1970s onwards, partly liberal, but partly connected to Russian nationalist opposition circles (see Mitrokhin 2003).

9 This discourse has been described by a number of sociologists and cultural and social historians, including Boris Dubin, Lev Gudkov, Mark Lipovetsky, Nikolai Koposov and Gasan Guseinov.

10 The author of this blog is Flavian (Matveev), an Orthodox monk and priest, the abbot (hegumen) of a monastery in Yekaterinburg.

11 The author of this comment, **billy_madbull**, lives in St Petersburg (which he calls by its Soviet name, Leningrad). He is an amateur poet and writer, admirer of Stalin, Soviet socialism and Ernesto Che Guevara, and an active participant of offline role-playing games.

12 The 'Stalinobuses' campaign is the initiative of extreme right-wing public activist Viktor Loginov. Loginov created an independent foundation which paid for the campaign to decorate buses with portraits of Stalin in 40 towns of the former USSR, including Moscow, St Petersburg, Riga, Tallinn and Kyiv. The Stalin posters bore slogans glorifying the dictator as the 'organizer of Victory' in the Second World War. Loginov calls these 'Victory Buses' or 'Stalinobuses'. Loginov's 'Stalinobuses' were first launched on St Petersburg bus routes in 2010. Like the Kurskaia restoration, these 'public service announcements' provoked heated discussion; for example, in 2012 human rights activist and historian Arsenii Roginskii, Chairman of the 'Memorial' Society, called 'Stalinobuses' 'a disgrace to the country', and Mikhail Fedotov, head of the Presidential Human Rights Council, characterized them as 'provocative'.

13 He lives in the Russian city of Orel.

14 This is an allusion to the July 2009 OSCE resolution which 'expressed deep concern at the glorification of totalitarian regimes, including the holding of public demonstrations glorifying the Nazi or Stalinist past' (OSCE Resolution 2009). The Resolution was defined as an 'offensive anti-Russian attack' and 'an abuse of history' by representatives of the contemporary Russian political elites (Vodo and Taratuta 2009). It was also, of course, roundly condemned by Stalinist activists and bloggers on Runet.

15 On the sociological aspects of the late Soviet family sagas in literature, see Dubin and Gudkov 1994: 126–137.

16 This process of the migration of pictures and slogans from the Internet to 'offline space' was discussed at the seminar 'Hidden Values and the Language of New Social Protest Slogans' which was held on 30 December 2011 in Moscow at the Andrei Sakharov Museum and Cultural Centre. Political philosopher Mischa Gabowitsch and at least three groups of researchers are now studying the textual and visual representations of the protest social movements in contemporary Russia: 'The Folklore of the Snow Revolution', 'Scientific and Research Institute of the Rallies', and the working seminar 'The Political Development of Russia: A New Turn?' (see e.g. Lur'e 2012). In addition, a special issue of the online version of the Russian journal *The Anthropological Forum* (no. 16, 2012) was dedicated to the social anthropology of the protests (see especially Akhmetova 2012; Alekseevskii 2012; Arkhipova 2012; Moroz 2012).

References

Akhmetova, M. (2012) '. . . I banderlogi prishli: vyskazyvanie V.V. Putina i "narodnyi plakat"', *Antropologicheskii Forum* 16: 193–207. Online. Available: <http://anthropologie.kunstkamera.ru/files/pdf/016online/akhmetova2.pdf> (accessed 25 June 2012).

Alekseevskii, M. (2012) 'Kto vse eti liudi (s plakatami)?', *Antropologicheskii Forum* 16: 154–171. Online. Available: <http://anthropologie.kunstkamera.ru/files/pdf/016online/alekseevsky2.pdf> (accessed 25 June 2012).

Arkhipova, A. (2012) 'Anekdoty o Putine i vyborah 10 let spustia, ili Est' li fol'klor "Snezhnoi revoliutsii"?', *Antropologicheskii Forum* 16: 208–252. Online. Available: <http://anthropologie.kunstkamera.ru/files/pdf/016online/arkhipova2.pdf> (accessed 25 June 2012).

Aron, L. (2011) 'Nyetizdat: How the Internet Is Building Civil Society in Russia'. *American Enterprise Institute of Public Policy Research*, 28 June. Online. Available: <http://www.aei.org/files/2011/06/28/RO-Spring-2011-g.pdf> (accessed 25 June 2012).

billy_madbull (2009) Comments on blog post, September and October. Online. Available: <http://russos.livejournal.com/605782.html?thread=19731030#t19731030> (accessed 3 July 2012).

Brandenberger, D. (2009) *Natsional-Bol'shevizm: stalinskaia massovaia kul'tura i formirovanie russkogo natsional'nogo samosoznaniia, 1931–1956 gg.* St Petersburg: Akademicheskii Proekt.

Brandenberger, D. (2002) *National Bolshevism: Stalinist Mass Culture and the Formation of Modern Russian National Identity, 1931–1956.* Cambridge, MA: Harvard University Press.

Castells, M. (2009) *Communication Power.* Oxford and New York: Oxford University Press.

Cherepova, P. (2010) 'Rossiiane o Staline', *Levada-Tsentr,* 5 March. Online. Available: <http://www.levada.ru/05-03-2010/rossiyane-o-staline> (accessed 25 June 2012).

Chudakova, M. (1975) *Besedy ob arkhivakh.* Moscow: Molodaia Gvardiia.

Dolutskii, I. (2004) 'Sovremennaia idilliia'. *Neprikosnovennyi zapas* 4 (36).

Dubin, B. and Gudkov, L. (1994) 'Sotsial'nyi protsess i literaturnye obraztsy (o vozmozhnosti sotsiologicheskoi interpretatsii literatury i massovogo chteniia)', in B. Dubin and L. Gudkov, *Literatura kak sotsial'nyi institut. Stat'i po sotsiologii literatury.* Moscow: Novoe literaturnoe obozrenie, pp. 99–151.

Dubin, B. (2009) 'Vremia svidetelei isteklo', *Ogonek,* 21 September. Online. Available: <http://www.kommersant.ru/doc/1235879> (accessed 25 June 2012).

Dubin, B. (2010) 'Simuliativnaia vlast' i ceremonial'naia politika' (first published 2001), in B. Dubin, *Rossiia nulevykh: politicheskaia kul'tura, istoricheskaia pamiat', povsednevnaia zhizn'.* Moscow: ROSSPEN, pp. 233–252.

Etling, B., Alexanyan, K., Kelly, J., Faris, R., Palfrey, J. and Gasser, U. (2010) 'Public Discourse in the Russian Blogosphere: Mapping RuNet Politics and Mobilization', *Berkman Center Research Publication* 2010–2011, 19 October. Online. Available: <http://cyber.law.harvard.edu/sites/cyber.law.harvard.edu/files/Public_Discourse_in_the_Russian_Blogosphere_2010.pdf> (accessed 25 June 2012).

Ferro, M. (1984) *The Use and Abuse of History: How the Past is Taught.* London: Routledge & Kegan Paul.

Gudkov L. (2000, first published; 2004) 'K probleme negativnoi identifikatsii', in L. Gudkov, *Negativnaia identichnost'. Stat'i 1997–2004 godov.* Moscow: VTsIOM-A; Novoe literaturnoe obozrenie, pp. 169–261.

Ermol'tsev, D. and Koliagina, N. (2012) 'Igor' Dolutskii: "Nauchit' rebenka soprotivliat'sia"'. *Uroki istorii XX vek,* 11 April. Online. Available: <http://urokiistorii.ru/learning/edu/3215> (accessed 25 June 2012).

Iaroshenko, D. (2011) 'Nachinat' nado s sebia', 4 September. Online posting. Available: <http://gidepark.ru/user/2710392883/content/798968> (accessed 3 July 2012).

Koposov, N. (2011) *Pamiat' strogogo rezhima.* Moscow: Novoe Literaturnoe Obozrenie.

Kulikova, V.V. and Perlmutter, D.D. (2007) 'Blogging Down the Dictator? The Kyrgyz Revolution and Samizdat Websites'. *International Communication Gazette* 69: 29–50.

Kuraev, A. (**diak-kuraev**) (2009) 'Stalin na Kurskoi', 28 August. Online posting. Available: <http://diak-kuraev.livejournal.com/33678.html> (accessed 2 July 2012).

Lapina-Kratasiuk, E. (2009) 'Politika i mediareal'nost': formirovanie obshchestvennogo mneniia o poslednei kavkazskoi voine'. *Vestnik obshchestvennogo mneniia* 99 (1), January–March: 65–71. Online. Available: <http://ecsocman.hse.ru/data/2010/03/25/1210464065/vom_2009.1_x2899x29_65-71.pdf> (accessed 26 June 2012).

Levinson, A. (2009) 'Vsekh vremen i narodov'. *Neprikosnovennyi zapas* 6 (68).

Levinson, A. (2010) 'Zachem mertvyi Stalin nuzhen zhivym rossiianam?'. *Polit.ru*, 25 March. Online. Available: <http://www.polit.ru/article/2010/03/25/stalin/> (accessed 26 June 2012).

Letter to Yurii Luzhkov (2009) 'Kollektivnoe pis'mo meru g. Moskvy Luzhkovu Iu.M. o sokhranenii imeni Stalina na m. "Kurskaia"'. Online. Available: <http://www.za-stalina.ru/> (accessed 24 June 2012).

Lur'e, V. (ed.) (2012) *Azbuka protesta: narodnyi plakat: po materialam 15 mitingov i aktsii v Moskve i Sankt-Peterburge*. Moscow: O.G.I.; Polit.ru.

Mal'gin, A. (2011) Thread of online discussion. Available: <http://avmalgin.livejournal.com/2724097.html?thread=85235457> (accessed 6 July 2012).

Matveev, Flavian (**flavianos**) (2009) Comment on blog post, 28 August. Online. Available: <http://diak-kuraev.livejournal.com/33678.html?thread=4608398#t4608398> (accessed 3 July 2012).

Miller, A. (2012) 'Istoricheskaia politika v Rossii: novyi povorot?' in A. Miller and M. Lipman (eds) *Istorichekaia politika v XXI veke*. Moscow: Novoe literaturnoe obozrenie, pp. 328–367.

Mitrokhin, N. (2003) *Russkaia partiia: Dvizhenie russkikh natsionalistov v SSSR. 1953–1985*. Moscow: Novoe literaturnoe obozrenie.

Moroz, A. (2012) 'Protestnyi fol'klor dekabria 2011 g. Staroe i novoe'. *Antropologicheskii Forum* 16: 173–192. Online. Available: <http://anthropologie.kunstkamera.ru/files/pdf/016online/moroz2.pdf> (accessed 26 June 2012).

mozg_cow (2009) Comments on blog post, 31 August. Online. Available: <http://diak-kuraev.livejournal.com/33678.html?thread=4608398> (accessed 2 July 2012).

Nikolenko, K. (2011a) 'Berech' istoriiu. Nastupaet prozrenie'. Online posting. Available: <http://nikolenkokir33.livejournal.com/14646.html> (accessed 23 June 2012).

Nikolenko, K. (2011b) 'Istoricheskaia spravedlivost' nachinaet torzhestvovat''. Online posting. Available: <http://ru-stalinizm.livejournal.com/165826.html> (accessed 24 June 2012).

Nikolenko, K. (2011c) 'Zhdem novyi "Kratkii kurs VKP(b)"'. *Argumenty nedeli* (Vladimir-Ivanovo), 26 June. Online. Available: <http://argumenti33.ru/284-Kirill-NIKOLENKO-Zhdem-novyj-Kratkij-kurs-VKP-b.html> (accessed 26 June 2012).

Nosik, A. (2011) 'Look at Yourself', 20 August. Online posting. Available: <http://dolboeb.livejournal.com/2165941.html> (accessed 23 June 2012).

OSCE Resolution (2009) 'Resolution on Divided Europe Reunited: Promoting Human Rights and Civil Liberties in the OSCE Region in the 21st Century'. Online. Available: <www.oscepa.org/members/member-directory/doc_download/261-vilnius-declaration-english+&hl=en&pid=bl&srcid=ADGEEShGW26BDMMq8i9M0_oBrXdeQY19h8> (accessed 26 June 2012).

Otto Pohl, J. (1999) *Ethnic Cleansing in the USSR, 1937–1949*. Westport, CT: Greenwood Press.

Pavlovskii, G. (2012) *Genial'naia vlast'! Slovar' abstraktsii Kremlia*. Moscow: Evropa.

Pernavskii, G. (**Sirjones**) (2010) 'Pro Alekseevu i mordoboi', 1 April. Online posting. Available: <http://sirjones.livejournal.com/1231225.html> (accessed 23 June 2012).

Potapova, N. (2009) 'Shkol'nye uchebniki o noveishei istorii Rossii: poetika i politika'. An analytical report prepared for the project *The Bologna Process and the Democratization of Higher Education in Russia*, St Petersburg. Online. Available: <http://politmemo.ru/publication/school_history_book/> (accessed 23 June 2012).

pppdddnnn (2009) Comment on blog post, 20 March. Online. Available: <http://viklamist.livejournal.com/792653.html?thread=10836557&> (accessed 3 July 2012).

Rogoża, J. (2012) 'The Internet in Russia: The Cradle of Civil Society'. *OSW Commentary* 72, 21 March. Online. Available: <http://www.osw.waw.pl/sites/default/files/commentary_72.pdf> (accessed 26 June 2012).

rst37_2 (2009) Comment on blog post, 31 August. Online. Available: <http://russos.livejournal.com/605782.html?thread=19533398#t19533398> (accessed 2 July 2012).

Popov, A. (**russos**) (2009) '"Kurskaia-kol'tsevaia" – otkryt vestibul'', 25 August. Online posting. Available: <http://russos.livejournal.com/605782.html> (accessed 2 July 2012).

Samover, N. (2011) 'T'ma v kontse tonnelia – 2'. *Arkhnadzor*, 6 February. Online. Available: <http://www.archnadzor.ru/2011/02/06/t-ma-v-kontse-tonnelya-2/> (accessed 26 June 2012).

Schmidt, H. and Teubener, K. (2006) '(Counter)Public Sphere(s) on the Russian Internet', in H. Schmidt, K. Teubener and N. Konradova (eds), *Control + Shift. Public and Private Usages of the Russian Internet.* Norderstedt: Books on Demand, pp. 51–72.

Shliapentokh, V. and Gudkov, L. (2001) Letters to the editor. *Monitoring obshchestvennogo mneniia: ekonomicheskie i sotsial'nye peremeny* 2 (52), March–April: 46–51.

Sokolov, N. (2008) 'Vek surka, ili Kratkaia istoriia kolovrashcheniia rossiiskih uchebnikov istorii'. *Polit.ru,* 15 October. Online. Available: <http://www.polit.ru/article/2008/10/15/history/> (accessed 26 June 2012).

Stromer-Galley, J. and Wichowsky, A. (2011) 'Political Discussions Online' in M. Consalvo and C. Ess (eds), *The Handbook of Internet Studies.* Malden, MA: Oxford: Wiley-Blackwell, pp. 168–187.

Sveshnikov, A. (2004) 'Bor'ba vokrug shkol'nykh uchebnikov istorii v postsovetskoi Rossii: osnovnye tendentsii i rezul'taty'. *Neprikosnovennyi zapas* 4 (36).

Trubina, E. (2010) 'Past Wars in the Russian Blogosphere: On the Emergence of Cosmopolitan Memory'. *Digital Icons. Studies in Russian, Eurasian and Central European New Media* 4: 63–85. Online. Available: <http://www.digitalicons.org/issue04/files/2010/11/Trubina-4.4.pdf> (accessed 26 June 2012).

Vodo, V. and Taratuta, Y. (2009) 'Rossiia popala v plokhuiu istoriiu. OBSE priravniala stalinizm k natsizmu'. *Kommersant*, 2 July. Online. Available: <http://kommersant.ru/doc/1196402> (accessed 26 June 2012).

Yurchak, A. (2006) *Everything Was Forever, Until It Was No More: The Last Soviet Generation.* Princeton, NJ: Princeton University Press.

8 Building Wiki-history

Between consensus and edit warring

Hélène Dounaevsky

Introduction

The Wikipedia historical directory represents an online laboratory where history is continuously being written and rewritten. Hence the 'popular encyclopedia' appears to be one of the major frontlines of the 'memory wars' and at the same time a promising online playground for the study of this phenomenon. The national and linguistic virtual communities that have emerged from the Wikipedia environment compete with each other in terms of quantitative contribution to the project's development, as well as through the production of article content, especially on historical and political issues. These communities are pursuing a double purpose: their activity is an act of national self-assertion inside their own countries and simultaneously a self-representation in the worldwide context. Through Wikipedia's steady growth – and the increasing power of the Internet in general – their activity is making an ever greater impact on the public sphere. In this chapter, we propose to observe how the Wikipedia communal content is created and edited. To this end we will approach the site from the inside, by investigating the 'edit histories' and other behind-the-scenes elements of Wikipedia. More specifically, we will focus on some examples of entries of the Russian-language edition linked to controversial issues in Ukrainian history.[1]

Wikipedia, edit wars and post-Soviet space

Wikipedia is a user-written online encyclopedia freely available on the Web (wikipedia.org). Launched in 2001 as an experimental project, over the course of the next decade, Wikipedia became firmly established as an emblematic service of Web 2.0 and one of the most popular knowledge repositories on the Internet. Currently, in November 2012, Wikipedia contains nearly 23 million articles in 285 languages. Thanks to this unprecedented amount of information, it has become an irreplaceable reference source for many Internet users. The secret of its popularity lies without doubt in its open and interactive interface which invites collective collaboration.

It may be useful to provide some basic information here on how this original and innovative technological model works (for more background on wikis and

Wikipedia see Cunningham 2007; Cummings and Barton 2008: 1–17; Leuf and Cunningham 2001).

Wikipedia is currently the largest and most popular site relying on wiki technology. This application allows any user to become an author and editor of web page content, by creating a new entry or by changing an existing one. At the same time, erased or modified previous content can easily be reinstated through a wiki mechanism which is aimed at enabling the 'self-healing' of the page in question as well as protecting the viability of the project as a whole. In short, version control is the second key distinguishing feature of this wiki technology, after collective authorship.

This option of saving and reverting to previous versions is invaluable for many reasons, but it also has a regrettable side-effect: it enables and even encourages *revert wars* or *edit wars* between editors with disparate perspectives and standpoints. As defined by Wikipedia policy, an edit war occurs 'when editors who disagree about the content of a page repeatedly override each other's contributions, rather than trying to resolve the disagreement by discussion' (Wikipedia: Edit warring). Edit warring is further defined as an 'unconstructive' practice that 'creates animosity between editors, making it harder to reach a consensus' (ibid.). These wars may be more or less extensive, depending on the issue in question.

Objectively speaking, the most edited Wikipedia subjects do not necessarily deal with the most urgent issues that society faces. However, most of the time they reflect the intensity of the controversy in the outside world, as they are devoted to topics affecting people for a variety of different reasons (Wikipedia: List_of_controversial_issues). A similar paradox permeates Ukrainian public space, which has been agitated for years by a set of controversial issues related to the history of the past century. No national consensus having been found during the 20 years of independence in Ukraine, the debates are currently characterized by ongoing 'edit wars', not only on the pages of Wikipedia, but also in the form of official state historical policy. Recently, a number of the former president Victor Yushchenko's historical and commemorative initiatives have been 'cancelled' by the current chief of the Ukrainian state Viktor Yanukovych, elected in February 2010. In March 2010, during a visit to Russia, President Yanukovych announced his intention to reverse, 'before Victory Day' (9 May), his predecessor's decision to honour two controversial nationalists, Stepan Bandera and Roman Shukhevych, as 'Heroes of Ukraine' (*Reuters* 2010). One month later, in April 2010, the Ukrainian president said to the Parliamentary Assembly of the Council of Europe that it was 'unjust' to call the Holodomor (the 1932–1933 Great Famine in Ukraine) a genocide of the Ukrainian people. Yanukovych's statement was interpreted as a complete reversal of the policy of his predecessor Viktor Yushchenko, who sought international recognition of the Holodomor, as an instance of genocide *(RIA Novosti* 2010). A few months later, the designation of the Holodomor as a genocide was called 'an invention of foreign historians' by the Education Minister of Ukraine Dmytro Tabachnyk (*Ukranews* 2010). Under Dmytro Tabachnyk, a re-editing of history textbooks has been undertaken, and some recent interpretations related to modern Ukrainian history have been 'reverted' to earlier – 'Soviet' – versions *(Argumenty-I-Fakty.UA* 2010). Thus, in the new edition of one history textbook, the term 'Great Patriotic War'[2] is restored, and 'an objective picture' of the OUN (the Organization of Ukrainian Nationalists) and UPA (the Ukrainian Insurgent Army) history is drawn (for more details see V"iatrovych 2010). Moreover, an ambitious project aimed at creating a common Ukrainian-Russian history school book has been announced by Minister Tabachnyk.

This immanent openness (and exposure) to the Russian neighbour is another noticeable specificity of Ukrainian historical discourse. Ukraine and Russia are indeed culturally and linguistically close. Within the Internet, Ukrainian and Russian users, who share a common past and, to a greater or lesser extent, language, constitute a *digital diaspora*. The term 'digital diasporas' is used in most digital media studies to describe the online expatriate communities (Brinkerhoff 2009; Everett 2009). This definition makes an awkward fit with the reality of post-Soviet Ukraine, which rather witnesses a digital diaspora as recently revised by the research project *Web Wars*.[3] In this project's definition, digital diaspora, first, encompasses not only migrants but all web users in Russia and Ukraine, and second, it appears as a space of fierce tensions – one where languages of conflict and hatred often prevail over discourses of solidarity or post-colonial hybridity.

Ukrainian linguistic and cultural duality and ambiguity is manifested, within Wikipedia, through the significant contribution of editors from Ukraine (approximately 40 per cent of total edits) to the Russian-language edition (Wikimedia Traffic Analysis Report: Wikipedia Page Edits Per Country). It is especially noticeable through the clear preference of Ukrainian audiences for the Russian language Wikipedia (approximately 65 to 70 per cent of total page views from Ukraine) (Wikimedia Traffic Analysis Report: Wikipedia Page Views Per Country). These Ukrainian readers are presumably attracted primarily by the richer content of the Russian edition: for comparison, in August 2011, Wikipedia contained 307,573 articles in Ukrainian (1,636 active editors) versus 752,949 articles in Russian (11,328 active editors) (Wikimedia: Wikipedia Statistics: Article count). Needless to say, this imbalance is perceived as a challenge by those sections of the Ukrainian language community who are actively involved in the struggle for Ukrainian 'informational independence'. Indeed, in independent Ukraine, Russian remains the dominant language in many spheres of daily life, including the Internet.[4] Yuri Perohanych, Executive Director of Wikimedia-Ukraine, speaks in this connection of a 'neo-info-lingo-imperialism' (Perohanych 2011). As a counter to this imperialism, Perohanych holds up the historical model of the *Prosvita* ('enlightenment') society, created in the nineteenth century for the purpose of the preservation and promotion of Ukrainian culture in an unfavourable environment. Today, Perohanych argues, it is the mission of the Ukrainian Wikipedia to educate people and to continue Prosvita's struggle for the survival and viability of the Ukrainian language (*Slovo Prosvity* 2011).

If the Ukrainian Wikipedia is thus employed in national identity construction, the same is true for its Russian sibling. Russian speakers are enthusiastic contributors to Wikipedia, and the Russian Wikipedia ranks among the world's ten most developed editions (List of Wikipedias). Unlike the Polish Wikipedia,[5] which also features among the world's top ten Wikipedias, the Russian Wikipedia does not benefit from direct support from the state, but it has triggered significant interest from the Russian authorities. In June 2011, for example, at the initiative of Russian President Dmitrii Medvedev, the *RIA Novosti* media agency jointly with Wikimedia-Russia launched the *Eternal Values* project. Under this project, images from the *RIA Novosti* archive are released to the public under free licences. The first batch of materials to be transferred under the scheme was a collection of photographs from the Great Patriotic War (*Sociable.co* 2011). Reportedly Dmitrii Medvedev himself uploaded some images to the site (*Wikipedia Signpost* 2011). The President has underlined the great importance of the project for preserving the memory of the war and the sacrifice of Soviet soldiers *(RIA Novosti* 2011).

For the Russian-language community, the large-scale presence of Ukrainian editors is profitable in terms of quantitative contribution. Russian users produce the majority of edits to the Russian Wikipedia (approximately 70 per cent), but Ukrainian users also make a substantial contribution here, producing the second-highest number of edits by country (roughly 12 per cent) (Wikimedia Traffic Analysis Report: Page Edits Per Wikipedia Language). The Ukrainian presence has, however, generated tensions over some sensitive issues related to Ukrainian history and politics. As a transnational space open to the intervention of any Russian speaker (Russian remains *lingua franca* of the post-Soviet space), the Russian Wikipedia is distinguished by intensive and virulent edit wars, in particular related to entries dealing with the recent shared Russian-Ukrainian past. Below, we will observe how these debates take shape by examining some examples of controversial historical entries. Without attempting to directly evaluate the quality of the content of these entries, we will rather focus on so-called *meta pages*,[6] examining the 'edit history' of the entries and active contributors' profiles.

A survey: post-Soviet Wikipedia and memory wars

Note first that Wikipedia constitutes extremely rich source material for the researcher studying the post-Soviet memory wars. Through its very large dataset and its transparent structure, the site makes it possible to follow page history in detail – discussion ('talk') pages are archived – and to trace each conflict history and each editor's contribution (through the 'edit history' pages). Through user profile pages, the site also provides a vast amount of information, more or less reliable, on its editors: place of birth, native language, country of residence, education level, political leanings, interests and hobbies, personal contribution to the project, awards granted by the Wikipedia community, etc. Frequently, one can also find less relevant information, including preferences about music, books, and even eating habits.

To judge from these profile pages, the post-Soviet users would appear to be characterized by especially high levels of performativity. Many of them do not hesitate to exhibit, through so-called *userboxes*, their strong identity rooting, along with ostentatious proclamations of their ideological commitments. A userbox is a small coloured box on a Wikipedian's user page, which serves as a communicative notice about the user (Wikipedia: Userboxes). Conceived to help the collaboration on articles, userboxes can, however, be potentially divisive. Often they boast provocative content that is capable of generating significant tension among Wikipedia editors and of increasing the temperature of the debate. Currently, this *userbox-mania* is tending to decrease on Russian Wikipedia, being systematically repressed by administrators, but it is still thriving in the Ukrainian edition.[7] Here are some examples of 'political' userboxes used by members of the Russian and particularly Ukrainian Wikipedia communities: *This user identifies as a Communist; This user is against communism; This user identifies as a Ukrainian Nationalist; This user is a Russian patriot; This user supports the independence of Chechnya; This user opposes the independence of Kosovo*, etc.

Within Wikipedia, the debates frequently focus on various controversial issues related to Ukraine, starting from simple disagreements over the spelling of geographical names, which may differ depending on the reference language, Russian or Ukrainian: *Kiev/Kyiv, Kharkov/Kharkiv, na Ukraine/v Ukraine*,[8] etc. It is interesting to note that the case of Kiev/Kyiv (the capital of Ukraine) is also quoted within Wikipedia's list of the lamest edit wars in the English edition (Wikipedia: Lamest edit wars).

Tensions can take the shape of ongoing drawn-out conflicts on a transnational scale (unofficially called *holyvory* in Russian Internet parlance, from the English 'holy wars'); online 'battles' of various kinds (the Battle for the Ukrainian State Navy,[9] the Battle for Khar'kov,[10] the Mazepa Campaign[11]), and multiple foci of long-term warfare.

The military analogy that resounds in these terms is also embodied in the system of awarding Wiki Barnstars to the most active contributors. Our examples include the *Ukrainian Barnstar* ('I give you this Ukraine Barnstar for improving the Russia–Ukraine gas disputes article'); the barnstar *For Bravery* ('You are hereby awarded this Ukrainian National Award "For Bravery" in recognition of your contributions to Ukraine-related historical articles, insistence on credibly sourced statements, and fight against vandalism'); the *Russian Order of Glory Dedicated to WW2, National Merit – Russia*, etc.

Traditionally, subjects linked to Ukrainian history are among the most edited entries within the Russian-language Wikipedia. A list of the hottest historical topics (excluding individual historical figures) is given below. Here one can find the inevitable UPA (Ukrainian Insurgent Army) and Holodomor (Great Famine in Ukraine) entries, devoted to the most divisive issues of current Russian–Ukrainian political and historical debates. It is also relevant to note that the overwhelming majority of the top 15 most edited historical entries either deals explicitly and elaborately with the Russian–Ukrainian relationship, or affects, in one way or another, both Russian and Ukrainian camps (for instance, the *Armed conflict in South Ossetia* is a topic of discord between Russians and Ukrainians and one of the sensitive areas of their confrontation).

In theory, a growing number of edits should normally lead to an improvement in the content (see Lih 2004). When applied to wiki articles, however, this general

Table 8.1 The most edited historical articles of Russian-language Wikipedia (for the integral list of pages with the most revisions see: Wikimedia: Wikipedia Statistics Russian: Most edited articles)

Total number of edits	*Percentage of edits by registered users*	*Registered users–unregistered unique IP addresses*[12]	*Entry title*
5446	15	38–39	History of the Lak people
4396	96	384–102	Armed conflict in South Ossetia (2008)
2496	77	261–265	Civil War in Russia
2448	92	222–116	Katyn' Massacre
2147	75	348–370	Great Patriotic War
2053	71	356–383	Second World War
2048	92	194–111	Russian Language in Ukraine
2013	82	384–211	USSR
1986	83	188–151	Ukrainian Insurgent Army (UPA)
1895	98	45–15	Territorial-Political Expansion of the Third Reich
1852	82	209–147	Holodomor in Ukraine
1744	82	167–150	Dissolution of Russian Supreme Soviet
1697	99	66–6	Austrian-Prussian-Italian War
1651	97	208–33	Red Army's Polish Campaign
1651	98	43–19	Jews in Second World War

rule seems to show its limits in the case of those articles which have become the casualties of severe edit wars. Such articles often make their way into Wikipedia's 'NPOV Disputes' category. 'NPOV' stands for 'Neutral Point of View', and is one of Wikipedia's three core principles. This basic rule states that 'all Wikipedia articles and other encyclopedic content must be written from a neutral point of view', representing significant views 'fairly, proportionately and as far as possible without bias' (Wikipedia: Neutral Point of View). When an article is deemed to have failed to meet these criteria, it may be listed in Wikipedia's 'NPOV Disputes' category, and many Ukrainian history pages have indeed made their way into this category.

When an instance of imbalanced coverage is identified on Wikipedia, the page or section in question is flagged as likely to contain controversial content. Special banners are intended to alert readers: this is a controversial topic provoking heated disputes between participants. We can go further and measure the temperature of the debate by taking some technical information from the edit history pages. Table 8.2 presents this information for a number of key contested topics. Here, one can see the following picture: thousands of revisions (cf. the Russian edition's mean number of 34 revisions per article [Wikimedia: Wikipedia Statistics: Edits per article]), hundreds of participants, and dozens of mobilized watchers. The watchers are members having added the given page to their *watch-list*. A watch-list works as an alerting mechanism allowing close monitoring of pages deemed to be vulnerable to vandalism and edit warring.

Table 8.2 Examples of disputed topics (based on data from 10 August 2011).

Subject entries (nodes)	*Number of edits*	*Number of unique editors*	*Number of watchers*
Ukrainian Insurgent Army	2444	469 (228 IP addresses)	78
Holodomor	1982	413 (147 IP addresses)	92
Russian Liberation Army	506	238 (111 IP addresses)	34
October Revolution	1653	357 (179 IP addresses)	75

It is obvious from this table that the Ukrainian history problematic tends to affect members of the Russian-language Wikipedia community more strongly than some disputed subjects of modern Russian history (such as the Russian Liberation Army and the October Revolution). One explanation for this paradoxical observation may lie in the strong political use and abuse of sensitive issues of Ukrainian history inside both countries. The high temperature of the debate may also be a symptom of the presence of Ukrainian *POV-warriors* within the Russian Wikipedia. The position of these warriors, promoting their biased 'points of view', frequently collides with the prevailing Russian vision (shared by a considerable part of the Ukrainian population) of the historical realities in question that hardly seems impartial either.

We can flesh the picture out further through an analysis of the user profiles of these pages' editors. In the case of the UPA entry, the four most prolific users were identified as having contributed an unusually large number of edits (over 100) (History statistics: User statistics for UPA page). These 'very active' contributors show, however, diverging positions and highly conflicting ideological values: two of them defend 'Ukrainian nationalist' positions and the other two are opponents of 'Ukrainian nationalism' and proponents of Soviet or *gosudarstvennicheskii* (in favour of a strong Russian state) historical narratives. One of these users is also actively involved in the Holodomor page, where he has produced the greatest number of edits (History statistics: User statistics for Holodomor page), promoting his content and advancing his strong 'points of view' (a practice known as *POV-pushing)*. This author, as we can see from his edits list below, maintains a strong conscious focus on the Ukrainian problematic and shows a systematic bias toward subjects linked to the most sensitive Ukrainian history issues.

228 – Holomodor_in_Ukraine
216 – Ukrainian Insurgent Army
88 – Collectivization
84 – Shukhevych_Roman Iosypovych (Ukrainian nationalist leader, commander-in-chief of the UPA)
70 – 14th Grenadier Division of the SS 'Galician' (1st Ukrainian) (currently *Diviziia SS Galichina*)
64 – Ukrainian Collaborationism in the Second World War
64 – Organization of Ukrainian Nationalists (Banderite movement)
52 – Holodomor_in_Politics

47 – USSR Census of Population (1937)
42 – *Prodrazvërstka* (the Bolshevik forced food-requisitioning policy)

(The figures in the left column indicate the number of edits.)

On 25 December 2009, this user was blocked for an indefinite period as an undesirable author (Wikipedia: Special: Block Log: User: Jo0doe), but he will likely go down in the history of the Russian Wikipedia as the member making one of the most controversial contributions to the project, through unethical editing, destructive attitude, edit warring, and the online practice known as trolling.[13]

Finally, pages themselves may be blocked by administrators with the purpose of protecting them against vandalism and edit warring (see Wikipedia: Protection policy). Thus, today the Holodomor page has 11 (since 2005, when the article was started) (Wikipedia: Special: Protection Log: Holodomor-na-Ukraine) and the UPA page has 12 (since 2005) protections (Wikipedia: Special: Protection Log: UPA). The very large number of page protections clearly highlights the strong conflict potential of the topics in question and their vulnerability to persistent edit warring. Protected pages are no longer publicly editable, while the warring parties are invited to discuss their differences on the talk page, where they can (in theory) reach consensus. In protecting a page, the administrator is normally attempting to prevent an edit war. Sometimes, however, the decision to protect or 'unprotect' a page depends on the administrator's own position in content disputes and on his individual preferences for one or another article version. In such cases, the protection is in fact nothing more than yet another offensive in a drawn-out war.

Wikipedia's 'exercises in history'

Clearly, this kind of content should be evaluated not in terms of final product quality, but rather as an ongoing act of collective creativity. For our purposes, the most fascinating aspect of this online collaboration is embedded in the process itself, rather than in the result. This process may be defined as 'Exercises in History', to cite the title of Ukrainian historian Andriy Portnov's recent book (Portnov 2010) devoted to the 'Ukrainian style' of debates about history. Portnov argues that the concurrence of different models of memory preserves the pluralism of Ukrainian public space: since neither competing camp is in a position to attain a definitive hegemonic status for its point of view, this public space remains 'pluralistic by necessity'.

At the same time, Wikipedia itself could be depicted as an ideal laboratory where a special type of historical knowledge is being produced – uncertain, doubting, fundamentally pluralistic, polyphonic, constantly changing, and never finalized, accomplished, definitive or hegemonic. This 'non-expert knowledge' (see Foglia 2008) would appear to be completely foreign to the descendants of totalitarian ideologies, but at the same time it seems to offer the promise that this stale mentality may eventually be overcome.

To conclude, we would like to turn back to the initial question animating the authors of this volume: *How is the Soviet experience mediated in digital spheres?* How could our observation of Wikipedia memory-related practices contribute to this discussion? Thus, what does wiki-mediated memory look like? And, more specifically, what does wiki-mediated memory of the Soviet past look like? How does this memory evolve in this new digital environment of Web 2.0 services? And what does it become in this 'global memory place' (Pierre Nora: *lieu de mémoire*) in cyberspace that is Wikipedia, according to Christian Pentzold (2009)?

The present study is far from having the ambition to provide any definitive or clear-cut answer to these complex questions. Instead, we might note – as a preliminary and rather intuitive observation – that this web-mediated memory certainly has more in common with a flowing river than it does with the Bronze Soldier[14] standing guard over the sacrosanct Soviet past. Fluid, dynamic and transient, it stands in opposition to the traditional, 'archaic' memory embodied in the frozen monuments of stone and bronze, erected once and for all, for eternity. Mobile, unstable and multi-facial, 'constructed on-the-fly', it appears closer to 'a living archival memory' as described by Andrew Hoskins (2011: 92). This new kind of memory that emerges from the online environment develops according its own – 'digital network' – logic, emancipated from traditional memory-related practices. Thus, it does not need to be 'protected',[15] and nor does it fear any 'falsification',[16] since being constantly written and rewritten is in its very nature. Indeed, for some online memory warriors, this very fluidity of digital content, along with the immanent openness and interactivity of Web 2.0 in general, may be something that only serves to heighten anxiety. Their memory about the past could be figuratively likened to the famous Brest Fortress, and the Wikipedia practices described here are aimed precisely at protecting this 'memory fortress'. The whole fight for one's own version of the past history, animated by old totalitarian reflexes, appears, however, to be in dramatic contradiction with the very nature of the new digital environment, where, once again metaphorically speaking, rock is slowly but surely eroded by dripping water.

Despite the fact that the picture drawn in this chapter may look a little gloomy, we do remain optimistic about the future – or maybe even utopian, since we are going to quote Richard Buckminster Fuller and his famous line on the power of technology: 'If you want to teach people a new way of thinking, don't bother trying to teach them. Instead, give them a tool, the use of which will lead to new ways of thinking.' The Wiki-tool, by structurally inviting communal editing (*wiki writing*), tolerating dissent and favouring consensus building (Cummings and Barton 2008), seems to be just such an instrument: a kind of simulator for 'exercises in history'.

Notes

1 This chapter is based on empirical data from August 2011.

2 The term is used inside the former Soviet Union to describe, from the official Soviet perspective, the events that took place in the period from 22 June 1941 to 9 May 1945 during the Second World War.

3 Web Wars: Digital Diasporas and the Language of Memory in Russia & Ukraine, project description available online on <www.web-wars.org>.
4 For further information on this problem see, among others, Besters-Dilger 2009.
5 As a Polish NGO, Wikimedia Polska benefits from a part of the funds – 1 per cent – coming from Polish taxpayers. For further details see: <http://opp.wikimedia.pl/> (accessed 20 April 2012). See also Public benefit organization <http://en.wikipedia.org/wiki/Public_benefit_organization> (accessed 20 April 2012).
6 Additional pages associated with every main content page and containing meta-information about this page.
7 A picturesque example of this userbox-mania: <http://uk.wikipedia.org/wiki/Користувач:Тарас_Чекан/Юзербокси> (accessed 20 April 2012). See also <http://uk.wikipedia.org/wiki/Вікіпедія:Шаблони/Користувачі/Переконання> (accessed 20 April 2012).
8 In Russian and Ukrainian, preposition usage with the name of this country is often an ideological rather than a linguistic choice.
9 Bitva za ukrainskii derzhavnyj flot *(Битва за Украинский Державный Флот)* is an editing conflict surrounding the entry devoted to the Ukrainian Navy during the period 1917 to 1919. In the Russian edition, the article is still disputed. At the same time, its Ukrainian language version is quoted among featured articles of Wikipedia.
10 Bitva za Khar'kov *(Битва за Харьков)* is a Wikipedia conflict about the spelling of this Ukrainian city, the name of which differs depending on the language, namely Russian or Ukrainian.
11 Mazepa-kampaniia (*Мазепа-кампания*): this large-scale dispute deals with the contribution of the user **Mazepa11**, devoted to the controversial Ukrainian historical personality Ivan Mazepa.
12 Wikipedia can be edited by both registered and anonymous users. Registered users are logged under their user names, while anonymous contributors are identified only by IP address.
13 'Trolling is any *deliberate and intentional* attempt to disrupt the usability of Wikipedia for its editors, administrators, developers, and other people who work to create content for and help run Wikipedia. Trolling is a violation of the implicit rules of Internet social spaces and is often done to inflame or invite conflict' (Wikimedia: What is Troll?).
14 Soviet monument in Tallinn centre, cause of a large-scale conflict between Russian and Estonian communities.
15 For example, the initiative of ex-president Yushchenko concerning the public denial of the Holodomor as an instance of genocide.
16 We have in mind primarily the Russian Presidential Commission to Counter Attempts to Falsify History to the Detriment of Russia's Interests, created in May 2009 and disbanded in 2012.

References

Argumenty-I-Fakty.UA (2010) 'Reformy ot Tabachnika' (Реформы от Табачника), 28 May. Online. Available: <http://www.aif.ua/politic/article/19382> (accessed 20 April 2012).

Besters-Dilger, J. (ed.) (2009) *Language Policy and Language Situation in Ukraine: Analysis and Recommendations*. Frankfurt am Main: Peter Lang.

Brinkerhoff, J. (ed.) (2009) *Digital Diasporas: Identity and Transnational Engagement*. Cambridge: Cambridge University Press.

Bryant, S.L., Forte, A. and Bruckman, A. (2005) 'Becoming Wikipedian: Transformation of Participation in a Collaborative Online Encyclopedia'. *Group'05, Sanibel Island, FL, USA*.

Cummings, R.E. and Barton, M. (eds) (2008) *Wiki Writing: Collaborative Learning in the College Classroom*. Ann Arbor: University of Michigan Press.

Cunningham, W. (2007) *Wiki Design Principles*. Online. Available: <http://c2.com/cgi/wiki?WikiDesignPrinciples> (accessed 20 April 2012).

Everett, A. (2009) *Digital Diaspora: A Race for Cyberspace*. New York: State University of New York Press.

Foglia, M. (2008) *Wikipédia média de la connaissance démocratique? Quand le citoyen lambda devient encyclopédiste*. Limoges: FYP éditions.

Garde-Hansen, J. *et al.* (eds) (2009) *Save as ... Digital Memories*. Basingstoke: Palgrave Macmillan.

Hoskins, A. (2009) 'Digital Network Memory', in A. Erll and A. Rigney (eds), *Mediation, Remediation, and the Dynamics of Cultural Memory*. Berlin: Walter de Gruyter, pp. 91–106.

Hoskins, A. (2011) 'Anachronisms of Media, Anachronisms of Memory: From Collective Memory to New Memory Ecology', in M. Nieger, O. Meyers and E. Zandberg (eds) *On Media Memory: Collective Memory in a New Media Age*. Series: Palgrave Macmillan Memory Studies. Basingstoke: Palgrave.

Leuf, B. and Cunningham, W. (2001) *The Wiki Way: Quick Collaboration on the Web*. Boston, MA: Addison-Wesley Professional.

Lih, A. (2004) 'Wikipedia as Participatory Journalism: Reliable Sources? Metrics for Evaluating Collaborative Media as a News Resource'. *Proceedings of Fifth International Symposium on Online Journalism*, 16–17 April, UT Austin.

List of Wikipedias (2012) Online. Available: <http://s23.org/wikistats/wikipedias_html> (accessed 20 April 2012).

Olick, J.K. (2003) 'Introduction', in J.K. Olick, *States of Memory. Continuities, Conflicts, and Transformations in National Retrospection*. Durham, NC, and London: Duke University Press, pp. 1–16.

Pentzold, C. (2009) 'Fixing the Floating Gap: The Online Encyclopaedia Wikipedia as a Global Memory Place'. *Memory Studies* 2(2): 255–272.

Perohanych, Y. (2011) 'Neoinfo/lingvoimperializm v Evropi' (Неоінфо/лінгвоімперіалізм в Європі). Paper presented at the International Conference *Information Technologies and Security*, 26 May, Kyiv. Online. Available: <http://wikimediaukraine.files.wordpress.com/2011/05/wiki-neo-info-imperializm-2011.ppt> (accessed 20 April 2012).

Portnov, A. (2010) *Uprazhneniia s istoriei po-ukrainski* [Exercises in History Ukrainian-Style]. Moscow: OGI, Polit.ru, 'Memorial'.

Reuters (2010) 'Yanukovych to Strip Nationalists of Hero Status', 5 March. Online. Available: <http://www.kyivpost.com/news/nation/detail/61110/> (accessed 20 April 2012).

RIA Novosti (2010) 'Yanukovych Reverses Ukraine's Position on Holodomor Famine', 27 April. Online. Available: <http://en.rian.ru/exsoviet/20100427/158772431.html> (accessed 20 April 2012).

RIA Novosti (2011) 'Medvedev zapustil proekt, otkryvaiushchii dostup k fotoarkhivu RIA Novosti', 23 June. Online. Available: <http://ria.ru/ria70_news/20110623/392115320.html> (accessed 20 April 2012).

Slovo Prosvity (2011) 'Yuri Perohanych: "Vid Vikipedii zalezhyt' maibutnie movy"', *Slovo Prosvity* 31 (616), 4–10 August 2011, p. 10. Online. Available: <http://slovoprosvity.org/pdf/2011/slovo2011–31.pdf > (accessed 20 April 2012).

Sociable.co (2011) 'Wikimedia Uploads Previously Unpublished Photographs from the Second World War', 22 August. Online. Available: <http://sociable.co/web/wikimedia-uploads-previously-unpublished-photographs-from-the-second-world-war/> (accessed 20 April 2012).

Ukranews (2010) 'Tabachnyk: Holodomor 1932–1933 rokiv v Ukraini ne buv henotsydom ukrains'kogo narodu', 31 August. Online. Available: <http://ukranews.com/uk/news/ukraine/2010/08/31/25948> (accessed 20 April 2012).

V"iatrovych, V. (2010) 'Back to URSS, abo mystetstvo vytynanky z pidruchnyka istorii'. *Ukranews*, 1 September. Online. Available: <http://ukranews.com/uk/article/2010/09/01/228> (accessed 20 April 2012).

Wikimedia Traffic Analysis Report – Page Edits Per Wikipedia Language – Breakdown. Online. Available: <http://stats.wikimedia.org/wikimedia/squids/SquidReportPageEditsPerLanguageBreakdown.htm> (accessed 20 April 2012).

Wikimedia Traffic Analysis Report – Wikipedia Page Edits Per Country – Breakdown. Online. Available: <http://stats.wikimedia.org/wikimedia/squids/SquidReportPageEditsPerCountryBreakdown.htm> (accessed 20 April 2012).

Wikimedia Traffic Analysis Report – Wikipedia Page Views Per Country – Breakdown. Online. Available: <http://stats.wikimedia.org/wikimedia/squids/SquidReportPageViewsPerCountryBreakdown.htm> (accessed 20 April 2012).

Wikimedia: What is Troll? (2012) Online. Available: <http://meta.wikimedia.org/wiki/What_is_a_troll%3F> (accessed 20 April 2012).

Wikimedia: Wikipedia Statistics: Article Count (2011) Online. Available: <http://stats.wikimedia.org/EN/TablesArticlesTotal.htm> (accessed 20 April 2012). Data from 10 August 2011.

Wikimedia: Wikipedia Statistics: Edits per Article (2011) Online. Available: <http://stats.wikimedia.org/EN/TablesArticlesEditsPerArticle.htm> (accessed 20 April 2012).

Wikimedia: Wikipedia Statistics Russian: Most Edited Articles (2011) Online. Available: <http://stats.wikimedia.org/EN/TablesWikipediaArticleEditsRU.htm> (accessed 20 April 2012). Data from 29 May 2011.

Wikipedia: Wikipedia (2012) Online. Available: <http://en.wikipedia.org/wiki/Wikipedia> (accessed 20 April 2012).

Wikipedia: Edit Warring. Online (2011) Available: <http://en.wikipedia.org/wiki/Wikipedia:Edit_warring> (accessed 20 April 2012).

Wikipedia: Lamest Edit Wars (2011) Online. Available: <http://en.wikipedia.org/wiki/Wikipedia:Lamest_edit_wars> (accessed 20 April 2012).

Wikipedia: List_of_Controversial_Issues (2011) Online. Available: <http://en.wikipedia.org/wiki/Wikipedia:List of_controversial_issues> (accessed 20 April 2012).

Wikipedia: Neutral Point of View (2011) Online. Available: <http://en.wikipedia.org/wiki/Wikipedia:Neutral_point_of_view> (accessed 20 April 2012) .

Wikipedia Page History Statistics: User Statistics for UPA Page (Russian edition) (2011) Online. Available: <http://vs.aka-online.de/cgi-bin/wppagehiststat.pl?lang=ru.wikipedia&page=Украинская_повстанческая_армия> (accessed 20 April 2012). Data from 10 August 2011.

Wikipedia Page History Statistics: User Statistics for Holodomor Page (Russian edition) (2011) Online. Available: <http://vs.aka-online.de/cgi-bin/wppagehiststat.pl?lang=ru.wikipedia&page=Голодомор_на_Украине> (accessed 20 April 2012). Data from 10 August 2011.

Wikipedia: Protection Policy (2011) Online. Available: <http://en.wikipedia.org/wiki/Wikipedia:Protection_policy> (accessed 20 April 2012).

Wikipedia Signpost (2011) 'Russian President Uploads to Wikimedia Commons; Brief News', 28 June. Online. Available: <http://en.wikipedia.org/wiki/Wikipedia: Wikipedia_Signpost/2011-06-27/In_the_news> (accessed 20 April 2012).

Wikipedia: Special: Block Log: User: Jo0doe (2011) Online. Available: <http://ru.wikipedia.org/w/index.php?title=Служебная:Журналы&page=Участник%3AJo0doe&type=block> (accessed 20 April 2012).

Wikipedia: Special: Protection Log: Holodomor-na-Ukraine (2011) Online. Available: <http://ru.wikipedia.org/w/index.php?title=Служебная:Журналы&type=protect&user=&page=Голодомор+на+Украине&year=&month=-1&tagfilter=&hide_review_log=1> (accessed 20 April 2012).

Wikipedia: Special: Protection Log: UPA (2011) Online. Available: <http://ru.wikipedia.org/w/index.php?title=Служебная:Журналы&type=protect&user=&page=Украинская+повстанческая+армия&year=&month=-1&tagfilter=&hide_review_log=1> (accessed 20 April 2012).

Wikipedia: Userboxes (2011) Online. Available: <http://en.wikipedia.org/wiki/Wikipedia:Userboxes> (accessed 20 April 2012).

9 News framing under conditions of unsettled conflict

An analysis of Georgian online and print news around the 2008 Russo–Georgian War[1]

Doreen Spörer-Wagner

Introduction

With the formal dissolution of the Soviet Union in December 1991, 15 former Soviet republics became independent states. Among the many challenges faced by these new states was the task of creating a common national identity. This task is especially urgent, but also especially complex in ethnically divided societies with their heightened potential for violent conflict (Holsti 1996; Talentino 2004; see also Deutsch and Foltz 1966; O'Loughlin and Toal 2009).

In the post-Soviet space, we can find several examples of war-torn societies. One of them is Georgia. Since its early days of independence, the status of South Ossetia and Abkhazia has been an issue of conflict. While the two regions see themselves as independent political entities, Georgia considers them to be integral parts of its state territory. This clash of viewpoints resulted in secessionist movements which led to civil wars in the separatist regions in the early 1990s. Although ceasefire agreements were signed in the 1990s, neither side accepted the other's claims to sovereignty. This frozen ethno-territorial conflict resulted in the 2008 Russo–Georgian War, after Russia moved to provide armed support to the separatists.[2] The war demonstrated that the Georgian, South Ossetian and Abkhaz people had failed to create an overarching national identity, and, furthermore, it obscured the fact that under Soviet rule the ethnic groups on Georgian territory had lived together peacefully. In addition, the 2008 war renewed Georgian fears of Russian hegemony. The question that arises, then, is how the affected people's attitudes towards each other can be shaped favourably, especially when they are struggling to overcome the divisive legacy of past conflicts.

This is where the media come into play. The transfer of information between groups of people is crucial for the creation of a shared national consciousness (Hippler 2005; Anderson 2006). Various channels of communication enable people to 'think together, see together, and act together' (Taylor 2000: 188). Even though each new mode of communication allows more rapid dissemination of national ideas (Kuntsman 2010), it is an open empirical question whether new media work in a similar way to traditional media, such as the press, in promoting national unity.

In times of crisis, when people have more need for information, online as opposed to print news media offer instant and less censored access to political information. Online technologies also allow the cheap storage of information (Dimitrova *et al.* 2005; Garde-Hansen *et al.* 2009) which enables journalists – and, indeed, members of the wider public – to easily recall events of the past (see Reljic 1998). Through journalists' news framing, people are provided with interpretations of events and issues such as conflict situations, ethnic differences or past terrors. Yet to create a shared national identity among the former warring parties, news needs to be reframed to incorporate and value/evaluate differences and pluralities of past enemies. This is a difficult endeavour in situations of unsettled conflict – situations in which mistrust and fear of new violence characterize daily life. The decentralization and diversity of new media allow all opposing groups to present and promote their versions of events and points of view. Print media, by contrast, are more limited to official interpretations, which result from the complex transition of political and economic institutions in post-socialist countries (see Karklins 1994).

This study seeks to clarify whether and to what extent Georgian online and print news media differ in framing the unsettled conflict between Georgia, its separatist regions and Russia. I selected 784 news articles from Civil.ge (online) and *Rezonansi* (press) in the years 2006 to 2010 and approached this material with two hypotheses: first, under conditions of violent conflict, news is more likely to be presented in memory-related frames than in situations of non-violent conflict; and second, online news media as opposed to print news media are more likely to present news in memory-related frames. My key finding was that memory-related frames play a minor role in both selected Georgian news media. What is more, online and print articles have similar framing patterns, although variations across them may be found along with the phases of the unsettled conflict.

News framing in times of war and peace

It is widely held in conflict research that the news media contribute to the outbreak and course of wars (see Reljic 1998). Looked at another way, this means that peace building can also be affected by the news media. If they facilitate the free flow of information and the dissemination of ideas within society, then this may increase the possibilities for holding free and fair elections, controlling the government, making civil society's voices heard and, at best, building a shared national identity regardless of citizens' ethnic backgrounds (Howard 2002a). Nevertheless, nationalistic ideas can also flourish under conditions of media freedom (Morozov 2011).

In times of war, old and new media can serve as an instrument of power for the conflicting parties to strengthen intra-group relations and to legitimize intergroup violence (Wimmer 2008; Kuntsman 2010; Morozov 2011). War reporting is conflict-biased and partisan news tends to cause distortions and misperceptions in the public which (further) incite fear, hatred and violence (Reljic 1998; Lynch and McGoldrick 2005; Peleg 2006). But online media can also intensify tensions between conflicting groups as they enable group members to come together and to disseminate their own versions of reality relatively easily (Morozov 2011). In line with this rationale, traditional media peace researchers who do not distinguish between old and new media – and, as a consequence, do not consider the diversity of new media, which varies from blogs to online news – stress that media which represent different views on any conflict situation can create opportunities for reconciliation as they allow the public to make reasonable political choices (McCombs 1994; Howard 2002a; Lynch and McGoldrick 2005).

News media provide a framework for the interpretation of political events and issues. These news frames are an 'organizing mechanism for media content' (Dimitrova and Connolly-Ahern 2007: 155) and contribute to the construction of social reality by giving meaning to words (McCombs and Ghanem 2003). By emphasizing certain aspects of an issue or an event while neglecting others, news frames serve as conceptual tools to transfer, interpret and evaluate information (Entman 1993). They represent beliefs held by the public at large and are shaped by social factors such as culture and tradition (Jha-Nambiar 2002). News frames affect public perceptions of risk and of political issues, each of which is crucial for successful nation building (Kahneman 1984; Saris 1997).

News content differs significantly in times of war and peace. War news is characterized by increased patriotism; it emphasizes the arena of conflict as opposed to other topics, and it proceeds from a closed space and limited time frame, and so makes the war opaque (Reljic 1998; Peleg 2006). News media also tend to focus on shared group ideas such as collective memory and history which are expected to disturb the prospects for the creation of a common national identity (Reljic 1998).

Based on the general assumption that news frames can change over time, in transitions from war to peace the reframing of conflict-oriented news into de-escalating news is not only crucial but also likely (Iyengar 1991; Howard 2002b). Journalists who take into account the causes and courses of conflict start the reframing process with a critical but neutral reporting before they completely avoid news frames which prevailed in times of war. More precisely, instead of stressing the terrors of war inflicted by the former enemies, causes, responsibilities and consequences of the conflict are explored; instead of blaming only one side for war crimes, untruths and suffering on all sides are identified; and instead of insisting on pre-war political goals, new approaches to conflict resolution are considered (Kempf 2002; Lynch and McGoldrick 2005; Peleg 2006).

Unfortunately, (news) media research does not specify transitions from war to peace to an adequate extent either theoretically or empirically. As observed in Georgia, it is possible that even after a civil war has ended, the resolution of underlying disputes (ethno-territorial claims) may be delayed and may cause a recurrence of violence at any time (as in the August 2008 war). I therefore suggest specifying situations of unsettled conflict by distinguishing periods of violence (ranging from single armed incidents to war) and non-violence (frozen conflict or cold peace). Furthermore, since we might reasonably expect that collective memory and history tend to play a more important role in phases of violent conflict than in peacetime for societies with heavily contested national identities, I posit the following hypothesis (which I propose both for the Georgian case and as a globally applicable paradigm):

Hypothesis 1

Under conditions of violent conflict, news is more likely to be presented in memory-related frames than it is in situations of non-violent conflict.

I use the term *memory-related frames* to refer to news media tools that allow for an interpretation of events and issues from the perspective of the past. I hypothesize that frequent references to past conflicts and contested views of history make conflict resolution more difficult. From a political point of view the war may be at an end, but whether or not the underlying conflict can be settled effectively remains an open question. I am sceptical on this point because I anticipate an intensification of the hitherto tense relations between the conflicting groups, hampering the formation of a shared national identity.

Conflict framing in online and print news media

In wartime, people experience a stronger need for information in general, and for interpretations of information in particular. The online revolution has significantly improved people's access to political information. However, it has also established a platform for diverse interpretations of events and issues that can polarize rather than unify people under conditions of conflict.

The Internet creates a virtual public sphere.[3] It allows users to question and comment on mainstream information disseminated by traditional media which are subject to constraints such as privileged access for political elites as opposed to other social groups (Dimitrova *et al.* 2005). By offering a vast amount of extra information such as expert opinions, background stories or source documents, it exposes users to different viewpoints which exceed the capacities of print media. However, the downside may be that inexperienced users cannot manage the flood of information and may thus become a target of manipulation.

Due to the structural characteristics of the Internet, which include easy access and storage of information about past and current events and issues, users of online news media may be exposed to different memories. In situations of conflict, the terrors of past wars, secessionist efforts or the involvement of third parties in the conflict (such as Russia, in the case of the conflict in Georgia, which evokes the traumatic past of Soviet socialism) are discussed in public, which strengthens rather than overcomes the boundaries between ethnic groups (Matheson and Allan 2009). But references to the past can also include positive aspects, such as the peaceful coexistence of ethnic groups before the outbreak of violent conflicts. Therefore, as regards the public representation of memories, the simultaneous transition of political and economic institutions that is characteristic of the reorganization of post-socialist states has left online news media in a more favourable situation. Print news, by contrast, tends to be subject to more state/government control, which implies that opposing memories cannot be reflected and discussed to such an extent as in online news media (see Kuntsman 2010; Rutten 2010). This reasoning leads me to my second hypothesis:

Hypothesis 2

Online news media as opposed to print news media are more likely to present news in memory-related frames.

Online news media represent alternative platforms for the circulation of political news. They allow more diverse interpretations of events and issues from the perspective of the past. Even though the public representation of opposing memories may confront users of online news with a dilemma when it comes to deciding which points of view are (not) acceptable, it at least provides a less restricted public platform than print news media to discuss and reflect conflicts and contested views of history. If memory-related frames in online news media cover negative and positive references to the past, the creation of an overarching national identity is more likely than if there is a bias towards conflict-loaded events and issues of the past. Admittedly, this approach is quite idealistic, for two reasons. First, online news media may also be manipulated by the state; second, expectations of online news users' ability to differentiate manifold interpretations of memories are too high. Nevertheless, from a theoretical point of view, new media open up the possibility of successful nation building by overcoming ethnic polarization.

Research design and methodology

As stated earlier, the goal of this study is to analyse in what respects framings of Georgian online and print news differ under conditions of unsettled ethno-territorial conflict. Online news media in particular may challenge reconciliation processes as they are expected to have a stronger backward/retrospective orientation. This postulated effect may occur to an increasing degree in times of armed conflict.

Case selection

To test my hypotheses I use data from a quantitative frame analysis of Georgian online and print news around the 2008 Russo–Georgian War. Besides political power struggles after Georgia's breakaway from the Soviet Union in 1991, which were partly violent, the territorial status of South Ossetia and Abkhazia has been a constant bone of contention (Closson 2010). Under Soviet rule, both South Ossetia and Abkhazia had been classified as autonomous regions of Georgia. Shortly after the country's declaration of independence and following Georgia's nationalist politics, both these regions asserted claims for self-determination and sovereignty. While Georgia insisted on maintaining its territorial integrity, Russia actively supported the separatist regions in their claims. This conflict over the status of South Ossetia and Abkhazia resulted in severe wars in the beginning of the 1990s, frozen conflict in the periods that followed and a military clash between Georgia and Russia in 2008. This situation raises apprehensions and fears on all sides, and brings back memories of both the terror of civil war in the early 1990s and dependence on Russia during Soviet times.

Period of study

To account for the dynamics of the unsettled Georgian conflict, my frame analysis focuses on the years 2006 to 2010 and distinguishes between three periods of conflict. The *war period* covers 4 to 17 August. I have chosen these dates in order to include military incidents which took place before and after the war formally started and ended. This period includes the start of fighting on 7 August and the official termination of military action on 12 August. Based on EU mediation, a ceasefire agreement was signed by Georgia on 15 August and by Russia on 16 August.

The *pre-* and *post-war periods* comprise situations of non-violent (and frozen) conflict. The *pre-war period* dates back to 2006 when relations between Georgia, the separatist regions and Russia deteriorated noticeably. Relations between Georgia and South Ossetia declined due to rival elections which were held by the separatist regime and the Georgian government on the territory of South Ossetia. Negotiations between Abkhazia and Georgia stalled as a result of an anti-crime police operation by Georgia in the Kodori valley, which was strongly condemned by the Abkhazian side. As the result of a series of economic and political events, relations between Georgia and Russia worsened. The *post-war period* covers the years 2008 until 2010. After fighting formally ended, Russia recognized both separatist regions as independent countries on 26 August. In October 2008, the Geneva talks were launched at the international level to negotiate the future of the breakaway regions. After two years, the conflict parties faced the crucial decision of how to proceed.

Media sample and unit of analysis

For the frame analysis, two news media outlets were selected: Civil.ge and *Rezonansi*.[4] Civil.ge is the Georgian daily online news platform with the most visitors per day.[5] Founded in July 2001 by the United Nations Association of Georgia (UNAG), a Georgian non-governmental organization, it delivers quality news about Georgia in Georgian, Russian and English.[6] News is presented in eight different sections, and articles are available from 2001 to date. *Rezonansi* is the Georgian daily newspaper with the highest circulation.[7] Even though it has an online version, I refer here to the traditional print version. *Rezonansi* has been published since 1990 and is disseminated all over Georgia. This independent daily focuses largely on social and political issues, and contains, among other things, sections covering Georgian news, economics, business, justice, culture and international affairs.

The unit of analysis in this study consisted of articles from the selected news media. I selected *all* issues that were published in the *war period* and chose one day randomly in every fourth month in the *pre-* and *post-war period*. I included *all* articles that appeared on the front page of *Rezonansi* and on the main website of Civil.ge. I also counted all other articles published elsewhere in the media outlets which referred to the separatist regions, Russia, conflicts between Georgia and the separatist regions, the 2008 war, and international or regional organizations involved in the unsettled conflict.

Coding measures and process

Based on the theoretical discussion and the peculiarities of the Georgian case, Table 9.1 summarizes the frames considered for the content analysis by distinguishing between memory- and non-memory-related frames. Memory-related frames are characterized as conceptual media tools that imply an interpretation of issues and events in past or retrospective terms, connoted either positively (HistoryPos) or negatively (HistoryNeg, Russia, Integrity, Ethnicity, Friend–Foe). Non-memory-related frames make no reference to the history. All frames were dichotomously coded (articles which mentioned the defined frame were coded with the value 1, otherwise with 0).

Each article was coded for the presence/absence of these frames. Articles were analysed by a trained student coder, who is fluent in the Georgian language. For the purpose of intra-coder reliability, Percent Agreement was calculated.[8] It showed that the average Percent Agreement is 0.98, which is significantly high.[9]

Table 9.1 Summary of (non-)memory-related frames

	Frame	*Definition*
Memory-related frames	HistoryNeg	The article refers to separating claims stated by the conflicting parties in the (recent) past.
	HistoryPos	The article mentions good relations between the conflicting parties in the (recent) past.
	Russia	The article mentions Russia as a threat to Georgia's national existence.
	Integrity	The article mentions territorial integrity as Georgia's main political goal.
	Ethnicity	The issue of ethnicity is mentioned in the article.
	Friend-foe	The article mentions victims and perpetrators of war and conflict.
Non-memory-related frames	Military conflict	The article mentions the military conflict or military actions.
	Non-military conflict	The article mentions political, economic, administrative or legal disagreements between the conflicting groups.
	Human interest	The article mentions human participants in the war.
	Violence	The article mentions human and material costs of the war.
	Responsibility	The article mentions actors responsible for the conflict or the war.
	Diagnosis	The article mentions reasons for the war.
	Prognosis	The article mentions political outcomes of the war.
	Conflict solution	The article mentions possible solutions of war or conflict.

News framing in pre- and post-war Georgia

To test my hypotheses, frequency analyses were run for each of the relevant variables. For the frame analysis a total of 1,145 articles were *pre*selected from Civil.ge (N 379) and *Rezonansi* (N 766). Chart 9.1 displays the issue coverage of the selected media outlets in the selected periods of analysis.

Chart 9.1 shows that conflict-related articles prevail over other topics in the news, regardless of whether or not a violent conflict is underway at the time. This finding applies mainly to *Rezonansi*, which addresses the conflict issue more frequently than Civil.ge. The largest number of conflict-related articles was observed during the war period. Differences between the selected media samples may be found in the non-war periods: *Rezonansi* was more conflict-oriented than Civil.ge in both the pre- and post-war phases, but addressed non-conflict-related issues more often in the pre- than in the post-war period.

To summarize, the empirical evidence mirrors the deep concerns of the Georgian people, which result from the unsettled ethno-territorial conflict. At the same time, there are indications that online news media provide a more diverse perspective on news, i.e. on events and issues of overall interest for society. Provided that print news media tend to be subject to more state control than online news media in transition countries, the empirical findings may also be interpreted as the government's attempt to keep the unsettled conflict constantly alive as a topic of public debate. This may hamper exchanges and, ultimately, reconciliation between the opposing groups, Russia included.

As I assume conflict-related news (i.e. news that refers to the 2008 war, Georgian–Russian relations, separatist regions and Russia and its politics and

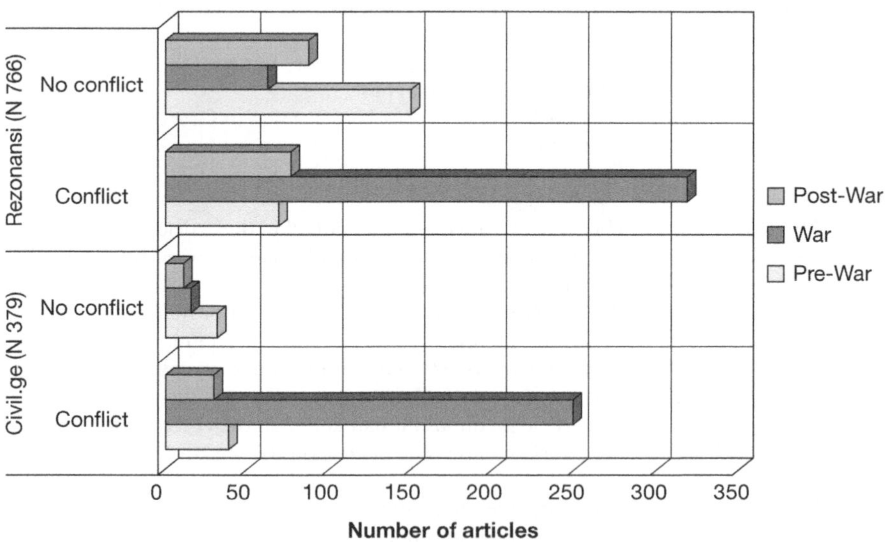

Chart 9.1 Issue coverage of Civil.ge and *Rezonansi* across time

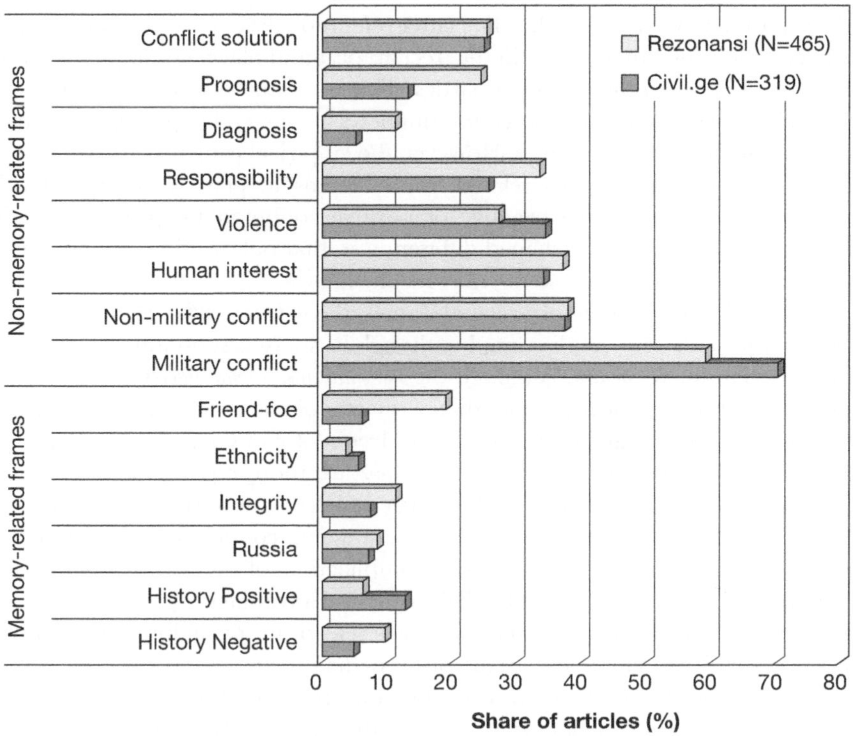

Chart 9.2 Distribution of (non-)memory-related conflict frames across news media

economy) to have more frames with a memory orientation than non-conflict-related news, I made a further selection of 319 articles from Civil.ge and 465 articles from *Rezonansi* from the pre-sample, in total 784 articles. The extent to which the framing of this news differs across online and print news media, and the role played by memory-related frames as opposed to non-memory-related frames, is shown in Chart 9.2. I expect online news media to be characterized by more memory-related information than print news media.

Chart 9.2 displays quite strikingly that memory-related frames occur less frequently than alternative frames, irrespective of the selected news media. This finding is surprising inasmuch as the development of the Georgian ethno-territorial conflict would appear to imply a more frequent occurrence of the memory-related frames in general. The minimal relevance of memory-related frames in both media samples suggests, however, that news media show more interest in present than past issues and thus provide some ground for conflict settlement, undisturbed by 'bad' memories.

Significant differences in the representation of past events and issues cannot be identified between *Rezonansi* and Civil.ge. However, on closer inspection of the memory-related frames, it is evident that articles published by *Rezonansi* have a slightly stronger inclination towards accusation, stereotyping and bad memories of the past than Civil.ge articles. The latter refer more frequently to good relations between the conflicting parties in the (recent) past and place less emphasis on the differences between the opposing parties. These findings disprove my hypothesis that online news media as opposed to print news media tend to present news more often in memory-related frames. However, the empirical evidence also shows that the content of the memory-related frames seems to play an important role. Whether or not they have negative or positive connotations, parties' attitudes towards each other can be shaped differently so that polarization may become a result of news framing, but so too may reconciliation.

As regards the non-memory-related frames, the *military conflict* frame was found regularly in both news media samples, though its share is substantially higher for Civil.ge than for *Rezonansi*. Although the *non-military*, *human interest*, *conflict solution* and *violence* frames appear in more than a quarter of the articles from both media samples, the latter may be observed more frequently in Civil.ge. As regards the remaining non-memory-related frames, they are more often used by *Rezonansi* than by Civil.ge. As a general trend, Civil.ge articles show a stronger bias towards the representation of violent aspects of the ongoing conflict, while print articles focus more on the political dimension and implications of the overarching conflict. This may be due to online news media's structural advantage, namely that it offers political news more or less in real time, whereas print journalism focuses much more on political analyses due to the print media time lag.

Next, I explored the extent to which memory-related frames were presented in the selected online and print news media by distinguishing the different phases of the unsettled conflict (see Table 9.2). My expectation was that memory-related frames would occur more often in times of war than peace.

As expected, in times of war, news is more frequently represented in memory-related frames. Negative references to the past (i.e. the HistoryNeg, Russia, Integrity, Friend–Foe and partly the Ethnicity frames) dominate war reporting in Civil.ge and *Rezonansi*. Still, their relevance is evidently less significant in periods of relative stability; this applies to both news media samples. Nevertheless, it is worth noting two other striking aspects. First, even in times of war, positive

Table 9.2 Memory-related frames in times of (non-)violence across news media

Frame	*Civil.ge*			*Rezonansi*		
	Pre-war (N 39)	*Post-war (N 30)*	*War (N 250)*	*Pre-war (N 69)*	*Post-war (N 77)*	*War (N 319)*
HistoryNeg	2 (5.1 %)	0	14 (5.6 %)	5 (7.2 %)	4 (5.2 %)	36 (11.2 %)
HistoryPos	14 (35.9 %)	1 (3.3 %)	25 (10.0 %)	9 (13.0 %)	4 (5.2 %)	16 (5.0 %)
Russia	0	2 (6.7 %)	27 (10.8 %)	0	3 (3.9 %)	39 (12.2 %)
Integrity	2 (5.1 %)	1 (3.3 %)	21 (8.4 %)	4 (5.8 %)	5 (6.5 %)	43 (13.5 %)
Ethnicity	0	3 (10.0 %)	15 (6.0 %)	1 (1.4 %)	2 (2.6 %)	14 (4.4 %)
Friend-foe	2 (5.1 %)	3 (10 %)	45 (18.1 %)	3 (4.3 %)	10 (13 %)	76 (23.8 %)

references to good relations between the conflicting parties in the past (HistoryPos) may be identified. Although at a lower level than before the war, this finding suggests at least minor efforts made by both media to provide balanced reporting. After the war, however, the HistoryPos frame disappeared almost completely: this is best illustrated by Civil.ge news articles. Second, the public image of Russia has deteriorated over time, but less strongly than one might expect. While Russia's direct involvement in the 2008 war caused a serious deterioration in Russo–Georgian relations, Civil.ge and *Rezonansi* mirrored it during but not after the war.

The final comparison extends the previous analysis by investigating the occurrence of non-memory-related news frames in Civil.ge and *Rezonansi* (Table 9.3) in times of war and peace.

The *military conflict* frame is the most dominant frame during the war period in both Civil.ge and *Rezonansi* articles. Yet differences were found in the pre- and post-war phases. While the *military conflict* frame was of minor relevance before the war, it achieved significantly higher levels of usage after the armed conflict, particularly in *Rezonansi*. This is in contrast to the *non-military conflict, prognosis* and *diagnosis* frames which occurred in Civil.ge articles less frequently during the war, but more extensively afterwards. Similar patterns of news framing across the selected media samples could be identified with regard to the *human interest, violence* and *responsibility* frames. They played a crucial role in times of war, but became less important in the post-war period. By taking into account the pre-war phase, however, differences between Civil.ge and *Rezonansi* appeared inasmuch as these frames were used more frequently in articles in the former than in the latter.

Another interesting finding is the usage of the *conflict solution* frame in articles from Civil.ge in all the non-violence phases. But even more striking is the constant decline in the coverage of the *conflict solution* frame, which is more intensive in Civil.ge (from 38.5 per cent to 16.7 per cent) than *Rezonansi* news (17.4 per cent to 11.7 per cent). In the post-war phase, Civil.ge's focus clearly shifted towards discussion of the outcomes of the 2008 war and the underlying ethno-territorial conflict, whereas *Rezonansi*'s framing of political news did not have a clear focus. As a consequence, it is mainly the online news platform that provides some ground for further public debate about the still unsettled ethno-territorial conflict.

Conclusion and discussion

My study found some empirical evidence that the framing of news, on the one hand, and its mediation through online news media, on the other, allow for some rapprochement between the conflicting parties under conditions of unsettled conflict. More specifically, the study showed that war stories attracted most attention from both Civil.ge and *Rezonansi*. However, print news articles that focused on the Georgian ethno-territorial conflict were published more frequently than online news articles in the pre- and post-war periods. This finding may imply that print news media rather than online news media stick to a relatively fixed news agenda. One reason for such editorial inflexibility may be seen in newspapers' political dependence on state authorities, which is typical for post-Soviet space.

Table 9.3 Non-memory-related frames in times of (non-)violence across news media

Frame	*Civil.ge*			*Rezonansi*		
	Pre-war (N 39)	*Post-war (N 30)*	*War (N 250)*	*Pre-war (N 69)*	*Post-war (N 77)*	*War (N 319)*
Military conflict	1 (2.6 %)	5 (16.7%)	218 (87.2 %)	8 (11.6 %)	18 (23.4 %)	249 (78.1%)
Non-military conflict	21 (53.8 %)	20 (66.7 %)	78 (31.2 %)	40 (60.0 %)	27 (35.1 %)	109 (34.2 %)
Human interest	8 (20.5 %)	7 (23.3 %)	94 (37.6 %)	6 (8.7 %)	14 (18.0 %)	153 (50.0 %)
Violence	0	3 (10.0 %)	107 (42.8 %)	0	9 (11.7 %)	118 (37.0 %)
Responsibility	7 (18.0 %)	6 (20.0 %)	69 (27.6 %)	5 (7.3 %)	19 (24.7 %)	132 (41.4 %)
Diagnosis	0	2 (6.7 %)	15 (6.0 %)	1 (1.4 %)	4 (5.2 %)	48 (15.0 %)
Prognosis	1 (2.6 %)	14 (46.7 %)	27 (10.8 %)	0	17 (22.1 %)	97 (30.4 %)
Conflict solution	15 (38.5 %)	5 (16.7 %)	61 (24.4 %)	12 (17.4 %)	9 (11.7 %)	97 (30.4 %)

Empirical support could be found for my first hypothesis that, irrespective of the news media, memory-related frames are more relevant in times of violent conflict than in times of peace. Another result is that the content of frames that interpret events and issues through the lens of history seems to play a significant role. While memory-related frames with negative connotations prevailed in times of war, those with a positive connotation were found under conditions of frozen conflict. This finding suggests that it may be appropriate to adopt a more nuanced approach to the relevance of memories and histories in media reporting. News framing in memory-related terms may not per se be a problem for reconciliation; what matters is the content of memory-related frames.

In contrast to my second hypothesis, memory-related frames play a minor role in both online and print news media. Civil.ge articles in particular were less likely to present events and issues in memory-related frames. These empirical findings are in line with the assumption that many post-Soviet states prefer to forget rather than reappraise the past (see Novak 2008). At the same time, the empirical evidence contradicts the assumption that in online media, the past is as alive as the present (see further the Introduction to this volume). One reason may be that online news media function according to principles that are more similar to traditional news media than to other news media.

Against the background of convergent framing patterns across the selected news media samples, the empirical findings of this study provide only a small window of opportunity to launch a broader public discussion about the future of the separatist regions within the borders of Georgia. Moreover, as regards Georgia in particular and the post-Soviet space in general, the prospects for a lasting solution to unsettled ethno-territorial conflicts which are closely related to the construction of national identities and the revival of the Soviet legacy are mixed. Arguing from the frame perspective, negative references to the past culminate in times of violent conflict, especially in print news media, which leaves enough room for the interpretation of conflict-related events and issues in alternative frames during phases of non-violence. From a more structural point of view, it is the online news media that are less easy to control than print news media. As a consequence, online news media have more structural potential than print news media to enhance a solution in frozen conflicts.

Notes

1 The author wishes to thank the Academic Swiss Caucasus Net and Nino Abzianidze for support in data collection and analysis. Valuable feedback was provided by Lars-Erik Cederman, Frank Esser, Gesine Fuchs, Simon Hug, Galina Nikiporets-Takigawa, Manuel Vogt, Martin Wettstein, Anne Wetzel, and anonymous reviewers. The study is based on research conducted as part of the Institutional Strategies for Post-Conflict Democratization project at the Swiss Center of Competence in Research 'Challenges to Democracy in the 21st Century' (NCCR Democracy), and funded by the Swiss National Science Foundation.

2 In general, Russia as the formal successor to the Soviet Union is more sympathetic to separatists' political goals than to the new states' territorial integrity (Sokolow 1997). In

line with this policy, Russia openly attacked Georgia's territorial integrity by recognizing South Ossetia and Abkhazia as independent states.

3 Not all new media scholars accept that the Internet presents an analogue of the classical 'public sphere', especially when it comes to the post-Soviet segments of the Internet (Schmidt *et al.* 2006; Panchenko 2011).

4 To identify the most relevant online and press news media, five criteria were applied: The media outlets are: (1) available in the predefined period of analysis; (2) published on a daily basis; (3) accessible all over Georgia; (4) published in Georgian, and (5) have the highest circulation/the most visitors per day.

5 According to Civil.ge (May 2011), it achieves 300,000 views per month, i.e. 10,000 views per day.

6 Civil.ge is currently supported by the Eurasia Partnership Foundation (EPF) and the Friedrich Ebert Foundation (FES).

7 The circulation of the newspaper is 4,000 to 5,000 (May 2011). Although this is only half the circulation figure of Civil.ge, *Rezonansi* was selected as the most influential daily newspaper.

8 Inter-/intra-coder reliability tests show the extent to which multiple coders who apply the same coding scheme agree on the coding of text data. Percent Agreement is frequently used to estimate inter-/intra-coder reliability.

9 Values above 0.60 are acceptable for the Percent Agreement test.

References

Anderson, B. (2006) *Imagined Communities. Reflections on the Origin and Spread of Nationalism*, (3rd edn). London and New York: Verso.

Closson, S. (2010) 'Networks of Profit in Georgia's Autonomous Regions: Challenges to Statebuilding'. *Journal of Intervention and Statebuilding* 4(2), Summer: 179–204.

Deutsch, K.W. and Foltz, W.J. (1966) *Nation-Building.* New York: Atherton Press.

Dimitrova, D.V. and Connolly-Ahern, C. (2007) 'A Tale of Two Wars. Framing Analysis of Online News Websites in Coalition Countries and the Arab World during the Iraq War'. *The Howard Journal of Communication* 18: 153–168.

Dimitrova, D.V., Kaid, L.L., Williams, A.P. and Trammell, K.D. (2005) 'War on the Web. The Immediate News Framing of Gulf War II'. *The Harvard Journal of Press/Politics* 20(1), Spring: 22–44.

Entman, R. (1993) 'Framing. Toward Clarification of a Fractured Paradigm'. *Journal of Communication* 43(4): 51–58.

Garde-Hansen, J., Hoskins, A. and Reading, A. (eds) (2009) *Save As . . . Digital Memories.* Basingstoke and New York: Palgrave.

Hippler, J. (ed.) (2005) *Nation-Building. A Key Concept for Peaceful Conflict Transformation?* London: Pluto Press.

Holsti, K.J. (1996) *The State, War, and the State of War.* Cambridge: Cambridge University Press.

Howard, R. (2002a) *An Operational Framework for Media and Peacebuilding.* Vancouver: Institute for Media, Policy and Civil Society.

Howard, R. (2002b) *Conflict Sensitive Journalism.* Vancouver: Institute for Media, Policy and Civil Society.

Iyengar, S. (1991) *Is Anyone Responsible?* Chicago, IL: University of Chicago Press.

Jha-Nambiar, S. (2002) *Reframing Frame Analysis. Gaps and Opportunities in Framing Research.* Paper presented to the Cultural and Critical Studies Division at the Association for Education in Journalism and Mass Communication (AEJMC), Miami Beach, FL.

Kahneman, D. (1984) 'Choice, Values, and Frames'. *American Psychologist* 39: 341–350.

Karklins, R. (1994) 'Explaining Regime Change in the Soviet Union'. *Europe-Asia Studies* 46(1), Spring: 29–45.

Kempf, W. (2002) 'Conflict Coverage and Conflict Escalation', in W. Kempf and H. Luostarinen (eds), *Journalism and the New World Order. Studying the War and the Media.* Gothenburg: Nordicom, 59–72.

Kuntsman, A. (2010) 'Online Memories, Digital Conflicts and the Cybertouch of War'. *Digital Icons: Studies in Russian, Eurasian and Central European New Media* 4: 1–12.

Lynch, J. and McGoldrick, A. (2005) *Peace Journalism.* Stroud: Hawthorn Press.

Matheson, D. and Allan, S. (2009) *Digital War Reporting.* Cambridge: Polity Press.

McCombs, M. (1994) 'News Influence on our Pictures of the World', in J. Bryant and D. Zillman (eds), *Media Effects. Advances in Theory and Research.* Hillsdale, NJ: Lawrence Erlbaum Associates: 1–17.

McCombs, M. and Ghanem, S.I. (2003) 'The Convergence of Agenda Setting and Framing', in S. Reese *et al.* (eds), *Framing Public Life. Perspectives on Media and Our Understanding of the Social World.* Mahwah, NJ: Lawrence Erlbaum Associates: 67–81.

Morozov, E. (2011) *The Net Delusion. The Dark Side of Internet Freedom.* New York: Public Affairs.

Novak, A. (2008) *History and Geopolitics. A Contest for Eastern Europe.* Warsaw: Polish Institute for International Affairs.

O'Loughlin, J. and Toal, G. (2009) 'Accounting for Separatist Sentiment in Bosnia-Herzegovina and the North Caucasus of Russia. A Comparative Analysis of Survey Responses'. *Ethnic and Racial Studies* 32(4), Winter: 591–615.

Panchenko, E. (2011) 'Convergence of Internet News Media and Social Networks on Runet. A New Public Sphere or a Space of Control?' *Digital Icons: Studies in Russian, Eurasian and Central European New Media* 5: 87–118.

Peleg, S. (2006) 'Peace Journalism Through the Lense of Conflict Theory. Analysis and Practice'. *Conflict & Communication Online* 5(2), Summer: 1–17.

Reljic, D. (1998) *Killing Screens. Medien in Zeiten von Konflikten.* Düsseldorf: Droste.

Rothberg, R. (2004) 'The Failure and Collapse of Nation-States', in R. Rothberg (ed.), *When States Fail: Causes and Consequences.* Princeton, NJ: Princeton University Press: 1–49.

Rutten, E. (2010) 'Web Wars: Digital Diasporas and the Language of Memory'. *Digital Icons: Studies in Russian, Eurasian and Central European New Media* 4: 171–176.

Saris, W.E. (1997) 'The Public Opinion about the EU Can Easily be Swayed in Different Directions'. *Acta Politica: International Journal of Political Science* 32: 406–435.

Schmidt, H., Teubener, K. and Konradova, N. (eds) (2006) *Control + Shift. Public and Private Uses of the Russian Internet.* Norderstedt: Books on Demand.

Sokolow, A. (1997) 'Russian Peace-Keeping Forces in the Post-Soviet Area', in M. Kaldor and V. Basker (eds), *Restructuring the Global Military Sector. New Wars.* London, and Washington, DC: Pinter: 207–230.

Talentino, A.K. (2004) 'The Two Faces of Nation-Building. Developing Function and Identity'. *Cambridge Review of International Affairs* 17(3), Autumn: 557–575.

Taylor, M. (2000) 'Toward a Public Relations Approach to Nation Building'. *Journal of Public Relations Research* 12(2), Summer: 179–210.

Wimmer, A. (2008) 'The Making and Unmaking of Ethnic Boundaries. A Multilevel Process Theory'. *American Journal of Sociology* 113(4), Winter: 970–1022.

10 Rust on the monument

Challenging the myth of Victory in Belarus

Aliaksei Lastouski

Introduction

On 29 May 2011, the premiere of the animated film *Budz'ma Belarusami* (*Let's Be Belarusians*) took place in the city of Minsk. The film was the result of a joint project by the civic cultural campaign 'Budz'ma' ('Let's Be') – aimed at the promotion of the Belarusian language and culture – and the most popular Belarusian Internet portal, tut.by. The film presents a very vivid picture of the history of Belarus: in five minutes it provides a hip-hop version of the main events of the country's national history, from the mythological werewolves Nevres mentioned by the Ancient Greek historian Herodotus, through to 1991, when Belarus gained independence following the collapse of the Soviet Union.

In this animated film, the Second World War fits into the chronologically ordered narrative as just one link in a long chain of events stretching back to ancient times. The war itself is described as follows:

> After that, one more hell – WWII.
> There were invaders, there were partisans,
> the country was torn apart again . . .
> Belarusians fought with Belarusians again,
> shedding each other's blood.
>
> (Budz'ma 2011)

This description is completely devoid of victorious fervour; the war appears more like a tragic event, which had a detrimental impact on Belarusian sovereignty and which in fact resembled a civil war, with Belarusians fighting on both sides.

As such, the film's representation of the Second World War stands in sharp contrast to the Belarusian state cult of Victory, which holds that the most important historic achievement of the Belarusian people is the Victory in the Great Patriotic War, and which has become the basis for the post-Soviet official Belarusian national identity project. The central role of this Victory doctrine is fixed not only in the speeches of the President and in official commemorations. Belarusian sociological studies conducted by the Institute of Sociology in 2008; Novak in 2009; and IISEPS in 2012 indicate that Belarusian memory of the Soviet past is dominated by the emphatic and expressive cult of the Victory in the Great Patriotic War, in whose shadow all other events of this period appear insignificant (Lastovskii [Lastouski] 2009: 83).

In this chapter, I focus on the variety of Belarusian strategies for remembering the past and the diversity of the sources upon which they draw. I concentrate in particular on the representational possibilities for controversial and oppositional versions of the past – that is, those (mostly online) versions that evade the near-complete control of the Belarusian state over the country's public space. In contrast to other researchers, I am interested not so much in the content and argumentation of oppositional narratives of the past as in their transformation under the influence of the media environment.

Belarus and the Second World War memory

In the development of the official memory narrative of the Republic of Belarus, two key milestones may be highlighted. The first is 1991, the year that marked the collapse of the Soviet Union and the creation of an independent Belarusian state, along with the restoration of a national Belarusian historiography that was repressed during the Soviet period. This historiography has followed three key paths:

1. Delving into the 'glorious' historical past with a view to tracing the roots of Belarusian national statehood back to the early medieval Principality of Polatsk; that is, rejecting the Soviet narrative which posited Kievan Rus as the cradle of the three East Slav nations, namely Belarus, Russia and Ukraine.
2. Focusing on Europe: treating Belarusian history as part of European history, with common processes and characteristics, and therefore opposed to Russian history.
3. Demonstrating the negative influence of Russia on Belarusian history.

The other event that radically changed the fate of Belarusian politics of memory is the election of Aliaksandr Lukashenka as the President of Belarus in 1994. In contrast to the early post-Soviet period, the Lukashenka period has seen Belarusian historiography turn back to its pan-Slavic, Russophile *and* Soviet roots (Kuzio 2002: 254). Historian David Marples has argued that Lukashenka 'recognizes the historical legacy of Belarusians only selectively – strictly in the Russian context' and that under Lukashenka, 'history as a form of public policy is limited to the Soviet period, at the expense of important fundamental periods of the Grand Duchy of Lithuania and the Polish Commonwealth' (Marples 2007). Thus, for example, since 1996, Belarusian Independence Day has been celebrated on 3 July, the date when Soviet troops liberated Minsk in 1944. The main political opponent of Lukashenka in the early 1990s was the nationalist opposition for which the ethno-national historical narrative reconstituted in the early 1990s was of fundamental importance; as a result, the political confrontation moved to the sphere of history. Under Lukashenka, Belarusian historiography has thus bifurcated into the official (state) line, on the one hand, and an unofficial, nationally oriented one, on the other (Lindner 1999).

These two versions of history employ radically different chronological frames and foundation myths. The national historiography traces the roots of the Belarusian state back to the Principality of Polatsk, a feudal principality of the ninth to twelfth centuries that achieved a significant political influence in the region. The official state historiography, by contrast, features a myth of origins that is based primarily on the partisan resistance during the Second World War, and on the figure of the partisan as heroic defender of the state against an external aggressor. This myth was put in place in the Soviet period. After the Second World War, the former commanders of the partisan groups went on to become local leaders in communist Belarus, and the mythologized image of the 'partisan republic' allowed them to legitimize their own authority and acquire symbolic prestige in the general Soviet hierarchy (Urban 1989). The heroic Belarusian 'Partisan Myth' was fixed in historical memory and turned out to be beneficial to the government in the post-communist period too (Leshchenko 2008: 1420).

In the Soviet Union, the Second World War was called the Great Patriotic War, and its chronological framework was also different from that prevalent in the Western world: it started on 22 June 1941 (the German attack on the Soviet Union) and ended on 9 May 1945 (celebration of the Victory over Germany in the Soviet Union). This war was the hardest trial for the communist state – and even harder for its people.

During the first post-war years, the war was not a remote past approached through art films; its memory was still raw, fresh and painful. The complicated and bloody twists and turns of the war included many aspects which did not lend themselves to inclusion in the official Soviet war narrative: extermination of the Jewish population, the experience of life under Nazi occupation, the fate of the POWs (perceived by the Soviet authorities as 'traitors'), the phenomenon of Nazi collaboration, nationalist insurgency, etc.

Under Brezhnev (1964–1982), the monumental and heroic image of the war was eventually formed, but it took a long time to smooth out its basic contours, to settle on a way of handling these controversial aspects and suppressing uncomfortable memories, and to elaborate a common language for describing and making sense of the past. The Ukrainian historian Vladimir Grinevich writes about the importance of this unified model of the memory of the war in terms of the drive to create a common Soviet identity:

> War with its numerous real and mythical manifestations of heroism and sacrifice was excellent material for the creation of patriotic symbols and patterns of collective memory. Moreover, the common struggle of the Soviet peoples gave an opportunity to create a model of common patriotism – a common Soviet identity not ignoring, but rather on the contrary, focusing on local specificity.
>
> (Grinevich 2005)

From the Brezhnev era onwards, the Victory Myth acquired a leading role in the production and expansion of Soviet memory politics. Its symbolic structure has proven so stable that even the storms of post-communist transformations could not break it. In Russia and Belarus, the Soviet Victory Myth not only survived, but it became even more significant for the collective memory of these societies and the self-legitimization efforts of the ruling authorities.

Many researchers have noted the importance of a key set of ideas about the Great Patriotic War in the development of Belarusian national identity (Pershai 2006; Marples and Padgol 2008; Rudling 2008). Memory of the war continues to be actively reproduced in contemporary Belarusian society. The state uses virtually all possible channels of cultural policy to spread and consolidate this memory. The authorities pay particular attention to patriotic education – for instance, school textbooks contain heroic examples drawn from the Great Patriotic War (Smalianchuk 2008), and in many universities a special course on the 'History of the Great Patriotic War' is now compulsory for students across all fields of study. Finally, the most important national holidays in the Republic of Belarus – that is, Independence Day and Victory Day – are both directly related to triumphant moments in the Great Patriotic War. It is therefore far from surprising that, according to the results of a sociological survey conducted in 2008[1] (Lastovskii [Lastouski] 2009), the victory in the Great Patriotic War ranks as the most significant and pride-inspiring event in the history of Belarus.

The most striking thing about these data is the extraordinary shallowness of the historical memory that they indicate – all of the most significant events that made it into the top list belong to the twentieth century. Even though the questionnaire was asking about *history*, the respondents remembered primarily the *current achievements* of the modern Belarusian state, topics that are constantly circulating and reproduced through the media. In fact, only the Myth of Victory is capable of generating the depth and intensity of emotion required to sustain historical memory and engender a sense of national pride.

But while the Belarusian image of the war coincides in many ways with the Soviet myth of the Great Patriotic War, there are also important ways in which it differs from the Soviet version. It has its own specificity, which took shape even

Table 10.1 Themes in the history of Belarus that arouse pride among the country's residents

Themes in historical memory of the residents of Belarus	*Number of answers*
Victory in the Great Patriotic war	567
Gaining independence	200
Construction of new buildings	76
Sports achievements	70
Victories in 'Eurovision'	56
Festivals	52
Economic well-being	51
Presidential rule of A Lukashenka	34

under Soviet rule. First of all, the Belarusian war myth foregrounds the huge number of casualties among the Belarusian people. Within the local version of the myth, the Belarusian nation acquires an aura not only of heroism, but also, and equally, of martyrdom. The tragic price that the Belarusian nation paid for victory is underlined and echoed in the continuous playback of one rhetorical statistical figure: every fourth Belarusian, we are constantly being reminded, died during the war. Moreover, in recent years it is also increasingly common to hear it said that every third inhabitant of Belarus died in the war (the fact that ethnic and territorial definitions are constantly confused nullifies any attempt to verify these figures, but in no way diminishes their emotional significance). Second, the Belarusian version highlights the exceptional role of the Belarusian people in the victory over fascism. Here again, the 'Partisan myth' comes into play, with its emphasis on the huge (unprecedented, according to some accounts) scale of the Belarusian anti-Nazi resistance movement. In this way, the Belarusian war myth places the popular notion of 'the Soviet people as the conqueror of fascism' into the shadows, with the Belarusian people taking up this place of honour instead.

Thus, the Great Patriotic War appears in the consciousness of Belarusians as an event that is simultaneously tragic (a terrible test, proving the people's right not only to exist, but also to earn universal respect) and heroic, in roughly equal parts. Within this vision of war memory, then, the event has its negative sides too – huge losses, the disastrous defeats at the beginning of the war, the brutal occupation period, and the related problem of collaborationism. In fact, the partisan movement itself looks quite controversial in the unofficial memory translated primarily via family channels in Belarusian villages (Shatalava 2008). These negative moments were widely debated in the media in the late 1980s and early 1990s, but in recent years they have virtually disappeared from official public discourse, both in Belarus and Russia. A partial return to the norms of the Soviet era has taken place, whereby only a convenient and unified memory of the war is allowed to exist in the public space controlled by the state; anything that does not fit this schema now functions only at the level of personal memories and family legends.

It is noteworthy that the War myth actualizes the connection between the past and the present. Victory in the war is seen as the people's heritage of which one can and should be proud today. The simplicity and non-contradictory nature of this image in official discourse only enhances its strength and prominence in public consciousness. Thus, it is possible to agree with other researchers that historical memory of the Great Patriotic War is the key to the formation of the contemporary Belarusian national identity, and that it forms the most sustained and articulated complex in representations of the past among the residents of Belarus. This being said, some authors (such as Kuzio and Smalianchuk) focus so one-dimensionally on the continuity between the Belarusian and the Soviet war myth that they overlook the fact that in contemporary Belarus, the memory of the Second World War has its own idiosyncrasies. Most importantly, as we have seen, Belarusian war memory rhetoric differs from its Soviet counterpart in that it serves to strengthen national identity by concentrating on the role of Belarusian people in the victory over fascism.

Alternate voices: old memories, new media

The scale of the official representation of Victory, and the repressive stance taken by the authorities when it comes to this particular historical theme, leads to an almost complete marginalization and exclusion of alternative interpretations of the past. Pompous and heroic descriptions are praised and used by the ruling powers as a resource for consolidating their position.

Perhaps as a result of this official infatuation with war memory, attempts to review the history of the war are inevitably politicized. A good example is the case of the movie *Occupation. Mysterium* ('Akupacyja. Misteryji'). In *Occupation*, which was filmed in 2004 by the independent Belarusian filmmaker Andrei Kudzinienka, the wartime partisan movement was interpreted in a very unconventional way – thus, for example, the film features a sharply negative depiction of a Soviet partisan commander. The film was banned shortly after its completion, and the ban was lifted only in 2010. Another example is the criminal case brought against the newspaper *Narodnaia Volia* ('People's Will') that published 'inconvenient' memories about the partisans in 2010. Finally, we might mention an incident involving a cross erected in 2008 to the memory of victims of the Soviet partisans in the village of Drazhna, where in 1943 partisans killed several dozen local residents who were suspected of collaboration with the Germans. The cross was destroyed the following day, and the initiators of its installation were punished with administrative arrests and fines.

Even though they draw upon the content of individual memories, such attempts at challenging the official Myth of Victory are conditioned by the context of political confrontation in Belarus, where the marginalized opposition minority is opposed to the powerful state propaganda machine. Accordingly, any unofficial interpretations of the memory of the war face severe restrictions when it comes to their expression in the public space. This means that, as political scientist Alexandra Goujon has argued, while

> [T]here has been some criticism of the official war narrative [in Belarus], mostly from within the academic and artistic communities . . . [t]he public is not really aware of this dissent . . . since it is expressed primarily on unofficial Web sites and in independent newspapers that are poorly distributed.
>
> (Goujon 2010: 12)

A preliminary hypothesis is that in the Belarusian segment of the Internet, in contrast to the dominant norms and beliefs, a critical response to state-initiated commemorations (and to the Victory Myth) prevails over approval of the official historical policy. New media have contributed to the appearance of a quite isolated 'space of freedom' – one which is increasingly fenced off from other forms of public communication, and where new rules of representation and debate are being born. As in many other countries that witness attempts at top-down mass media control, alternative views in Belarus have the best opportunities to appear here. As the German scholar Imke Hansen points out, today the Belarusian opposition discourse has moved almost entirely to the Internet (Hansen 2006).

On the other hand, due to the increasing importance of new media for all spheres of life in Belarus, as well as for political mobilization (Zorina and Avison 2011), it has become clear that this alternative public space cannot be left untouched by government control. Indeed, Belarus is often mentioned as an example of a country where active state intervention in the free flow of information takes place (Ponomarev and Lefter 2012). The Belarusian government has even been listed as an 'enemy of the Internet' (Reporters Without Borders 2012: 15–16).

This pessimistic picture is not incorrect, although it needs some qualification. First, the percentage of Internet users in Belarus is quite high (47 per cent of the total population), and of course, total censorship or monitoring of this immense group is impossible.

Second, it should be noted that if we examine national variations of mediated memory, we must always bear in mind that online space combines two contradictory features: on the one hand, it is fundamentally international, since old borders are crossed and principally new relationships and communities are created; on the other hand, it is also potentially local in its scope, since communities that were created offline can be preserved and sometimes even grow stronger with the help of online communications.

For the scholar of Internet usage in Belarus the most significant problem is the socio-linguistic situation in the country, where the Russian language dominates in virtually all social spheres (Woolhiser 2011). Naturally, this leaves its imprint on online language usage – the majority of Belarusian-made sites are Russian speaking, and most users tend to collect information from Russian sites: from popular Russian search engines and portals, mail services, news sites, etc. In addition, most of the social networks created on Runet – such as V Kontakte (*In Contact*), Odnoklassniki (*classmates*), or Moi Mir *(My World)* – are also widely used in Belarus. Whenever we speak of digital memory in Belarus, we must thus bear in mind that this memory is woven into the complex and conflicting relationships with Runet, just as the country of Belarus itself cannot break free of its eastern neighbour's geopolitical embrace.

On the other hand, it is obvious that any statement made on the Internet, even if, in theory, it targets a global audience, in practice always addresses an audience that is limited linguistically or topically; messages usually appear in the context of communication within small communities. Therefore, in principle, we will identify those sites that are primarily focused on the reader from Belarus.

Belarusian digital memory and Victory Day

In this analysis, I review the basic forms of web-based responses to Belarusian official memory politics. The topic for analysis is 9 May, or Victory Day, the Soviet-era holiday which has morphed into one of the major state holidays in post-Soviet Belarus, accompanied by a grand parade and mass festivities.

Reactions to this holiday will be studied in two segments of the Internet:

1 The Belarusian segment of LiveJournal, a popular platform for personal blogs in our country.
2 The user forum of tut.by, the most popular Belarusian website which acts as a huge web portal, collecting and producing news, and providing mail services and even web TV.

LiveJournal

The most popular blogging platform in Belarus is LiveJournal (LJ). LJ attracts a considerably smaller number of users than Belarus' favourite social media networks (vkontakte.ru, facebook.com, odnoklassniki.ru), but it is widely used by intellectuals. The majority of Belarusian writers, and many scholars and politicians, may be found here. LJ, with its systems of branched comments, is considered an optimal platform for lengthy texts and extensive discussions. It should be noted that LJ has its own rules for communicating and presenting information. Perhaps the most important characteristic features of LJ discussion are a sceptical position towards the world and a somewhat cynical attitude towards mainstream culture.

Again, here we observe similar processes to those occurring on Runet (Alexanyan 2009). As in Russia, where 'the views of LiveJournal groups tended to be more oppositional or polar than attitudes found in the general population' (MacLeod 2009:19), in Belarus LJ is mainly used to express oppositional political views and to conduct various public campaigns against the authorities. A prime example is the campaign in support of political prisoners in Belarus that followed the crackdown of 19 December 2010 in the wake of protests against fabrication of the presidential election results. Many of those protesting were arrested and sentenced to prison. Oppositional activists first published the lists of detainees in LJ, and then used this platform to coordinate the material and symbolic support for the prisoners.

Not surprisingly, it is precisely in this space of the Internet that one finds the sharpest evaluations of the past. The most vivid example is the diary of a user named **lesnoi-slon** ('the forest elephant'). **Lesnoi-slon** criticizes not only the Belarusian authorities, but also the established political opposition in a provocative, accusatory style. His harsh words have often led to confrontations; in one of these verbal skirmishes he received the nickname 'shame and disgrace of the Belarusian blogosphere' from a *Radio Liberty* Internet observer. One recurring motif in **lesnoi-slon**'s diary is his criticism of the 9 May celebrations and his tough attacks on the 'parade' memory of the war. Characteristic is his post on 8 May 2008, which deals with the upcoming holiday and which he calls the 'sabbath':

> What is 9 May for us, the people of Belarus? What kind of Victory are we talking about? What are we celebrating? The German occupation was

> replaced by the Soviet occupation. Which one is better? Is there such a thing as a better occupation? Which is more fun – living without a kidney or without a lung? My answer: it's better to be healthy. The 9th of May is the day of mourning for the innocent victims of a foreign war. The veterans clanking with commemorative medals are no better than SS troops marching on the same streets – none of them have ever been Belarusians, both of them are invaders.
>
> (**lesnoi-slon**, 8 May 2008)

This rather lengthy post unravels the fake character of the modern celebration of 9 May and the use of veterans for legitimizing purposes that are quite far removed from the war, such as the support of the government or the promotion of state lotteries. In addition, a revisionist line is taken in the post in relation to the official version of history. **Lesnoi-slon** glorifies the Belarusian nationalist forces that cooperated with the Nazis during the Second World War. Soviet Russia is presented as a more terrible enemy than the German invaders, while the Belarusian nationalist partisans are presented as real heroes.

Written in a lively and sharp style, **lesnoi-slon**'s post caused a stormy reaction in the Belarusian blogosphere and generated a large number of comments (190 at the time this chapter was written). The overwhelming majority of comments either contained words of encouragement and/or indicated that users were re-posting the article in their own diaries. This may be the sharpest and most powerful statement against the political use of war memory that can be found in the Belarusian information space.

In LJ one may also find messages that oppose official memory politics, not via a nationalist approach, but rather from a family memory perspective, embodying a more realistic or personal perspective on events. User **prychynets**, for instance, wrote in his diary on 9 May 2011:

> May 9 is a regular day for me. During the war, neither the Soviet government, nor the Red Army, nor the so-called partisans did any good to my family. On the contrary, I would say: they delivered a lot of damage and harm which still lives in the heart of my grandmother.
>
> (**prychynets**, 9 May 2011)

A characteristic visual form used in the Belarusian segment of LJ for challenging the triumphant image of war victory is the so-called *demotivator*. The name refers to pictures that share a common style – black background, picture or image in the centre, and text at the bottom (see also, on *demotivators*, Maria Pasholok, Chapter 11, this volume). Typically, the point of a demotivator lies in the dissonance of meanings between the image and the text, and they are often used for satiric purposes. In Belarus demotivators have also proved to be a handy tool for debunking the official image of the war. They emphasize the indifference that is hidden behind the demonstrative care for veterans or the commercial exploitation of the Victory cult.

An ideal occasion for the creation of demotivators was provided by a civic campaign initiated by the authorities aimed at using the St George's Ribbon as a symbol of memory of the war. The campaign was launched by the Russian government in 2005, but then spread into Belarus and Ukraine, where the myth of the Great Patriotic War is most enduring. The campaign was aimed at consolidating war commemorations on a micro-social level. The St George's Ribbon made a convenient symbol for the campaign for a number of reasons. First, the ribbon, which dates to the pre-revolutionary period, offers a less controversial and less overtly ideological alternative to Soviet symbols such as the red Victory Banner (on the ribbon and related symbols, see also Galina Nikiporets-Takigawa, Chapter 3, this volume). At the same time, it is also firmly established in memory as a state symbol of the Soviet Union, having been among the Russian imperial military decorations that were revived during the Second World War. The St George's Ribbon was used to decorate the so-called Order of Glory, which was awarded only to soldiers and sergeants. As a consequence, the ribbon has long been a symbol of the heroism of the simple soldier on the battlefield.

At the same time, in contemporary Belarus the top-down reintroduction of these ribbons, the artificial nature of the official commemorations and the use of military symbols in numerous contexts that had no relation to memorialization of the war whatsoever (commercials, entertainment, etc.) predictably led to their rejection by the frondeur and sarcastic LJ public. The result was a series of demotivators, whose most popular motif was the biographies of the chevaliers from the tsarist-era Order of Saint George who cooperated with the Germans and/or fought against the Soviet Union during the Second World War. In this way, users foregrounded the notion of this popular symbol's falsity, built on a weak public knowledge of the complex and intricate past.

Meanwhile, the website of the newspaper *Nasha Niva*, a well-known oppositional newspaper that is highly committed to the ideology of ethno-nationalism, published a special article dedicated to the question of 'whether or not Belarusians should wear St. George's ribbons'. The author, referring to the fact that the symbol originally emerged in the times of the Russian Empire, concludes:

> If we want to honour the courage of Belarusians and citizens of other nations who laid down their lives in the war, it is more appropriate to do so with the national colours – white, red and white or red and green, whichever is accepted.
>
> But not the colours of the Empire that was an invader of Belarus, deprived Belarusians of their liberties, destroyed our town halls and our culture and turned our country into one of the poorest in Europe.
>
> (Bugai 2011)

This comment points to an interesting parallel in processes of transnational memory proliferation in post-Soviet online space. On the one hand, the distribution of ribbons shows that the practices of Russian state regulation and control over memory are willingly adopted in neighbouring countries; on the other hand, the forms of protest that this attempt generates are also spread internationally.

The St George's Ribbon controversy offered yet another opportunity to remember past conflicts, and, by articulating the historical opposition to a 'foreign' and 'falsified' version of the past, to reaffirm the uniqueness of Belarusian national identity. Thus, the memory of the Victory in the Second World War, instead of uniting the victors – which, of course, was the original motivation for the creators of this memory icon – became an occasion to consolidate isolated national projects.

L'viv incident: Belarusian reflection

In 2011, however, the liveliest debate on the Internet was caused not by the ribbons, but by the civic clashes that took place on 9 May in the West Ukrainian city of L'viv (for details, see Galina Nikiporets-Takigawa, Chapter 3, this volume). **Lesnoi-slon** commented on this incident as follows:

> Well that was not a lie about the armed assholes sent from Odessa to L'viv, judging by the photos and reports. The cult of fucking victory requires new blood.
>
> (**lesnoi-slon**, 9 May 2011)

More than LiveJournal, however, the ultimate platform for discussion of the riots was Belarus' most popular Internet portal (it attracts around 1.4 million visits a day) tut.by, where the L'viv events were highlighted in several news reports borrowed from Russian sources (lenta.ru, korrespondent.net). Ironically, despite the domination of the post-Soviet victory cult in the historical memory of Belarusians and despite the fact that Belarusian media tended to borrow from sources that framed the events in accordance with the official Russian standpoint, the tut.by discussions show quite a different picture. An overall analysis of the comments suggests that the dominant position in the discussion (in numerical terms, at least) was one of support for the actions of the Ukrainian nationalists. Here are some representative examples:

> Well done guys that you did not allow this red-brown sabbath to unfold. One day the streets of Minsk will also be free from all red rags.
>
> (**Ja-pamru**)

> The question is not about Nazism as the Russian part wants to present it, but the question is in the inadmissibility of the revival and spread of the communist ideology and Russian chauvinism in the territory of a state which is moving towards the European community. This is a provocation by chauvinists.
>
> (**pilj**)

> The Russian red-browns were also shooting rubber bullets from pistols. Not to mention the fact that these provocateurs brought with them banned Russian and red flags.
>
> (**Nmmmo**)

Naturally, there were also opposing views (although in smaller quantities) appealing to the notion of a sacred imperative to honour the veterans who 'saved the country':

> Another [instance of] disrespect for the people who fought so that your grandmother could live, and so that, in the future, you could be born. Shame on you man for thousands of Belarusians died for the country, for our land, so that you and I and we all lived.
>
> (**PrYYYYvet**)

> Fascists have to be killed! They shouldn't live on the earth! BIG THANKS to the veterans!
>
> (**hanno4ka**) (tut.by Forum 2011)

It is noteworthy that this forum discussion about current events immediately provoked an intensified debate of the historical past. The events triggered assessments by forum users not merely of military events and the partisan movement, but also of the attitude towards the communist regime. The opinions expressed by these 'amateurs' represented the Belarusian past in ways that are clearly different from its representations in official historiography and school textbooks.

It is important to underline here that in digital discourse about the past and present, geographical boundaries acquire configurations that are different from their offline counterparts. LiveJournal creates a common discussion platform for bloggers from Belarus, Russia and Ukraine, which allows information to flow freely from one country to another and the establishment of communication between representatives of various nationalities. This is why it is not surprising that demotivators that were originally created in Russia are used with great pleasure by bloggers from other countries. This also explains why the events that took place in L'viv provoked such lively debate in the Belarusian segment of the Internet, while the gala celebrations in Minsk passed virtually unnoticed. This is not to say that all events are discussed on a transnational level; and despite the readiness of Belarusian bloggers to discuss events in Russia and Ukraine, the online situation in no way reproduces the myth of the trinity of the Russian people, according to which the Belarusian and Ukrainian identities are merely variants of Russianness. On the contrary, Belarusian national and state identity is constructed and reproduced on the Internet through a canvas of discussions which reproduce stereotypes of Russia and Ukraine as foreign and wild spaces, while Belarus is represented as a country of predictability and order.

Conclusion

To conclude, in Belarusian new media the following key strategies of challenging official memory discourse may be identified:

1. Ironic paraphrase based on hyperbolic exaggerations and sarcastic attacks.
2. Revisionist strategies based on alternative versions of the historical past.
3. Visual contestations of official memory politics that use new technologies to create a subversive iconography (with the help of such tools as the demotivator).

It should be emphasized that this list of examples (which could be expanded) shows not only that alternative memory can be represented on the Internet, where it is easier to avoid control; more importantly, it is clear that the very phenomenon of collective memory exists in digital space under new rules.

I agree with other researchers that memory acquires fundamentally different features online than it does in traditional media (van Dijck 2007; Erll and Rigney 2009; Garde-Hansen *et al.* 2009). The weakness of online censorship creates a new ethos of expression and debate, where rational argumentation gives way to provocation, visual impressiveness, cynicism and resonance. The new language of memory is no worse and no better than that used in scholarly books and reputable journals. Rather than assess its moral status, we should evaluate it using the criterion of efficiency. The form of communication in blogs and social networks makes optimal use of the technological capabilities of the media, and allows speakers to take maximum advantage of their resources and directly influence the emotions of the participants of communication. As such, digital memory is in a sense more 'alive', because it generates much more reaction than the strongly regulated and standardized official memory.

But the social significance of this online symbolic resistance remains controversial, since it seems to exist rather in the mode of an intellectual ghetto, where the protest sentiments are provided with an isolated ground and do not attract the attention of the general public. Moreover, it is difficult to speak of counter-memory as a coordinated challenge to official discourse, as a project with its own alternative vision of the past, or as a neatly defined project of national identity building. Cynicism and scepticism are suitable tools for destroying the monstrous constructs of official propaganda, but they prevent participants in the debate from building bonds of solidarity and sustainable forms of collective identity.

In short, in Belarusian digital media there is a realm of freedom, but this freedom is unlikely to spread beyond the boundaries of social networks. At any rate, the attempts to transfer the mobilization potential of social networks into offline protest capital in Belarus (by which I mean the wave of protests in Belarusian cities in 2011, which were coordinated through the V Kontakte social network) ended in failure. They ceased after the repressive actions of the authorities – an outcome which was quite predictable. Fragmented and provocative as it is, online counter-memory has its limitations. On the other hand, it does allow at least some degree of preservation of freedom of thought in the face of strong government pressure aimed at homogenization of cultural memory.

Notes

1 Some 1,147 respondents were interviewed in the study which was a national representative sampling for Belarus. Responses to the open question 'What events of Belarusian history are you proud of?' were used for analysis. Respondents were allowed to mention up to three events.
2 A metaphor that points to the similarity of the two totalitarian regimes – the Nazi and the communist regimes.

References

Alexanyan, K. (2009) 'Social Networking on Runet', *Digital Icons* 2. Online. Available: <http://www.digitalicons.org/wp-content/uploads/2009/11/Karina-Alexanyan-DI-2.1.pdf> (accessed 16 March 2012).

ARCHE (2011) 1–2 (Special issue: '19 December 2010').

Budz'ma (2011) *'Budz'ma Belarusians'*. Online. Available: <http://budzma.org/uncategorized/budzma-belarusans.html> (accessed 16 March 2012).

Bugai, M. (2011) 'Ci naliezhyc' bielarusam chapliac' gieorgieuskia lientachki?', *Nasha Niva,* 7 May. Online. Available: <http://nn.by/?c=ar&i=38180> (accessed 16 March 2012).

Erll, A. and Rigney, A. (eds) (2009) *Mediation, Remediation, and the Dynamics of Cultural Memory.* Berlin: De Gruyter.

Garde-Hansen, J., Hoskins, A. and Reading, A. (eds) (2009) *Save As . . . Digital Memories.* Basingstoke: Palgrave Macmillan.

Goujon, A. (2010) 'Memorial Narratives of WWII Partisans and Genocide in Belarus', *East European Politics and Societies* 24(1): 6–25.

Grinevich, V. (2005) 'Raskolotaia pamiat': Vtoraia mirovaia voina v istoricheskom soznanii ukrainskogo obshchestva', *Neprikosnovennyi zapas* 2–3. Online. Available: <http://magazines.russ.ru/nz/2005/2/gri24.html> (accessed 16 March 2012).

Hansen, I. (2006) 'Prastora bielaruskaga palitychnaga dyskursu i iago vizualnyia i pierfarmatyunyia eliemienty', in V. Bulhakau (ed.), *Gieapalitychnaie miesca Bielarusi u Europie i sviecie.* Warsaw: Publishing House of Lazarski University.

Kuzio, T. (2002) 'History, Memory and Nation Building in the Post-Soviet Colonial Space'. *Nationalities Papers* 30(2): 241–264.

Lastovskii [Lastouski], A. (2009) 'Spetsifika istoricheskoi pamiati v Belarusi: mezhdu sovetskim proshlym i natsional'noi perspektivoi', *Vestnik obshchestvennogo mneniia: Dannye. Analiz. Diskussii* 4: 88–99.

Leshchenko, N. (2008) 'The National Ideology and the Basis of the Lukashenka Regime in Belarus', *Europe-Asia Studies* 60(8): 1419–1433.

lesnoi-slon (2008) '9 maia', 8 May. Online posting. Available: http://lesnoi-slon.livejournal.com/227248.html?page=2&cut_expand=1#cutid1 (accessed 16 March 2012).

lesnoi-slon (2011) 9 May. Online posting. Available: <http://lesnoi-slon.livejournal.com/829871.html> (accessed 16 March 2012).

Lindner, R. (1999) 'Besieged Past: National and Court Historians in Lukashenka's Belarus', *Nationalities Papers* 27(4): 631–647.

MacLeod, H. (2009) 'Examining Political Group Membership on LiveJournal', *Digital Icons* 2. Online. Available: <http://www.digitalicons.org/issue02/heather-macleod/> (accessed 16 March 2012).

Marples, D. (2007) 'Sila i slabas'c' bielaruskaga autarytaryzmu', *ARCHE* 4. Online. Available: <http://arche.bymedia.net/2007-04/marplez704.htm> (accessed 16 March 2012).

Marples, D. and Padgol, U. (2008) 'Palityka pamiaci u drugoi rasijskamounai dziarzhavie', *ARCHE* 11: 91–100.

Pershai, A. (2006) 'Questioning the Hegemony of the Nation State in Belarus: Production of Intellectual Discourses As Production of Resources', *Nationalities Papers* 34(5): 623–635.

Ponomarev, A. and Lefter, H-V. (2012) 'Belarus and the Internet: Beyond the Misunderstanding, Still a Web Under Control', *Social Science Research Network*. Online. Available: <http://papers.ssrn.com/sol3/papers.cfm?abstract_id=1998404&> (accessed 16 March 2012).

prychynets (2011) 'Dlia mianie 9 maia dzien' smutku i boli'. 9 May. Online posting. Available: <http://prychynets.livejournal.com/42044.html> (accessed 16 March 2012).

Reporters Without Borders (2012) 'Internet Enemies Report 2012', *Reporters Without Borders*. Online. Available: <http://en.rsf.org/IMG/pdf/rapport-internet2012_ang.pdf> (accessed 16 March 2012).

Rudling, P.A. (2008) '"For a Heroic Belarus!": The Great Patriotic War as Identity Marker in the Lukashenka and Soviet Belarusian Discourses', *Sprawy Narodowościowe (Nationalities Affairs)* 32: 43–62.

Shatalava, V. (2008) 'Cieni vajny: paliceiskija i partyzany u pamiaci nasiel'nictva bielaruskaj vioski', *Homo Historicus*: 384–389.

Smalianchuk, A. (2008) 'Shkol'ny padruchnik gistoryji iak "miesca pamiacci/miesca zabyccia" pra Druguiu Susvietnuiu vainu', *Homo Historicus*: 370–383.

tut.by Forum (2011) Online. Available: <http://forums.tut.by/showthread.php?t=13720086&pp=1000000> (accessed 16 March 2012).

Urban, M. (1989) *An Algebra of Soviet Power: Elite Circulation in the Belorussian Republic, 1966–1986*. Cambridge: Cambridge University Press.

van Dijck, J. (2007) *Mediated Memories in the Digital Age*. Stanford, CA: Stanford University Press.

Wikipedia (Russian version) (2012) 'Naimenovaniia belorusskogo gosudarstva'. Online. Available: <http://ru.wikipedia.org/wiki/Наименования_белорусского_государства> (accessed 16 March 2012).

Woolhiser, C. (2011) '"Belarusian Russian": Sociolinguistic Status and Discursive Representation', in R. Muhr (ed.), *Non-dominating Varieties of Pluricentric Languages: Getting the Picture. In Memory of Prof. Michael Clyne*. Vienna: Peter Lang Verlag.

Zorina, A. and Avison, D. (2011) 'Discovering New ICT-Enabled Models: The Case of Grassroots Development of Internet Access in Belarus'. *ECIS 2011 Proceedings*. Online. Available: <http://is2.lse.ac.uk/asp/aspecis/20110218.pdf> (accessed 16 March 2012).

Part Three

Images of memory

If revolving mostly around language and words, several of the preceding chapters also have a prominent visual component. This component is highlighted in some contributions, but, even to studies that focus exclusively on texts, language's visual presentation and composition is of increasing importance. After all, with digitization the primarily text-oriented 'constellation of writing and book [has] been overtaken by the new constellation of image and screen' – and 'the processes of making texts and reading texts are both processes of design' (Kress 2004). When online we never look *exclusively* at words, even when we visit a text-only site or blog. The same site or blog also inevitably includes *images* or visual components – a term we use here in the broad sense: a web page's visual ingredients can range from flashy (audio)visuals and videos to plain navigation menus or a tiny 'Tweet' button.

Images merit special attention from the scholar of Russian media. The latest generation of online media leads us away from the myth of Russian media as logo- and literaturo-centric by nature. Rather than revolving around 'the word', Russian online media culture is increasingly visual. Most new media scholarship on Russia has so far tended to focus on Russian blogging, but since the advent of YouTube, broadband Internet and cameraphones, we have seen a decline in the importance of language-based textual blogs in the Russian media space. Oppositional activity has been largely migrating from LiveJournal to other platforms, and there has been a huge growth in audiences for video blogging on YouTube, for example.

The chapters in Part Three allocate a prominent space to the increasingly important domain of visual online expression. In some way or other, all deal with (audio)visual responses to the Soviet and socialist past. Some do so in passing, while visualization is a prime interest for others – including the author of Chapter 11, cultural historian-cum-journalist Maria Pasholok. Pasholok analyses online portals, blogs and social networks whose users debate the geopolitical status of the Crimea, an autonomous republic within Ukraine. Exploring such visual memory tools as conceptual maps and *demotivators*,[1] she argues that post-socialist web wars boil down to infinite symbolical reinterpretations of the past.

Pasholok's claim is confirmed by the chapters that follow. Investigating the visually spectacular attempts to re-create the Soviet past in two Russian digital games, literary historian Gernot Howanitz (Chapter 12) examines the memory potential of gaming. Contrary to popular views on gaming and violence, Howanitz argues that, if the two games did trigger minor web wars, ultimately the computer game industry may well be conducive to the consolidation of a new, post-socialist identity.

Equally cautiously optimistic conclusions on online memory are drawn by political scientist Caterina Preda (Chapter 13) in a study of digitally mediated commemorations of dictator Nicolae Ceauşescu. According to Preda – who maps Ceauşescu memorializations in state-funded web archives, on amateur and artists' sites, blogs, and in social-networking platforms – in Romania, 'online media counterbalance the offline unidirectional construction of the past'.

Pasholok, Howanitz and Preda all primarily ponder counter-official memory iconography. Political communications scholar Jussi Lassila, by contrast, is interested in the political use of memory in a top-down history event: a project dedicated to the Second World War launched by state-driven online TV network *Russia Today*. Lassila's analysis of *Russia Today*'s visual and rhetorical memory strategies demonstrates that, apart from accommodating alternative voices, digital media also offer an excellent locus for the production of politically viable memory narratives.

In Chapter 15, cultural historian Dieter De Bruyn focuses on the 2010 Smolensk air crash, in which many of Poland's leading figures met their deaths, and which triggered fierce debates on the nation's socialist past. Using visual and verbal Facebook responses to the Smolensk tragedy to theorize on the idiosyncrasies of online memory practices, De Bruyn argues that in our digitized age, 'Polish memory of communism is now being exposed and put into perspective in ways that open up possibilities for new critical assessments of Polish history'.

De Bruyn's conclusion shares with that of most chapters in this section an inclination to ponder the socio-political implications of digital commemoration. In post-socialist space, its contributors wonder, does digital memory trigger more cosmopolitan, polyphonic approaches to historical traumas? Or do they offer, in Lassila's words, 'even better options for emulating the transnational world in the service of national goals'? If the answer to these questions is still pending, the coming pages do demonstrate that – to cite the author whose chapter follows next – 'visualizing becomes an integral part of the way in which online wars are fought'.

Note

1 *Demotivators* are image–caption combinations whose meanings tend to contradict one another, and that circulate in social media (see also Lastouski, Chapter 10, this volume).

Reference

Kress, G. (2004) 'Reading Images: Multimodality, Representation and New Media'. *Expert Forum for Knowledge Presentation*. Online. Available: <http://www.knowledgepresentation.org/BuildingTheFuture/Kress2/Kress2.html>.

11 Between Runet and Ukrnet

Mapping the Crimean web war

Maria Pasholok

Introduction

The Crimean peninsula occupies a unique place in the Russian–Ukrainian relationship, where it has long been the point of departure for sharp national, historical, cultural and political debates. The Crimea became part of the Russian Empire in 1783 during the reign of Catherine the Great. Later, after the Bolsheviks took power, Crimea was incorporated into the Russian Soviet Federative Socialist Republic (RSFSR), where it remained for over three decades. On 19 February 1954, the Soviet leader Nikita Khrushchev presented the Crimean peninsula to the Ukrainian SSR as a 'gift' from the RSFSR. This historical fact initiated a long and exhaustive national discourse on the territory.

Although currently Crimea has the special status of an autonomous republic within independent Ukraine, many Russians insist on the illegitimacy of this status and believe that Crimea should be 'given back' to Russia. At the same time, Ukrainians have been making every effort to refill Crimea's cultural space with their own national values. This process is even more evident today, as the Internet has radically changed both the way Soviet memory is transferred between generations and communities and the way the territory is represented in cyberspace. Under these modern conditions, a new digital 'Crimean war' has been proclaimed.

The historical Crimean war took place on the Crimean peninsula from October 1853 to February 1856. It was a conflict for the influence over the territories of the Ottoman Empire that was, at that time, in decline. The participants in the conflict were the Russian Empire, on one side, and the British Empire, the French and Ottoman Empires and the Kingdom of Sardinia, on the other. As the result of the conflict, the Treaty of Paris, signed on 30 March 1856, made the Black Sea neutral territory. The 'Crimean Web war' to which I refer in this chapter borrows only its name from the real Crimean war. Unlike the latter, it deals not with the real space of Crimea, but with its imaginary representations on the Web. Its participants are Russian and Ukrainian Web users – defined here not by nationality, citizenship or residence in Crimea, but by their relationship to an identity: the Russian or Ukrainian digital representation of the peninsula.[1]

Through a close-reading study of online resources – such as the 'Russian Crimea' news agency (www.RusCrimea.org) and the online portal about

'Ukrainian life in Sevastopol' (www.ukrlife.org), as well as relevant discussions in personal blogs and social networks – this chapter investigates the strategy and tactics of this online war. It analyses how the Soviet trauma of a 'lost Crimea' is mediated both digitally and visually.

Virtual and visual

The unique form of the peninsula,[2] and its favourable geographical position on the north coast of the Black Sea, offering easy access to the Sea of Azov, has made Crimea an object of desire in many military conflicts throughout history. It is no wonder that it is precisely the geography of the peninsula that has become the main topic of the online conflict.

However, the geographies and cartographies of cyberspace are different from their prototypes in 'geographic' space proper. Unlike the physical Crimea, the peninsula's imaginary representations on the Web share one important quality with all virtual spaces – they are in fact 'antispatial': their reconstruction as territorial systems is entirely visual in nature (Mitchell 1998: 205). As Kambiz Memarzia has stated, in cyberspace there are no rules, no gravity, no scale, no dimensions, and no spatio-temporal qualities – nothing of what is common for 'normal' spatial architecture (Memarzia 1997).

In order to describe the spatiality of virtual geographies, Marcos Novak has coined the term 'liquid architecture', defined as 'an architecture whose form is contingent on the interests of the beholder':

> It is an architecture that opens to welcome you and closes to defend you; it is an architecture without doors and hallways, where the next room is always where it needs to be and what it needs to be. It is an architecture that dances or pulsates, becomes tranquil or agitated. Liquid architecture makes liquid cities, cities that change at the shift of a value, where visitors with different backgrounds see different landmarks, where neighbourhoods vary with ideas held in common, and evolve as the ideas mature or dissolve.
>
> (Novak 1991: 251–252)

Following Novak, I would argue that Crimean virtual space is embodied in two forms of liquid architectural construction that are 'contingent' upon the interests of their two 'beholders' – those who want to see a Russian Crimea, and those who prefer to see it as a Ukrainian peninsula. I choose the verb 'to see' deliberately, as the two forms of Crimean online architecture discussed here are constructed, first and foremost, by a constant reinterpretation of the *visual* representation of Crimea's shape, and not so much by narratives, or historical and political slogans.[3]

Re-imagining space and mapping its borders is essential for constructing any kind of national identity, especially for countries as vast as Russia in both its Soviet and federal manifestations (Franklin and Widdis 2004). Crimea, as an important part of the Russian imaginary – if no longer geographical, then definitely cultural

(Hokanson 1998; Liusyi 2003) – is certainly true to this principle. As this chapter will demonstrate, symbolic interpretations and reinterpretations of the peninsula's shape have become the dominant tool for discovering and constructing Crimean national identity on the Web.

Along with exploring Crimean virtual geography, this chapter analyses the relationship between online conflict and visuality. In doing so, it aims to find out how the matter of visualizing becomes an integral part of the way in which online wars are fought. My other goal is to show how the virtual conflict is addressed as a visual spectacle in contrast to political, social and historical narratives. If these narratives have already attracted much scholarly attention (Beloff 1997; Kuzio 2007), I focus my attention on the largely overlooked deployment of the visual as a specific weapon in this online war for Crimean virtual space.

Digital maps of the conflict

Visiting Moscow for the first time in 1926 to 1927, at a time when maps were being used intensively as part of the drive to shape and project the identity of the Soviet Union, Walter Benjamin noticed that 'the map is almost as close to becoming the centre of the new Russian icon cult as is Lenin's portrait' (Benjamin 1986: 51). Those who try to browse 'Russian' or 'Ukrainian Crimea' on the Web are likely to find themselves similarly overwhelmed by the strikingly dominant presence of maps in Crimean digital space. Different kinds of geographical models of the peninsula, some highly creative, are very popular among Internet users and seem to have acquired an iconic significance for those engaged in defining and re-establishing Crimean identity on the Web.

However, navigating this virtual territory (which, as we saw above, is in fact a 'non-territory') is a difficult matter. Specialists in virtual mapping Jiang and Ormeling have classified cybermaps according to their function: they can serve for cyberspatial analysis, which helps us understand the structure of the online territory; for navigation, which helps one find one's way in the digital spaces; and for persuasion, which acts as a tool to influence the users (Jiang and Ormeling 1997). Virtual maps of Crimea largely fall into the latter category. Most of them use specific tools and rhetorical elements to defend one out of two basic positions: Crimea belongs to Ukraine; or Crimea belongs to Russia. Dodge, who has written a lot on virtual mapping, has divided 'cybermaps' into a number of types, including geographical metaphors, conceptual maps, topology maps, virtual cities and navigation tools (Dodge 1997). The agents of the Crimean Web conflict over Crimea employ all of these types, but the most controversial is the mixture of the first two – geographical metaphors and conceptual maps.

Exemplary are those Web users who believe in a 'Ukrainian Crimea'. They employ the cartographic image of Crimea as a part of Ukraine in order to create a concept of a united and undivided country. This fact is indeed hard to refute: Crimea *is* an integral part of Ukraine's present territory. However, those who still believe in a 'Russian Crimea' try to argue this state of affairs by introducing a conceptual virtual map of Ukraine. On this map, the country has its contemporary borders; as on a political map, different regions of the country are highlighted in different colours. However, each of Ukraine's parts is also provided here with a new legend. This legend presents several descriptions of carefully selected episodes and historical events that are designed to explain how and when this particular territory became Ukrainian.

The explanations provided on this alternative map serve a political goal: they are aimed at calling into question the legitimacy of Ukraine's claim to this territory. The anonymous authors of this map assert that every piece of the territory that belongs to contemporary Ukraine was in fact 'gifted' to Ukraine by one or another of the Soviet or Russian leaders. On this map, the New Russia[4] is depicted as a gift from Lenin presented in 1922; Western Ukraine and Northern Bukovina become gifts from Stalin given in 1939 to 1940; central Ukraine is represented as a series of gifts from the Russian Tsars during the period 1654 to 1917. Crimea finishes the series of 'territorial' presents being 'gifted' in 1954 by Nikita Khrushchev.[5] Moreover, following this map's logic, Ukraine itself did not exist before the first gift was presented.

Depicting Crimea as part of the territory of Ukraine in its entirety is one of the most vivid ways of visually asserting Ukrainian ownership of the peninsula. The maps that represent the peninsula on its own, however, require more creativity from the online cartographers in order to highlight its national identity. In one such map, which is framed as a so-called *demotivator*[6] – pictures popular on the Internet, which consist of image and caption, usually opposite or contradictory in meaning – Ukrainian virtual cartographers use a red line to highlight Crimea's borders. The caption reads: 'The national border of Ukraine is inviolable.' Additional statements such as 'Crimea is Ukrainian' are also drafted across the image of the peninsula, and the body of the peninsula itself is shaded in the colours of the Ukrainian flag. To add to this statement of belonging, the lower caption is addressed to the 'Muscovites' (*москалі*, in Ukrainian) – a commonly used pejorative label for Russians living in Ukraine. This second caption reads: 'Muscovites, remember that Crimea is Ukrainian. In case you forget, write it on your forehead, or on your ass'. The offensive tone of the message is common to both sides of this online conflict.

The same virtual battle is extended in the group 'Sevastopol-Crimea-Russia' on the popular social network V Kontakte. This community is dedicated to 'the Russian Crimea' and has stipulated several rules for its users and guests. One of the most important rules states that this is a 'gathering for educated people', and that hence both swear-words and Ukrainian language are forbidden. For the creators of this group, the Ukrainian language itself becomes 'obscene', and those who speak it are compared to 'uneducated people' who use swear-words in public.

In the 'Sevastopol-Crimea-Russia' community's image gallery, one may find a lot of visual responses to the virtual maps of Crimea that represent the peninsula as a part of Ukraine. These maps are usually decorated with the attributes of the wars fought by Russian troops on Crimean soil. Illustrative is one map featuring a caption with a simple question: 'Is Crimea Ukrainian?' – together with the answer: 'But the blood that was spilt there is Russian!' Other maps of Crimea are decorated with the St Andrew's Cross or St George's Ribbon – martial symbols that also appeal to the heroic defence of Sevastopol both during the Crimean War and the Second World War, and that invite commentators to use military metaphors for the description of the online conflict over Sevastopol – the 'city of Russian glory'.

Urban practices

Virtual cities comprise one of the most important categories of virtual mapping. If we look for examples of the representation of different cities on the virtual maps of Crimea, we may be led to believe that the peninsula has only one city: Sevastopol. Sevastopol is consistently the key focus of online 'battles' for Crimean identity.[7]

In real-life Sevastopol, a common urban practice consists of decorating spaces with Russian flags or attaching ribbons in the colours of the Russian flag to cars and clothing. As the number of Internet users in the city increases, this practice gradually moves into virtual space. Many Web users take photos of the Russian flags displayed throughout the city and upload them. The result is a virtual Sevastopol that, like the real city, is aggressively overloaded with Russian flags.

Another sign of urban national identity heritage that has moved from offline urban space to its virtual representation is graffiti stating that Sevastopol is a Russian city. Photographs of such graffiti are also eagerly uploaded online. The Web thus provides an excellent opportunity to discover a Sevastopol existing within Russian space just by typing the words 'Russian Sevastopol' in Russian or Ukrainian into a search browser. One might easily be overwhelmed by the image of the city that the visual results for this search term yield. They create the impression that every corner of the virtual city is marked with the line: 'Sevastopol is Russian'. In fact, there are no white clear walls in this virtual Russian Sevastopol. 'Sevastopol is Russian' becomes the landmark of the virtual city.

Against the online dominance of pro-Russian imagery, those participants in the online conflict who believe that Sevastopol is Ukrainian invent highly creative methods of 'counter-attack'. As a response to the common slogan that Sevastopol is the city of Russian glory, those citizens of virtual Sevastopol who want to create their own Ukrainian city – cleansed of any Russian presence – set out to reveal the 'dark' sides of urban life with a view to rebranding the Russian Sevastopol as a city of misery and destitution. One of the most popular photographs expressing this alternative view depicts a wall with graffiti that reads 'Glory to Russia'. Under this wall lies the body of a presumably drunk, homeless man – an image that, without words, implies the counter-message: 'This is what is left of your glory'. This picture creates a natural *demotivator*, in which the meaning of the image (the real person lying on the street) deconstructs the meaning of the caption (in this case, the lines written on the wall).

Conclusion

If the real Crimean War had its winners, and every offline contemporary political conflict over Crimea has resulted in concrete political decisions, treaties and legislation,[8] the online Crimean war seems to be endless. For every digital 'attack' from one side there is a response from the other that deconstructs (or 'demotivates') the attack. The participants of the conflict wage online battles on the level of constant symbolic reinterpretations of the images of the peninsula. As we have seen, the image of Crimea becomes a subject of creative visual transformation, and is the main 'weapon' which the virtual 'soldiers' of this war employ. In this constant changing of virtual representations, the Crimean digital war has no linearity, no beginning and no end.

In 1984, in the novel *Neuromancer*, the inventor of the term *cyberspace*, science fiction writer William Gibson, describes the new concept as 'the nonspace of mind . . . a consensual hallucination' (Gibson 1984: 51). This is what the virtual Crimea becomes in the space of the Russian and Ukrainian segments of the Internet. To use computing scientist Michael Benedikt's vocabulary (Benedikt 1991: 3), in cyberspace, the peninsula turns into 'a common mental geography' for Crimeans. Its virtual territory of abstract imagination is 'swarming with data and lies, with mind stuff and memories of nature, with a million voices and two million eyes in a silent, invisible concert of enquiry, dealmaking, dream sharing, and simple beholding'. Its digital war never ends.

Notes

1 Here, I limit my study to the Russian-Ukrainian rivalry, excluding the Crimean Tatars, who also claim a right to the territory as a result of the Stalinist deportation of Crimean Tatars from the region in 1944. For a discussion on the Crimean Tatars and the question of Crimean national identity, see Brian Glyn Williams' monograph *The Crimean Tatars: The Diaspora Experience and the Forging of a Nation* (2001).

2 Crimea is commonly referred to in the local tradition as a 'medal' on the chest of the Earth.

3 Even those narrative slogans that appear on the Web in relation to Crimean identity are represented through a visual medium – photography or collages.

4 New Russia, or Novorossiia, is a term that came into use following the Russian annexation of the Crimean Khanate in 1783 to refer to a territory that included today's Southern Ukraine.

5 This map of gift-giving could act as an interesting addition and analogy to Nikolai Ssorin-Chaikov and Olga Sosnina's innovative work on gift-giving to Stalin (2006), which covered not only gift objects, but also symbolic and metaphorical gifts of memory and concepts.

6 On demotivators see also Lastouski (Chapter 10, this volume).

7 For an excellent discussion of the image of the city in Russian off-line culture, see Plokhy (2000).

8 For example, on the status of the Russian language in Crimea, or the Russian naval base in Sevastopol.

References

Beloff, M. (ed.) (1997) *Beyond the Soviet Union: The Fragmentation of Power*. Aldershot: Ashgate.

Benedikt, M. (1991) *Introduction to Cyberspace: First Steps*. Cambridge, MA: MIT Press.

Benjamin, W. (1986) *Moscow Diary*, Cambridge, MA, and London: Harvard University Press.

Dodge, M. (1997) 'A Cybermap Atlas: Envisioning the Internet'. *TeleGeography 1997/97*: 63–68.

Dodge, M. and Kitchin, R. (2000) *Mapping Cyberspace*. London: Routledge.

Franklin, S. and Widdis, E. (2004) *National Identity in Russian Culture: An Introduction*. Cambridge: Cambridge University Press.

Gibson, W. (1984) *Neuromancer*. New York: Ace Books.

Jiang, B. and Ormeling, F.J. (1997) 'Cybermap: The Map for Cyberspace'. *The Cartographic Journal* 34(2), Summer: 111–116.

Hokanson, K. (1998) 'Pushkin's Captive Crimea: Imperialism in *The Fountain of Bakchisarai*', in Monika Greenleaf and Stephen Moeller-Sally (eds), *Russian Subjects: Empire, Nation, and the Culture of the Golden Age*. Evanston, IL: Northwestern University Press, pp. 123–148.

Kuzio, T. (2007) *Ukraine—Crimea – Russia: Triangle of Conflict*. Stuttgart: Ibidem-Verlag.

Liusyi, A. (2003) *Krymskii tekst v russkoi literature*. St Petersburg: Aleteiia.

Memarzia, K. (1997) 'Towards the Definition and Applications of Digital Architecture', in M. Dodge and R. Kitchin (2000), *Mapping Cyberspace*. London: Routledge.

Mitchell, W.J. (1998) 'Antitectonics: The Poetics of Virtuality', in J. Beckmann (ed.), *The Virtual Dimension: Architecture, Representation and Crash Culture*. New York: Princeton Architectural Press.

Novak, M. (1991) 'Liquid Architecture in Cyberspace', in M. Benedikt (ed.), *Cyberspace: First Steps*. Cambridge, MA: MIT Press.

Plokhy, S. (2000) 'The City of Glory: Sevastopol in Russian Historical Mythology'. *Journal of Contemporary History* 35(3), Autumn: 369–383.

Ssorin-Chaikov, N. and Sosnina, O. (2006) *Dary vozhdiam – Gifts to Soviet Leaders*. Moscow: Pinakoteka.

Williams, B.G. (2001) *The Crimean Tatars: The Diaspora Experience and the Forging of a Nation*. Leiden, Boston, MA:, and Koln: Brill.

12 Repeating history?

The computer game as historiographic device

Gernot Howanitz

Introduction

Computer games offer a wide range of possibilities for those with an interest in history. In Russian – and Ukrainian[1] – games, for example, one can play a thirteenth-century boyar (*13 vek. Slava ili smert'* 2007), a seventeenth-century Cossack (*Kozaki* 2000), an infantry soldier in the Second World War (*V tylu vraga* 2004) or a tank commander in the Afghanistan war (*Liniia fronta: Afganistan '82* 2010). Regardless of the different strategies these games follow to deal with the past, they can obviously be used as tools for commemoration. But how are such games reshaping post-socialist memory and identity? What strategies do they employ in dealing with the past? Are there grounds for viewing digital gaming as yet another front of the East European memory wars?

Most of the Russian and Ukrainian games strive – just like their Western counterparts – to faithfully re-create the past. Illustrative is the 'game documentary' ('dokumental'naia igra') *The Truth about the Ninth Company* (*Pravda o deviatoi rote* 2008) which with painstaking effort tries to give the player the possibility to re-enact one specific historical battle in the Afghanistan war.[2] On the other hand, quite a few Russian games offer obviously distorted versions of the past. In one of the first-ever Russian computer games, *Times of Trouble: Living Dead* (*Smuta: Ozhivshie mertvetsy* 1997), the player has to kill zombie boyars. More recent games following this strategy include *Stalin vs. Martians* (*Stalin protiv marsian* 2009), in which aliens try to invade Siberia; *Metro-2* (2005), where the chief of the secret police, Lavrentii Beriia, wants to kill Stalin with an atomic bomb; and *You Are Empty* (2006), where Stalin has turned the whole Soviet populace into zombies. Other examples blend the future with the past. These include *S.T.A.L.K.E.R.: Shadow of Chernobyl* (*Ten' Chernobylia* 2007), which relocates Arkadii and Boris Strugatskii's cult science fiction novel *Roadside Picnic* (*Piknik na obochine* 1972) to the mutant-infested premises of the crippled Chernobyl power plant. *Metro 2033* (2010), an adaption of Dmitrii Glukhovskii's dystopian bestseller novel of the same title, is set in the catacombs of the post-apocalyptic Moscow Metro, which is also threatened by – surprise, surprise – Mutants. These features – distorted versions of the past, cyclical time, monsters – are not exclusive to Russian games; they may be found in contemporary Russian literature as well. The tendency of Russian writers to resort to mythical elements in order to deal with a traumatic past has been described in detail by one of this book's co-authors, the cultural historian Alexander Etkind, as *magical historicism* (Etkind 2009) – a literary weapon in an ongoing inner-Russian memory war.

This chapter concentrates on the virtual renditions of the Stalin era in a less elaborately explored cultural field: that of digital gaming. Zooming in on the two computer games *Metro-2* and *Stalin vs. Martians*, the chapter consists of four parts. First of all, recent research concerning computer games and history is summarized. Second, I map out the plot and overall characteristics of the two games in question. Third, I examine the relations between computer games, repetition and history with a special emphasis on one of the core questions of computer game theory: the relationship between interaction and narration. To conclude, I examine these games in the context of the digital memory wars that this book explores. I argue that, despite their obvious potential as weapons in East European memory wars, in fact these games tend to be perceived by their players rather in terms of Cold War binary categories of East vs. West.

Computer games and history

Compared to other, more traditional media, computer games facilitate visual re-creations of the past with the added bonus of user interaction. The player is immersed in the virtual reality and experiences a state of mind that has been described by psychologist Mihály Csíkszentmihályi as 'flow'. This term characterizes a state of high concentration and total absorption, a 'holistic sensation that people feel when they act with total involvement' (Csíkszentmihályi 2000: 36). Moreover, in digital games virtual space is experienced as the Real; the brain readily accepts virtual renderings as a real spatial experience, as the Georgia Institute of Technology's virtual acrophobia experiment has shown. Larry Hodges and his research group created virtual models of high places and showed them to known acrophobics. The research subjects exhibited syndromes such as weak knees, sweaty palms, etc. when exposed to these virtual simulations (Bolter and Grusin 2000: 165). Given the combined effects of 'flow' and virtual reality, then, one might argue that a digital re-creation of past environments may serve as a kind of time machine. By means of playing (i.e. interacting with a virtually re-created historical space), the player may experience a sense of actually *repeating history*.

Alluring as this idea may be, however, recent research has shown it to be false. In fact, the games' key feature – interactivity – does not mix well with history. We might go so far as to argue that digital gaming poses an important challenge to history, as traditionally understood. Media scholar William Uricchio notes that 'the interaction between a present-day player and the representation of a historically specific world would seem to challenge any notion of . . . historical "fact" and "fixity"' (Uricchio 2005: 327). According to him, the possible spectrum of historical games is confined by the following two poles:

> One sort . . . is specific in the sense that it deals with a particular historical event . . . allowing the player to engage in a speculative or 'what if' encounter

> with a particular past. In these games, efforts are usually taken to maximize the accuracy of historical detail, allowing the setting and conditions to constrain and shape game play. At the other extreme are games that deal with historical process in a somewhat abstracted or structural manner. . . . In both cases, history in the Rankean sense of 'wie es eigentlich gewesen ist' is subverted by an insistence on history as a multivalent process subject to many different possibilities, interpretations, and outcomes.
>
> (Uricchio 2005: 328)

This counterfactual quality of computer games parallels the developments of poststructuralist historiography, which challenges 'notions of facticity, explanatory hierarchies, master narratives, and . . . the interpretive authority of the historian' (Uricchio 2005: 328). In this regard – so Uricchio argues – historical computer games 'offer a new means of reflecting upon the past, working through its possibilities, its alternatives, its "might-have-beens"' (Uricchio 2005: 336).

Very much like Uricchio, media historian Wulf Kansteiner is convinced that computer games reshape our understanding of history. According to him, games are bound to transfigure the idea of collective memory, because they allow us to 'invent the content of our memories *and* the collectives which sustain them in such a compelling fashion that we will no longer need others to develop a psychologically functional sense of self' (Kansteiner 2007: 132; italics in original). In the future, users will no longer depend on centralized, official institutions for shaping collective memory. Using the games' counterfactual potential, they will be able to try out all sorts of different histories without the reality check of established institutions (Kansteiner 2007: 143). Of course, the current level of technology prevents computer games from realizing the full potential of the 'new' collective memory that Kansteiner describes; at present, it is still possible to distinguish between so-called *non-player characters* controlled by the computer and *avatars* of other players, so no perfect simulation of virtual collectives exists (Kansteiner 2007: 142).

Claudio Fogu, the last media theorist whom I want to cite, emphasizes that with computer games, the end of representation has been reached – historical computer games do not reference the past, and they do not reference the Real:

> The digitalization of history in video games thus brings together spatialization, virtualization, and simulation to complete the elimination of representation as the medium that anchored historical action to historical consciousness. Without representation, the Aristotelian opposition between history and poetry comes to a point of reversal. For Aristotle the former was inferior to the latter because it only spoke of what *had* happened, rather than what *may* happen. Digital history enters the twenty-first century exclusively under the sign of the possible; we are now interested only in what may happen and are no longer concerned with what has happened.
>
> (Fogu 2009: 121; italics in original)

Fogu points out that '[d]igital technology may have already produced a reconfiguration of what we mean by "historical" in the first place' (Fogu 2009: 106). As regards counterfactual representations of the past, he mentions two feature films, Oliver Stone's *JFK* (1991) and Robert Zemecki's *Forrest Gump* (1994), which by means of digital imagery 'blur the boundary between the historically real (that is, recorded) and the historically fictional' (Fogu 2009: 111f.).

To conclude: computer games share a common ground with the theories of poststructuralist historiography. Rather than facilitating a repetition or restaging of history, they are always history-altering devices, because the player's freedom automatically leads to a rewriting of the past.

The games: a brief overview

Let us pause now to examine *Metro-2* and *Stalin vs. Martians*, the two games that interest me here. Following Uricchio's spectrum, both of these games deal with specific historical events rather than mimicking general historic processes. The crucial point is, however, that the rewriting of history already starts during the process of their initial development – history here is rewritten by the designers, not the players. It is not so much that the players can try out different possibilities – quite the contrary: they have to follow the designers' vision quite closely, as the plots of both games are absolutely linear.

Metro-2, to begin with, is a so-called *first-person shooter* (FPS, 'shuter ot pervogo litsa'). This computer game genre features two main distinctive traits: it uses a first-person view and implements violent game play – the player's main means of interacting with the game world is a gun (see Figure 12.1). Because of the perspective and the fact that the player's character is not visible, first-person shooters are regarded as being highly *immersive* – that is, they offer a direct, capturing experience (Rehak 2007: 187). It should be noted that *Metro-2*'s setting as a whole and especially the positive portrayal of Stalin promote a Stalinist point of view. The game's main protagonist is Gleb Suvorov, a low-ranking officer of the Soviet secret police, who has to save Stalin from an assassination attempt conducted by Lavrentii Beriia in 1952. In order to achieve this goal, Gleb fights legions of defected secret police soldiers in a Moscow-based secret government transportation system called *Metro-2*.

Here, the game mixes fact and fiction: the notion of a second, secret Moscow subway belongs to the realm of urban myth.[3] The mythical locations are clearly considered to be the game's main appeal – hence the title. On the other hand, the blurb on the back cover also stresses the game's authenticity: it features 'real Moscow places, recreated with photorealistic accuracy: subway stations, the Kremlin, Moscow State University; a carefully recreated atmosphere from the middle of the 1950s'. And indeed, *Metro-2* offers convincing experiences of environments modelled after real Moscow locations. *Maiakovskaia*, one of the featured Metro stations which were built in the Stalinist period, includes, for example, faithful virtual reproductions of Soviet artist Aleksandr Deineka's ceiling mosaics. But *Metro-2* does not only visually re-create the past. The programmers

Figure 12.1 Screenshot from *Metro-2* (Russia, G5 Software/Orion Games 2005)

also tried to evoke the atmosphere of Moscow in 1952 by means of including ambient sounds, such as Vasilii Agapkin's famous march *The Slav Woman's Farewell* (*Proshchanie Slavianki* 1941) and Stalin speeches.

Stalin vs. Martians, on the other hand, exemplifies what, in gaming jargon, is called a *real-time strategy* (RTS, 'strategiia v real'nom vremeni'). This genre is not as immediate and immersive as FPS, as the player is not in control of a single protagonist, but rather of a whole army. The same difference affects the player's point of view: the first-person perspective is replaced by a bird's-eye view (see Figure 12.2).

The *Stalin vs. Martians'* plot is both trivial and strange: in the course of the Second World War, Martians invade Siberia, and as Stalin is occupied with fighting Nazi Germany, he appoints the player to defend Mother Russia against extraterrestrial invaders. The player commands tanks, infantry and a variety of other 'units' such as a Special Forces ('Spetsnaz') team, nuclear physicist Andrei Sakharov, or a 50-metre-tall Stalin. The decisive battle occurs on Mars, when giant Stalin confronts the Martian overlord – who is a half-octopus, half-Hitler hybrid.

As the above plot description evinces, *Stalin vs. Martians* is a parody rather than a serious representative of the RTS genre. Given its much more 'cartoonesque' style – the Martians are displayed as cute toy-like monsters – historical accuracy cannot have been this game's primary aim, in spite of lead designer Aleksandr

Figure 12.2 Screenshot from *Stalin vs Martians* (*Stalin protiv marsian*) (Russia/Ukraine, Black Wing Foundation/Dreamlore/N-Game 2009)

Shcherbakov's playful claim that '[t]he Russian units are 100% historically accurate (we even use the early version of T-34 tank, since it's 1942 in the game) [whereas] . . . Martian units are less historically accurate, only about 80%' (Gillen 2008). The Red Army units are indeed faithfully re-created, ranging from the lightweight tank BT-7 and the self-propelled anti-aircraft gun ZSU-37 to the tanks T-70, T-34, T-35, and the famous 'Katiusha' rocket launcher. These realistic characteristics, however, cannot change the game's basic parodical undertone.[4] The loading screens, which are displayed when the game initializes the virtual world, may be regarded as a metaphor for its creative strategy: they challenge the player to spot the difference between historical photographs from the Second World War and their distorted 'Martian' versions.

Corollaries of repetition

Repetition plays an important role both in computer games and history. In this section, I want to present some instances of repetition in both history and computer games, and to spell out the interconnections between them. The first corollary of repetition, namely that of *trial and error*, arises from the way computer games tell stories. The issue of the relationship between narration and interaction is a core question not just for the examination of historical computer games, but for Game Studies as a whole. American game designer Greg Costikyan notes that there is a

> conflict between the demands of story and the demands of a game. Divergence from a story's path is likely to make for a less satisfying story; restricting a player's freedom of action is likely to make for a less satisfying game.
>
> (Costikyan 2007: 6)

Costikyan has tried to negotiate between these two opposites and describes how they are balanced in different kinds of interactive media. According to him, the possible spectrum ranges from stories with only a few game elements to games with only a few narrative interspersions. One example of a story with ludic elements is Julio Cortázar's novel *Hopscotch* (1963), which offers the reader two different paths to traverse the text and thus features a small amount of interactivity. Tabletop role-playing games, on the other hand, are considered to be the most 'free-form', since there is no pre-established plot, and the narration is performed and controlled entirely by the players (Costikyan 2007: 9). Costikyan's most notable theoretical contribution to game theory is the so-called beads-on-a-string analogy, which perfectly describes the relationship between narration and interaction not only for *Metro-2* and *Stalin vs. Martians*, but also for a broad range of games:

> [G]ames tend to be 'beads-on-a-string': small areas where there is some freedom of action until some event occurs, at which point a transition to the next bead is opened. While there is some freedom within the beads, the overall game is a linear progress through the beads.
>
> (Costikyan 2007: 8)

In Costikyan's view, the background story of a game is a linear and non-branching string, which is told via short movie sequences, so-called 'cut scenes', where no interaction takes place. This string connects the beads, i.e. non-linear, branching parts where the user has the possibility to interact with the game world; (s)he can choose different ways to move through it. The interactive parts must be traversed successfully in order to reach the next linear fragment of the background story.

One consequence of the 'beads-on-a-string' principle which Costikyan does not address is the resulting repetitive gaming experience. In the – frequent and recurring – event of the player's virtual death, (s)he has to begin anew. One has to repeat her or *his story*, or rather *history*, until the right outcome has been achieved – that is, until the main character's victory is certain.

In *Metro-2* and *Stalin vs. Martians*, repetition is pivotal as well. In both, only one possible ending exists, because in both cases no narrative branch covers the player's death and its ultimate consequences – Beriia killing Stalin or the Martians conquering Siberia. If the player dies, the game simply falls back on the last successfully completed 'bead'. In other words, the game's 'reality' has to be repeated *until the 'right' ending or the 'right' history has emerged.* The two Russian games discussed here offer the player only one possibility: to win – of course, the player could also simply stop playing, but this would mean leaving the game world altogether. This perspective of the player who *will* be the victor because the game offers no other chance reminds us of the Stalinist perspective on history, which Slovenian philosopher Slavoj Žižek has described as follows:

> Actual history occurs . . . on credit; only subsequent development will decide retroactively if the current revolutionary violence will be forgiven, legitimated, or if it will continue to exert a pressure on the shoulders of the present generation as its guilt. . . . By contrast, the Stalinist perspective is that of a *victor* whose final triumph is guaranteed in advance by the 'objective necessity of history'.
>
> (Žižek 1989: 159f.; italics in original)

Of course, the games presented here do not actively and consciously promote Stalinist ideology – at any rate, the parody *Stalin vs. Martians* is certainly exempt from this accusation; the question is somewhat more complex when it comes to *Metro-2*. Nonetheless, the structural parallels between the Stalinist view on history and the two games' attitudes towards the player-victor should not be overlooked, especially since it is explicitly referenced in *Stalin vs. Martians*. One of the weapons offered by the game is a super-weapon called 'historical inevitability', which instantly kills all enemies, guaranteeing that the game's historical inevitability is fulfilled and the user wins owing to the 'objective necessity of history'. In this way, the game playfully draws attention to and parodies its 'Stalinist perspective'.

The notion of an 'objective necessity of history' is one of the concepts of 'traditional' historiography which have been challenged by contemporary theorists, Slavoj Žižek included. His remarks concerning historical necessity directly lead on to the second corollary of repetition: that of *historical (non-)necessity*. As he points out,

> repetition is the way historical necessity asserts itself in the eyes of 'opinion'. . . . What is lost in this notion is the way *so-called historical necessity itself is constituted through misrecognition*, through the initial failure of 'opinion' to recognize its true character – that is, the way truth itself arises from misrecognition. . . . [O]nly through repetition is . . . [an] event recognized in its symbolic necessity – it finds its place in the symbolic network.
>
> (Žižek 1989: 64; italics in original)

Žižek underlines the fact that there is no historical necessity – only if an event is repeated does its apparent 'necessity' surface. The 'true' character, the 'true' meaning of an event, is always determined in retrospect. We cannot directly transfer this idea to the Russian games in question, but it is worth pointing out that repeated events change their symbolic status in games, too. As stated above, if the players do not succeed, the games jump back in time to start anew. From the player's point of view, (s)he repeats those events, but from the game's point of view, all these repeatedly failed attempts simply *have not happened*. In this regard linear computer games like *Metro-2* and *Stalin vs. Martians* are perfect – even exaggerated – examples of a historical necessity so strong it no longer even needs repetition.

The third corollary of repetition – that of *historical trauma* – can be linked to the above-mentioned concept of *magical historicism*. Alexander Etkind has coined this term to describe strategies – especially in literature – for dealing with the traumatic Soviet experience by means of a unique form of cultural expression. He notes that

> [p]ost-traumatic culture works in repetitive, vacillating movements that simultaneously reconstruct the shock of the past, as it supposedly happened, and defamiliarize it in such a way that the new returns of this past take different, and therefore engaging, forms.
>
> (Etkind 2009: 644)

As literary examples of magical historicism, Etkind analyses, among others, Vladimir Sorokin's phantasmagoria *Blue Lard* (*Goluboe salo* 1999) or Viktor Pelevin's satirical novel *Empire V* (*Ampir V* 2006). The two texts share plots that revolve around 'unmotivated distortions of history, semi-human monsters, manipulations of the body, fantastic cults, circular time, and the resulting interpenetration of epochs' (Etkind 2009: 658). Admittedly, *Metro-2* is no picture-perfect example of magical historicism in computer games: only its heavy propagation of urban myths – the secret subway system – might be interpreted in such a fashion. *Stalin vs. Martians*, on the other hand, and the examples mentioned in the introduction to this chapter, illustrate the fact that magical historicism is without doubt an important factor for the emerging Russian and Ukrainian computer game industry. Russian and Ukrainian game developers seem intuitively – perhaps even unconsciously – to follow the creative strategy for dealing with the past developed by renowned Russian literary writers. This connection does not come as a surprise, because texts employing magical historicism have to a certain extent the same goals as computer games: they are 'designed . . . as experimental settings, transforming the identities of [the authors'] characters and, implicitly, themselves into an alternative cast of historical products' (Etkind 2004: 44).

The unconscious focus on magical historicism is not exclusive to the Russian and Ukrainian gaming industry. Similar games may be found in Poland, too. Examples include *Mortyr 2093–1944* (1999), which features time-travel and a Nazi victory in the Second World War; *Gorky Zero: Beyond Honor* (*Gorky Zero: Fabrika Niewolników* 2003), where the Soviets create zombie super-spies in the small Polish town of Lublin; and *Afterfall: InSanity* (2011), which offers a post-apocalyptic world reminiscent of *Metro 2033* and *S.T.A.L.K.E.R.* To my knowledge, to date no 'magical historicist' games have been produced in the other post-socialist countries. This lack may be partly attributed to the fact that, in some cases, a domestic computer game industry has yet to develop. Both Kazakhstan and Georgia, for example, have to date produced only one game each: *Astana Racer* (2009), a racing game located in Kazakhstan's capital, and *Geo Police* (2011), which simulates the everyday work of Georgia's police force. The Czech Republic, on the other hand, is renowned for its vivid gaming industry, but my findings indicate that no Czech games follow the patterns of magical historicism. Similarly, I could identify only two American games rewriting the past in a grotesque way: *Fallout* (1997), which takes place in a twenty-second-century dystopian post-nuclear world modelled after 1950s American utopias, and *Bioshock* (2007), which presents a 1960s underwater society experiment gone wrong. Although both games were tremendously successful and have sparked a long line of successors, overall, magical historicism does not appear to be a prominent phenomenon in the American computer game industry.

Memory games – memory wars

Given that the computer game is, thanks to its interactivity, a user-centred medium – or, to borrow Roland Barthes' phrase, a 'writerly text' ('texte scriptible', Barthes 1970: 11) whose reader has full control over the text – the act of interpretation is very important. Non-interactive literature also offers interpretive freedom, but not to the degree of the computer game (Kansteiner 2007: 141). Thus, the process of interpreting a game facilitates all sorts of memory wars. Beauty, or in this case Stalinism, lies in the eye of the beholder, and here, as in literary writing, 'the very act of interpretation . . . constitutes an act of memory as significant as carving a statue or writing a memoir' (Etkind 2004: 39).

How, in our two games, do the players engage in the interpretive acts of memory to which Etkind refers? In *Metro-2*, for instance, one of the past environments is the Moscow State University building site, where barbed wire, watch towers and barracks 'narrate' a forced labour background.[5] The player, however, might also interpret the university's impressive main corpus as an emblem of Stalinist grandeur. Another example is the frequent occurrence of *Maiakovskaia* Metro station in *Metro-2*. We do not know whether the programmers decided to use the station because of its beauty, because of its status as a communist icon, or because of the station's namesake, the poet Vladimir Maiakovskii, and his ambivalent relation to the Stalinist regime – there is no hint whatsoever to the intended interpretation, and this opens up a space for all kinds of memory wars. But which ones exactly are fought by the two games in question?

Both games reference the reign of former dictator Joseph Stalin. Given how sensitive this topic is, any answer to the question posed above must seek to explain why, of all possible settings, the game designers chose this specific period. In an interview, *Metro-2*'s lead designer Nikolai Sitnikov stated: 'Yes, of course, it was a dreadful time, but we thought it would be very interesting to show Stalin.' Playing this game may even be regarded as a 'little excursion into the history of our motherland'. It seems as if the main driving force behind *Metro-2* is a certain nostalgia for Soviet times – a phenomenon described, among others, by anthropologist Serguei Oushakine. According to Oushakine, 'the cultural logic of [nostalgic] reincarnations [of Soviet times] has more in common with the act of mechanical retrofitting (facilitated by the digital age) rather than with the process of political restoration' (Oushakine 2007: 453). Oushakine argues that nostalgic reincarnations of the past are not only apolitical but also ahistorical, because 'revived or retrofitted forms bring with them no history' (Oushakine 2007: 482). The main function of these nostalgic renditions consists in their answer to a 'striving for a recognized and a recognizable shape, for a set of automatized perceptions, and for a common repertoire of cultural references' (Oushakine 2007: 482).

In short, on the one hand, *Metro-2* seeks to present familiar images – real Moscow locations – but, on the other hand, it leans towards the exotic – think of the mythical secret subway system. After all, magical historicism is a form of *orientalization*: it presents the 'past . . . as an exotic and unexplored [country], still pregnant with unborn alternatives and imminent miracles' (Etkind 2009: 656).

For the game's players, nostalgia also plays a certain role – but there is another, arguably more important reason why players cherish the game. In 2005, the year *Metro-2* was released, virtually no genuinely Russian computer games existed. On the game's subpage on the popular online webshop ozon.ru, this fact is discussed at some length; most reviewers are quite forgiving towards the game's severe faults and bugs, because, they argue, at least the game offers a *Russian* setting as opposed to all the 'Western' games (ozon.ru 2005). On the popular Russian IT message board overclockers.ru, the discussion is quite similar. User 'Intelligence', for example, is fond of the game because 'it's not every day that Russians publish games about Russians' (Konferentsiia overclockers.ru 2004). The same attitude resonates in longer reviews of the game. Illustrative is a review by Aleksei Cheberda, who heavily criticizes the gaming experience but notes that 'it was precisely the plot that seemed to be the most attractive part of the game' (Cheberda 2005). Critical comments regarding the game's positive portrayal of Stalin are nowhere to be found.

Stalin vs. Martians has a different motivation for reviving the Stalin era. According to a statement published on their official website, the developers were simply tired of the heated nature of the debates over the figure of Stalin. They claim to be opting out of this memory war:

> It's possible to have very long discussions about Stalin's personality, and about the costs of the unmasking of the cult of personality – when a scapegoat was found on whom basically everything was written off. But we have no intention of engaging in such discussions now. . . . The editorial staff strives to avoid entering into correspondence with dumbasses and gasbags.
>
> (*Stalin protiv Marsian* website 2009)

It is of course disingenuous to deny one's own participation in a memory war and then to produce a game featuring Stalin which further fuels this very war. Indeed, *Stalin vs. Martians* has provoked some quite heated reactions, for example, on the review page of games-tv.ru (2009). The better part of statements here indicates that the players simply understood the game as a joke ('igra-shutka'), but other opinions may be found as well. User 'Bul ly', for example, asks 'if not for Stalin, where would we be today?' Next (s)he enters Cold War mode and speculates that the game was made for American audiences, 'so that the Yanks could have a laugh at the Russians', and notes that in Stalin's time, the game's designers would have been shot for this. In truth, it would be far more 'logical' to interpret the game in light of Russian–Ukrainian antagonism, since *Stalin vs. Martians* is the offspring of a Russian–Ukrainian cooperation. The memory gap between these two post-socialist countries is especially manifest in the assessment of Stalin and the Holodomor tragedy associated with him, so we may expect that a game mocking Stalin could easily be used as a 'memory weapon'. Nonetheless, this second, 'inner-Slavic' opposition does not seem to matter at all for the commentators.

Although the players' comments are deeply rooted in the 'East' vs. 'West' dichotomy, the players do not seem to be aware of or concerned by the fact that the medium of the computer game as a whole is structured by 'Western' paradigms. Kansteiner has pointed out that most games are programmed in the United States and are thus heavily influenced by American moral standards and taboos – they follow the principle of American heroism and do not contain any sexual scenes (Kansteiner 2007: 142). Another example of a bias in the game mechanics is described by Uricchio, who brings to our attention the fact that process-oriented games 'are built upon notions such as societal coherence, progression, and increasing complexity as a sign of advance' (Uricchio 2005: 335). A similar implicit ideological bias applies to the two games in question. Both *Metro-2* and *Stalin vs. Martians* may be regarded as subscribing to elements of a 'Western' perspective. The player's character in *Metro-2* is a lone ranger with such *Übermensch* traits as a health and strength that are superior to those of his opponents. *Stalin vs. Martians*, on the other hand, plays out an aggressive capitalist mechanism: killing enemy units yields money, which may be used to buy reinforcements for the player's army. It stands to reason that this 'Western' genre lens to a certain extent distorts the virtual re-creations of the Stalin era and its socialist background.

Conclusion

In this chapter, two quite different games dealing with the Stalin era were analysed. *Metro-2* mixes faithfully re-created past spaces with urban mythology and offers a very positive portrayal of Stalin. The second game, *Stalin vs. Martians*, is a parody mocking Stalin, Hitler, and the Great Patriotic War. By means of analysing the two games in question, I was able to characterize other problems concerning the use of history in computer games as well. As current research literature demonstrates, in spite of its medial features – immediate, immersive, photo-realistic scenarios – the computer game cannot be considered a virtual time machine. Due to the complex relationship of interaction (playing) and narration (telling history), the player is unable to repeat history, because (s)he is always rewriting it. For a number of Russian, Ukrainian and Polish games – including *Metro-2* and *Stalin vs. Martians* – this rewriting of history starts at the design stage and bears the hallmarks of a contemporary literary strategy of dealing with the traumatic socialist past: that of magical historicism. Unfortunately, within the confines of this chapter it was not possible to tackle the question of the extent to which these games could be used to overcome the Stalin era in the spirit of magical historicism – further research is necessary to address this essential problem.

The corollary of *historical trauma* is not the only corollary of repetition to be found in *Metro-2* and *Stalin vs. Martians*. Another corollary – that of *trial and error* – arises from their special narrative structure, which may be described as 'beads on a string' – that is, a linear background story interspersed with interactive sections. Thus, these games offer a highly repetitive gaming experience. Finally, the last corollary of repetition concerns the idea of *historical (non-)necessity*. Because of the games' linearity – they do not even provide a narrative framing for the player's failure – their point of view may be compared to a Stalinist perspective on history, where the player's victory becomes 'historically inevitable'.

Aside from these theoretical considerations, I also attempted to outline the impact of the two games on collective memory and came to the conclusion that they may be considered salvos in an ongoing internal Russian memory war. *Metro-2* was intended by its designers to be a kind of history lesson, and *Stalin vs. Martians* to be a critique of the current discussion about Stalin. And both games indeed triggered (albeit small) web wars. Somewhat surprisingly, most players of both games did not seem to care that much about Stalin proper. Likewise, even though players expressed the desire for a home-grown Russian computer game industry, they seemed to be unconcerned by the fact that a lot of Russian games are actually programmed in Ukraine. The main discussion point revived the old Cold War antagonism of 'East' vs. 'West', or rather Russian computer games vs. American ones.

As Wulf Kansteiner has argued, historical computer games seem certain to reshape our idea of collective memories. In the post-socialist world, it may well be the case that a domestic computer game industry will prove vital not only for the establishment and propagation of collective memories. In addition, it could also lead to the stabilization of a new, post-socialist identity.

Notes

1 Most of the Russian-language games are actually developed in Ukraine.

2 The game's creators are in fact fighting a memory war against Fedor Bondarchuk's controversial feature film *The Ninth Company* (*9 rota* 2005) and its historical inaccuracies.

3 The beauty and distinctiveness of Moscow's metro combined with former secret Cold War objects such as the *Taganka* bunker seem to spark people's imagination. Russian popular culture is full of references to the mythical metro system (e.g. Dmitrii Glukhovskii's blockbuster novel *Metro 2033*). Moreover, so-called diggers ('diggery') risk their lives and trespass into the metro tunnels to find the secret system. For more information on both the myths and reality of the Moscow subway system, see Cherednichenko 2010.

4 During the final battle on Mars, the realistic tanks are joined by a vehicle suspiciously reminiscent of the fictitious Soviet 'Mammoth' tank depicted in one of the most successful RTS of all times, *Command & Conquer: Red Alert* (1996). Thus, the makers mix

historical accuracy not only with cartoon stylistics, but also with references to other computer games.

5 Places can tell stories, too – see Harry Jenkins' concept of 'environmental storytelling' (Jenkins 2004: 129).

Games

13 vek. Slava ili smert' (Russia, Unicorn Games 2007)
Afterfall: InSanity (Poland, Intoxicate 2011)
Astana Racer (Kazakhstan, Arta 2009)
Bioshock (USA/Australia, 2K Boston/2K Australia 2007)
Command & Conquer: Red Alert (USA, Westwood 1996)
Fallout. A Post Nuclear Role Playing Game (USA, Black Isle 1997)
Geo Police (Georgia, Ministry of Internal Affairs 2011)
Gorky Zero: Fabrika Niewolników (Poland, Metropolis Software 2003)
Kozaki (Ukraine, GSC Game World 2000)
Liniia Fronta: Afganistan '82 (USA/Russia, Apeiron/Battlefront/Snowberry Connection 2010)
Metro-2 (Russia, G5 Software/Orion Games 2005)
Metro 2033 (Ukraine, 4A Games 2010).
Mortyr 2093–1944 (Poland, Mirage Interactive 1999)
Pravda o deviatoi rote (Russia, Extreme Developers/KranX Productions 2008)
Smuta: Ozhivshie mertvetsy (Russia, Gelios 1997)
Stalin protiv marsian (Russia/Ukraine, Black Wing Foundation/Dreamlore/N-Game 2009)
S.T.A.L.K.E.R.: Ten' Chernobylia (Ukraine, GSC Game World 2007)
V tylu vraga (Russia, Best Way 2004)
You Are Empty (Ukraine, Mandel ArtPlains/Digital Spray Studios 2006)

Bibliography

Barthes, R. (1970) *S/Z*. Paris: Seuil.

Bolter, J.D. and Grusin, R. (2000) *Remediation. Understanding New Media*. Cambridge: MIT Press.

Cheberda, A. (2005) 'Mertvo 2. Obzor igry Metro 2'. Online. Available: <http://www.overclockers.ru/games/20291.shtml> (accessed 31 October 2011).

Cherednichenko, O. (2010) *Metro 2010. Putevoditel' po podzemnomu gorodu*. Moscow: Ėksmo.

Costikyan, G. (2007) 'Games, Storytelling, and Breaking the String', in P. Harrigan and N. Wardrip-Fruin (eds), *Second Person. Role-Playing and Story in Games and Playable Media*. Cambridge, MA: MIT Press, pp. 5–14.

Csíkszentmihály, M. (2000) *Beyond Boredom and Anxiety: Experiencing Flow in Work and Play*. San Francisco, CA: Jossey-Bass.

Etkind, A. (2004) 'Hard and Soft in Cultural Memory: Political Mourning in Russia and Germany'. *Grey Room* 16: 36–59.

Etkind, A. (2009) 'Stories of the Undead in the Land of the Unburied: Magical Historicism in Contemporary Russian Fiction'. *Slavic Review* 68(3), Autumn: 631–658.

Fogu, C. (2009) 'Digitalizing Historical Consciousness'. *History and Theory* 47(5): 103–121.

games-tv.ru (2009) 'Video obzor igry Stalin protiv marsian'. Online. Available: <http://www.games-tv.ru/reviews/stalin_protiv_marsian/obzor_kenny_&_dziha> (accessed 11 April 2012).

Gillen, K. (2008) 'RPS vs. Russians: The Stalin vs. Martians Interview'. Online. Available: <http://www.rockpapershotgun.com/2008/05/07/rps-vs-russians-the-stalin-vs-martians-interiew> (accessed 31 October 2011).

Jenkins, H. (2004) 'Game Design as Narrative Architecture', in P. Harrigan and N. Wardrip-Fruin (ed.), *First Person. New Media as Story, Performance, and Game*. Cambridge, MA: MIT Press, pp. 118–130.

Kansteiner, W. (2007) 'Alternate Worlds and Invented Communities: History and Historical Consciousness in the Age of Interactive Media', in S. Morgan, K. Jenkins and A. Munslow (eds), *Manifestos for History*. London: Routledge, pp. 131–148.

Konferentsiia overclockers.ru (2004) 'The Stalin Subway – Metro-2'. Online. Available: <http://forums.overclockers.ru/viewtopic.php?f=13&t=57012> (accessed 11 April 2012).

Oushakine, S. (2007) '"We're Nostalgic But We Are Not Crazy". Retrofitting the Past in Russia'. *Russian Review* 66(3): 451–482.

ozon.ru (2005) 'Metro-2'. Online. Available: <http://www.ozon.ru/context/detail/id/7033218/?item=2427885> (accessed 11 April 2012).

playground.ru (2004) 'Metro-2. Tainy sovetskoi imperii'. Online. Available: <http://www.playground.ru/articles/8051> (accessed 11 April 2012).

Rehak, B. (2007) 'Genre Profile: First-Person Shooting Games', in M. Wolf (ed.), *The Video Game Explosion: A History from PONG to PlayStation and Beyond*. Westport, CT: Greenwood Press, pp. 187–195.

Stalin protiv marsian website (2009) 'FAQ'. Online. Available: <http://stalinvsmartians.com/ru/faq.html> (accessed 31 October 2011).

Uricchio, W. (2005) 'Simulation, History, and Computer Games', in J. Raessens and J. Goldstein (eds), *Handbook of Computer Game Studies*. Cambridge, MA: MIT Press, pp. 327–338.

Žižek, S. (1989) *The Sublime Object of Ideology*. New York: Verso.

13 The digital (artistic) memory of Nicolae Ceauşescu

Caterina Preda

Ever since the fall of the communist dictator Nicolae Ceauşescu in 1989 after almost 35 years in power, anti-Ceauşescu discourses have dominated Romanian public space. Romania witnessed a violent end to its communist regime and Ceauşescu himself was executed, his death being announced on the radio with the proclamation 'the anti-Christ is dead!', while the images of his execution shocked the world. Nowadays, in offline mainstream Romanian media, there is no pro-Ceauşescu discourse.[1] Ceauşescu is anathema, and has been, since December 1989, portrayed primarily in the double hypostasis of caricature and tyrant.[2] One of the first reactions in December 1989 was to erase the memory of him. We may recall, for example, the images of people burning his portrait, or tearing out of books the obligatory frontispieces bearing his picture. The diabolized portraits of Nicolae and his wife Elena dominated the traditional media in the 1990s.

At the same time, Ceauşescu's image is omnipresent in public life in post-socialist Romania. In this context, this chapter asks: How is the memory of Ceauşescu organized online? How does his online image differ from *offline* memorializations of the dictator? Do online media create more space for competing discourses, and might we find a range of alternative memories and images here: the tyrant, the illiterate, the man, the great leader, etc.?

Offline, throughout post-socialist space, hegemonic narratives have tended to dominate in the wake of the collapse of the socialist bloc. By contrast, online practices of memorialization have generally offered greater scope for and been characterized by the presence of multiple, often conflicting versions of the past. Romania is no exception here, starting with new perspectives on the communist leader Nicolae Ceauşescu – perspectives that are plural and multifaceted, compared to the offline media, where his image is mostly negative.

Even a quick glance at the relevant online media makes it clear that the digital world offers a more complex view of Ceauşescu as well as new sites of memorialization which do not have corresponding 'real' or offline equivalents. There are several discourses about the former Romanian dictator in this free – accessible to almost half the population[3] – digital world, on blogs, personal websites, and social networks' encomiastic pages. This multiplicity is congruent with a related overlapping phenomenon in contemporary artistic discourse about the dictator.

Recent artworks, some using new media, seek to bring forth a new image of the communist leader: an image that is more complex, and does not conform to the standard tyrant/caricature dichotomy. Their intention is to provoke a true discussion about the nature of the communist regime, identified primarily, at the moment of the December Revolution, with the figure of Ceauşescu.

This chapter focuses on alternative images of Ceauşescu as they are mediated digitally. My discussion explores institutional, personal and artistic forms of this image. Online it is manifested, first of all, in the official discourse of state institutions. These include national archives, such as the online Photo-archive of Communism project (Fototeca Online Website 2011), a research institute dedicated to the study of the communist regime (Institute of Research of the Crimes of Communism and Memory of the Romanian Exile website 2011), and national museums (see, for example, links to the various exhibitions organized by the National History Museum or the Museum of Contemporary Art).[4] Several amateur websites offer glimpses into the private life of the dictator and his family, as well as his public persona. One more peripheral example involves a nostalgic digital *re*construction of the myth of Ceauşescu. Finally, artistic renditions of the dictator may also be found online; they express a need to re-evaluate the past and place this major historical figure in a new light.

As I shall try to demonstrate, this plurality of digital representations helps enrich the way Ceauşescu is remembered nowadays, breaking with the conventional diabolic portrait. If at the beginning of the 1990s the past was recalled based on the (neo)communist/anti-communist cleavage, subsequently, the desire to integrate with Euro-Atlantic structures gradually took over as a dominant topic. Increasingly, in the mid-2000s, the articulation of the memory of communism crystallized as multiple points of view that contribute to the creation of a memory that sees communism as a multilayered reality. The sharply polarized public responses to President Traian Băsescu's condemnation of the communist dictatorship in December 2006[5] showed that the communist/anti-communist cleavage is still strong in Romanian society.

Digital memories and Romania: theoretical background

In recent years, post-communist studies – political science, history and sociology – have devoted increasing attention to the memory of communism, especially from around the year 2009, which marked 20 years since the downfall of the communist regimes (Brown 2009; Kotkin 2009; Tismăneanu and Iacob 2012). The intricate interweaving of nostalgia for the bygone epoch and commemoration of crimes of the past, both institutional and private, has been analysed in increasing detail. Scholars have shown a growing interest in non-official, non-institutional media, and have been turning their attention to 'softer' cultural spaces: to popular-culture and contemporary art reactions to the past and the different versions of memory that they enable and project (Saunders 2000; Pence and Betts 2007; Todorova 2010; Todorova and Gille 2010).

The emerging field of East European memory studies, which draws upon a range of disciplines including cultural history and anthropology, is another subfield specifically dedicated to the study of memorialization practices after the end of communism, which it examines in relation to the more developed study of the memory of the Western experience of the Second World War, the Holocaust and Nazi dictatorship. According to the literature on digital memory, post-Soviet space boasts idiosyncrasies that are not registered by writings on Western societies (Rutten 2011).

Social-media theory has acknowledged how cyberspace allows the creation of new communities that can help individuals consolidate their identities (Kitchin 1998: 386; Dodge and Kitchin 2001: 167). Kitchin underlines the fact that cyberspace 'renders place meaningless, identities fluid and reality multiple' (1998: 398), while digital memory scholars also observe how 'versions of events' are replacing the accounts of events as such and may lead to the re-articulation of the past and the transformation of how we perceive it (Wilson 2009: 195). This instability and mutability of digital memory underlines the ever-changing character of memory more broadly (Garde-Hansen *et al.* 2009: 15). The possibilities for establishing other types of accounts of the past in online space are quite important for the memorialization of Ceauşescu, as they provide a space that is missing in the offline memory.

In this chapter I attempt to blend insights from the scholarship on online memory in Western societies with studies of post-Soviet digital memory – which overlap to a substantial extent with the Romanian case – with a view to drawing some preliminary conclusions. I follow Garde-Hansen's definition of digital memory here; that is, 'memory as it is mediated and produced in online as opposed to analog media' (Garde-Hansen *et al.* 2009). I set out to ascertain to what extent this counter-position of the online to the offline may be seen in the case of the memorialization of Ceauşescu, and whether, as Rutten states, 'the Internet generates previously unrecorded strategies of commemoration' (Rutten 2010: 174). Therefore, my chapter is framed within the emerging trans-disciplinary field of post-socialist digital memories, as this makes it possible to comparatively situate the Romanian case in the broader perspective of the post-Soviet landscape.

In this study I refer to Alexander Etkind's concept of the *memory event.* Etkind uses this concept for various types of cultural remembering that range from celebrations and historical debates, to films, novels and websites (Etkind 2010b: 4). In this concept, Etkind combines Pierre Nora's '*lieux de mémoire*' and Alain Badiou's concept of the 'event'. In contrast to Nora's *lieux de mémoire,* the concept of the memory event suggests a singular moment and does not emphasize the continual or static presence of these cultural expressions (Etkind 2010a). This aspect is also relevant to my analysis because many artistic and cultural expressions are momentary – think, for example, of the ephemeral character of the graffiti stencils that I discuss below. Unlike more traditional monumental expressions, these works do not necessarily translate into long-term projects. This analysis uses these multidisciplinary resources as tools to better understand, and situate in a regional context, the process of remembering and forgetting Ceauşescu.

Nicolae Ceauşescu: brief historical reminder

Nicolae Ceauşescu (1918–1989) was president of Romania between 1965 and 1989, following in the footsteps of his predecessor, the first Romanian communist leader Gheorghe Gheorghiu Dej. If Ceauşescu's first period in power (1965–1971) was relatively mild, from the beginning of the 1970s, however, he began to strengthen control. He was designated the first president of Romania in 1974 and carried a sceptre at his nomination by the Great National Assembly. In the 1980s, after Ceauşescu decided to pay off Romania's foreign debt, penury became a fact of life for most Romanians. From the mid-1980s onwards, 'a chronic lack of food was accompanied by an energy crisis' (Kunze 2002: 387). For the overwhelming majority of the population this meant living in the dark and cold, without private transport: in 1985, citizens were forbidden to drive owing to petrol shortages.

The Ceauşescu regime was based on an extreme degree of personalization of power while its ideology combined Marxism-Leninism with nationalism and a set of Ceauşescu's own personal ideas such as the concept of 'the multilateral developed society', which meant applying socialist principles to all segments of life and thus ensuring the transition from socialism to communism. Analysed as dynastic socialism (by Vladimir Tismăneanu), 'Ceauşescuism' (by Trond Gilberg), and sultanism (by Linz and Stepan), an extreme personalization of power is the key defining feature of the Ceauşescu regime in the period 1974 to 1989.

Nicolae and his wife Elena Ceauşescu were tried in secret by an extraordinary military tribunal coordinated by the revolutionary leaders in the days that followed the take-over of power on 22 December 1989. They were then executed on 25 December 1989. In those days of controlled confusion, the revolutionary leaders used the chaotic atmosphere to justify the necessity to eliminate Ceauşescu in order to rule out the possibility of his return. To this end, lurid and sensationalist images of Ceauşescu were circulated. Ceauşescu was commonly presented in the mass media of the time as a vampire sucking the blood of innocent children, for example (Preda 2005). Other mass media representations depicted him as a clumsy, weird-looking, illiterate puppet who was controlled by his diabolical wife Elena. Making fun of Ceauşescu had been one of the few outlets for political commentary available to Romanians during his regime. Now, however, these jokes no longer had to be told in secret, and the rapid growth of mass media opened up new possibilities for self-expression. The first free newspapers were founded in January 1990, and these, together with the new private TV stations and radio stations that followed, gradually enshrined freedom of speech. Yet throughout all the dramatic changes in the Romanian mediascape over the past two decades, making fun has remained a key way of dealing with the past. Thus, after 1990, two paradigmatic portrayals of Ceauşescu were dominant: the tyrant/dictator versus the caricature/clown.

The many faces of Ceauşescu online

Ceauşescu is still very present today in many public spaces, from popular culture to scholarly literature. It is still very much his *image* that is predominant: the mass-media discourse commonly uses the standard portrait of Ceauşescu, in which his carefully airbrushed face smiles benevolently. This image was omnipresent in socialist Romania. From the mid-1970s it appeared on the frontispiece of all Romanian books, and it was ubiquitous on the walls of all Romanian public institutions in Romania up until 1990. This same portrait reappeared once a new memory mechanism was set in place and it may be seen, since 2006, in the famous street-art stencils, in which it is combined with the tags: 'I'll be back' or 'Back in 5 minutes'. Famous as they have become, these stencils are nowadays only to be found online and are no longer present on the actual walls of Bucharest. Their digital availability and their use in online spaces (blogs, personal websites or Facebook profiles) makes for a different ongoing memorialization of Ceaușescu, often more ironical and 'cool' or laid-back than the one supported by offline media. In fact, the structure of the memory of Ceaușescu is not restricted to this smiling, optimistic image, and may be understood as comprising several overlapping and often contradictory layers.

In academic circles – among historians or political scientists – there is no pressing interest in establishing an alternative portrait of Ceaușescu to replace the one created by the previous regime of Ion Iliescu (1990–1996; 2000–2004) who, himself a former member of the nomenclature, sought to present Ceaușescu as the sole person responsible for the wrongdoings of the communist regime. Very few biographies have been written after 1990, and the most interesting of them are by non-Romanians.[6]

In Romanian society at large, Ceaușescu is still a deeply divisive subject. In looking back on his regime, two groups oppose each other: those who are nostalgic – arguing that Romania enjoyed a higher international status during the period – and those who emphasize instead the human rights violations, hardships and lack of freedom that characterized Ceaușescu's rule. The idea that the Ceaușescus were not really buried in the two graves, exhumed in 2010 so as to verify their identity through DNA testing, has been a constant of the nostalgic, vindictive discourse claiming that they are either alive in Cuba or buried in secret somewhere else.

At the same time, recently the symbol of Ceaușescu has enjoyed a resurgence – a development which should be understood in the context of the ongoing results of the 2008 financial crisis. His well-known portrait was displayed by participants of mass protests against the government's economic austerity measures in 2010, and thereafter his disinterment in July made the former dictator a constant presence in both traditional media (newspapers, TV and radio shows) and new media (online news, blogs and Facebook pages). A few days later, the results of a public survey[7] (26 July 2010) indicated that over 40 per cent of Romanians would vote for him today. Democratic disenchantment coupled with the economic crisis has shown that the past is still present.

Institutional/official

In Romania there is no state-sponsored museum of communism[8] – since the 1990s, only temporary exhibitions have been organized at the official level. One of them was dedicated to the cult of Ceaușescu and reunited several objects typical of the period together with gifts received by Ceauşescu from Romanians and foreigners (Golden Epoch Website 2012). No Museum of Ceauşescu exists either, although the former Memorial House of Scorniceşti is still in existence. This memorial presents the 'humble life' of Ceauşescu's youth in his native village. In addition, there is the kitsch-nostalgic Museum of the Republic of Socialist Romania, located near the city of Craiova. Established by a Romanian businessman-cum-politician who is a self-professed admirer of the dictator, it displays several statues, paintings and sculptures of Ceauşescu.[9]

If offline museums thus present a limited picture of the dictator, official institutions offer a more nuanced portrait on the Web. *The Photo-archive of Communism*, an online project of the National Archives of Romania, has become the main repository of images both of the period of communism and of Ceauşescu. When it was first launched in 2008 it provoked a wave of public interest. It brought to light several images showing Nicolae and Elena Ceauşescu accompanied by the post-revolutionary leader (and former nomenclature member) Ion Iliescu playing games such as quoits together. Iliescu, who served two terms as president of post-communist Romania, and who had previously tried to distance himself from the former dictatorial couple and to position himself as a dissident, was now caught by images that eloquently revealed his privileged status during the Ceauşescu regime.

Figure 13.1 'Nicolae and Elena Ceauşescu in Moldova and the Danube delta in the summer of 1976', *Fototeca online a comunismului românesc (Online Photo-archive of Communism)*. The photo shows Ion Iliescu standing at the centre, watching as Elena and Nicolae Ceauşescu throw their quoits.

The Institute for the Investigation of Communist Crimes and the Memory of Romanian Exile (IICCMER), created in 2009, is the main state-sponsored institution dedicated to the study of the communist regime.[10] The website of IICCMER is an important interface that presents several projects related to the communist regime. None of them centres on the person of Nicolae Ceaușescu, however: the perspective of the current researchers is broader and grants pre-eminence to the role of the Communist Party more broadly, rather than to Ceaușescu himself.

Ceaușescu does play first fiddle in a webpage created by the National History Museum (MNIR) called 'Communism in Romania'. It offers viewers an entire section dedicated to the personality cult around Ceaușescu (Ceaușescu Personality Cult 2011). The series includes photographs and descriptions of the various gifts received by Ceaușescu from world leaders and different state institutions in Romania; a collection of images of Ceaușescu celebrations (26 January, his birthday, was increasingly celebrated as a national holiday) and of mass rallies glorifying the leader; paintings portraying Ceaușescu; and photographs of the book covers of his official biographies, translated into several languages. Besides this cult-devoted page, Ceaușescu also appears in other sections of the museum's site. Samples include a section dedicated to the dictator's 'working visits' throughout the country, as well as 'Different Aspects of Political Life' – a section that also centres on images of Ceaușescu (National History Museum Communism in Romania website).

In addition, online versions of major Romanian newspapers have published or are currently publishing series about Ceaușescu, communism, and especially the still controversial end of the Ceaușescu regime (*Jurnalul*, *Adevărul*, *Evenimentul Zilei*). The quality newspaper *Adevărul* has recently inaugurated a series about 'The True Ceaușescu' that unveils daily 'truths' about the former dictator (Adevăratul Ceaușescu *Adevărul* Series Website 2011). It touches upon several formerly forbidden topics, such as the issue of his homosexuality.[11] Finally, the latest trend in Romanian online media is to dissect and discuss in detail the personality of Elena Ceaușescu, in what amounts to be an ever-growing collection of invented stories, real factual details and media exploitation.

Personal/private – nostalgic and hateful

On blogs and personal sites, web users construct a more privately oriented digital memory of Ceaușescu. Prevalent is a nostalgic discourse about the 'true Ceaușescu' – one that zooms in on certain aspects of the personality and biography of the former leader: his private life, the 'good' decisions he made, and especially his violent death in December 1989 and the so-called 'coup d'état' that overthrew him.[12] The idea that the 1989 revolution was a coup d'état carried out with the involvement of foreign secret agents reiterates the diagnosis issued by Nicolae Ceaușescu himself during his staged trial in December 1989. Today, this reading of the events is kept alive by partisans of the former dictatorial regime.

Pro-Ceauşescu blogs tend to be highly standardized: they recycle the same images and discuss similar topics, making them part of one overarching corpus of nostalgia, claiming to re-establish historical truth. This trend in Romanian online space is similar to what Ellen Rutten and Vera Zvereva discuss in the Introduction to this volume about the web wars of post-socialist societies dedicated to settling truths about the still present past. A comparable approach may be found in other media. Characteristically, one of the most popular TV stations in Romania, OTV (*Oglinda* TV or Mirror TV) uses a nostalgic tone so as to gather an audience of disenchanted, disillusioned democrats. The TV station privileges the voice of its viewers and centres its nightly show on the owner of the station, Dan Diaconescu, who engages in direct discussion with the callers. Those without a space for expression may say what they want in these two forums: online blogs and websites, or the OTV talk shows. Diaconescu seems to provide an offline channel for this kind of energy, whereas blogs offer a refuge online.

But in digital media, representations of the dictator are not limited to nostalgic affirmation. An interesting example of the multiple points of view that coexist online is the blog of Serghei Niculescu-Mizil, the son of a former nomenclature member and minister of the Ceauşescu regime. Along with registering Mizil's public appearances as a socialite, the blog also invokes Serghei's past and his close friendship with Nicu Ceauşescu, the son of the dictatorial couple.[13] Besides his relationship with Nicu, Serghei recalls his own life during communism, the life of a privileged member of the nomenclature which contrasts with most Romanians' reflections on the period. Serghei posts photos from lavish socialist-era parties and a photo of himself in Paris at a time when, for most Romanians, travelling abroad was almost impossible. The image of Nicolae Ceauşescu that he presents is filtered through the prism of Serghei's father, who eventually fell from favour and was demoted by the communist leader. According to Serghei, Ceauşescu was mistaken, but he had good intentions and he also did positive things. We could say that the presence of Mizil in the online space articulates competitive memorial practices and breaks with the linear, anti-Ceauşescu discourse.

The web page Ceauşescu.org, created in 2000, aims to offer a yet more comprehensive and objective image of the Ceauşescu era. It includes texts, images of the Ceauşescus, photos of the period (comprising details such as coins, flags, etc.), and a collection of links to bibliographical resources. Compared to the other sites discussed here, this page offers a more neutral tone, and a non-biased perspective on the dictator. Its bibliography, for example, includes links to volumes that discuss the nature of the regime from a range of different positions, and also contains scholarly literature.

These sites exemplify the growing interest in the past, usually in the form of a nostalgic look back at one's youth, which has been characteristic of Romanian digital discourse from the mid-2000s onwards. A range of blogs and web pages has been dedicated to the collection of material objects that evoke the user's socialist-era childhood or youth. These objects range from games and cartoons via comic books to food and iconic communist advertisements. One of the country's most famous blogs, entitled *past tense* (latrecut.ro, launched in 2006) has today established a fine collection of all sorts of memories belonging to the author and other contributors.[14]

Social networks such as Facebook also register the presence of Ceauşescu. A simple search on Facebook yields several pages (15) and profiles (148)[15] under the name of Nicolae Ceauşescu (Apostol and Slujitoru 2011), each of which has a few hundred friends/fans. The dominant tone of these fake identities is ironical. Indeed, what is surprising is precisely their multiplicity, together with the consistently satirical form of the nostalgia expressed here. One such page belongs to the New Communist Party of Romania and links to the party's website. The former Communist Party of Romania (PCR) was dissolved and banned after 1990, but it still exists online (New Communist Party of Romania Committee of Reorganization Website 2011). Some of these Facebook pages link back to the blogs and personal pages dedicated to the memory of Ceauşescu discussed above. Their satirical tone notwithstanding, most include comments and posts whose authors are quite nostalgic about Ceauşescu and, more broadly, the communist era. The current political situation in Romania, where public rhetoric is violent and the opposition has branded the president a dictator, and the ever-worsening quality of education in state schools, are factors that at least partially explain the nostalgia felt by people who have no direct experience of communism.

Recently, Ceauşescu has also made his debut on Twitter, where fake Ceauşescus use the idiosyncratic language – brimming with grammatical mistakes and outdated expressions – for which the dictator was famous. The same language was used to ironize about him during his rule (through jokes), and, following the collapse of the regime, as a way of healing/dealing with the past. In addition, the memory of Ceauşescu circulates in the form of videos on YouTube, where previously unreleased footage may be found alongside official speeches (from Party congresses, national holidays, daily news programmes, etc.), and Ceauşescu's trial and subsequent execution. These videos have lively comment sections. Exemplary is the video 'Romania in 1989 vs Romania in 2010', which compares speeches by Ceauşescu with those by the current Romanian leader, Traian Băsescu. The video compares Ceauşescu's promises to increase revenues to the current president's decision to cut salaries by 25 per cent in 2010 in view of the current economic crisis. The conclusion of the commentators is clear: life was better before, there were more opportunities; freedom is dispensable when no jobs or opportunities are available. Many authors of the comments posted here demand the execution of the current leaders. This type of markedly violent, vindictive and at the same time nostalgic discourse is also rampant in other online media: online forums, newspaper articles' comments, blogs, politicians' personal web pages, etc.

In short, if at the official level during Iliescu's first term in 1990 to 1996, and in general public discourse after 1990, the Ceauşescus were diabolized and morphed into scapegoats bearing sole responsibility for the communist period, the digitalization of memory has enabled a less unequivocal, albeit often violent perspective on the period.

Artistic: the art of memorialization and obsessive Ceauşescu

Digital media also offer a fruitful platform for artistic commemorations of the Ceauşescu era. While the digital world is not the first medium of Romanian contemporary artists, it is an important place for displaying their artworks – in personal blogs, for example, or on the websites of contemporary art galleries (which often receive more visitors than the galleries themselves).

From stencils to traditional painting and beyond, Romanian visual arts have seen, especially in the 2000s and mainly via the creation of what I call the *art of memorialization*, a resurgence of the image of Ceauşescu. The art of memorialization as a corpus is establishing an alternative memory to the one supported at the official level by post-1990 political institutions, using artistic means to present a novel image of the dictator. Most importantly, artists have started humanizing the former dictator in their works. While this is a broad phenomenon – as the art critic Cosmin Năsui recalls, 'Ceauşescu still sells' – on the following pages I zero in on five examples produced by some of the most in-vogue contemporary artists who exemplify quite different yet complementary approaches to the former dictator, namely: Dragoş Burlacu (*Understanding History*, 2009), Adrian Ghenie (*Study for Boogyman,* 2010), Ion Grigorescu (*Posthumous Dialogue with Nicolae Ceauşescu*, 2007), Ion Bârlădeanu (most of whose collages consist of a humorous treatment of Ceauşescu), and Andrei Ujică (*The Autobiography of Nicolae Ceauşescu*, 2010). These examples of the art of memorialization may be linked to Alexander Etkind's concept of the 'memory event' because they spark interest in the past but are temporary; they do not occupy specific, definitive places; and their meanings are also subject to change and different interpretations.

Dragoş Burlacu, in his *Understanding History* series, has constructed a reinterpretation of Ceauşescu and his persona through the use of archival material, such as the *Photo-archive of Communism* presented above, and video footage of the trial and shooting of the Ceauşescus. One may interpret Burlacu's gesture to redraw or paint inspired by photographs and a video that registered events 'as they happened' as an attempt to discuss these events in a new light, to critically engage this recent past. In line with this analysis, the playful image of Ceauşescu (the caricature) and the tyrant who is punished (the execution) are the images chosen to illustrate Burlacu's artistic approach. The artist's intention, as the art critic Cosmin Năsui observes, is to provoke a new inquiry into the *true* significance of the regime of Ceauşescu and to discuss its *genuine* nature – questions that were too quickly abandoned during the transition to democracy, when looking to the future was more important.

Andrei Ghenie, one of Romania's bestselling and most highly acclaimed contemporary artists, has also worked with the image of Ceauşescu. Ghenie's is a dark universe, nightmarish even, with clear influences of Francis Bacon's painting, in which a recurrent theme is the abuse of power. See, for example, his *Study for Boogyman* (2010) or *Ceauşescu* (2007), or even his *The Trial* (2010) that shows him together with his wife Elena.[16] The image of the *Boogyman* is the closest to that of

Figure 13.2 Dragoş Burlacu, *U.H. 9* (2009) (Dragoş Burlacu's website 2011)

'Ceauşescu the tyrant' and portrays him as almost erased; the colours seem to melt, to fade away. The scary image of the dictator fades away, leaving nothing but a sad, destroyed portrait.

One of the most important artists of the Romanian neo-avant-garde, Ioan Grigorescu, has recently *re*worked one of his earlier pieces. In 2007 the artist produced a video called *Posthumous Dialogue with Nicolae Ceauşescu*, which offered a continuation of his 1978 *Dialogue with Comrade Ceauşescu*. In the first work, a video presentation superimposed with the transcript of a fictitious interview with the dictator, the artist adopted the double posture of interviewer and interviewee, wearing a mask of Ceauşescu. Both the questions and answers transgressed the boundaries of the permissible for the epoch.

The 2007 video departed from the same idea of an invented interview with the now forgotten dictator. The video, which offers 'Ceauşescu's vision of present-day Romania', is set against the backdrop of the House of the People. This enormous building was the result of a megalomaniac architectural project conceived by Ceauşescu. Begun in the early 1980s and never finished, its construction necessitated the demolition of an entire neighbourhood and completely altered the capital city's articulation. Today, it still dominates downtown Bucharest. The artist goes even further than imagining Ceauşescu's response to the transformations Romania has seen since 1990, and signals that the demonization of Ceauşescu has invalidated critical perspectives not only by ignoring the positive outcomes of his 34-year-long dictatorship, but also by shifting the discussion to a level that obscures the truly important questions.[17]

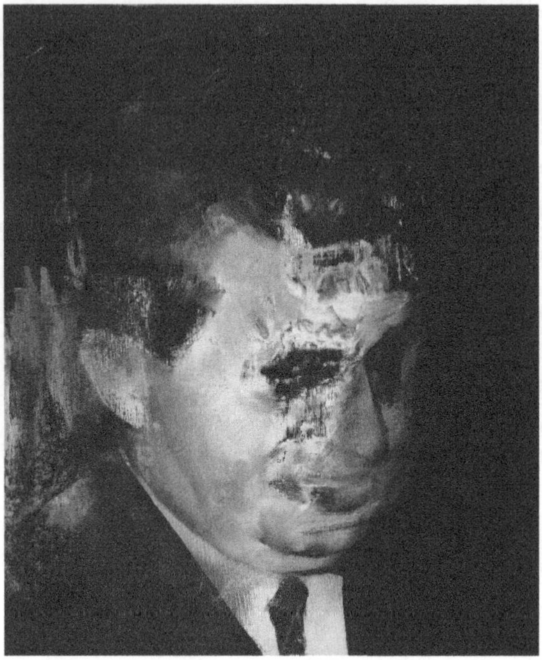

Figure 13.3 Adrian Ghenie, *Study for Boogyman* (2010) (Plan B Gallery website 2011)

Ion Bârlădeanu, a non-professional artist who was discovered in 2008 by the owner of the Bucharest-based H'Art Gallery, is evocative of another conceptualization of the Romanian leader. In one of the collages released in the 1970s to 1980s, outside of the officially controlled public space, at a time when state artists were producing canonical socialist-realist images, Ceauşescu is still presented at the centre of the image. He is smiling and waving, but he is now smaller than the dancers, who dominate and determine the rhythm of the ensemble, and he appears as a caricatured image of himself. Bârlădeanu has created a whole series of collages centred on the figure of Ceauşescu. If Bârlădeanu's works were realized in their majority under the socialist regime and not after its demise, their discovery in 2008 and circulation online has fuelled the creation of the new image that the former leader has been given by artists in recent years (H'Art Gallery website 2011). Bârlădeanu also has a Facebook page that is quite popular (with more than 7,000 fans in 2012) and his images often accompany the ironical treatment of the past in online media.

A final example I want to discuss is that of the documentary film produced by the Romanian film director Andrei Ujică. His film *The Autobiography of Nicolae Ceauşescu* (2010) was the most important event relating to the rewriting of the history of Ceauşescu's rule in recent years. Using only archival film material of Ceauşescu that was previously inaccessible to the public, the film shows the dictator in both official and private settings. Ujică redraws the portrait of the dictator as he himself would have rendered it, and this recalls the 'videology' concept of historian Adrian Cioroianu; that is, the 'ideology that tends gradually but unavoidably to be restricted to the exhibition of the same effigies, to the display of a single portrait' (Cioroianu 2006: 251). This 'obsession with the self-portrait' (all the artistic representations of Ceauşescu's cult seem as if he would have painted them himself, if only he knew how) led to the repetition of the same idealized image of the leader (Cioroianu 2006: 251). They create the same effect as the photographs that inspired the painter Burlacu and which show Ceauşescu in all kinds of hypostases (playing games, making official visits, unwinding with his family): that of creating a more inclusive and complex image of the man than the demonized and caricature versions which dominated the period immediately following 1990. The film has been uploaded to YouTube and is available to a larger public; the online comments on the video/trailers fit in with the broader discussion about Ceauşescu recalled above. Easy access to a source like Ujică's film may prove beneficial for the young generations that were raised on the binary images of Ceauşescu as either extremely negative or ridiculous. By contrast, the film offers viewers raw images of the reality designed by the dictator himself. Online media resources, most often wielded by young Romanians, thus open up new possibilities for understanding the past as something more complex than the traditional media would have us believe.

Conclusion

Twenty-one years after his dramatic end, the former dictator Nicolae Ceauşescu is still very much present in Romanian society, public discourse, and new and old media. Ceauşescu's persona has been understood in several ways: as a dictator, as a tyrant, but also as a visionary, and as a better statesman than his democratic successors. Ceauşescu the man and not the leader has also been brought into discussion, as politicians and other public figures have sought to reclaim him. His shortcomings, his speech impediment, his clumsiness, were and still are ridiculed through jokes. The digital world presents all these understandings of Ceauşescu and participates in the ongoing memorialization of his regime. As a consequence, the digital versions of Ceauşescu are diverging, and they are introducing a more comprehensive image of the character than the ones available offline.

Thus, different descriptions of the past are made possible through online resources and participate in the 'versioning of the past' (Wilson 2009: 195) and the simultaneity of digital horizons (Hoskins 2009: 28). The Romanian experience here is comparable to that of other former socialist states: online media counterbalance the offline unidirectional construction of the past. But whereas in the Russian context, many newspapers and TV programmes adopt a positive view of the socialist past, the Romanian press has been characterized by a largely negative view of the Ceauşescu regime and even more of his persona. The offline media in Romania are very uniform and polarized (especially in recent years) when it comes to representing the communist past. The cleavage for and against the existing government may also be identified in the discussions of the memory of communism. For example, newspapers closer to the current government with its sharply negative stance on the communist past tend to favour a memorialization of that past which lays a heavy emphasis on the repressive character of the regime. The media close to the opposition, on the other hand, generally dismiss such rhetoric as hypocritical and meaningless posturing; instead, they tend to emphasize the common guilt shared by all of society for the communist period – a position which serves to elide the differentiated participation in the former communist regime, thereby avoiding difficult issues surrounding, for example, the presence of former secret police collaborators within the opposition's leadership. The highly divided and divisive nature of the Romanian public space is noticeable here and helps explain why digital space provides several points of view of the past that cannot be expressed in traditional media.

To summarize, new forms of memory-making are emerging in online spaces, evoking the 'connective memory' conceptualized by Andrew Hoskins. But, as Rutten and Zvereva remind us in their Introduction to this volume, online information is scattered and presented in fragments. This is an important reminder of the fact that online memorialization has to accompany the offline forms of memory-making; the two are mutually dependent. Online memories must be situated in relation to offline memories if they are to help us reach a new understanding of the recent past.

Notes

1 A partial exception is the discourse conducted by the now marginal, extremist Great Romania Party (PRM) led by a former sycophant of the Romanian leader, Corneliu Vadim Tudor.

2 Among the myths of the revolution were those of Ceauşescu as a monster, reincarnation of Dracula. See Ramonet (1990).

3 According to a December 2011 article that quotes a Eurostat study, 47 per cent of Romanians have access to the Internet while 57 per cent have never used a computer. This places Romania in one of the lowest positions when it comes to Internet access and use within the European Union (Pescaru 2011).

4 'The museum of painting', Museum of Contemporary Art, Bucharest (16–22 May 2005). Curator: Florin Tudor. For a collection of texts see Museum of Contemporary Art website 2008.

5 The Presidential Commission for the Study of the Communist Dictatorship (also called the Tismăneanu Commission, after its head, political scientist Vladimir Tismăneanu) issued a Report on Analysis of the Communist Dictatorship in 2006. This Report formed the basis for the presidential speech before the reunited chambers of Parliament in December 2006. President Băsescu eased access to the documents of the former secret police of the communist regime, the *Securitate*, and provided the National Council for the Study of the Securitate Archives (CNSAS) with resources to study this enormous archive. This constituted an important break with the past, as during the presidencies of Ion Iliescu (1990–1996 and 2000–2004) no effort had been made to develop an understanding of the past, Iliescu himself being part of the former regime.

6 For example, Thomas Kunze's *Nicolae Ceauşescu. A Biography* (2000); Dennis Deletant's *Romania under Communist Rule* (1998); or Adam Burakowski's *Dictatorship of Nicolae Ceauşescu 1965–1989. Genius of the Carpathians* (2010).

7 A public survey by IRES (Institutul Român pentru Evaluare şi Strategie) conducted during the period 21–23 July 2010 interviewing 1,460 persons found that 41 per cent would vote for Ceauşescu in presidential elections, while only 26 per cent doubted that the Ceauşescus were buried where they were (Ursu 2010).

8 Admittedly, there are private initiatives dedicated to the memorialization of communism. See Sighet Memorial website (2012), whose virtual tour section includes, for example, a room dedicated to the 'Golden Era', as the regime of Ceauşescu was called, and the cult of his personality.

9 Inaugurated in 2004, and nowadays called the Palace of the Republic of Socialist Romania, it has been transformed into a club/restaurant. Unfortunately, the club website no longer shows images of the Ceauşescu relics. See Palace of the Republic of Socialist Romania Museum website (2011). For a gallery of images see Photogallery RSR Museum (2011).

10 IICCMER was created in 2009 by the fusion of two previous research institutes: IICCR (Institute for the Investigation of the Crimes of Communism, established in 2005) and the INMER (Institute of National Memory and the Romanian Exile). Another official source that provides access to online documents from the former secret police Archive is the National Council for the Study of the Securitate Archives (CNSAS), first established in 1999 but much more active since 2006. This body also has a website that includes many references to Ceauşescu (CNSAS website 2012). The other research institutes dedicated to the study of the communist regime (or which include it among their interests) do not display very much information online.

11 Most of these articles, in both newspapers, are written by the same person, Lavinia Betea. Famous for publishing extensive interviews with some of the former communist leaders, Betea was dismissed from the University of Bucharest after being accused of plagiarism.

12 For an example, see the Ceauşescu Nicolae website (2011). This blog is one of the websites dedicated to Ceauşescu that includes many photographs in both official and private contexts. It has six sections: Autobiography; Literary Critic (a book about Ceauşescu's speeches to writers); Florin Velicu (an interview with a close collaborator of Ion Iliescu who took power in 1990); The Coup in 1989; and Târgovişte (the place where the Ceauşescus were shot).

13 See the section 'My past' on the Serghei Niculescu Mizil website (2012), and also the section dedicated to Nicu ('The Life of Nicu Ceauşescu', with extensive interviews and articles), who was tried for genocide together with his sister Zoia Ceauşescu. Mizil is trying to reposition their post-1989 memory, and it is interesting to see how the blog's commentators are drawn to differentiating between the good communists and the bad communists. Mizil was one of the good ones, of course.

14 The webpage is subtitled 'Naïve Memories from the Red Period'. See La Trecut website 2011.

15 According to a recent article about Ceauşescu's presence on Facebook there were 148 profiles of Ceauşescu, both nostalgic and satirical, making him the Romanian personality with the most important presence on Facebook in terms of profiles/pages created by fans. See Apostol and Slujitoru 2011.

16 For more images of Ghenie's artworks, see Plan B Gallery website 2011.

17 Ion Grigorescu at the public meeting 'Arte marţiale', organized by the Romanian Cultural Institute, Bucharest, 27 November 2007.

References

Adevăratul Ceauşescu Adevărul Series website (2011) Online. Available: <http://www.adevarul.ro/actualitate/adevaratul_ceausescu/> (accessed 24 August 2011).

Adevãrul website (2012) Online. Available: <http://www.adevarul.ro> (accessed 12 March 2012).

Apostol, M. and Slujitoru, C. (2011) 'Nicolae Ceauşescu are 148 de profile pe Facebook', *Adevãrul* (6 March 2011). Online. Available: http://www.adevarul.ro/locale/bucuresti/Tovarasi-frumoasa_e_viata_pe_Facebook-_Ceausescu_este_romanul_cu_cele_mai_multe_profile_create_de_simpatizanti_0_439156159.html> (accessed 12 March 2012).

Brown, A. (2009) *The Rise and Fall of Communism*. New York: Harper Collins.

Ceauşescu Personality Cult (2011) 'Communism in Romania', *National History Museum* website. Online. Available: <http://www.comunismulinromania.ro/Arhiva-foto/Cultul-personaltatii.html> (accessed 19 August 2011).

Ceauşescu Nicolae website (2011) Online. Available: <http://ceausescunicolae.wordpress.com> (accessed 18 August 2011).

Cioroianu, A. (2006) '"Videologia" lui Nicolae Ceauşescu. Conducãtorul şi obsesia autoportretului', in R. Cesereanu (ed.), *Comunism şi represiune în România*. Iaşi: Polirom, pp. 251–265.

Council for the Study of the Securitate Archives (CNSAS) website (2011) Online. Available: < http://www.cnsas.ro> (accessed 12 March 2012).

Dodge, M. and Kitchin, R. (2001) *Atlas of Cyberspace*. London: Pearson Education.

Dragoş Burlacu's website (2011) Online. Available: <http://www.dragosburlacu.ro/work/16-Understanding_History.html> (accessed 23 August 2011).

Etkind, A. (2010a) 'Memory Events in the Transnational Space'. Paper presented at the Memory at War Inaugural Workshop, Cambridge, June. Online. Available: <http://www.memoryatwar.org/pdf/Etkind%20memory%20events%20paper%20June%202010.pdf (accessed 12 March 2012).

Etkind, A. (2010b) 'Mapping Memory Events in the East European Space'. *East European Memory Studies* 1: 4–5.

Foarfã, C. (2006) 'Interview with Dumitru Gorzo'. *Metropotam.ro*, 7 November. Online. Available: http://metropotam.ro/La-zi/Interviu-Dumitru-Gorzo-art7977512042 (accessed 12 March 2012).

Fototeca Comunismului Online [Online Photo-archive of Communism] (2011) Online. Available: <http://fototeca.iiccr.ro/> (accessed 28 October 2011).

Fraser, N. (2007) 'Transnationalizing the Public Sphere'. Online. Available: <http://eipcp.net/transversal/0605/fraser/en> (accessed 12 March 2012).

Garde-Hansen, J., Hoskins, A. and Reading, A. (eds) (2009) *Save As . . . Digital Memories*. Basingstoke: Palgrave Macmillan.

Gilberg, T. (1990) *Nationalism and Communism in Romania. The Rise and Fall of Ceauşescu's Personal Dictatorship*. Boulder, CO: Westview Press.

Golden Epoch. Between Myth and Reality (2007) Exhibition organized by the Ministry of Culture and Cults, the Romanian Museum of National History in collaboration with the Association Civic Media, the National Philatelic Museum, the Romanian Service of Informations, A.N.P. ROMPRES, '15 November 1987' Association, Polish Institute, National Council for the Study of Securitate Archives (CNSAS) (*Romanian Museum of National History*, 26 January to 26 February 2007). Online. Available: <http://www.mnir.ro/ro/ExpozitiiTemporare/ExpozitieArhiva.aspx?IDExpozitieTemp=40> (accessed 12 March 2012).

H'Art Gallery website (2011) Online. Available: <http://www.hartgallery.ro/index.php?page=artist&id=11&section=works> (accessed 16 October 2010).

Hoskins, A. (2009) 'The Mediatisation of Memory', in J. Garde-Hansen *et al.* (eds), *Save As . . . Digital Memories*. Basingstoke: Palgrave Macmillan.

Institute of Research of the Crimes of Communism and Memory of the Romanian Exile website (2011) Exile. Online. Available: <http://iiccmer.ro/en/> (accessed 28 October 2011).

Kitchin, R. (1998) 'Towards Geographies of Cyberspace'. *Progress in Human Geography* 22(3): 385–406.

Kotkin, S. (2009) *Uncivil Society.* New York: Modern Library.

Kunze, T. (2002) *Nicolae Ceauşescu. O biografie.* Bucharest: Ed. Vremea.

La Trecut website (2011) Online. Available: <http://www.latrecut.ro/> (accessed 18 August 2011).

Linz, J. and Stepan, A. (1996) *Problems of Democratic Transition and Consolidation.* Baltimore, MD: The John Hopkins University Press.

Museum of Contemporary Art website (2008) Online. Available: <http://www.mnac.ro> (accessed 23 June 2008).

National History Museum Communism in Romania website (2012) Online. Available: <http://www.comunismulinromania.ro> (accessed 19 June 2012).

New Communist Party of Romania Committee of Reorganization Website (2011) Online. Available: <http://npcr.ro/> (accessed 18 August 2011).

Pence, K. and Betts, P. (eds) (2007) *Socialist Modern: East German Everyday Culture and Politics.* Ann Arbor, MI: The University of Michigan Press.

Pescaru C. (2011) 'România la coada clasamentului UE privind accesul la internet'. Ziare.com, 15 December. Online, Available: < http://www.ziare.com/internet-si-tehnologie/acces-internet/suntem-pe-primul-loc-in-ue-la-lipsa-de-acces-la-internet-1139879> (accessed 12 March 2012).

Photogallery RSR Museum (2011) Online. Available: <http://www.newsin.ro/muzeul-rsr-nicolae-ceausecu.php?cid=view&nid=73f4ae52-5a97-4fe1-b1f9-37e03c956c03&hid=foto> (accessed 19 August 2011).

Plan B Gallery website (2011) Online. Available: <http://www.plan-b.ro/index.php?/adrian-ghenie/> (accessed 23 August 2011).

Preda, C. (2005) 'La révolution roumaine de 1989 dans la presse écrite belge'. *Studia Politica Romanian Political Science Review* 5(2): 427–459.

Preda, C. (2010) 'Looking at the Past through an Artistic Lens: Art of Memorialization', in *History of Communism in Europe. Politics of Memory in Post-communist Europe*, new series, Vol. 1. Bucharest: Zeta Books, pp. 129–148.

Ramonet, I. (1990) 'Télévision nécrophile'. *Le Monde Diplomatique*, March. Online. Available: <http://www.monde-diplomatique.fr/1990/03/RAMONET/18658> (accessed 14 March 2012).

Rutten, E. (2010) 'Web Wars: Digital Diasporas and the Language of Memory'. *Digital Icons* 4: 171–176.

Rutten, E. (2011) 'How New Media Affect Eastern Europe's Memory Wars Or How Eastern Europe's Memory Wars Affect New Media Studies'. Paper presented at the King's College Memory and Theory in Eastern Europe Conference, Cambridge, July.

Saunders, F.S. (2000) *The Cultural Cold War: The CIA and the World of Arts and Letters.* New York: The New Press.

Serghei Niculescu Mizil website (2012) Online. Available: <http://sergheiniculescumizil.blogspot.com/p/trecutul-meu.html> (accessed 12 March 2012).

Sighet Memorial website (2012) Online. Available: <http://www.memorialsighet.ro/> (accessed 12 March 2012).

Stencil Archive (2012) Online. Available: <http://www.2020.ro> (accessed 12 March 2012).

The Palace of the Republic of Socialist Romania Museum website (2011) Online. Available: <http://www.palatul-rsr.ro/palat/index.html> (accessed 25 August 2011).

Tismăneanu, V. (2003) *Stalinism for all Seasons. A Political History of Romanian Communism.* Berkeley: University of California Press.

Tismăneanu, V. and Iacob, B.C. (eds) (2012) *The End and the Beginning. The Revolutions of 1989 and the Resurgence of History*. Budapest: CEU Press.

Todorova, M. (2010) *Remembering Communism: Genres of Representation.* New York: Social Science Research Council.

Todorova, M. and Gille, Z. (eds) (2010) *Post-communist Nostalgia.* New York: Berghahn Books.

Ursu, I (2010) '41% dintre români l-ar vota pe Nicolae Ceauşescu preşedinte – sondaj IRES'. ziare.com, 26 July 2010. Online. Available: http://www.ziare.com/nicolae-ceausescu/comunism/41-la-suta-dintre-romani-l-ar-vota-pe-nicolae-ceausescu-presedinte-sondaj-ires-1031471 (accessed 12 March 2012).

Wilson, S. (2009) 'Remixing Memory in Digital Media', in J. Garde-Hansen *et al.* (eds), *Save As . . . Digital Memories*. Basingstoke: Palgrave Macmillan.

14 Witnessing war, globalizing victory

Representations of the Second World War on the website *Russia Today*[1]

Jussi Lassila

Introduction

The public memory of the Soviet Union's victory in the 'Great Patriotic War' in 1945 lies at the heart of history debates between Russia and countries of the former Soviet bloc, notably the Baltic States, Poland and Ukraine. A special media project entitled *War Witness – WWII Victory Tribute*, launched by the Russian state-driven global television news network *Russia Today* in 2010, provides an illuminating perspective on one aspect of these debates: the political use of memory and identity in transnational digital media. In this chapter I examine the symbolic practices of *War Witness* in order to figure out how the project and its forum, *Russia Today*, aim to translate the national importance of the 'Great Patriotic War' for an international audience.

Regardless of the importance that parents may attach to a child's first words, steps or birthday parties, the processes of choosing and preserving them for future remembering are shaped by cultural conventions (van Dijck 2004: 263; van Dijck 2007: 37–38). By the same token, the national commemorative practices employed by states are likewise heavily dependent upon socio-cultural, political and technological circumstances. As Jeffrey K. Olick has pointed out, 'differences between the commemorations of important state events respond not only to the politics of the present or to immediate historical precedents, but they are interdependent with the forms and media available at different moments as well' (Olick 1999: 383). It follows that the specific historical and political identity information about these events is not only distributed by the media: it is, crucially, constructed in and through them.

With its location at the intersection of transnational digital media and the attempt to distribute particular state-driven views, *War Witness* represents an empirical case that may be framed using James Rosenau's concept of *fragmegration*. This concept refers to a complex dynamism of simultaneous processes of fragmentation and integration which, according to Rosenau, have become particularly apparent in the post-Cold War globalization (Rosenau 2006: 15–17). More importantly for our purposes, dimensions of fragmentation and integration may be desirable or undesirable depending on viewpoint, and thus uncertainty is an elementary feature of fragmegration. For instance, the Internet's capacity to accelerate and expand the spread of the official interpretation of the key event in Russia's history is undoubtedly a desirable feature from the point of view of *Russia Today*, given the latter's status as a representative of Russia's official voice on the global stage. In addition to the Internet's capacity to strengthen Russia's political order in this regard, it may help to integrate Russia's official views on the Second World War with other states' commemorative narratives, and vice versa.

However, at the same time, the Internet's capacity to disseminate information not only beyond national borders but also beyond traditional hierarchies of information flows – that is, the Internet's ultimate openness, as distinct from relatively closed media such as newspapers, television and radio – also has deeply undesirable characteristics for state-run projects of this kind. In other words, in contemporary media space the various representations of official state history and national identity are completely beyond any limits that could allow their maintenance, development and control within a 'national vacuum'.[2] Instead, they are doomed to be available in the space that Anna Reading (Chapter 1, this volume) calls 'the globital memory field' (Reading 2011: 380). This field 'enables new connectivities and assemblages of memories in unevenly globalized and localized contexts' which challenges the previous order(s).

Russia Today: background

In line with the domestic patriotic programmes that have characterized Vladimir Putin's rule, the Russian state has visibly invested in the country's foreign image. A turning point in this respect was a speech given by Putin in 2004, when he addressed Russian ambassadors on the necessity to create a favourable image for the country (Feklyunina 2008: 608). Scholars of Russia's international relations have discussed these image projects in terms of 'soft power' (for a critical discussion of this concept in terms of Russia, see Hudson 2011). These range from various media projects and the establishment of foundations aimed at promoting Russian language and culture abroad, to public defences of particular interpretations of history as pillars of national identity (Feklyunina 2008: 621–622; Hudson 2011). *Russia Today* is the largest and the most expensive of these state image projects. Commonly abbreviated as *RT*, this global television news network was launched in December 2005 ('RT Corporate Profile' 2012), and in 2007 its budget was approximately US$80 million ('"Svoboda slova" obkhoditsia vse dorozhe' 2006). Besides Moscow headquarters, *RT* has offices in Washington, DC, London, Tel Aviv and Tskhinvali, South Ossetia, the epicentre of the August 2008 Russo-Georgian war ('Broadcast Engineering' 2012). In addition to English, which is its primary language, *RT* broadcasts in Spanish and Arabic. The channel is potentially available all around the world, whether via free online streaming, cable or satellite.

RT definitely figures as a simple state-sponsored media project that mediates politically biased views in English for the outer world, loosely based on the familiar format used by global networks like *CNN*, *BBC World News* and *Al-Jazeera*. However, if we follow the concept of fragmegration with its focus on the tension between the desirable and undesirable effects of integration (and order) and fragmentation (and chaos), then *RT* provides an illuminating case of the negotiation of communicative practices linked to nationally important themes for a global audience.

Online exclusive: *RT's War Witness*

> Luckily, for most of those reading this text, 'war' is only a word. A word from school lectures, history books, newspaper articles; something they would never want to happen to them in life.
>
> But there are those for whom war was a reality. They had no choice. There was only one thing for them to do – go to that war and defend their countries. They did it for people like us to have 'war' as nothing more than part of history. They fought so that you could now be reading these words. For them the war was real, and now it is hard and painful for them to remember.
>
> For the Soviet Union, World War II was known as the Great Patriotic War. It was truly patriotic, as the Soviet people were fighting on their own land trying to save their homeland and the whole world from the terrible menace that was the Nazis. And, as we know, they did it, having won that war and forced Nazi Germany to capitulate.
>
> (Online exclusive *War Witness 2012*)

The first two paragraphs of *War Witness'* introduction text frame the 'Great Patriotic War' as an instance of the universal human experience of war. A distinction is set up between 'us' (presumably, the post-war generations) and 'them' (those who lived through the war and are thus able to mediate this experience to us, and to whom we owe a debt). Finally, in the third paragraph, a bridge is built between the universal dimensions of the war and the Russian national viewpoint. These witnesses are made to straddle this divide, and to justify Russia's claim to a special right to take pride in this universal achievement. In other words, we all owe our existence to those first-hand war witnesses, but at the same time the link between the universal war and our universal existence was made possible first and foremost specifically by the Soviet war effort.

The project's opening passage is revealing, not only in its use of a transnational forum (the English-language Internet) for the dissemination of particular national views, but also in its apparent drive to reconcile the transnational and the national. In her article on Russian bloggers' negotiations of national versus cosmopolitan war memory, Elena Trubina asks to what extent forms of national memory find themselves in a dialogue with transnational ones (Trubina 2010: 66). Trubina's question is highly relevant when it comes to the discursive strategies employed by *War Witness*. These strategies exemplify the management of the tension between the nation and the transnational through symbolic forms. Consider, for example, the following blurb from the project site:

> What makes the project unique is that it is really international: our correspondents went to interview war witnesses not only from Russia, but also from Belarus, Georgia, Latvia, Finland, Poland, the Czech Republic, Germany, the UK, France and the US. RT has been searching for those who could share their memories via veteran organizations, museums and personal contacts internationally. Most of the materials collected are truly unique. For instance, there are only two surviving non-USSR citizens who were awarded 'The Hero of the USSR' – the country's highest honor – during wartime. One of them resides in France, and now you have the opportunity to watch RT's interview with him on our website.
>
> (*War Witness:* Voices of War 2012)

The professed international focus of this 'export' version of the 'Great Patriotic War' sits somewhat uneasily alongside the evident (and understandable) bias towards Russian witnesses, who make up the vast majority of the roughly one hundred protagonists featured in the video clips. Other countries are also represented here, but in much smaller number. Within its transnational context it is worth pointing out that the English term *Russian* can have one of two meanings: Russian as an ethnic category in the multinational Russian (and previously, Soviet) Federation, or Russian as a citizen of this multinational federation. In terms of internationalizing Russia's national, and to some extent ethnically-driven memory, the use of English blurs the distinction between these two categories.

These video clips, all of which are made available in English, operate at the nexus of the technological possibilities of the global digital media, memory politics, and national identity. This, too, presents particular problems for the project's designers, who must strive to balance the use of high-tech media against the need to project 'authentic' unmediated memory. Andrew Hoskins has argued that the case of Holocaust-memory in the contemporary mediated age also 'implies a search for an authentic historical memory as the antithesis of a debased and mediated relation to the past' (Hoskins 2003: 10). This statement applies equally to *War Witness*, which simultaneously harnesses all the contemporary technological possibilities for audiovisual mediation of individuals' memories while aiming to deliver the 'truth' about the war. Arguably, the challenge posed by this dilemma is recognized, or 'anticipated,' – in Pierre Bourdieu's sense (Bourdieu 1991) – in the project creators' assertion that:

> Going through the videos on the site you will hardly come across pathetic speeches or heroic descriptions. You will mostly hear ordinary people talking about everyday life, with the only remarkable thing being that their lives went on during the war . . . These are simple folk, not used to talking on camera. That's the most precious thing about these interviews.
>
> (*War Witness*: Voices of War 2012)

The focus on 'simple folk' is sharply at odds with another section of the *War Witness* project, 'War Fact Files', which consists of descriptions of the 'Great Patriotic War's' most famous heroic figures (*War Witness:* War Fact Files 2012). This section focuses exclusively on Soviet heroes. Most of these are military figures, though certain prominent civilians, most notably from the siege of Leningrad, some of which have only been canonized in the post-Soviet period, are also featured. Alongside these traditionally monolithic, person-centred representations of the war, the primary content of *War Witness* relies heavily on the large quantity of 'ordinary war witness voices'. We might argue, then, that the project aims to transcend the tension between national narratives' unchallenged mythic images and audiovisually mediated ordinary voices by creating a credible combination of mutually reinforcing sources: the heroic Soviet-Russian narrative is not upstaged, cancelled out or contradicted by the project's audiovisual mediation of 'international' individual memories; rather, it is animated, 'brought to life', by this mediation. Consequently, a collection of international individual memories may be framed by particular nation-bound sources, which in turn gives these memories official 'scholarly' or 'scientific' historical value. This strategy offers a means of neutralizing the criticism that any 'Grand Narrative' activates in the contemporary international arena, and in particular, the vociferous attacks that the narrative of the 'Great Patriotic War' inevitably prompts in that arena's 'East European corner'.

From this standpoint, today's global 'Internet generation' is offered a collection of universal voices representing the rapidly vanishing war generation, and embodying that generation's suffering and sacrifice. This transnational constellation of war memories is one that can credibly serve Russia's official national memory project. Indeed, potential critiques of Russia's national viewpoint on the Second World War may readily be countered with these ultimate living documentary voices of the war. This is apparent in the following description of the witness talks by the site creators:

> 65 years after the victory, some of those who brought it to us agreed to share their memories – not for us to savour the inhuman and shocking atrocities of that time, nor to scavenge for naturalistic descriptions of their life, but to try and grasp at least a tiny part of meaning of what the word 'war' means for those who took part in it.
>
> (*War Witness* 2012)

When viewed in the context of Eastern Europe's transnational memory wars, this passage is highly revealing. Typifying the descriptions of war horrors that many of the talks mediate, this characterization would appear to anticipate potential conflicts that representations of the war typically evoke in the space of post-socialist digital memories in particular (see Introduction, this volume). By using emotive and heavily value-laden language such as 'scavenge' in connection with 'atrocities', the passage implicitly paints a demonic portrait of those who strongly oppose Russia's official interpretation of the war (a position most often associated with the Baltic States, Ukraine and Poland). In other words, the project initiators employ seemingly universal suffering in order to deflect potential attempts at questioning Russia's viewpoint.

Each video clip is titled with a quote from the given clip. The choice of quotes here is quite instructive, since it provides us with an insight into which aspect or key 'message' of the clip the project creators have chosen to highlight. For instance, a talk by one Russian war witness is entitled: 'One German soldier called us, put us on his lap and gave us chocolate bars', with the subtitle 'I have seen bad German soldiers, who robbed, shot and killed. I have seen them. But I have also seen good Germans' ('One German Soldier' 2012). In a similar vein – but now to defend the honour of Soviet soldiers – a talk by a Finnish veteran is entitled 'Life is precious. It doesn't matter what army you serve, what country you defend' ('Life is Precious' 2012). A shift from the universal viewpoint of this title to a nation-bound perspective occurs immediately in the opening sentence of his talk: 'A Soviet soldier was a very good soldier. It's indisputable and this fact is recognized not only in Russia' (ibid.). These quotes have evidently been selected with a view to furthering the project's attempt to reconcile national memory with the anticipated cosmopolitan memory.

Despite the project's ambitious nature and evidently large budget, it does not seem to have evoked much response or commentary. In April 2012, approximately two years after the project's launch, there were only 86 comments on the project's dedicated online discussion forum (*War Witness:* Forum 2012). On the project's separate discussion forum there are no references to particular video clips either. All comments concern general opinions about the war, or personal responses to the *War Witness* project. The majority of the 86 comments are supportive. Characteristically, user Thomas Brown writes, 'Thank you Russia. If it wasn't for you, I would not be able to experience the freedom that I enjoy today. Spasiba!'

On the one hand, this positive overall tone notwithstanding, it would be simplistic to assume that *War Witness* applies strict moderating policies by allowing only supportive or even naïve appraisals of the project. Negative views are also present. Moreover, these critical views are by no means all standard defences of the old Soviet line on the war, with its narrative of 'good Soviet-Russians' versus the 'fascists'. Instead, some commentators give a more detailed view of the weaknesses of the project's constructed objectivity. For instance, user Anthony centres his critique on Stalin when he writes:

> I agree the Soviet Union did the bulk of the fighting to destroy the German war machine, but the US did give them a lot of support with weapons, materials, and other items to support a huge army. Armies are not just created and moved with tanks and guns. They need trucks, jeeps, etc. Food and fuel are also essential. So it took a united effort to beat Germany, in 1941, Hitler came real close to winning the war, but he screwed up by misdirecting his panzer armies away from Moscow and toward Kiev. Giving the Russians time to set up their defenses. Then winter set in and it was over for the

> Germans. I wonder what Russian producers are doing about what Stalin did, killing millions of Russians too. Makes me wonder.
>
> (*War Witness:* Forum, Discuss the Project 2012)

On the other hand, even Anthony's comment cannot avoid those stereotypical extremes that prevail in Russia's memory politics regarding the 'Great Patriotic War'; for example, the supposed worldwide admiration for the Soviet victory (as in Thomas' comment above), and Stalin's calamitous mistakes (as in Anthony's comment). Given the stereotypical features present here, it is possible that both comments are staged. However, staged or not, both alternatives illustrate the project's drive to reconcile Russia's official national memory with the anticipated transnational critique of it, either by allowing such critical views to be aired, or by manufacturing such views. Either way, the intended effect is presumably at least in part to demonstrate the fact that contemporary Russia has rejected the old totalizing Soviet discourse on the memory of the war and is willing to adhere to the conventions of global digital space.

Managing Stalin for a global audience

The figure of Stalin is a major stumbling-block when it comes to packaging Russia's national war narrative for a global audience. On the one hand, Stalin is obviously a central protagonist in this story, but on the other, any perceived glorification of Stalin damages Russia's international reputation. The producers of *War Witness* had to find a way to craft a war narrative that would be acceptable and credible to the global audience, but without undermining the foundations of the Soviet–Russian narrative.

The strategies adopted by *War Witness* in response to this dilemma take several different forms. The figure of Stalin is rather conspicuously absent from many of the project's key texts, but simply omitting Stalin altogether would be an unsustainable and counter-productive strategy. Thus, in addition, the project also includes sections that are evidently aimed at re-negotiating the figure of Stalin and his place within the war narrative. For instance, the project features the video version of an interview with President Medvedev that was published in the newspaper *Izvestiia* on the eve of Russia's commemorative victory holiday, Victory Day, in 2010 ('Russian President Gives his View on WWII' 2010). In this interview Medvedev pointedly reframed the Soviet-Russian victory in 1945, not as the victory of Stalin and the Red Army, but as a victory of the Russian people, with an explicit critical overtone directed against Stalin. Given Stalin's central role in the traditional patriotic framework of the 'Great Patriotic War' myth, it is no wonder that Medvedev's views prompted noisy criticism by many readers of *Izvestiia*'s online version ('Dmitrii Medvedev' 2010). For *War Witness*, by contrast, given its transnational role and its drive to attain global recognition for the national narrative, the emphasis on Stalin's criticism is a plausible and less controversial strategy.

Elsewhere, too, *War Witness* appears to take its cue from Medvedev's May 2010 speech when it comes to the difficult question of handling the figure of Stalin. For example, the *War Witness* website features a short film, *Brest Fortress Defenders: Betrayed Heroes*, which constructs an explicitly heroic version of Soviet fighters who were abandoned by Stalin, and it elaborates openly on Stalin's political mistakes ('Brest Fortress' 2012).

The battle of the Brest Fortress in 1941 represents a kind of ideal symbol of the self-sacrifice by those who ultimately won out in 1945. It provides an example of the relatively successful conversion of the national into the transnational image, in which 'natural' national sacrifice in defence of one's motherland combined with critical attitudes towards Stalin may be said to resonate with global views. Nonetheless, there are examples where the conversion is less smooth. Consider, for instance, the section 'War Fact Files', which presents a chronological overview of the events of the Second World War (*War Witness:* War Fact Files, War Overview 2012). The timeline begins with the date generally accepted as marking the beginning of the war: 1 September 1939. For the year 1939, the list does include those events for which the Soviet Union is commonly criticized, and which were suppressed or distorted in the Soviet narrative; for example, the Soviet occupation of eastern Poland and the Soviet invasion of Finland. The fact that the Soviet Union was expelled from the League of Nations as a result of its attack on Finland is also acknowledged. However, while these basic factual events are recognized, their labelling and classification bear the hallmarks of the Russian–Soviet narrative. Thus, for example, it is asserted that the 'Winter War' was not 'part of the Second World War', though no explanation or justification is provided for this assertion (ibid.). What is more, a thumbnail sketch of the map depicting Operation Barbarossa in 1941 is attached to these events of the year 1939. This pictorial link clearly implies a partial legitimization of the Soviet invasions as strategic necessities. In other words, the site presents these 'Soviet sins' that are largely condemned by the outer world as necessary moves by the Soviet political leadership (i.e. Stalin) in terms of anticipating Hitler's attack.

The 'War Fact Files'' depiction of the war's key protagonists struggles with the related challenge of finding a way to simultaneously retain and downplay the figure of Stalin. The text accompanying the entry on Stalin reveals the difficulty that the project faces when tackling this central war character. The text reads:

> Historians still have not come to a consensus about Stalin's role in World War II, but one thing is certain – the Soviet army, commanded by Stalin, not only pushed the Germans back from the Soviet borders, but also liberated many European countries and occupied Berlin.
>
> (*War Witness*: War Fact Files, Personalities 2012)

The section of the project dealing with the February 1945 Yalta Conference is perhaps most revealing of the challenges associated with the project's drive to embed Stalin within a reconstituted transnational version of the national Great Patriotic War narrative. The related *RT* video is subtitled *End of One War, Beginning of Another* ('End of One War' 2012). The emphasis is placed here on the ways in which the Western commemoration of the Yalta Conference fails to pay due respect to the Soviet Union's role in these events. The video focuses on the 'Allies' statue on Bond Street in London, which depicts Winston Churchill and Franklin D. Roosevelt (but not Stalin) seated on a bench, in conversation with one another.

The *RT* footage features two vox populi comments by random members of the British public, both of whom say that Stalin should not be included with the leaders of the Western allies in the statue – and thus implicitly the footage admits that Stalin is a controversial figure. However, the makers of the video also air the viewpoint of a Russian military historian, who states that 'it is wrong to equate the image of one man with the actual achievements of the entire country'. For Russia, a central challenge that such a critique of Western criticism on Stalin brings to the fore is related to the question of the temporality of the framing of the figure of Stalin. Whereas it is understandable from Russia's viewpoint that Stalin should be included on the Allied victors' bench, this is less justifiable when viewed from the perspective of the long-term consequences of Yalta: the establishment of the dictatorial socialist bloc and all its inhuman ramifications. This video appears to reach for a solution to this problem by imposing a selective temporal frame in order to make its implicit claim that in 2010, now that the Cold War is over, Stalin should work as a flexible and internationally recognized symbol of the mythical Soviet-Russian achievement of defeating Nazi Germany and liberating Europe. In effect, this requires the bracketing out of the entire history of Eastern Europe from 1945 to 1989 (on concepts of time linked to the memory of the Great Patriotic War, see Wolfe 2006; see also Kangaspuro 2011; Kangaspuro and Lassila 2012). The final sentence of the video's voice-over also appears to tackle this difficulty by recasting the 'Soviet legacy' as something that is 'the West's problem': 'The Cold War may be over but democratic powers don't seem ready to recognize the Soviet legacy.'

By contrast, other sections of the project place a heavy emphasis on the supposed global recognition of Russia's victory. A long series of video clips available in the section entitled 'On Air Specials' cover manifestations of Western admiration of Soviet heroism and worldwide Victory Day celebrations at great length (*War Witness:* On Air Specials 2012). This line of reporting clearly clashes with the 'Yalta Conference' video's critique of the West's alleged refusal to recognize the Soviet contribution to the 1945 victory. The only exception in this series, compatible with the Yaltaclip in terms of posing a critique against critique of Russia's national memory, is a clip which reports on Russia's initiative in the UN General Assembly in 2009 protesting the destruction of the Second World War monuments in Estonia and Georgia.[3]

An illuminating manifestation of the supposed global recognition of Russia's victory – and its usage specifically for transnational media practices – is presented in the clip entitled 'Victory Day Parade is a Sign of Russia Opening to the West – Expat' (*War Witness*: Victory Day Parade 2012). The video shows an *RT* reporter interviewing foreign tourists on the streets of Moscow immediately after Victory Day. The report is framed by a *CNN*-style casual dialogue between the reporter and *RT's* studio hosts. The topics discussed with the three interviewees range between football, the weather, the euro crisis and Moscow's cultural activities. The reporter's first target is a tourist from New York who comments that, for him, the participation of Western troops in the Victory Day Parade on Red Square was a sign of Russia's opening up to the West. It is unsurprising – given *RT's* evident intention to subsume all of the various positively valued events and practices surrounding the commemoration of Russia's victory (for more on this 'subsuming', see Bell 2003) – that it was this interviewee's casual remark that was selected as the title for the video.

Conclusion

The *War Witness* project, with its evident tension linked to the quest for suitable memory representations, may be framed as an empirical case of Rosenau's fragmegration. When reconciling the state-driven need of nation building with the digital space of fragmenting grand narratives, it is this space that evidently provides a desirable horizon for the new national order. At the same time, however, the project inevitably exposes itself to the undesirable effects of fragmentation that are inherently present in digital space.

Within this tension the project offers a fruitful angle on memory politics in digital space and the use of post-socialist digital memories in particular. According to Claudio Fogu and Wulf Kansteiner, the politics of memory always interact with specific poetics of history (Fogu and Kansteiner 2006: 284). They argue that the intensity of this interaction may constitute the major variable in the evolution of collective memories. At least in terms of the evolution of collective memories, *War Witness* demonstrates how the national politics of memory has found an effective channel to a global audience, while at the same time it is irrevocably conditioned by this channel. The project illustrates how this national poetics of history appears as a particular form of 'web poetics'. The symbolic resources of this global web poetics may be harnessed for the national memory narrative of the 'Great Patriotic War', but they must also be calibrated between national and transnational conventions.

Whereas digital media certainly play a major role in the evolution of collective memories, Andrew Hoskins has convincingly shown that this evolution poses a challenge when it comes to the use of contemporary technology in order to exhibit the memory of the Holocaust (Hoskins 2003: 7). He points out that 'the continuous feeding of memory has more to do with the connectivity of the electronic media than with any sustained social consensus about the past' (ibid.). In the same way, the *War Witness* website exhibits how this digital feeding of memory (texts, images, voices, sounds and especially audiovisual footage) becomes the central symbolic resource of the project.

Just like the Holocaust museum exhibition strategies that Hoskins describes (ibid.: 13), *War Witness'* large-scale audiovisual collection of living history aims to 'punctuate history because of its extraordinary nature, and thus to provide a time out of time'. In light of the project's high-level technical functionality and design, the technological possibilities of digital media are especially well suited for enabling various constellations of past events, as well as 'anticipating' their counterpoints. To apply Fogu and Kansteiner, *War Witness* aims to close the evident gaps in the project's politics of memory – that is, the national underpinnings of memory in a transnational forum – with the help of web poetics. These gaps are most notably centred in the role of Stalin.

An important feature of this web poetics is a potentially endless scope for attaching different materials in the service of one's own memory politics. In addition to the unrestrained possibilities that digital space offers for attaching one's own viewpoint(s) to a variety of potentially supporting views, this strategy requires a recognition of opposing views. Richard Rogers and Noortje Marres label this sort of 'viewpoint-management' a 'debate-scaping' technique (Rogers and Marres 2000: 146). This means the recognition of the issue's contested nature in which an actor is involved, and is realized by providing hyperlinks to 'the semblance of an epistemic network' that would serve the actor's viewpoints. More importantly, 'the semblance of an epistemic network can be visualized as a debate only if actors acknowledge other actors by linking to them' (ibid.).

To be sure, as *War Witness* illustrates, hyperlinking to opposing viewpoints in memory debates that rage around the Second World War – and notably in post-Soviet space – is not a common practice. Instead, links are constantly made to 'Western examples' that provide a connection to Russia's memory politics and its 'punctuated' history (for example, in the form of references to the Soviet Union's Western allies in the Second World War). The main problem is, however, that although digital space provides tools for simulating such punctuation, it is the digital space itself that crucially restricts this simulation. Is it thus the case that particular 'Grand Narratives' related to nations' commemorative practices – born and largely maintained within the development of print capitalism (Anderson 2006) – are today being forced to adapt their forms to the pressure exerted by the Internet's technological possibilities and social force? Or, do these technological possibilities and social forces offer even better options for emulating the transnational world in the service of national goals, as the producers of *RT's War Witness* seem to believe?

Notes

1 I am grateful to Julie Fedor, Ellen Rutten and Vera Zvereva for helpful comments on earlier versions of this chapter.

2 For example, in studies of geopolitics traditional nation state-bounded geographical space is contrasted with cyberspace, and the latter does not follow traditional geographical borders. These notions may be applied here, although it seems that the scholarship's views are sometimes overly generalizing in describing these two realms. See, for example, Spiegel (2000).

3 According to the footage, 'the document drew the support of 127 countries, and while 54 delegations abstained, the US voted against saying the resolution questions freedom of expression' (see General Assembly). This initiative was primarily motivated by Russia's outrage against Estonia's decision to remove the Soviet-era 'Bronze Soldier' statue from central Tallinn in late April 2007. The statue was moved from a central district to the military cemetery located on the outskirts of the city.

References

Anderson, B. (2006) [1983] *Imagined Communities*. London and New York: Verso.

Bell, D.S.A. (2003) 'Mythscapes: Memory, Mythology, and National Identity'. *British Journal of Sociology* 54(1): 63–81.

Bourdieu, P. (1991) *Language and Symbolic Power*. Cambridge: Polity Press.

'Brest Fortress Defenders: Betrayed Heroes' (2012) *War Witness:* On Air Specials. Online. Available: <http://victory1945.rt.com/on-air/brest-fortress-defenders-war/> (accessed 13 April 2012).

'Broadcast Engineering' (2012) Online. Available: <http://broadcastengineering.com/hdtv/rt-adds-washington-dc-0910/> (accessed 13 April 2012).

'Dmitrii Medvedev: Nam ne nado stesniat'sia' (2010). *Izvestiia*. 7 May. 2010. Online. Available HTTP: <http://izvestia.ru/news/361448#ixzz2JCHU1Zyv> (accessed 27 January 2013).

'End of One War, Beginning of Another' (2012) *War Witness:* On Air Specials. Online. Available: <http://victory1945.rt.com/on-air/yalta-end-war-allies/> (accessed 13 April 2012).

Feklyunina, V. (2008) 'Battle for Perceptions: Projecting Russia in the West'. *Europe-Asia Studies* 60(4): 605–629.

Fogu, C. and Kansteiner, W. (2006) 'The Politics of Memory and Poetics of History', in R.N. Lebow, C. Fogu and W. Kansteiner (eds), *The Politics of Memory in Postwar Europe*. Durham, NC: Duke University Press.

'General Assembly Condemns Destruction of WWII Monuments', *War Witness:* On Air Specials. Online. Available: <http://victory1945.rt.com/on-air/general-assembly-destruction-monuments/> (accessed 13 April 2012).

Hoskins, A. (2003) 'Signs of the Holocaust: Exhibiting Memory in a Mediated Age'. *Media, Culture & Society* 25(1): 7–22.

Hudson, V. (2011) 'Locating Russian Soft Power: An Examination of Current Trends in the Discourse'. Paper presented at the Aleksanteri Institute Visiting Fellows Seminar, Helsinki (3 March).

Kangaspuro, M. (2011) 'The Victory Day in History Politics', in E. Kahla (ed.), *Between Utopia and Apocalypse: Essays on Social Theory and Russia*. Helsinki: Aleksanteri Series 1, pp. 292–304.

Kangaspuro, M. and Lassila, J. (2012) 'Naming the War and Framing the Nation in the Russian Public Discussion'. *Canadian Slavonic Papers/Revue Canadienne des Slavistes*, Vol. LIV, Nos. 3–4, September–December: 61–84.

'Life is Precious. It Doesn't Matter What Army you Serve, What Country you Defend' (2012) *War Witness:* Voices of War. Online. Available: <http://victory1945.rt.com/witnesses/life-army-soviet-soldiers/> (accessed 13 April 2012).

Olick, J.K. (1999) 'Genre Memories and Memory Genres: A Dialogical Analysis of May 8, 1945 Commemorations in the Federal Republic of Germany'. *American Sociological Review* 64: 381–402.

'One German Soldier Called Us, Put Us on His Lap and Gave Us Chocolate Bars'. (2012) *War Witness:* Veterans Remember. Online. Available: <http://victory1945.rt.com/memoirs/soldier-lap-germans-chocolate/> (accessed 13 April 2012).

Online exclusive *War Witness – WWII Victory Tribute* (2012) Online. Available: <http://victory1945.rt.com/> (accessed 13 April 2012).

Reading, A. (2011) 'Identity, Memory and Cosmopolitanism: The Otherness of the Past and a Right to Memory?' *European Journal of Cultural Studies* 14(4): 379–394.

Rogers, R. and Marres, N. (2000) 'Landscaping Climate Change: A Mapping Technique for Understanding Science and Technology Debates on the World Wide Web'. *Public Understanding of Science* 9: 141–163.

Rosenau, J.N. (2006) *The Study of World Politics. Vol.2: Globalization and Governance.* London and New York: Routledge.

'Russian President Gives his View on WWII', *War Witness:* On Air Specials. Online. Available: <http://victory1945.rt.com/on-air/war-president-events-lived/> (accessed 13 April, 2012). This interview was originally published in *Izvestiia* on 7 May 2010. Online. Available: <http://izvestia.ru/news/361448> (accessed 13 April 2012).

'RT Corporate Profile' (2012) *RT.* Online. Available: <http://rt.com/about/corporate-profile/> (accessed 13 April 2012).

Spiegel, S.L. (2000) 'Traditional Space vs. Cyberspace: The Changing Role of Geography in Current International Politics'. *Geopolitics* 5(3): 114–125.

'"Svoboda slova" obkhoditsia vse dorozhe' (2006) *Nezavisimaia gazeta,* 5 September. Online. Available: <http://www.ng.ru/politics/2006-09-05/1_svobodaslova.html> (accessed April 13, 2012).

Trubina, E. (2010) 'Past Wars in the Russian Blogosphere: On the Emergence of Cosmopolitan Memory'. *Digital Icons: Studies in Russian, Eurasian and Central European New Media* 4: 63–85.

van Dijck, J. (2004) 'Mediated Memories: Personal Cultural Memory as Object of Cultural Analysis'. *Continuum: Journal of Media & Cultural Studies* 18(2): 261–277.

van Dijck, J. (2007) *Mediated Memories in the Digital Age.* Stanford, CA: Stanford University Press.

War Witness: Forum, Discuss the Project (2012) Online. Available: <http://victory1945.rt.com/forum/discuss-project/page-3/> (accessed 13 April 2012).

War Witness: Forum, Share your Thoughts (2012) Online. Available: <http://victory1945.rt.com/forum//> (accessed 13 April 2012).

War Witness: On Air Specials (2012). Online. Available: <http://victory1945.rt.com/on-air/> (accessed 27 January 2013).

War Witness: Voices of War (2012) Online. Available: <http://victory1945.rt.com/witnesses/> (accessed 13 April 2012).

War Witness: War Fact Files: Personalities (2012) Online. Available: <http://victory1945.rt.com/war-facts/personalities/> (accessed 13 April 2012).

War Witness: War Fact Files, War Overview (2012) Online. Available: <http://victory1945.rt.com/war-facts/war-overview/> (accessed 13 April 2012).

War Witness: 'Victory Day Parade is a Sign of Russia Opening to the West – Expat' (2012) *War Witness:* On Air Specials. Online. Available: <http://victory1945.rt.com/on-air/victory-day-west-expat/> (accessed 13 April 2012).

Wolfe, T.S. (2006) 'Past as Present, Myth, or History? Discourses of Time and The Great Patriotic War', in R.N. Lebow, C. Fogu and W. Kansteiner (eds), *The Politics of Memory in Postwar Europe.* Durham, NC: Duke University Press, pp. 249–283.

15 From 'the second Katyn' to 'a day without Smolensk'

Facebook responses to the Smolensk tragedy and its aftermath

Dieter De Bruyn

On Saturday, 10 April 2010, a Tupolev Tu-154M aircraft of the Polish Air Force crashed near Smolensk (Russia), killing all its passengers including the Polish president, Lech Kaczyński, his wife, and many of the nation's leading political, military and civic figures. At first glance, the Smolensk catastrophe may seem to have little if anything to do with online commemorations of the socialist experience. Yet, if we keep in mind Alexander Etkind's concept of an East European cultural memory that continues to be 'haunted' by the traumatic history of the twentieth century (Etkind 2009), this case may be able to teach us more about the particular role which the socialist past plays in the Polish present than any direct engagement with this topic.

When we take a closer look at the multitude of commemorative gestures that the tragedy and its aftermath have stirred in the Polish public sphere, we will perceive that these gestures often engage more with deeply rooted historical and sociocultural divisions than one might expect, given that the tragedy itself was a mere accident (albeit a highly deplorable and disastrous one). Of course, the fact that the president and his entourage were heading to Katyn, a site of memory saturated with national trauma, has been influential in shaping the perception of this event. To understand this phenomenon, however, we also need to take account of the current extension of the public sphere to the digital realm, including the bottom-up creation of commemorative practices on social media platforms such as Facebook. Therefore, my account of the various Facebook responses to the Smolensk catastrophe and its aftermath will not only focus on the role that historical memory in general is currently playing in the Polish public sphere, but first and foremost on the specificities of the medium through which these particular responses are articulated.

Poland and historical memory

My claim is that the Smolensk case is highly exemplary of the omnipresence of historical memory in the Polish public sphere following decades of communist distortions of the national past. In the last decade, and especially since the brief political hegemony of Lech (President 2005–2010) and Jarosław (Prime Minister 2006–2007) Kaczyński and their conservative Law and Justice (Prawo i Sprawiedliwość, or PiS) party, historical memory in Poland has developed into a key political concern. The Kaczyńskis set out to resuscitate and commemorate selected episodes of Polish history as part of their project aimed at establishing a so-called 'Fourth Republic' that would represent a definitive break with Poland's communist past. In addition to the overt 'politics of history' (in Polish, *polityka historyczna*) waged by PiS and (albeit in a more moderate way) other political groups, the re-emergence of the Romantic paradigm of Polish history has also resulted in a remarkable 'memory boom' (Huyssen 2003: 18) or 'upsurge of memory' (Nora 2002) within the increasingly mass-mediated and pop cultural public sphere.[1]

Yet, as historian Robert Traba has argued, the idea that the current omnipresence of historical memory is a function of 'a single politics of history that joins together a uniform "memory community"' (Traba 2009: 73) tends to obscure the pluralization of memory discourses in Poland since the 1990s.[2] Without this pluralization, for instance, it would have been easier for Jarosław Kaczyński and other supporters of the new 'politics of history' to unilaterally reinterpret the tragic plane crash as a 'Second Katyn'[3] – thus once more transforming the memory of the 1940 mass murder of more than 20,000 Polish prisoners by the Soviet secret police (NKVD) in the forests near Katyn (Russia) and elsewhere into a tool for (geo)political agitation against Russia.

Admittedly, a series of striking coincidences made it very tempting to apply the Katyn 'schema' or 'template'[4] to the evolving Smolensk narrative: the improbable fate of the nation's top figures on their way to Katyn inevitably called forth parallels with the very event that they were about to commemorate. Given these circumstances, it is not surprising that, in the minds of Jarosław Kaczyński and his allies, the slightest sign of Russian involvement or manipulation has been easily transformed into solid evidence of yet another political plot against the ill-fated Polish Eagle. Yet, those who fear that these conspiratorial interpretations of the recent past will marginalize others just as they did in the days of Soviet hegemony tend to forget that – as Timothy Garton Ash remarks in his comparison of both 'Katyns' – 'the historical circumstances [of the two events] are like night and day' (Garton Ash 2010).[5] First of all, whereas the communist authorities in the Soviet Union and their allies in Poland were often successful in silencing or distorting the truth about the Katyn massacre, at least when it came to public memory, such totalitarian control over the production of historical memory seems to be impossible in contemporary Poland. Indeed, the failed attempts by PiS to capitalize on the Smolensk disaster are themselves eloquent testimony to the pluralized nature of the contemporary Polish memoryscape.

With regard to the Smolensk catastrophe, this lack of control works in two directions. On the one hand, the PiS camp can only watch both the immediate institutionalization of its memory (through all kinds of ceremonies, memorial tablets, etc.) and the meticulous investigation of its causes, and thus has difficulties substantiating any accusations of Soviet-like manipulations by their supposed adversaries. On the other hand, the ongoing cooperative and mutually supportive relations between the Polish and Russian governments have seriously frustrated the same group of non-believers in their attempts to construct and circulate their own conspiracy narrative. Of course, conspiracy theories on the crash have gained a certain popularity, but they have never developed into anything even remotely resembling a commonly shared national belief.

Second, we should be aware of the changing ways in which historical memory has been mediated since Poland, as of the early 2000s and especially during the EU accession process, experienced the same kind of shift from history to memory which Pierre Nora had earlier diagnosed with reference to France and other traditional nation states. According to Nora, contemporary nation states are losing control over traditional memory institutions (such as the school, the museum and the monument), as a result of which an 'internal decolonization' and subsequent 'democratization of history' may take place (Nora 2002).

The shift to which Nora refers may be perceived most prominently in (or may even be said to be contingent upon) the plurality of the forms and agents mediating historical memory. Or, as Nora puts it in another essay:

> National memory cannot come into being until the historical framework of the nation has been shattered. It reflects the abandonment of the traditional channels and modes of transmission of the past and the desacralisation of such primary sites of initiation as the school, the family, the museum, and the monument: what was once the responsibility of these institutions has now flowed over into the public domain and been taken over by the media and tourist industry.
>
> (Nora 1998: 636)

Not surprisingly, these 'primary sites of initiation' are precisely the ones targeted by the Kaczyńskis – key examples being the politicization of the Institute of National Remembrance (IPN), the creation of the 2004 Warsaw Rising Museum, which was one of Lech Kaczyński's main projects as President of Warsaw, and the establishment of the 2006 'Patriotism of Tomorrow' (*Patriotyzm jutra*) educational programme spearheaded by the former Minister for Culture and National Heritage (and then member of PiS), Kazimierz Ujazdowski. What such attempts at taking control over prominent memory institutions illustrate most vividly is precisely the fact that these are no longer taken for granted by a public that has become aware both of the mediated nature of their experience of historical reality, and of the role that they can play themselves in its production and distribution.

Polish memory and social media

This new centrality of media in the production and distribution of memory brings me to my main point of interest: the commemoration of the Smolensk catastrophe on the popular social network site (SNS)[6] Facebook, the specificities of this medium, and the ways in which it has shaped the articulation of responses to the Smolensk catastrophe.

In a recent series of articles, Andrew Hoskins has drawn attention to the increasing 'mediatization' and even complete renewal of memory resulting from the revolutionary transformation of our current 'mediascape' and of the digital technologies through which it is shaped. More specifically, Hoskins argues that:

> in the post-broadcast age the temporalities and simultaneities of our immediate present, although seemingly overwhelming and obliterating in one way, also effect a far greater intensive and extensive *connectivity*, between the forms and agents and discourses of memory. As the resources of memory-making in the form of digital data become more fluid and accessible but also more revocable and diffused, individuals locate their own pasts and those of their groups and societies through their *immersion* in emergent networks that blur if not transcend the personal and the public, the individual and the social and the particular and the collective.
>
> (Hoskins 2009a: 40)[7]

In other words, with our 'everyday life increasingly embedded in the mediascape' (p. 29), where 'new horizontal connections – peer-to-peer' are being established on what Hoskins proposes to call the 'interstitial level of social life' (pp. 40–41), we may eventually welcome 'a new social network memory: fluid, de-territorialised, diffused and highly revocable, but also immediate, accessible and contingent on the more dynamic schemata forged through emergent sociotechnical practices' (p. 41).

Taking her cue from Hoskins' insightful diagnosis of what he labels our new *digital media ecology*, José van Dijck focuses on the particular role of SNSs within what she prefers to call our current *culture of connectivity*. More specifically, she points to three elements that are central to the 'performative infrastructure' of the SNSs we use, but which tend to be overlooked when assessing the social practices that these engender (van Dijck 2010: 3). These elements are:

1 the presence of a 'technological unconscious' (i.e. the often covert influence of the particular interface of each SNS);
2 the idea that SNSs facilitate a 'connective' rather than a truly 'collective' experience;
3 the problem that, on SNSs, memory is produced and circulated in a 'continuous present', as a result of which it can hardly be reconstructed after the fact.

(van Dijck 2010: 3–4)[8]

We need to bear all three elements in mind when assessing the ways in which SNSs are reshaping historical memory. But at the same time, no matter how hard it may be to recover be it only traces of the memory work that is being performed in the 'continuous present' of an SNS such as Facebook, we may at least be certain that the resultant historical memory – having been produced horizontally (not vertically) on Hoskins' 'interstitial level of social life' – largely evades the potentially 'harmful' dominance of traditional memory agents (such as museums, newspapers, television, etc.). Furthermore, what the following more or less chronological overview of the various Facebook responses to the Smolensk catastrophe and its aftermath should illustrate is precisely the fact that SNSs appear to challenge the very possibility of individual or institutional control over the production of memory.

Facebook and the Smolensk tragedy

As with any disastrous public event, especially since the 2005 London bombings, the Smolensk plane crash on 10 April 2010 instantly yielded all kinds of real-time news coverage and commemorative rituals on Facebook and other popular websites that support Web 2.0 features. Among the first commemorative practices were condolences posted on both new and existing *'like'* pages[9] devoted to the victims of the crash, but also typical performative gestures such as the burning, on one's profile *status*, of a digital candle (signified by [*] or [′]) in memory of those who died, or the addition to individual profile pictures of small mourning symbols – think a black ribbon or a Polish flag.[10] In sum, in the immediate aftermath of what was immediately perceived as a national tragedy, Poles united in deep mourning, on- no less than offline.[11]

This state of unity, however, soon came to an end. A few days later, after the controversial decision had been taken to bury Kaczyński and his wife in the crypt of Wawel Cathedral in Kraków (a place otherwise reserved for the Polish kings and other national heroes), an avalanche of pages and groups were created on Facebook in response. Some of these supported the plan, but the vast majority were opposed to it. These online protest initiatives included not only serious pages (e.g. *YES* and *NO to the burial of the Kaczyńskis on Wawel Hill*),[12] but also – quite typically for SNSs such as Facebook – more playful groups (e.g. *I want to be buried on Wawel Hill too!* or *Yes to the burial of the Kaczyńskis in the Pyramid of Cheops*).[13] The *YES* and *NO to the burial* communities proved to be important as serious mediators and even lobbyists generating nationwide support for their respective positions on the entombment issue (though with considerable differences in their number of fans);[14] but it was the latter, more ironic types of groups and communities that continued to leave their mark on Facebook activities long after the actual burial. The 'Yes to (the burial of)' and 'No to (the burial of)' templates, for instance, kept generating new pages of all kinds (e.g. *Yes to the burial of the Kaczyńskis on the moon*, *Yes to the burial of Jarosław Kaczyński on Wawel Hill*, *Yes to the burial of Jarosław Kaczyński anywhere, as long as it is done right away*, *Yes to the burial of the Kaczyńskis in the National Stadium*), including ongoing creative reworkings of the Egyptian motif (e.g. *Yes to the burial of the Kaczyńskis in the Valley of the Kings*, *No to the burial of Cheops in the National Stadium*) – especially as the Arab Spring burst out in early 2011. Later, such pages even started to allude to current (national or international) events: *Yes to the burial of [Polish politician Andrzej] Lepper on Wawel Hill*, *Yes to the burial of Amy Winehouse on Wawel Hill* (after the tragic deaths of both figures), and *No to the burial of [Polish racing driver] Robert Kubica's hand on Wawel Hill* (after the latter's car crash).

In other words, the exposure of Facebook users to the Wawel controversy generated a number of 'templates' through which other news events could now be mediated. What is behind such performative gestures, I would argue, is a growing awareness among those immersed in social networks of the 'mediatedness' of their online performances or, put differently, the increasing reflexivity of commemorative and other social experiences taking place on the Internet. The message that may be drawn from even the most unpopular (in terms of number of fans) or remote (by virtue of their questionable sense of humour) examples of this type is that people were increasingly critical of the exposure that the catastrophe in all its aspects was given by politicians and traditional news media alike.

Similar instances of both support and protest – the former generally serious and not terribly popular, the latter increasingly playful and often receiving a lot of attention – reappeared on a regular basis in the ongoing aftermath of the plane crash, most notably on the occasion of related public controversies. Of particular interest are the Facebook responses to three public debates on which I shall briefly focus here: the conflict over the memorial cross in front of the presidential palace; the plans for a statue in memory of President Kaczyński; and the conspiracy theories regarding the causes of the crash.

The cross controversy arose in the second half of July 2010, after the president elect Bronisław Komorowski issued an order to remove the memorial cross (subsequently called the *krzyż smoleński* or 'Smolensk cross') from the presidential palace on Krakowskie Przedmieście in Warsaw and move it to a nearby chapel. This wooden cross had been placed outside the palace by a group of scouts five days after the plane crash as an appeal to the authorities to erect a permanent monument at the same location. In the subsequent months, the ordinary cross was itself transformed, as it were, into a substitute memorial to the victims of the catastrophe. The presidential order was contested by a group of ardent supporters of the cross who physically obstructed its removal, and pledged to continue to do so until the authorities complied with their demand for a permanent monument. On 16 September 2010, after a summer full of vehement discussions and even physical fights, and 151 days after its erection, the cross was finally removed. Again, the most popular Facebook communities that gathered people commenting on this brand-new controversy were playful ones: *We're moving the presidential palace away from the cross – that will be easier*; *I don't sleep because I'm holding the cross* (later also parodied as *I don't sleep because I am waiting for the truth*); *Have Cross Will Party*; *Let's move the cross one metre to the left each day*; and even *Appeal to call in David Copperfield to solve the problem of the cross.*[15] After the cross was finally removed, a new series of derisive pages appeared, such as *I am the one who hid the cross.*[16]

As we might expect, the demand for a statue in memory of Lech Kaczyński, which underlaid the crusade of many defenders of the cross, also aroused a lot of commotion on Facebook. Whereas an early page in support of this idea (*A statue in memory of President Lech Kaczyński*) failed to attract many fans, the protest page

I don't want a statue of Lech Kaczyński became quite popular and for months garnered discussions and jokes about the topic.[17]

Lastly, one of the most remarkable pages was called *I don't rule out the intervention of a UFO in the tragedy in Smolensk.*[18] This page reflected the ironic stance of so many people towards the most improbable conspiracy theories emerging around the crash (some of which were nurtured by a video clip circulated online which purportedly comprised footage filmed at the crash site immediately after the plane went down, showing what appeared to be armed men moving among the victims and shooting survivors).

From SNS to offline intervention

Of course, during the ongoing aftermath of the catastrophe Facebook also served as an organizing medium in order to raise broad public support for all kinds of offline interventions. This was especially the case at the time of the cross saga, when the fierce campaign against its removal spawned reactions in the form of happenings and other carnivalesque activities.[19] The most influential action, however, took place soon after the MAK (*Mezhgosudarstvennyi aviatsionnyi komitet* or Interstate Aviation Committee) investigation report was made public by the Russian authorities in January 2011. In the report the two pilots were blamed for having ignored bad weather warnings, most probably due to the psychological pressure caused by the president's determination not to alter his schedule. The publication of the report raised a fresh round of commotion among politicians and the general public, and a new flood of 'Smolenskomania' emerged. This new controversy was most likely what prompted two Polish students to set up the Facebook event *A Day Without Smolensk*. Their brief manifesto read as follows:

> Are you already tired of the words Smolensk, Katyn, catastrophe, air traffic controllers, MAK? You don't want to incite an uprising? Are you tired of the hunt for blame? Yes? That's great! There's an ideal solution! Take part in an initiative in support of your psychic and emotional health! We declare 3 February the Day Without Smolensk![20]

Within two days the event attracted more than 100,000 participants and in no time it became the talk of the town. Predictably, a few members of PiS protested against the initiative, while politicians from other parties supported it. In this way, what started out as a campaign against the politicization of the catastrophe itself became a politicized act.

The group was soon removed by its initiators owing to this political appropriation, and a small set of successor groups attracted much less attention. Its rapid closure notwithstanding, however, the initiative may be said to count among the most reliable barometers of the way in which the Polish public prefers to remember the catastrophe. Indeed, between the small group of ardent supporters of the ongoing 'Smolenskomania' and the equally small group of rather nihilistic opponents, there seems to be a huge majority of Poles who do want to show respect for the memory of all 96 casualties, but without letting this tragic event overshadow the more urgent problems facing Poland.

Conclusion

What conclusions, then, may we draw from the various modes in which SNSs such as Facebook leave their mark on the public sphere? As many of the examples have shown, due to the idiosyncrasies of its interface (allowing for the 'viral' distribution of certain data) and its performative features (one-click reactions), which turn it into an extremely popular forum for what is still highly normative behaviour,[21] Facebook manages to forge effective and reliable connections between collectively shared opinions, thus creating a collective (or 'connective'?) experience that is unlikely to occur in the real world. Given the high degree of playfulness of most Facebook communities, even a group of more than 100,000 members will not immediately translate into offline street protests. What Facebook does achieve is to give each of these members a real face; as a result, what would otherwise remain *communicative memory* (to use Jan Assmann's famous distinction) may now 'objectify' into *cultural memory*.[22]

The importance of such alternative forms of cultural memory became obvious during the first anniversary of the Smolensk crash. Offline, two opposed series of public commemorations – one organized by the government, another by the PiS camp – further strengthened the impression of a deeply divided Polish society.[23] On Facebook, however, the anniversary caused substantially less animosity, and the reactions that it did engender typically leaned towards irony and cynicism (invitations to join barbecue parties rather than one of the many ceremonies, for instance).[24]

In other words, due to the multitude of memory forms and discourses that Facebook and other SNSs allow to solidify in one way or another, it has become more difficult for traditional memory agents – governments, political groups, and possibly also traditional media – to monopolize the construction of cultural memory. One of the stereotypes that these Facebook examples help to modify, for instance, is the idea that opposite views on dealing with the socialist past (i.e. the 'thick line' or 'gruba kreska' of the Third Republic versus the lustration plans of the Fourth)[25] are conducive to the alleged chasm dividing present-day Polish society. As the Smolensk case reveals, although the socialist past continues to offer useful narrative schemata (e.g. the 1940 Katyn crime) for those trying to capitalize on important public events, in the 'continuous present' of our increasingly self-conscious digital mediascape such schemata tend to collide both with their own ironic transformations and with so many other, often opposing narrative forms.[26] As a result, instead of becoming a stable political tool in the present, Polish memory of communism is now being exposed and put into perspective in ways that open up possibilities for new critical assessments of Polish history.

Notes

1 On the increasing pop culturalization of Polish national memory, cf. Czubaj (2005); for particular examples within the context of historical comics and the Internet, cf. De Bruyn (2010a, 2010b).
2 For an interesting case in point, cf. Ochman (2009).
3 One of the first to come up with the idea of a second Katyn was no less a figure than Lech Wałęsa himself. In an interview with the leading Polish newspaper *Gazeta Wyborcza* immediately after the crash, he declared that it was 'the second Polish tragedy of this size', a 'Katyn nr. 2' (Wałęsa 2010). Cf. also Dabrowski (2010).
4 For an interesting take on the instrumentalization of past events as (media) 'schemata' or 'templates', cf. Hoskins (2009a: 36–41).
5 For a similar emphasis on the differing historical circumstances between the 'two Katyns', cf. Snyder 2010.
6 Social network sites such as Facebook, Twitter and Google+ were accurately defined by boyd and Ellison as 'web-based services that allow individuals to (1) construct a public or semi-public profile within a bounded system, (2) articulate a list of other users with whom they share a connection, and (3) view and traverse their list of connections and those made by others within the system' (boyd and Ellison 2007).
7 Cf. also Hoskins (2009b).
8 Cf. Hoskins (2009: 102); cf. also Wulf Kansteiner's early critique of memory practices in our new media landscape: 'Since the consumption of history becomes more and more discontinuous and fragmented in time and space, communities of memory might only rarely be constituted on the basis of shared interpretations of specific events. Increasingly, consumers are only linked through the media that they access individually and very selectively. Consequently, the media, their structure, and the rituals of consumption they underwrite might represent the most important shared component of peoples' historical consciousness, although this non-confrontational, semi-conscious, non-referential, and decentralized process is *extremely difficult to reconstruct after the fact*' (Kansteiner 2002: 195; emphasis added).
9 A '*like*' page (formerly also known as '*become a fan*' page) may be created on Facebook in order to encourage individual users to publicly 'like' an individual (e.g. a celebrity), organization (e.g. a political party) or product (e.g. Belgian chocolate).
10 Similar 'performances' also appeared on the home pages of Polish online news and other websites. Another remarkable commemorative gesture on the latter pages was the use of black-and-white layout in the period of national mourning.
11 For an interesting take on the first months of mourning in Poland after the crash and more particularly on the evolution from an initial 'shock of the absurd' over a temporary state of 'communitas' to the political recuperation of the tragedy through Lech Kaczyński's controversial burial and his brother's candidacy for the upcoming presidential elections, see Niżyńska (2010).
12 'TAK dla pochowania Kaczyńskich na Wawelu' <http://www.facebook.com/pages/TAK-dla-pochowania-Kaczyńskich-na-Wawelu/114428748583085> (accessed 13 October 2011); 'NIE dla pochowania Kaczyńskich na Wawelu' <http://www.facebook.com/pages/NIE-dla-pochowania-Kaczyńskich-na-Wawelu/108910729145050>.
13 'Ja też chcę być pochowany/na na Wawelu'<http://www.facebook.com/group.php?gid=108999352469162>; 'Tak dla pochowania Kaczyńskich w piramidzie Cheopsa' <https://www.facebook.com/group.php?gid=1105633 12310831>.
14 On 13 October 2011, the '*YES to*' page had 1,689 fans, and the '*NO to*' community 41,165. Whereas the former community served for some time as a forum for serious support of the burial, the latter evolved into a virtual meeting point for the organization of all kinds of protest actions throughout the country.

15 'Przenosimy pałac prezydencki spod krzyża, będzie prościej' <http://www.facebook.com/pages/Przenosimy-palac-prezydencki-spod-krzyza-bedzie-prosciej/124760110904270?ref=ts> (accessed 14 October 2011); 'Nie śpię bo trzymam krzyż' <http://www.facebook.com/trzymam> (accessed 14 October 2011); 'Jest krzyż jest impreza' <http://www.facebook.com/pages/Jest-krzyz-jest-impreza/122075611173502> (accessed 14 October 2011); 'Przesuwajmy codziennie krzyż o 1 metr w lewo' <http://www.facebook.com/pages/Przesuwajmy-codziennie-krzyz-o-1-metr-w-lewo/100518466676776> (accessed 14 October 2011); 'Apel o sprowadzenie Davida Copperfielda aby rozwiązał problem krzyża' <http://www.facebook.com/group.php?gid=148704448488 680> (accessed 14 October 2011).

16 'To ja schowałem krzyż' <http://www.facebook.com/pages/To-ja-schowalem-krzyz/147938501911426> (accessed 14 October 2011).

17 'Pomnik dla śp. Prezydenta Lecha Kaczyńskiego' <http://www.facebook.com/group.php?gid=1426248124200 51> (accessed 14 October 2011); 'Nie chcę pominka [*sic*] Lecha Kaczyńskiego' <http://www.facebook.com/ pages/Nie-chce-pominka-Lecha-Kaczynskiego/117635268288679> (accessed 14 October 2011).

18 'Nie wykluczam udziału UFO w tragedii w Smoleńsku' <http://www.facebook.com/UFOpl> (accessed 14 October 2011).

19 The *Have Cross Will Party* page, for instance, was used for promoting playful happenings at the same location on Krakowskie Przedmieście where the cross was being defended 24 hours a day. One of the most remarkable results of these public actions was the erection of an alternative (mock) cross composed of empty Lech beer cans. For the story behind the cross made of beer cans, cf. Leszczynski (2001).

20 'Męczą Cię już słowa: Smoleńsk, Katyń, katastrofa, kontrolerzy, MAK? Nie chcesz wzniecać powstania? Masz dość polowania na winnego? Tak? To świetnie! Jest idealne rozwiązanie! Weź udział w inicjatywie na rzecz zdrowia psychicznego i emocjonalnego! Ogłośmy 3 lutego dniem bez Smoleńska!' Although the original manifesto can no longer be retrieved, it has been reproduced on numerous web pages commenting on the initiative.

21 For an insightful analysis of Facebook as 'a forum for the policing and establishing of normative behavior, more than the imagined forum of deviant exhibitionism', cf. Westlake (2008: 35).

22 Cf. Assmann (1995).

23 Cf. the way in which the commemorations were covered by both Polish and foreign (traditional) media, which echoed the idea of a deeply divided country.

24 Cf. a (seemingly not very successful) public counter-event in Koszalin entitled 'A campfire instead of Smolensk!' ('Ognisko zamiast Smoleńska').

25 The main argument employed by the PiS camp in support of their call to set up a 'real' (Fourth) post-communist state was that their predecessors had failed to settle scores with former communists – thus supporting the historic proposition of the first prime minister of post-communist Poland, Tadeusz Mazowiecki, to draw a 'thick line' under the past.

26 Cf. Hoskins (2009a: 28): '[T]he digital era opens up conflicting and simultaneous horizons (or even "fronts" on the past) that are rapidly being assembled, torn up and reassembled in more self-conscious and reflexive ways by individuals, groups, nations, politicians, news organisations, terrorists, etc. in other words by all those who have ready access to the increasingly affordable tools of digital recording and production, editing and dissemination.'

References

Assmann, J. (1995) 'Collective Memory and Cultural Identity'. *New German Critique* 65: 125–133.

boyd, d.m. and Ellison, N.B. (2007) 'Social Network Sites: Definition, History, and Scholarship'. *Journal of Computer-Mediated Communication* 13(1). Online. Available: <http://jcmc.indiana.edu/vol13/issue1/boyd.ellison.html> (accessed 17 April 2010).

Czubaj, M. (2005) 'Pop pod flagą biało-czerwoną'. *Sprawy Narodowościowe* 27: 119–129.

Dabrowski, P. (2010) 'Why the Polish Plane Crash is Called "Katyn 2"'. *GlobalPost*, 14 April. Online. Available: <http://www.globalpost. com/dispatch/worldview/100413/katyn-polish-history?page=full> (accessed 13 October 2011).

De Bruyn, D. (2010a) 'Patriotism of Tomorrow? The Commemoration and Popularization of the Warsaw Rising Through Comics'. *Slovo* 22(2): 46–65.

De Bruyn, D. (2010b) 'World War 2.0. Commemorating War and Holocaust in Poland Through Facebook'. *Digital Icons* 4: 45–62.

Etkind, A. (2009) 'Post-Soviet Hauntology: Cultural Memory of the Soviet Terror'. *Constellations* 16(1): 182–200.

Garton Ash, T. (2010) 'A Glimmer in Poland's Darkness'. *Guardian*, 12 April. Online. Available: <http://www.guardian.co.uk/commentisfree/2010/apr/12/glimmer-polish-gloom-second-katyn> (accessed 13 October 2011).

Hoskins, A. (2009a) 'The Mediatisation of Memory', in J. Garde-Hansen, A. Hoskins and A. Reading (eds), *Save As . . . Digital Memories*. Basingstoke: Palgrave Macmillan, pp. 27–43.

Hoskins, A. (2009b) 'Digital Network Memory', in A. Erll and A. Rigney (eds), *Mediation, Remediation, and the Dynamics of Cultural Memory*. Berlin: Walter de Gruyter, pp. 91–106.

Huyssen, A. (2003) *Present Pasts. Urban Palimpsests and the Politics of Memory*. Stanford, CA: Stanford University Press.

Kansteiner, W. (2002) 'Finding Meaning in Memory: A Methodological Critique of Collective Memory Studies'. *History and Theory* 41: 179–197.

Leszczynski, A. (2001) 'A Very Polish Protest Party'. *Guardian*, 6 April. Online. Available: <http://www.guardian.co.uk/commentisfree/2011/apr/06/polish-protest-cross-of-beer> (accessed 1 November 2011).

Niżyńska, J. (2010) 'The Politics of Mourning and the Crisis of Poland's Symbolic Language after April 10'. *East European Politics and Societies* 24(4): 467–479.

Nora, P. (1998) 'The Era of Commemoration', in *Realms of Memory: Constructions of the French Past (Vol. III: Symbols)*. New York: Columbia University Press, pp. 609–637.

Nora, P. (2002) 'Reasons for the Current Upsurge in Memory'. *Eurozine*, 19 April. Online. Available: <http://www.eurozine.com/articles/2002-04-19-nora-en.html> (accessed 12 October 2011).

Ochman, E. (2009) 'Municipalities and the Search for the Local Past: Fragmented Memory of the Red Army in Upper Silesia'. *East European Politics and Societies* 23(3): 392–420.

Snyder, T. (2010) 'Czy katastrofa polskiego samolotu może na zawsze pogrzebać stalinizm?' *Res Publica Nowa*, 28 April. Online. Available: <http://publica.pl/teksty/duchy> (accessed 13 October 2011).

Traba, R. (2009) *Przeszłość w teraźniejszości. Polskie spory o historię na początku XXI wieku*. Poznań: Wydawnictwo Poznańskie.

van Dijck, J. (2010) 'Flickr and the Culture of Connectivity: Sharing Views, Experiences, Memories'. *Memory Studies*, 18 October: 1–15. Online. Available: <http://mss.sagepub.com/content/early/2010/10/12/1750698010385215> (accessed 13 October 2011).

Wałęsa, L. (2010) 'To Katyń nr 2. Jestem zdruzgotany'. *Gazeta Wyborcza*, 10 April. Online. Available: <http://wyborcza.pl/1,76842,7753298,To_Katyn_nr_2__Jestem_zdruzgotany.html> (accessed 12 October 2011).

Westlake, E.J. (2008) 'Friend Me if You Facebook'. *TDR: The Drama Review* 52(4): 21–40.

Conclusion

Julie Fedor

In early 2012, the Ukrainian social psychologist and public intellectual Oleh Pokal'chuk noted ironically that Ukrainian online media culture was characterized by such high degrees of political hysteria and verbal aggression that it was now being exported abroad as an exotic specimen to be studied and dissected by Western and Russian academics. Pokal'chuk evidently had low expectations of how accurate or enlightening the results of such studies would likely prove to be. It would be foolish, he warned, to attempt to draw easy conclusions about the state of Ukrainian society based on, say, blog post comments, often produced to order by trolls, robots, provocateurs and political technologists. In fact, the overwhelming majority of everyday online activities of Ukrainians suggested a much healthier (if less dramatic) picture (Pokal'chuk 2012).

Here, Pokal'chuk puts his finger on an important challenge facing scholars working with online sources: how do we assess the meaning and influence, the authority and authenticity of digital texts? As many commentators have pointed out, digital objects, as compared to traditional media such as books or archives, present particular sets of problems for the researcher (see e.g. Rosenzweig 2003; Winget and Aspray 2011). These new sources can be extremely rich, but they need to be approached with extreme caution. There are ways in which this applies especially to the terrain of post-socialist digital memories, which has its own distinctive pitfalls and complexities. In this volume, we have presented some preliminary, pioneering attempts at developing and testing tools for approaching this dynamic and rapidly shifting terrain – tools which take account not only of the structural features of digital media, but also of the cultural and historical specificities of post-socialist space.

A brief reminder of some of the basic assumptions underlying this volume is perhaps in order here. First, for all their diversity, post-socialist societies, like their socialist predecessors (Verdery 1996: 12), share certain family resemblances, including a heightened proclivity to (both transnational and internal) *memory wars* – fraught and highly contested processes of remembering, defining and debating past experiences as part of the struggle to build present and future identities.[1] Re-membering, re-collecting, protecting against fears of dismemberment and disintegration, mourning the victims of past catastrophes and making sense of their deaths – these are processes that carry a special importance and a special emotional charge in a region that has undergone such dramatic and far-reaching upheavals in the recent past.

Second, post-socialist modes of remembrance have entered a new period of flux with the advent of digital media throughout the region. Memory wars are increasingly fought online. Secret police archival documents posted on a website can rapidly reach audiences of millions, as in Poland in early 2005 (see Machcewicz 2007); government decisions on moving Soviet monuments or banning the display of Soviet symbols now bring the risk of large-scale cyber-warfare in their wake, as in Estonia and Lithuania in 2007 and 2008 respectively; video footage of offline street clashes over memory is instantly disseminated and debated online, as in Ukraine in May 2011 (see Nikiporets-Takigawa, Chapter 3, this volume); and Twitter and social networking services are used as key platforms for high-profile celebrity arguments over the correct way of interpreting and narrating the past, as in Russia on Victory Day in 2012 (see Karelova 2012). These web wars are waged using a common set of new media tools, languages and practices. None of these are neutral; they are actively framing and fashioning the ways in which users engage with their past and present experiences and realities. Media and memory mutually shape one another, to the point where, as van Dijck puts it in a seminal text, they 'increasingly coil beyond distinction' (van Dijck 2007: 2 and 15). The commemorative practices described in this book cannot be separated either from the media that enable and constitute them, or from the identities that they perform and negotiate.

A key overarching aim of this volume is to launch an exploration of how we might use the powerful online research tools and databases now available in order to develop new ways of gauging the extent to which the past is still present in post-socialist space. As Etkind notes (Chapter 2, this volume), it is now possible to map the online terrain of cultural memory with unprecedented speed, reach and precision. There are many ways in which this territory nevertheless remains opaque; so far, we know very little about how search engine bias and filtering may skew our results, for example.[2] But the contributors to this volume have made an energetic start at using this potential to explore which historical figures and events are on people's minds and at their fingertips, and how the shifting dynamic of their presence and visibility is intertwined with current events and future scenarios for the post-socialist space.

High levels of verbal aggression are one striking feature of post-socialist online culture, and of post-socialist online debates about memory in particular, that requires explanation. The contributors to this volume do not ignore online hysteria, hate speech and posturing, but they aim to put these phenomena in context and perspective, asking where this violence comes from, and what it means. They anchor their analysis in offline and online realities, in close readings and 'thick descriptions' of texts and practices, and in-depth case studies. In other words, they engage with Rogers' call for 'online groundedness' – for Internet research that acknowledges the intimate, complex and mutually transforming nature of the relationship between the Web and the ground (Rogers 2009). Thus, some chapters in this volume develop tools not only for understanding the role played by new media tools such as Facebook (De Bruyn), Twitter (Paulsen), computer games (Howanitz) and Wikipedia (Dounaevsky) in mediating transnational conversations about the past, but equally for examining how these media are being appropriated, transformed and adapted to fit specific needs and cultural practices.[3]

Another salient feature of post-socialist online memory-scapes has to do with the legacy of the systematic radical violence that was done to memory during the socialist period, as well as its flipside: the long counter-cultural struggle to recover and preserve this memory. This dual legacy is one of the causes of the aggressive speech behaviour mentioned above, but it also has a host of other ramifications. Perhaps most obviously, the relative lack of established sites of memory in the form of national museums and monuments combined with the sharply diminished freedom of traditional mass media in early twenty-first-century Russia, for example, has meant that Russian memories of socialist state terror have overwhelmingly tended to take up residence in online space. The gulag's afterlife in cyberspace may be read as a kind of uncanny postscript to Solzhenitsyn's monumental labour of memory, *Gulag Archipelago,* in which he outlined the contours of the 'almost invisible, almost intangible' geography of the Soviet gulag, fragmented in space, absent from maps, unacknowledged and disavowed in public, a kind of phantom country that did and did not exist (Solzhenitsyn 1973). Today, the little that has survived of the memory traces of that gulag has largely migrated to the Internet, where it has found a hospitable environment lacking in other domains of public life in Putin's Russia.[4]

An important feature of the post-socialist online terrain that many of the authors in this book explore comprises what Nancy Condee has labelled 'contiguity' (Condee 2009: 23); that is, the relative lack of uncontestable geographical and other boundaries within the space of the former Russian empire as compared to the maritime empires. This includes a relative lack of sharp linguistic discontinuities, a feature that is an important theme of this volume, and especially for the East Slavic transnational online conversations and conflicts described here. The volume's bias in favour of the East Slavic world is in part a consequence of the fact that, as Etkind notes in his contribution, Cyrillic makes for a 'naturally restricted universe' online.[5] This can be useful for scholars wishing to limit their data sets, but it also raises problems about how to track the flow of discourse within the Cyrillic online universe, where conversations seep through and float above the physical borders that now separate nations which were once part of the Soviet Union, shaping, in turn, the processes of forging and consolidating stable identities and relationships in this region.[6] The most important factor to be noted here, and one which is analysed by many of this book's contributors, is the ongoing online dominance of the Russian language beyond the physical borders of the Russian Federation (see e.g. Chapter 8 by Dounaevsky, Chapter 4 by Kulyk, Chapter 10 by Lastouski and Chapter 3 by Nikiporets-Takigawa). In general, the extreme fluidity of physical and imagined borders in the region since the collapse of communism and the eastward expansion of the European Union has intersected in manifold ways with identity and memory projects, for example, via the de- and re-territorialization of memory enabled by digital technologies. Maria

Pasholok (Chapter 11, this volume) gives a vivid description of how these technologies are being put to use as part of competing drives to map the post-socialist terrain.

While we often tend to think of the Internet as transcending and rendering less relevant offline geographical borders, it equally offers a home and a refuge for remembered borders that have long ceased to exist in the offline. Most strikingly, the Soviet Union itself still lives on online in the form of the top-level domain name .su, originally registered during the Soviet twilight and now not only still in existence (despite ongoing contestation of its legal status), but undergoing something of a renaissance.[7] It remains to be seen how the recent (2010) launch of the top-level Cyrillic domain .рф will further change the contours of post-socialist online space. It may well be that we shall see fresh attempts by the Russian government to ground the Internet nationally, through initiatives such as RuTube, the Russian rival to YouTube which aims to channel content nationally, in part as an antidote to the vibrant visual online oppositional culture that has sprung up on Runet in recent years.[8]

The vexed question of how to assess the authenticity of online sources given the ease of digital manipulation that van Dijck identifies (2007) has added layers of significance when considered in the post-socialist context; that is, coming after decades of the suppression, erasure, distortion, and sometimes whole-scale fabrication of the historical record, as well as the radical curtailment of the public sphere, such that alternative spaces for self-expression had to be carved out. Thus, for example, many of the online practices now current on Runet bear strong similarities to late Soviet counter-cultural traditions of 'kitchen-table conversations' and *samizdat*, which migrated into cyberspace as the freedom of other Russian mass media shrank in the 2000s (Gorny 2007). Likewise, we are currently witnessing top-down attempts at recycling and reconstituting Soviet-era techniques for controlling access to information and means of public self-expression (Deibert and Rohozinski 2010).[9] The socialist legacy thus also shapes the regional specificity of another set of borders: the shifting borders between the private and the public, a topic discussed by several of the authors in this volume (see e.g. Kukulin, Chapter 7, Preda, Chapter 13, Reading, Chapter 1, and Introduction).

The question of authenticity is one that plagues post-socialist online communications for other reasons, too. In post-Soviet space in particular, the ubiquity of 'political technologies' has further radically eroded trust in the reliability of digital media (Kulyk 2010; Wilson 2005). Revelations about the Kremlin's networks of paid bloggers (including oppositional ones) and other state interventions into online communications in Russia have greatly undermined the credibility and authority of online commentators. In some cases, we are apparently dealing here with deliberate state campaigns aimed at polluting online space to the point where conversation becomes impossible, for example, via the activities of Internet brigades paid by Russian state institutions to post abusive comments online with the long-term aim of creating 'a climate in comments which will force the publication to close down the comments service as such', to quote one of the activists allegedly engaged in these processes in Russia (cited in Mal'gin 2012; see further Fedor and Nikiporets-Takigawa 2012). More importantly for our purposes, political technologies are also frequently used with the aim of challenging the validity of any alternative versions of history by branding them as hopelessly compromised by their instrumentalization in the regional memory wars – again, a discursive move which is facilitated by the lack of reliable documentary knowledge on many aspects of the socialist past.[10]

Overall, researchers working in this field need to take painstaking care in unpicking the connections between state-sponsored and grass-roots memory projects. Grappling with this issue means, for example, striving to avoid confusing top-down memory politics and rhetoric with their reception, and with the ways in which individuals and communities remember and imagine the past. But equally, it means resisting the temptation of positing a neat divide between state and society, between official memory and dissident or counter-memories. Most often we are dealing with a more complex mix, in which initiatives aimed at the political instrumentalization of memory feed into and upon spontaneous grass-roots movements, for example. Several of the chapters in this volume challenge prevailing stereotypes about the state's role in dictating memories under and after socialism. Lastouski (Chapter 10) moves beyond the standard picture of a monolithic Belarusian memory, uncovering the multiplicity of memories in contemporary Belarus, as well as showing how they are entwined with and shaped by the official Belarusian discourse. De Bruyn's study of bottom-up commemorative practices challenges the received wisdom on Polish memory culture as deeply polarized, unremittingly serious, and conforming to the fault-lines laid down by politicians (Chapter 15). Lunde (Chapter 6) uses online personal reminiscences about Sovietisms to demonstrate 'the degree to which official and alternative linguistic practices of Soviet language culture were intertwined and interdependent', challenging the idea of a stark dichotomy between official and unofficial Soviet culture. Kukulin (Chapter 7) shows the ways in which the late Soviet dissident struggle to wrest memory from state control has unfolded in expected ways, with the discursive inversion and appropriation of Gorbachev-era liberal memory discourses and slogans in contemporary Russia.

It would be possible to expand this necessarily brief list of regional specifics much further. There are generational dimensions to the phenomena described here, for example. Young adults in the region are now not only the first generation to have no direct memory of socialism, but also the first to have grown up with the Internet.[11] As De Bruyn points out, this is a generation that is keenly aware of the mediated nature of historical reality. Meanwhile, as Lassila (Chapter 14) illustrates, the passing of the last generation to have lived through the landmark event in the post-socialist memory wars, the Second World War, has added urgency and pathos to memory projects aimed at fixing and consolidating competing narratives of that war.

What broad conclusions might we draw, then, about how digital media are shaping post-socialist engagements with the past? What kinds of conversations do these media enable? The picture that emerges from this volume is a mixed one. On the one hand, the Internet opens up new possibilities for mutual media monitoring and instantaneous translation, serving more often than not to fuel and perpetuate conflict (see e.g. Spörer-Wagner's discussion of the Internet's capacities for polarizing and/or manipulating populations (Chapter 9), or Kulyk on the Internet's tendency to increase the levels of contestation of the meaning of the past (Chapter 4)). The potentially corrosive and destructive effects of connectivity and exposure to one's neighbours are exemplified by the Russian imperialist ideologue Aleksandr Dugin's response to the site InoSMI.ru, which publishes Russian translations of foreign media reports on Russia. The creation of this site, Dugin claims, has brought about a change in the 'collective consciousness' in Russia, a change that he (characteristically) links to memory politics surrounding the Second World War. Dugin's reading of the role played by this site is testimony to the divisive potential inherent in digital connective media:

> The ordinary high-level manager . . . who wants to learn what the West is writing about Russia, turns to this site, to InoSMI. And what do they see? . . . That they hate us, that they have contempt for us, that they are constantly turning us into shit and they criticise even our own victories in our eyes [*sic*].
>
> ('A. Dugin' 2008)

Several of the authors in this volume investigate the form, content and patterns of online conversations about the past. Paulsen (Chapter 5) guides us through the circuits of Twitter conversations about the past, as well as analysing the specific forms they take in the Ukrainian context. Dounaevsky (Chapter 8) explores the mixed blessings of the workings of the Wikipedia editing process. Wikipedia's revert mechanisms and accessible edit histories make it a wonderfully rich and transparent source for scholars, but they can also foster long, repetitive cycles of stalemates and discursive impasses, as well as fuelling the drive to fence off and securitize memories viewed as being under threat by virtue of their vulnerability to being edited by neighbours. Nikiporets-Takigawa (Chapter 3) shows how the structural features of social media facilitate disjointed and disorienting conversations, with effects that can be, if not destructive, then certainly incapacitating. Several of the authors highlight the contradictory nature of what Anna Reading has called the globital memory field: at once cosmopolitan and local (Lastouski), constraining and enabling, and giving rise to new challenges linked to the imperative to package national memory for global audiences (Lassila).

If we think of this as a giant interlinked conversation about the past, how do the different media interact – who leads, and who follows? How is the agenda set? How do images of the past migrate, spread, shift and flow – can we track their movements through blogs and social networks? Can we develop ways of measuring their 'rating trends'? Several of the contributors share a focus on media ecologies and exploring how new media fit in and interact with other kinds of media. Nikiporets-Takigawa sets out to track the role played by different media in initiating or provoking the memory conflict in L'viv on Victory Day in 2011. She found that social media were the most active in preparing the ground for this conflict. Paulsen, on the other hand, concluded that older, established news media were still setting the agenda for Ukrainian Twitter exchanges on the Holodomor. Howanitz (Chapter 12) suggests that digital gaming industries can play a pivotal and hitherto unrecognized role in identity-formation.

The overall picture that emerges from this volume is by no means unremittingly grim. Approaching post-socialist memories through the prism of digital media uncovers a landscape that is heterogeneous and vibrant, and several of the chapters in this book offer optimistic prognoses for the future. De Bruyn, Dounaevsky and Preda, for example, all document the extent to which the old totalizing memory cultures are in various stages of erosion and decay, thanks in great measure to pressures brought to bear by the possibilities opened up by digital media. In these conditions, imposing and controlling a single narrative or vision of the past is no longer even remotely feasible. It remains to be seen where the ongoing process of adapting to these new realities will lead. It may well prove that the transformative power of online memories and, more broadly, the translation of post-socialist political, cultural and social forms into digital formats, together with the powerful feedback of these digital forms and practices offline, will accelerate a shift from the 'post-socialist' to some new, unknown condition.

Notes

1 For a recent study of the memory wars over Katyn, see Etkind *et al.* (2012); and for a study of Central East European memory wars that combines the agendas of oral history and memory studies, see Mark (2010).

2 The politics of search engines has received some attention, but this has largely been focused on the USA and the UK (see Introna and Nissenbaum (2000) for a useful survey of the relevant issues and the scholarship to date). In spring 2011, Russian bloggers claimed that Yandex (the Russian rival to Google) was manipulating image search results. They posted a video on YouTube comparing Google and Yandex search results to illustrate their point; see Yandeks tsenzura (2011). On the ways in which search results and other Internet services are being personalized for individual users based on their previous online activities, see Pariser (2011). In handling these sources, we need to take account of the ways in which both governmental and corporate actors determine how they are selected, stored, preserved, indexed, displayed, accessed, retrieved and used. Certainly, we cannot assume any kind of straightforward or transparent linear relationship between individual and group memories and online memories. For one historian's account of his concerns about the dominant role played by Google in digitizing primary source materials, see Noiret (2009) (thanks to Cate O'Neill for drawing this article to my attention).

3 On the ways in which the Internet is not only transforming but being transformed by local conditions, see also Rogers (2009) and Goldsmith and Wu (2006). The latter identify a global trend whereby the Internet is 'splitting apart and becoming borders. Far from flattening the world, the Internet — its language, its content, its norms – is conforming to local conditions' (Goldsmith and Wu 2006: viii).

4 Like the Soviet gulag memory on which it builds, this online gulag memory exists thanks to the efforts of networks of amateur memory enthusiasts. Impressive examples include the 'Memorial' Society's 'Virtual Gulag Museum' project (Virtual Gulag Museum website), and the Facebook community 'Remembering the Gulag'. Also like its Soviet counterpart, post-Soviet online gulag memory is often a cosmopolitan enterprise; see, for example, the European Memories of the Gulag website, or the Gulag: Many Days, Many Lives website.

5 As Kamusella points out, the Cyrillic alphabet is an extra-linguistic feature that was used to help bolster the separation of East Slavic from West Slavic languages, in the absence of any sharp linguistic discontinuity between them (Kamusella 2008: 169).
6 This is also, as Rutten and Zvereva have argued, a diasporic space; see further Rutten (2010).
7 Martin Paulsen delivered a paper on this topic to the 2011 Virtual Russia conference in St Petersburg and is currently reworking it as a book chapter in a volume to be co-edited by Paulsen, Ingunn Lunde and Michael Gorham.
8 As this volume went to press, new legislation was passed in Russia seemingly aimed at shutting down oppositional online media outlets in the wake of the dramatic wave of protests that began in winter 2011 to 2012 in Russia.
9 Deibert and Rohozinski note that some post-Soviet governments would appear to be drawing on and adapting previous late Soviet-era practices aimed at controlling access to information, and recycling them as part of new, often indirect and subtle techniques for controlling the Internet without resorting to blatant censorship.
10 This lack of knowledge is in turn a direct consequence of socialist-era archival policies; see further Etkind *et al.* (2012, chs 3 and 7).
11 For a more general study on this generation, see Palfrey and Gasser (2008).

References

'A. Dugin' (2008) 'A. Dugin: Kazhdyi den' my dolzhny ubivat' v sebe zapadnika'. *InoSMI. ru*, 10 June. Online. Available: <http://www.inosmi.ru/world/20080610/241918.html> (accessed 3 March 2010).

Classen, C. (2009) 'Balanced Truth: Steven Spielberg's *Schindler's List* among History, Memory and Popular Culture'. *History and Theory* 47, May: 77–102.

Condee, N. (2009) *The Imperial Trace: Recent Russian Cinema*. Oxford and New York: Oxford University Press.

Confino, A. (2011) *Foundational Pasts: The Holocaust as Historical Understanding*. Cambridge: Cambridge University Press.

Deibert, R. and Rohozinski, R. (2010) 'Control and Subversion in Russian Cyberspace', in J. Palfrey, R. Rohozinski and J. Zittrain (eds), *Access Controlled: The Shaping of Power, Rights, and Rule in Cyberspace*. Cambridge, MA: MIT Press.

Erll, A. and Rigney, A. (eds) (2009) *Mediation, Remediation, and the Dynamics of Cultural Memory*. Berlin and New York: Walter de Gruyter.

Etkind, A. (forthcoming 2012) *Warped Mourning: Stories of the Undead in the Land of the Unburied*. Palo Alto, CA: Stanford University Press.

Etkind, A., Finnin, R., Blacker, U., Fedor, J., Lewis, S., Mälksoo, M. and Mroz, M. (2012) *Remembering Katyn*. Cambridge: Polity Press.

European Memories of the Gulag website. Online. Available: <http://museum.gulagmemories.eu/> (accessed 10 July 2012).

Fedor, J. and Nikiporets-Takigawa, G. (2012) 'What's the Colour of Russian Protest?' *East European Memory Studies*: 10–11.

Goldsmith, J. and Wu, T. (2006) *Who Controls the Internet? Illusions of a Borderless World*. New York: Oxford University Press.

Gorny, E. (2007) 'The Russian Internet: Between Kitchen-table Talks and the Public Sphere', *ARTMargins*, 18 October. Online. Available: http://www.artmargins.com/index.php/2-articles/145-the-russian-internet-between-kitchen-table-talks-and-the-public-sphere (accessed 10 July 2012).

Gulag: Many Days, Many Lives Website. Online. Available: <http://gulaghistory.org/> (accessed 10 July 2012).

Introna, L. and Nissenbaum, H. (2000) 'Shaping the Web: Why the Politics of Search Engines Matters'. *The Information Society* 16(3): 169–185.

Judt, T. (2005) *Postwar: A History of Europe since 1945*. Harlow: Penguin.

Kamusella, T. (2008) *The Politics of Language and Nationalism in Modern Central Europe*. Basingstoke: Palgrave Macmillan.

Karelova, V. (2012) '"Vyskazyvanie Durova oskvernilo Den' Pobedy, poetomu ia ushel iz 'VKontakte'"'. *Izvestiia*, 10 May. Online. Available: <http://izvestia.ru/news/524032> (accessed 16 July 2012).

Kulyk, V. (2010) 'The Role of the Media in (Re)Shaping Historical Memory in Ukraine', a talk delivered to East European Memory Studies Research Group, Cambridge, 17 November.

Lévy, D. and Sznaider, N. (2006) *The Holocaust and Memory in the Global Age*. Philadelphia, PA: Temple University Press.

Machcewicz, P. (2007) 'Poland's Way of Coming to Terms with the Legacy of Communism'. *European Network for Contemporary History*. Online. Available: <http://www.eurhistxx.de/spip.php%3Farticle40&lang=en.html> (accessed 16 July 2012).

Mal'gin, A. (avmalgin) (2012) 'Iz otcheta: "Provedena nakrutka golosovaniia"', 6 March. Online posting. Available: < http://avmalgin.livejournal.com/2968304.html?thread=104800752&> (accessed 16 July 2012).

Mark, J. (2010) *The Unfinished Revolution: Making Sense of the Communist Past in Central-Eastern Europe*. New Haven and London: Yale University Press.

Noiret, S. (2009) 'The Digital Historian's Craft and the Role of the European History Primary Sources (EHPS) Portal'. *Archivi & Computer, Automazione e Beni Culturali* 19(2–3): 5–41.

Palfrey, J.G. and Gasser, U. (2008) *Born Digital: Understanding the First Generation of Digital Natives*. New York: Basic Books.

Pariser, E. (2011) *The Filter Bubble*. Harlow: Penguin.

Pokal'chuk, O. (2012) 'Grazhdanskoe obshchestvo No. 3, Ili zdorovyi pul's blogosfery', *Zerkalo nedeli. Ukraina* 4, 3 February 2012. Online. Available: <http://zn.ua/SOCIETY/grazhdanskoe_obschestvo_3,_ili_zdorovyy_puls_blogosfery-96689.html> (accessed 10 June 2012).

'Remembering the Gulag' Facebook group. Online. Available: <http://www.facebook.com/groups/memoryatwar/#!/groups/remembering.the.gulag/> (accessed 10 July 2012).

Rogers, R. (2009) *The End of the Virtual: Digital Methods*. Amsterdam: Amsterdam University Press.

Rosenzweig, R. (2003) 'Scarcity or Abundance? Preserving the Past in a Digital Era'. *The American Historical Review* 108(3), June.

Rutten, E. (2010) 'Web Wars: Digital Diasporas and the Language of Memory'. *Digital Icons: Studies in Russian, Eurasian and Central European New Media* 4. Online. Available: <http://www.digitalicons.org/issue04/ellen-rutten/> (accessed 16 July 2012).

Solzhenitsyn, A. (1973) *Arkhipelag GULag*. Paris: YMCA Press.

van Dijck, J. (2007) *Mediated Memories in the Digital Age*. Stanford, CA: Stanford University Press.

Verdery, K. (1996) *What Was Socialism, and What Comes Next?* Princeton, NJ: Princeton University Press.

Virtual Gulag Museum website. Online. Available: http://gulagmuseum.org/ (accessed 10 July 2012).

Wilson, A. (2005) *Virtual Politics: Faking Democracy in the Post-Socialist World*. New Haven, CT: Yale University Press.

Winget, M.A. and Aspray, W. (2011) 'Introduction', in M.A. Winget and W. Aspray (eds), *Digital Media: Technological and Social Challenges of the Interactive World*. Plymouth: Scarecrow Press, pp. v–xi.

Winter, J. (2006) *Remembering War: The Great War between Historical Memory and History in the Twentieth Century*. New Haven, CT, and London: Yale University Press.

Yandeks tsenzura (2011) *Yandex tsenzura. O chem molchit poisk*. Online. Available: <http://www.youtube.com/watch?v=IcQaDYv2pyY> (accessed 11 July 2012).

Timeline

1989 to 1991

- Communist governments fall throughout Soviet bloc (from Solidarity's landslide election victory in Poland in June 1989, to the dissolution of the USSR in December 1991).
- Memory activism (such as the reburial of martyrs of the 1956 Hungarian uprising, and the 'Baltic Way' protests marking the signing of the Molotov–Ribbentrop Pact in the summer of 1989) plays a prominent driving role in protest movements throughout the region.
- The collapse was largely peaceful, with major exceptions including: the Yugoslav Wars (1991–1995); the Chechen Wars (1994–1996 and 1999–2009); and armed conflicts in Nagorno-Karabakh (1988–1994); South Ossetia (1991–1992 and 2008); Transnistria (1992); and Abkhazia (1992–1993).

1990

- Country-code top-level domains registered for Hungary (.hu), Poland (.pl) and Soviet Union (.su).
- *World Wide Web* created.
- USSR: *GlasNet* Association of Users of Computer Networks created.
- Poland: Senate condemns 1947 'Operation Vistula' (Polish communist deportations of Ukrainian minority).
- *April:* USSR: government acknowledges NKVD responsibility for 1940 Katyn massacre.
- *October:* Germany: Post of Federal Commissioner for the Stasi Archives created to investigate history of Stasi crimes and preside over relevant archives. Joachim Gauck appointed head. The German or 'Gauck Office' would later serve as a model for similar institutions elsewhere in the region.
- Russia: Solovetskii Stone erected in central Moscow in commemoration of victims of Soviet political repressions.

1991

- Country-code top-level domains registered for Bulgaria (.bg), Czechoslovakia (.cs) and Romania (.ro).
- Estonia: Parliament creates State Commission to research history of atrocities committed by Nazi and Soviet occupying powers.
- Poland: Chief Commission for Investigation of Hitlerite Atrocities (est. 1945) is renamed and its brief expanded to cover Stalinist atrocities against Poles.
- Ukraine: Official ceremony marking fiftieth anniversary of 1941 Babii Yar massacre formally recognizes Jewish victims for the first time.
- Czechoslovakia: Lustration law (denying public office to former communists and collaborators) comes into force. This was the most radical of a series of such processes instituted throughout region.
- Russia: Law on Rehabilitation of Victims of Political Repressions passed. Day of Memory of Victims of Political Repressions instituted (18 October; previously, from 1974, unofficially marked as Political Prisoners' Day).

1992

- Country-code top-level domains registered for Estonia (.ee), Georgia (.ge), Lithuania (.lt) and Ukraine (.ua).
- Germany: Stasi records opened to public access. Parliament creates commission to investigate history of GDR. Similar commissions set up the same year in Albania, Bulgaria, Romania.
- Lithuania: Museum of Genocide Victims opened under auspices of Ministry of Culture.
- Poland: Scandals and allegations over secret police informer files lead to fall of Olszewski government.
- Russia transfers documents confirming Soviet guilt for 1940 Katyn massacre to Poland.

1993

- Country-code top-level domains registered for Azerbaijan (.az), Croatia (.hr), Latvia (.lv), Macedonia (.mk), and Slovenia (.si). Czech Republic (.cz) and Slovakia (.sk) replace pre-Velvet Divorce domain name for Czechoslovakia (.cs).
- First Polish website created.
- Latvia: Museum of Occupation of Latvia is created in Riga.
- Hungary: Ban on Soviet symbols passed.
- Poland: Russian President Yeltsin kneels before Katyn cross in Warsaw and asks Poles, 'Forgive us, if you can'.

1994

- Country-code top-level domains registered for Armenia (.am), Belarus (.by), Kazakhstan (.kz), Moldova (.md), and Russia (.ru).

- First Russian website created.
- Hungary: Lustration law passed.

1995

- Country-code top-level domains registered for Kyrgyzstan (.kg), Tajikistan (.tj) and Uzbekistan (.uz).
- First Polish web portal (*Wirtualna Polska)* launched.
- Russia: Celebrations of fiftieth anniversary of Victory in the Great Patriotic War. Poklonnaia Gora memorial park opened in Moscow. Stalin depicted on postage stamp for the first time in over four decades. President Yeltsin views parade from traditional Soviet vantage point on top of Lenin Mausoleum. Polish President Wałęsa declines invitation to take part in Moscow celebrations.
- Estonia: Parliament declares Stalinist deportations a crime against humanity. Archives opened to public.
- Russia: Foundation stones for memorial at Katyn are laid. President Yeltsin does not attend ceremony.
- Poland: President Wałęsa declares 1995 'The Year of Katyn'. Presidential election campaigns dominated by issue of communist past.
- Lithuania: President Brazauskas officially apologizes for Lithuanian atrocities against Jews in the Second World War. Harsh reactions in Lithuanian media.

1996

- First Russian search engine (*Rambler*) created.
- Russia: 22 June (beginning of Great Patriotic War) declared the official Day of Memory and Sorrow; 7 November (former Day of Great October Socialist Revolution) is renamed the Day of Accord and Reconciliation.
- Russia: President Yeltsin restores Soviet-era Victory Banner, now to be flown on key military dates alongside the Russian state flag.
- Belarus: Independence Day (3 July) instituted, marking memory of 1944 Soviet liberation of Minsk.
- Serbia: Large-scale protests over electoral fraud. When government moves to shut down independent radio station B-92, it moves online.

1997

- Country-code top-level domain registered for Turkmenistan (.tm).
- Hungary: President Sólyom vetoes decoration of Prime Minister Horn over latter's role in suppressing 1956 uprising.
- Poland: Passage of lustration law (amended and expanded in 1998).
- Russia: *Yandex* search engine launched, enabling Russian-language searches.
- *December* Russia: President Yeltsin radio address on eightieth jubilee of founding of state security organs calls for historians to take a more positive view on Soviet past.

1998

- Latvia: Latvian Legion Day (16 March) is declared an official memorial day, sparking widespread international condemnation, since the Legion was part of the Waffen-SS. This official date would later be abolished (in 2000).
- Poland: Parliament formally condemns 'communist totalitarianism'. Institute of National Remembrance (IPN) founded to investigate history of crimes against the Polish people.
- Lithuania: President Adamkus creates International Commission for the Evaluation of the Crimes of the Nazi and Soviet Occupation Regimes in Lithuania.
- Estonia: President Meri creates International Commission for the Investigation of Crimes against Humanity committed by Nazi and Soviet occupying forces.
- Ukraine: Day of Memory of Victims of Holodomor (last Saturday in November) instituted.

1999

- LiveJournal launched.
- Russia: SORM-II system enables monitoring of Internet traffic.
- Uzbekistan: President Karimov creates Commission for the Promotion of the Memory of Victims to investigate the history of communist repressions, in an apparent effort to shift blame for current abuses on to communist legacy.
- Ukraine: National Unity Day (22 January) instituted (marking 1919 unification of Ukrainian and West Ukrainian People's Republics).
- *December* Russia: Prime Minister Putin restores Andropov memorial plaque at the Lubianka in Moscow. The plaque had been defaced and removed by protesters in August 1991.

2000 to 2003

Russia: Broadcast media freedoms restricted as state wages ongoing campaign against independent TV and press, partly in response to critical media coverage of Second Chechen War (from 1999).

2000

- Russia: President Putin comes to power. Security services' powers to monitor online communications further expanded.
- Latvia: Latvian Legion Day abolished.
- Poland: Jan Tomasz Gross's book *Neighbours* about 1941 Jedwabne massacres of Jews by Poles sparks heated debates. IPN launches investigation into the case.

- Germany: Erika Steinbach lobbies for creation of Centre against Expulsion in Berlin, sparking crisis in German–Polish relations.
- Armenia: Inaugural annual processions in Yerevan to mark Armenian Genocide Remembrance Day (24 April).
- Ukraine: Day of Sorrow and Honouring the Memory of the Victims of the War (22 June, marking start of Great Patriotic War) instituted. Day of Memory of Victims of Holodomor (last Saturday in November) renamed Day of Memory of Victims of Holodomor and Political Repressions.
- Russia and Ukraine: Major memorial complexes opened at sites of Katyn and other Soviet massacres.
- *June* Belarus: Lukashenka signs decree to widen ring road around Minsk, threatening to destroy Kurapaty NKVD mass graves site. Demonstrations ensue, including a permanent vigil at the site.
- *August* Poland: Wałęsa cleared of the charge of lying in his lustration declaration.
- *September* Ukraine: murder of investigative journalist Heorhii Gongadze, the most high-profile of several such cases under Kuchma's Presidency (1994–2005).
- *October* Lithuania: memorial cross erected at site of Ponary Second World War massacres.
- *November* Czech Republic: Struggle for Freedom and Democracy Day instituted (17 November, marking student uprisings against both Nazi and Soviet regimes).
- *December* Belarus: Government recognizes Kurapaty as site of mass executions by NKVD. Parliament rejects bid to erect a monument there.
- Russia: Music of Soviet anthem restored (with new lyrics). Red banner restored as symbol of Russian armed forces. Tsarist double-headed eagle and tricolour retained and confirmed as state symbols.

2001

- Belarus: President Lukashenka declares Internet a security threat.
- Poland: Public access to communist-era security files opened up.
- Hungary: Holocaust Memorial Day introduced (16 April, marking creation of Budapest ghetto in 1944).
- Germany: Prussian Trust founded to lobby for German expellees' compensation from Poland.
- Poland: Permanent exhibition on destruction of European Roma opens at Auschwitz.
- Kazakhstan: Official initiative to create museum at site of former camp KarLag launched.
- Russia: Government criticism of school history textbooks focuses on Igor' Dolutskii's *Twentieth-century Russian History*. The book included an exercise in which students were asked to assess whether contemporary Russia was a 'police state'.

- *July* Poland: New memorial erected on sixtieth anniversary of Jedwabne massacre. President Kwaśniewski officially apologizes for the crime.
- *September*: Polish Wikipedia launched.
- *October* Georgia: Popular TV channel *Rustavi 2* raided by government security forces, prompting mass demonstrations and fall of cabinet.
- *November* Belarus: President Lukashenka takes part in ceremony to commemorate Minsk ghetto massacre by Nazi forces.

2002

- Slovakia: National Memory Institute created under Ministry of Justice; former dissident Ján Langoš later appointed head. A series of scandals over archival revelations about secret police collaborators follow.
- Hungary: Budapest House of Terror opens, with exhibits covering fascist and communist regimes.
- Russia: Moscow Mayor Yurii Luzhkov proposes restoring statue of founder of Soviet secret police Feliks Dzerzhinskii in central Moscow.
- *Summer* Hungary: Scandal over Prime Minister Medgyessy's past as a collaborator prompts calls for harsher lustration procedures.

2003

- Lithuania: Holocaust added to school curriculum.
- Slovakia: Access to secret police archives opened.
- Poland-Ukraine: Joint official ceremonies mark sixtieth anniversary of Volyn massacres.
- *June* Russia: Last remaining non-state-controlled countrywide TV channel *TVS* is closed down.
- *July* Estonia: Museum of Occupations opens in Tallinn.
- *November* Georgia: Rose Revolution brings President Mikheil Saakashvili to power.
- *December* Russia: President Putin calls for urgent review of school history textbooks in the wake of the 2001 controversy over the Dolutskii textbook.

2004

- Facebook created.
- Georgia: Series of mass media closures in what some label the 'Putinization' of Georgian media.
- Romania: Traian Băsescu elected President on strongly anti-communist platform, despite his own communist past.
- Poland: Museum of Warsaw Uprising opened.
- Russia: Beslan school hostage crisis. Series of political reforms aimed at centralizing power and tightening control over media follow.

- Ukraine: Orange Revolution brings Viktor Yushchenko to power. Online media play key role in reporting and sustaining protests, and the number of Internet users in Ukraine rises dramatically.
- Russia: Chief Military Procuracy investigation of Katyn is closed down.
- Poland: Polish Institute of National Remembrance opens its own Katyn investigation.
- Russia and Germany included in D-Day commemorations for the first time.

2005

- YouTube created.
- Poland: Scandal and ongoing controversy after 'Wildstein List' of names of possible informers from secret police archives is posted online.
- European Commission rejects proposals (primarily Hungary- and Lithuania-led) for Soviet symbols to be banned on a par with Nazi ones.
- Kyrgyzstan: 'Tulip Revolution' overthrows President Askar Akaev. Discussions held surrounding proposals (later rejected) to block all Runet sites with content 'offensive' to Kyrgyzstan and to ground Kyrgyz Internet nationally, restricting access to .kg domain.
- Azerbaijan: Murder of journalist Elmar Huseynov.
- Russia: St George's Ribbon instituted (a new commemorative ritual marking Victory in the Great Patriotic War, with the slogan 'We Remember, We Are Proud').
- Russia: Celebrations of sixtieth anniversary of Victory Day marred by conflict. The presidents of Estonia, Georgia and Lithuania boycott the ceremony.
- Ukraine-Poland: 'Young Eagles Memorial' unveiled in L'viv at the burial place of Polish defenders of L'viv during the 1918 to 1919 Polish-Ukrainian War, previously a heavily contested site of memory.
- Poland: Law and Justice (PiS) party comes to power and launches radical de-communization.
- Russia: Day of National Unity instituted (4 November, marking the expulsion of Polish-Lithuanian interventionists from Moscow and the end of the Time of Troubles; this date replaced 7 November, the Day of Great October Socialist Revolution still commemorated by many post-Soviet people). From 2005, the Day of National Unity is marked by the annual nationalist 'Russian March' under the slogan 'Russia for Russians'.
- International Holocaust Remembrance Day (27 January) instituted by UN General Assembly.
- Russia: *Russia Today* multilingual global government-funded TV and online media outlet launched.

2006

- Twitter created.
- Russia: Social networks V Kontakte and Odnoklassniki.ru launched.

- Poland: Nasza-Klasa.pl social network launched.
- Romania: President Băsescu is first Romanian president to officially condemn communism. He endorses the Tismăneanu Report produced by the Presidential Commission for the Analysis of the Communist Dictatorship (created April 2006, headed by political scientist Vladimir Tismăneanu).
- Estonia: Parliament debates draft law banning public display of Soviet and Nazi symbols.
- Georgia: Museum of Soviet Occupation opens in Tbilisi as part of Georgian National Museum. Ukrainian President visits in 2007 and calls for Ukrainian counterpart to be created.
- Albania: Parliament calls for secret police archives to be opened.
- Belarus: Access to oppositional websites blocked during presidential elections.
- Russia: Investigative journalist Anna Politkovskaia murdered.
- Hungary: Protesters clash with police in fiftieth anniversary 'rerun' of 1956 uprising. Protesters rely on Internet and mobile communications.
- Ukraine: Parliament adopts law declaring the 1932–1933 Holodomor a genocide of the Ukrainian people. Institute of National Memory created.
- Bulgaria: 'Dossier Act' opens up individual access to communist state security archives and establishes 'Dossier Committee' to oversee this process.
- Parliamentary Assembly of the Council of Europe Resolution 1481 condemns crimes committed by totalitarian regimes.

2007

- Country-code top-level domain names .me (Montenegro) and .rs (Serbia) introduced (replacing .yu previously used by Serbia and Montenegro).
- Russia: Defence Ministry makes database of Soviet soldiers killed during Great Patriotic War available online (www.obd-memorial.ru).
- UN General Assembly resolution condemns Holocaust denial.
- Estonia: 'Bronze Soldier' conflict over Estonian relocation of Soviet monument, including rioting, media war and cyber-attacks on Estonian government, banking, media and other websites.
- Russia: Ongoing controversy surrounding history textbooks. Putin criticizes authors writing textbooks on foreign grants. Scandal over draft state-sponsored teaching manual that describes Stalin as an 'efficient manager' (this phrase would later be cut from the final version).
- Poland-Ukraine: sixtieth anniversary of 'Operation Vistula'. Yushchenko visits Poland as gesture of reconciliation.
- Poland-Russia: Election of Donald Tusk as Polish Prime Minister leads to improvement in bilateral relations.
- Russia: DDoS attacks on oppositional online media begin. Plans to create a Cyrillic Web announced.
- Ukraine: President Yushchenko posthumously awards Roman Shukhevych (leader of the Ukrainian Insurgent Army) the title of Hero of Ukraine (the decoration was later annulled in 2011).

- Georgia: *Imedi TV* raided and its broadcasting licence suspended over accusations of conspiring against the government.
- Poland: Parliament institutes Worldwide Day of Memory of Victims of the Katyn Crimes (13 April, marking the anniversary of the 1943 German announcement of the Katyn massacres).

2008

- Ukraine: President Yushchenko declares 2008 a Year of Holodomor Remembrance.
- European Parliament resolution recognizes Holodomor as a crime against humanity.
- ICANN approves introduction of Cyrillic domains.
- Kyrgyzstan: National Day of Remembrance for victims of 1916 uprising against Russian imperial rule instituted (first Friday of August).
- Ukraine: President Yushchenko submits draft law 'On the Official Status of Fighters for Ukraine's Independence from the 1920s to the 1990s' (the draft was never voted on by parliament).
- Poland: Controversy over allegations that Wałęsa was a secret police collaborator revived by IPN historians Cenckiewicz and Gontarczyk.
- *June* Prague: Declaration on European Conscience and Communism calls for 'Europe-wide condemnation of, and education about, the crimes of communism'.
- Lithuania: Public display of Soviet and Nazi symbols banned. In response, hackers attack Lithuanian websites, defacing them with Soviet symbols.
- *August* Russo-Georgian war. Allegations of Russian cyber-attacks on Georgian sites, and Georgian filtering of Russian Internet content.
- Russia: President Medvedev launches videoblog.
- Russia: Moscow court refuses to judicially rehabilitate the victims of Katyn massacre. Relatives take case to the European Court of Human Rights.
- Ukraine: Security Service of Ukraine launches its Digital Archives Centre, providing online access to previously classified archival documents (including on Holodomor, OUN-UPA and Stalinist repressions).
- *November* Ukraine: High-profile commemorations of seventy-fifth anniversary of Holodomor.
- Russia: Authorities raid office of 'Memorial' Society in St Petersburg and confiscate digital archives on Stalinist repressions.
- *December* Russia: Popular protests in Vladivostok; security services attempt to remove online coverage of protests.
- Number of Internet users in Russia reaches 38 million.

2009

- European Parliament Resolution on European Conscience and Totalitarianism institutes European Day of Remembrance for Victims of Stalinism and

Nazism (23 August, marking anniversary of the signing of the Molotov–Ribbentrop Pact).

- OSCE Vilnius Declaration condemns totalitarianism.
- Poland: Restrictions on use of Soviet symbols introduced (later partly revoked).
- Belarus: State control over Internet stepped up via new media law.
- *April* Moldova: Protests over communist victory in parliamentary elections dubbed 'Twitter revolution'.
- *May* Russia: in his videoblog, President Medvedev speaks about 'vile and aggressive' attempts to falsify history against Russia. Presidential Commission for Counteracting Attempts at the Falsification of History Damaging Russia's Interests created (disbanded 2012).
- *June* Latvia: Soviet Occupation Day (17 June) instituted.
- *September* Poland: Putin attends ceremonies in Gdansk marking the beginning of the Second World War.
- *November* Ukraine applies for top-level Cyrillic domain name .укр.

2010

- Moldova: Attempt to institute Soviet Occupation Day (later overturned). President Ghimpu creates Commission for the Study and Evaluation of the Communist Totalitarian Regime of the Republic of Moldova.
- Ukraine: President Yushchenko posthumously awards OUN leader Stepan Bandera the title of Hero of Ukraine (later annulled by a court decision in January 2011).
- Ukraine: Court verdict declares Stalin and other Soviet leaders guilty of genocide against Ukrainians.
- Ukraine: Internet portal Historical Truth launched.
- Russia: United Russia party launches campaign to introduce a single approved history textbook for schools.
- *February* Ukraine: Yanukovych is elected president. Later he states that Holodomor was not genocide but a common tragedy of the Soviet peoples.
- *April* Russia: Polish presidential plane crashes on its way to Katyn memorial ceremony, killing all 96 passengers. The tragedy is followed by moves towards Russian–Polish reconciliation. Russian authorities post Katyn documents online and screen Wajda's film *Katyń* on prime-time nationwide TV.
- *May*: ECHR ruling on Kononov vs. Latvia case sets precedent in applying standards of Nuremberg law to victors in Second World War (i.e. USSR).
- Russia: Foreign Allied troops join Moscow Victory Day parade for the first time.
- *June* Russia: President Medvedev opens a Twitter account.
- Hungary: National Unity Day instituted (4 June, marking anniversary of 1920 Trianon Treaty which reduced Hungary's territory by two-thirds). Bill bans denial of communist crimes on a par with Holocaust denial.
- Georgia: Soviet Occupation Day instituted (25 February, marking anniversary of 1921 Red Army invasion).

- *Summer* Russia: Online civil society mobilizes to organize relief for forest fire victims.
- *July* Moldova: Museum of Victims of Communism opens.
- *September* Hungary: New media bill reduces media freedom.
- Russia: Another 'history textbook war' breaks out in response to a neo-Stalinist manual for higher education teachers published by Moscow State University historians Vdovin and Barsenkov.
- *October* Russia: Putin launches new version of Solzhenitsyn's *Gulag Archipelago*, adapted for schoolchildren at Putin's request and now included in school literature curriculum. Launch is timed to coincide with Day of Memory of Victims of Political Repressions (2010).
- Russia: Holocaust history added to compulsory school curriculum.
- *November* Russia: State Duma recognizes Katyn massacre as a crime of the Stalinist regime.
- *December* Hungary: One Million for the Freedom of the Press (Milla) Facebook campaign set up to protest against new draft bill on media.

2011

- *January* Germany: Roma play important role in Holocaust Day ceremonies for the first time.
- Arab Spring prompts growing concerns over revolutionary potential of social media.
- *February* Russia: Security services propose measures to increase responsibility for content on social networking sites. 'League of Internet Safety' launched.
- Russia: Working Group on Historical Memory, part of the Presidential Council for Assistance to the Development of Civil Society and Human Rights, presents President Medvedev with draft proposals on commemorating victims of Stalinism. These include the creation of nationwide memorial museum complexes.
- *April* Russia: Security officials express concerns over use of foreign Internet services such as Skype and gmail. President Medvedev calls for increased editorial responsibility for comments on online media sites.
- *April* Hungary: new constitution declares 1944 to 1990 a period of foreign occupation.
- Belarus: Terrorist act in Minsk metro prompts renewed calls to control Internet in Belarus.
- *May* Uzbekistan: New restrictions placed on Internet cafés in Tashkent.
- Ukraine: Clashes on Victory Day in L'viv.
- *Spring–Summer* Russia: Debates over proposals to increase control over Internet (e.g. by making editors of online media sites responsible for users' comments). Medvedev and Putin deny government plans to reduce Internet freedom.
- Azerbaijan: Parliament debates legislative initiatives aimed at controlling social media.

- Georgia: Soviet symbols banned.
- *June* Belarus: Revolution via Social Networks movement launched.
- *July* Poland: President Komorowski asks for forgiveness at ceremony marking seventieth anniversary of Jedwabne massacre.
- *October* EU: Platform of European Memory and Conscience created to raise awareness of totalitarian crimes.
- Poland: Hunger strikes over school history reforms. Opponents argue that the reforms will destroy Polish historical memory.
- Ukraine: Freedom Day (22 November, marking the Orange Revolution) is merged into National Unity Day (22 January).
- *October* Russia: Grass-roots ceremonies commemorating victims of Stalinism streamed live on Internet.
- *December and beyond* Russia: Dramatic wave of protests over electoral fraud, largely organized online, despite major cyber-attacks on oppositional online media. Security services attempt to exert pressure on social networks to close down oppositional groups.

2012

- Russia: Daily Internet usage exceeds TV viewers for first time.
- *January* Belarus: Legislation further increasing state control over Belarusian segment of Internet.
- Russia: President Medvedev declares 2012 the 'Year of Russian History'.
- *February* Estonia: Parliament discusses initiatives to acknowledge Waffen-SS veterans as fighters for Estonian freedom.
- Azerbaijan: Campaign against Radio Liberty journalist Khadija Ismailova waged via Internet.
- Russia: Scandal after Kremlin youth agencies' emails on programmes aimed at controlling and manipulating online media are hacked and posted online.
- *March*: Kazakhstan launches country-code top-level Cyrillic domain .каз.
- *May* Kazakhstan: President Nazarbaev denounces social media as 'spreading lies and propagating violence and evil'.
- Uzbekistan: YouFace.uz launched in an attempt to compete with Facebook.
- *July* Moldova: Communist symbols banned.
- Russia: New laws open path to censoring Internet.

Index

Page numbers in italics refer to figures and numbers in bold refer to tables.